MEDIA and SOCIETY

an introduction

SECOND EDITION

Michael
O'Shaughnessy

Jane
Stadler

OXFORD

UNIVERSITY PRESS

OXFORD

UNIVERSITY PRESS

253 Normanby Road, South Melbourne, Victoria 3205, Australia

Oxford University Press is a department of the University of Oxford.
It furthers the University's objective of excellence in research, scholarship,
and education by publishing worldwide in

Oxford New York

Auckland Bangkok Buenos Aires Cape Town Chennai
Dar es Salaam Delhi Hong Kong Istanbul Karachi Kolkata
Kuala Lumpur Madrid Melbourne Mexico City Mumbai Nairobi
São Paulo Shanghai Taipei Tokyo Toronto

OXFORD is a trade mark of Oxford University Press
in the UK and in certain other countries

National Library of Australia

Cataloguing-in-Publication data:

O'Shaughnessy, Michael, 1951–.
Media and society: an introduction.

2nd ed.
Bibliography.
Includes index.
ISBN 0 19 551402 5.

1. Mass media. I. Stadler, Jane Megan. II. Title.

302.23

Typeset by OUPANZS
Printed through Bookpac Production Services, Singapore

CONTENTS

Part 6 But They Keep Moving the Posts: Postmodern Perspectives

FIGURES AND PLATES

FIGURES

PLATES

ACKNOWLEDGMENTS

For my part, this book is the outcome of some 20 years' studying and teaching—it is truly a collective volume. Acknowledgments go to a large number of people who, over that time, have informed and inspired me in this work, and without whom none of this would have happened. In particular, I would like to thank my first film teachers, Mike Weaver and Mick Gidley; all those with whom I worked at the Centre for Contemporary Cultural Studies in Birmingham and at the British Film Institute, Open University, and Leicester Summer Schools; the two best teachers I've ever known, Stuart Hall and Richard Dyer; my colleagues at Warwick, Coventry, and De Montfort Universities; William West, Joachim Miekle, Leo Rutherford, Alex Wildwood, and the Sanyassins (who opened my mind and body to a whole new set of perspectives); Nathaniel and Bob Bennett, Simon Cheek, Claudia Defrene, Helen Stoddart, Rebecca Hiscock, Pat Kirkham, Kat Murch, Jonathan Kester, Persephone Arbour, Maddy Broekhuysen, Brian Eyres, Jim McCourt, and Julie Reddin—good friends who over the years have kept me sane and stimulated; Kay, Philip, and Tom; Peter Watkins, John Corner, and Ken Page; the numerous students who gave me fresh insights and have contributed so much to this book, especially Mario Minichiello, Ruth Collins, Joanne Whitehouse, and Astrid Ingham; most recently, all my colleagues at Edith Cowan University, who have in various ways encouraged me to keep going in this work and have supplied a truly supportive place of work—the Doctors David McKie (who actually got me writing) and Alan McKee, Kevin Ballantine, Norm Leslie, Ian Hutchison, Max Pam, Ivan Al-Azm, Robyn Quin, Brian Shoesmith, John 'go-write-a-book' Hartley, Hilaire Natt, Lelia Green, Beate Josephi, Deb Westerberg, Tim Burns, Rod Giblett, Sue Hayes, John Rapsey, John Duff, Bill McGlue, Paul Godfrey, Marc Deval, and Alan Hancock (who I also drum with); those tutors who worked with me on the Foundations course that inspired this book, especially Keith Smith and all the students at Edith Cowan University who have taken this course; from External Studies at Edith Cowan University, Heather Sparrow and Rhonda Draper; from Arts Enterprise at Edith Cowan University, Lisa Throssell; and from Oxford University Press, Jill Lane, Maggie Way, and Gillian Cardinal. My thanks to Drum-mania, who are great, and to my family, without whom none of this would have been possible. Thanks also to Debbie Rodan, for contributing gender theory references. Lastly, I am very grateful to Carol Muir, for her excellent help in getting permissions and especially to Michele Sabto, editor of this book at Oxford University Press. Michele has added greatly to the style and presentation of what follows, adding insight and precision throughout. She has a big hand in the final work. My thanks to her.

The ideas in this book owe much to the above individuals and to the many writers and critics in media studies and cultural studies who have developed these disciplines so fruitfully. However, responsibility for the way these have been presented here is ours alone.

The following people and institutions kindly agreed to give permission to reproduce photos and other textual materials, and Jane and I gratefully acknowledge their assistance and cooperation: 'African Mother Drop the Debt Image' reproduced courtesy of the photographer, Tif Hunter, and Red Cell; Disability Campaign images appear courtesy of the Disability Services Commission; thanks to Simplot for the 'CHIKO Roll' images; the 'Monoculture' cover is reproduced courtesy of *Colors* Magazine; the 'Young Designers Emporium' image appears courtesy of Jupiter; the Nike Blockade poster appears thanks to April-Jane Fleming and Jacob Black; the Nike email exchange is reproduced courtesy of Jonah Peretti; Avant Card images appear thanks to Nobody Denim and *Cosmopolitan*; 'Happy Christmas' article and photos from *Local News: Claremont*, 18 December 1996, reproduced courtesy of *Local News: Claremont*; 'Happy Wedding Day' advertisement 1994 reproduced with permission of Wedgwood, Barlaston, Stoke-on-Trent, England; 'Shameless' and 'Too Many People', words and music by Neil Tennant and Christopher Lowe © 1993, reproduced by permission of Cage Music Ltd/EMI Music Publishing Ltd, London WC2H OEA.

Every effort has been made to trace the original source of all material reproduced in this book. Where the attempt has been unsuccessful, the authors and publisher would be pleased to hear from the copyright holder concerned to rectify any omission.

Michael O'Shaughnessy

PREFACE

This book is a beginner's guide to media studies. Media studies is a complex discipline. It draws on a number of academic areas and, since the 1970s, has established an elaborate terminology and theoretical framework. This book introduces some of the main concepts and approaches, and explains key critical terms used in the discipline.

The first edition of *Media and Society* was written by me, Michael O'Shaughnessy. I have co-written this second, revised and expanded, edition with Jane Stadler. In many instances we have chosen to write from a first-person perspective, using the terms 'I/me/my' and 'we/us/ours'. Where I am writing from my own experience, the terms 'I', 'me', or 'my' are used. Where Jane and I share a viewpoint, the terms 'we', 'us', or 'ours' are used.

Throughout the book we use the expression 'media–world' to describe the connection between the media and society. We use 'media–world' in three senses: first, to describe a relationship between two separate areas (the media and the world in which they exist); second, 'media–world' points to the views of the world, the visions, that we find in media texts; and third, the term suggests that the world we live in is now so heavily influenced by the media that we do indeed inhabit a media–world.

We explore the media–world by looking at media texts and stories. We examine how and why we read them, and we explore the complex relationship between these texts and the 'real' world (in other words, the relationship between media and society). There are other aspects to media studies and these are indicated in Part 1 and elsewhere, but the focus remains on texts and how to read them. We make no apologies for this. Texts and stories are what draw us to the media; they are the fundamental staple of what we consume. It is important to offer ways of looking at and understanding them and their social role.

The book includes model essays (Appendices 1 and 2), as well as illustrations, practical exercises, and suggestions for further reading. It includes theoretical overviews and detailed examples. It encourages readers to reflect on their own identities. It is also informed by our experiences teaching media, film, and cultural studies, and by the input of the many students we have known. It is also important to acknowledge how my own personal learning journey has influenced my approach and slant on the media: I do not write from a neutral position.

Four major influences have contributed to my understanding of the media and the world. First, as a middle-class, White, male Westerner, I grew up deeply imbued with the ideology of liberal individualism. In global terms, I have been a privileged person. I believed in concepts such as democracy, freedom of the individual, and freedom of speech. I believed it was possible for individuals to control their own destiny. I therefore saw the media as an arena for individual creativity and expression.

Then, when I was in my twenties, I discovered the insights of Marx, and I saw, from other theorists, how his work could be developed in understanding the media.

This understanding showed me a world dominated by class struggle and economic necessity, a world in which individuals are determined by their class and social positions. I began to understand the media as one of the mechanisms through which the ruling classes try to maintain their domination over subordinate classes.

At the same time, I was in close contact with feminist thought and practice, which led me to look at gender issues and media representations of gender. I began to understand how the inequalities of class and race articulated by Marx were compounded by patriarchal oppression: the media could be understood as a site that maintained sexist and male-dominated views of the world. My initial focus on the oppression of women was followed by analysis of masculinity.

Finally, when I was in my thirties, an interest in Freud led me to the work of Wilhelm Reich and Carl Jung, to psychotherapeutic approaches, the growth movement, and the teachings of Native Americans. These gave me new insights into how people and societies work, and into the role of the media in our lives.

All four strands of influence have contributed to my perceptions and my work on the media. In some ways they are contradictory, but I accept these contradictions since I find they are useful, meaningful, and stimulating—they 'work' for me, and life itself is full of contradictions. I will try to show how these approaches can be used in understanding the media and I will suggest ways they can be brought together. They lead into social and psychological concerns that, as this book shows, are significant in terms of understanding the media.

Jane shares some of these influences and interests, but areas such as Jungian theory and masculinity are mine alone. Her own research and writing engage with questions related to the media and identity, political and subversive uses of the media, media technologies, globalisation, and ethical considerations surrounding film and media.

This book focuses on gender, the family, and ethnicity, with an emphasis on political considerations. In using the term 'political considerations' we are not only referring to the traditional party-political system, or the left-to-right spectrum of beliefs. Governance and the organisation of the state entail the exercise of power to obtain control, redistribute wealth, and affect the lives of citizens in myriad ways. Hence the term 'political' is not simply about politicians, political parties, and policies. It also encompasses various strategies for obtaining and using power, and these strategies include, but are not limited to, the use of the media. Politics is a term that encompasses power relations, small-scale and large, that contribute to the way in which society is structured and the way in which social power is distributed and exercised. Feminists coined the phrase 'the personal is political' when they realised how the everyday domestic lives of many women—staying at home, looking after children, doing poorly paid work—were part of the wider picture of women's political situation. All personal and social behaviour is political: the clothes we wear, the food we eat, how we work, what we do with our money, the media we consume, how we spend our leisure time, and so on. These actions are political because, through social and global interconnections, they relate to and affect how we and other people live in the world. Therefore, they are worthy of analysis.

Media studies can be either an attempt at neutral and descriptive analysis, trying to explain, from the outside, how the media work, or it can be politically engaged, aiming to challenge how the media work. Much of media studies has been idealistic—it has been a part of the search for a more equal society—and this aspect has given it its political slant. To use Marx's phrase, 'The point is not to understand the world but to change it'. We see media studies operating in this broad political arena of developing and encouraging social change and debate about political issues.

Gender and ethnicity are relevant to anyone who wants to understand his or her own identity. We are all positioned or constructed as gendered and ethnic subjects, whether as male or female, Black or White, and so on. Who we are is affected by this social positioning, and the health of society depends on how well we relate to each other from these positions. Exploring gender and ethnic issues in the media leads to a fascinating exploration and understanding of ourselves and others.

Gender is a significant political issue in two ways. First, gender is political because it involves issues of social power: it is not simply a question of the social oppression of women by men, but a more complex situation in which both men and women are constructed and oppressed by the patriarchal, competitive, and hetero-sexist values of society. The media play a key role in this.

The second way in which gender is political lies in the fact that gender involves questions of sexuality, one of the key human drives. While in many ways sexuality is repressed in Western culture, it is also, paradoxically, often at the centre of media representations. Sex sells, and the popular media return to issues of sexuality time and time again, making it an important area to examine. Questions of social power and sexuality are also relevant in understanding the family, a major institution of society, and one that is undergoing significant change.

The media examples we look at are mainly advertisements, television fictions, and film fictions; they are part of popular, or mass, culture. This focus is not for the purposes of either celebrating or denigrating popular culture. Rather, it recognises that popular culture is a central site from which we learn how to think and feel about the world in which we live. We use these fictions—rather than news, current affairs, and documentary—to explore the interesting intersections between pleasure, fictions, and 'real life'. They are mostly chosen from Australia, the USA, or the United Kingdom—our areas of media experience.

There are three key theoretical concepts running throughout the book: ideology, discourse, and hegemony. We introduce them gradually, with examples, so that readers can build up a sense of what they mean before we give full definitions. Alongside these, we use concepts drawn from psychology. The methods of analysis presented here can be applied to many other texts: for example, novels, plays, and paintings.

A number of films and television programs are cited in this book. Viewing them will help illustrate points made. Most significant are *Thelma and Louise* (explored in depth in Part 3) and *Blue Velvet* (analysed in the model essay, Appendix 2). All the films and television programs mentioned in the book are listed in the index.

Michael O'Shaughnessy
January 2002

Part I

GETTING READY:
THE MEDIA AND MEDIA STUDIES

Of course the first thing to do was to make a grand survey of the country she was going to travel through. 'It's something very like learning geography', thought Alice.

Lewis Carroll, Through the Looking-Glass

OVERVIEW OF PART 1

Chapter 1   Defining the Media

Chapter 2   Media Studies

Chapter 3   What Do the Media Do to Us? Media and Society

Chapter 4   What's in a Name? Language and the Social Construction of Reality

Chapter 5   Mediation and Representation

Chapter 6   Texts, Meanings, and Audiences

Part 1 presents an overview of what the media are and what media studies is trying to do. It presents initial definitions, approaches, questions, and assumptions. Then it explores issues of representation, language, the social construction of reality, and how we read media texts.

I Defining the Media

'The media' is a commonly used term, but what exactly is it (or are they)? The media include a whole host of modern communication systems, for example cinema, television, newspapers, magazines, advertisements, radio, and interactive multimedia. We can also include video games, computers, mobile phones and pagers, virtual reality, the Internet, even 'tamagochi' toy pets. Defining the media is not easy because the media are constantly changing with the development of new forms and technologies. However, there are a number of characteristics, historical developments, and economic and social determinants that delineate what the media are, and these can lead us towards a definition.

MEDIA CHARACTERISTICS

- The media are human communication systems.
- The media use processes of industrialised technology for producing messages.
- The media generally aim to reach large audiences and hence have sometimes been referred to as 'mass media' operating through 'mass production'; their success is often built on popularity.
- The media usually aim to allow communication across distance (and/or time) between people, or to allow communication in which the sender does not need to be present as the communication is both recorded and then transmitted.
- The media are called 'media' because they are literally in the middle, or are the middle chain, of this communication (*media* means 'middle' in Latin); they are the mechanisms that connect the sender and the receiver of messages.
- The media's development has been affected by commercial interests that recognise that the media are potentially highly profitable industries.

HISTORICAL DEVELOPMENTS

There are several important historical moments or periods in the development of the media:
1 The first major medium in Western culture was the printing press in the sixteenth century, which led to the reproduction and distribution of information and entertainment through pamphlets, books, and then newspapers. The development of the mass production of paper increased media output.
2 During the late eighteenth and nineteenth centuries, the industrial revolution in Europe saw new forms of power and manufacturing lead to rapid development of printing technologies. At the same time, there was a revolution in the communication systems of road, rail, and water transport. Major social changes

and new forms of industrial production led to a massive growth in urban populations and new patterns of work and leisure. Demand for rapid communication of information and entertainment increased, alongside rising literacy.

3 The last part of the nineteenth and the first half of the twentieth centuries saw a further explosion of communication systems and technologies, which has affected our daily lives in numerous ways. The advent of photography, film, sound recording, radio, and then television; the development of the telephone and telegraph; and the concurrent rapidly changing systems of travel, particularly the car and aeroplane, all combined to change the map of human culture forever. People living in industrial, developed countries accept all these as basic conditions for human life. The media are our main source of knowledge and entertainment and are part of the very structure of our lives. It has been estimated that in an average 70-year lifespan a Western person is likely to spend seven whole years viewing television. When we factor in the time spent engaged in computer-mediated communication (CMC), the average individual spends well over 10 per cent of their life focusing on a screen, consuming media of various forms. Whether it involves chatting and sending text messages on mobile phones, emailing, surfing or shopping on the Internet, listening to music on CDs or Internet radio while working on a PC, downloading news online, participating in Internet banking and being subjected to online ads, or watching *Survivor* on television and logging on to the Internet to check on developments between episodes, screen media are omnipresent in modern life. However, media access is not yet global. Many people and many cultures still do not have private access to television, computers, or the telephone.

4 Since about 1980, and as we move into the twenty-first century, we have undergone, and are undergoing, another revolution in communications—thanks to the development of new technologies, particularly the computer chip. Satellite and cable communications, digital television, computers, video games, virtual reality, and the Internet are again changing our patterns of behaviour, our modes of accessing knowledge, our entertainment, and our ways of seeing the world and interacting with one another. We truly live in a 'media-world'.

ECONOMIC AND SOCIAL DETERMINANTS

These developments depend on the use of industrial technology to produce, send, and receive messages. However, technological changes do not just happen magically. Media analysts need to ask: What brought about these technological changes and developments? What caused the media to be the way they are? What determined them? The main answer is that the media develop in economic and social frameworks, with economic and social determinants.

Most media changes have occurred in a capitalist economy, so their development has been influenced by profit motives: they have been developed privately, in the interests of making money. Media history shows that technological changes tend to be implemented when they are seen to be profitable.[1] However, notice that governments, concerned about the potential power of the media, have sought to retain some control through censorship laws, licensing, and so-called public ownership of the media. In relation to television, the result of this attempt to retain control over the media's power has often been a two-tiered system of public and private ownership: in Australia the ABC is a public broadcast system, while channels 7, 9, and 10 (and satellite and cable) are all private; in the United Kingdom the BBC channels are public broadcast, while ITV, channels 4 and 5, satellite, and cable are private. Most of the television channels in the USA are privately owned or are independent. Generally the private media, funded by advertising and thus linked to economic production and consumption, are much larger than the public systems, but they are still bound to uphold laws of decency and acceptability that are monitored through government legislation.

Technical and scientific developments, which have contributed to the development of the media (one of the latest being the digitalisation of television), are themselves determined by other factors: for example, the demands of warfare technology, particularly in World Wars I and II and the Cold War, contributed greatly to innovations in the media. The development of early video-camera technology, for example, was related to its use for American military surveillance. The Internet, cable, and satellite technologies were also originally developed for the military.

Because vested interests and power relations influence both the content and interpretation of media texts, questions about the relationship between media, profit, and ownership are important and constitute the basis for studying the political economy of the media (see pp. 13–17).[2]

CONCLUSION

While the complexity of the media makes definitions difficult, the following brief definition is a useful starting point: the media are technologically developed and economically profitable forms of human communication, held either in public or private ownership, which can transmit information and entertainment across time and space to large groups of people.

This transmission of information is not one-way. The recipients of media messages are also involved in the process of communication as part of a feedback loop that influences the production of media. While it is true that many media forms such as television, radio, film, and newspapers have an asymmetrical flow of communication from one sender to many receivers, the rise of more interactive media forms has changed this dynamic. Even in television, radio, and newspapers the audience contributes something to the communicative exchange (primarily through the process of constructing meaning, but also through ratings, research, talk-back, letters to the editor, and other feedback mechanisms). The 'one-to-many' model of mass communication is also being transformed by technological advances, as the following chapters demonstrate.

2   *Media Studies*

WHY STUDY THE MEDIA?

Why are you studying the media and what are you hoping to get out of this? Take time to think about this and write down your thoughts and feelings. There are no right or wrong answers to this question (or rather, all answers are right). It's useful for you to record your position so you can compare it with other people's and so you can look back on it later. When you have done the exercise, read the section entitled 'commentary' below.

Exercise commentary

Your answer might be about creativity and expressivity—you may want to make videos or television programs. It might also be vocational (you want to guarantee a good job as a journalist), financial (you see the media as an excellent way of making lots of money), critical (you may want to critique the manipulative power of the media and understand its potential as a mechanism of beneficial social change). Or it may simply be curiosity— you may be fascinated by these technological communication systems that take up such a large part of many people's lives today. Your answer may include aspects of all of these positions, or it may raise many other points. It will probably change while you are study- ing the media. Keep it as a reference point to look back on. If you can, spend about 15 minutes sharing your answer with three or four friends to give you an awareness of other people's interests and other ways of thinking about the media.

OVERVIEWS OF THE MEDIA

1 Take time to make a list of all the arguments you can think of for and against the media: that is, those that posit the media as a 'good' or a 'bad' thing.

2 Ask yourself: Whose interests do the media serve, or who benefits from the production, distribution, and consumption of media texts and messages? Also ask other people you live, work, study, or socialise with, and make a note of their different perspectives. When you answer these questions, try to include both general statements about the media and particular detailed examples that support these statements. Share and compare your answers with others.

These questions will show where you are starting from and will also go straight to the heart of many common discussions about the media. You will probably find strong arguments for and against the media that reflect commonly held opinions that are part of our culture's 'common sense'.

If you require a stimulus to answering these questions, try watching some episodes from Frontline, Drop the Dead Donkey, *or any other television programs that are about the media. These programs invariably have some insights into the role of the media, how they work, and their effects on audiences. When you have done the exercise, read the section entitled 'Exercise commentary' below.*

Exercise commentary

The question about 'good' or 'bad' media is designed to reveal the contradictory ways we think about the media, and the different ways the media are used. It may also point out the difference between how the media could be used in society, their *potential use*, and how they are used in society (their *actual use*). The potential power of the media, and their regulation and control, are a major concern for all contemporary societies.

The points in the table below suggest a number of different general positions for and against the media; they all contain some 'truth' and they highlight many of the concerns of media studies.

For	Against
The media's huge range of cultural information and entertainment contributes to the development of popular knowledge. People are more aware and better educated through the media than ever before.	The media offer people a repetitive diet of worthless trivia. Like bread and circuses, they cater to the lowest intellectual abilities.
The media can inspire and develop us, actively encouraging us to do new things in our lives.	The media make us passive observers—'couch potatoes'—and we thereby lose the ability to think or act for ourselves.
The media help us explore and develop our understanding of sex and violence by depicting social attitudes and inviting critique of the behaviours that are represented.	The media corrupt and pervert us and our children, desensitising our feelings and emotions, and encouraging immoral sexual behaviour and violent acts. The media therefore need to be heavily censored.
The media are truthful and informative, and they make a major contribution to democracy and social accountability, offering us a window on the world.	The media are a series of false constructions serving minority political interests.
The media are democratic, allowing all people a voice in the world.	The media serve commercial interests and are totally controlled by multinational corporations and advertisers.
The media enable free-thought and speech to be disseminated.	The media are in the business of controlling our consciousness, thereby controlling who we are and how we think. Access to the media is limited.
The media are shrinking the globe, uniting us and bringing us closer together, creating a 'global village'.	The media are making us all the same and destroying minority cultures.

Continued

For	Against
The media give space to the voices of different social groups and cultures.	The media are a form of cultural imperialism, whereby dominant cultures impose their values on less powerful cultures.
The media are an agent for social change.	The media maintain the status quo.

Two examples illustrate some of these arguments. John Hartley has noted how Nelson Mandela, in his autobiography, talks about his arrival in Canada where he was greeted by many Inuits who celebrated his arrival. They had witnessed his release from prison in South Africa on television. His freedom struggle connected with their own struggles for land and political rights in Canada, but it was television that had made possible the connection between these different and geographically very distant people. As Mandela said, 'Television had shrunk the world and had, in the process, become a great weapon for eradicating ignorance and promoting democracy' (Mandela, 1995, quoted in Hartley and McKee 1996, p. 74).

On the other hand, the media can be seen as part of a purely self-serving and profit-motivated consumerist culture. We can see this by looking at the *Star Wars* trilogy. The *Star Wars* trilogy was heavily promoted and packaged for re-release to a generation that had not seen the film on cinema screens. Huge amounts of money were spent advertising and promoting it around the world. This, combined with the system of film distribution and release, made the re-release commercially successful. Advertising, distribution, release strategies, and other marketing tools combined to make this re-release a veritable money-making machine. The original release of the first *Star Wars* movie also demonstrates the money-making capacity of Hollywood films. In the original release, the profits made from selling *Star Wars* merchandise—toys, models, sweets, and so on—exceeded the profits from the box office. The original *Star Wars* film can thus be seen as a long advertisement for other goods. It could be argued that this was a form of economic exploitation that preyed on children, who are often considered to be a very susceptible media audience. Recent documentaries such as *The Merchants of Cool* show how important the youth market is to advertisers. Advertising executives known as 'cool hunters' do extensive research in youth culture to identify emerging trends, and then use the media to market the subcultural phenomena they have 'discovered'. Their objective is to harness the aura of cool and create an association between it and a particular brand. Young people, whose incomes are not already committed to things such as mortgage repayments, are particularly vulnerable to such strategies because they are perceived to be impressionable and image conscious.

These cases are specific examples of arguments for and against the media. They help to flesh out the generalities evident in the statements in the table above. What specific examples did you come up with?

WHY TEACH ABOUT THE MEDIA?

Some of the reasons we teach about the media are shared by many media teachers and researchers. Many of these reasons demonstrate a love–hate relationship with the media.

1 We grew up watching television and films, reading comics and magazines, and getting lots of entertainment from the media. We spent a lot of our leisure time consuming media products. The media were a source of great pleasure. Today we still get huge enjoyment from the media, whether it's from reading *The Face*, using the Internet and email, watching *Big Brother* or *South Park*, or seeing Jane Campion's latest film at the cinema. We expect many students will also love some aspects of the media. Teaching about the media aims to enhance understanding, appreciation, and enjoyment of the media through understanding how they work.

2 We see the potentially positive social power of the media. Media communication systems are capable of sharing ideas across physical distances and of making them known despite cultural differences. They are capable of making information and aesthetic forms available in a truly global form to all people, and can therefore, in this capacity, be called democratic. The media have also been termed democratic because, like a representative democracy, media can provide a 'voice for the people' and can be used to represent the political views of minority groups as well as those of the majority of the population. The media are used to publicise political issues and events, making it possible for pressure groups to unite around a common issue or injustice, thus overcoming the disempowering effects of isolation in ways that would not have been feasible without mass communication. For the media to be able to fulfil these 'democratic' roles in public life, freedom of expression is crucial.[3] The media can contribute beneficially to the development of our future world, and it's important to demonstrate this.

3 However, we are extremely critical and distrustful of the ways the media are actually working. We believe that in key structural ways these powerful means of communication are often misused by the people controlling them. Consequently, it can be said that through their use of the media these people are abusing us, contributing to many of the problems of our society and helping to maintain a status quo of global social inequality. Teaching about the media can raise awareness of this negative side of the media, and can develop ways of challenging and changing the media at the same time as celebrating their positive aspects. This social concern gives a critical agenda to media studies. It looks forward to social change and it means that media studies operates in a social and political framework.

With its love–hate relationship to the media, our approach reflects some of the contradictions of the media suggested above. These contradictions make media studies a stimulating discipline! Understanding the media will help you to develop skills that will equip you to work creatively in the media, and it will also lead you to a critical awareness of how the media function, so you can engage as an informed citizen with the ongoing social debates about the media and the powers they have.

THE HISTORY OF MEDIA STUDIES

My views of the media grew out of the work I did as a student. I was influenced by previous writing and research on the media. One recurrent theme to emerge in work that attempts to understand the relationship between media and society as a whole (how the media function, what social power and influence they have) is fear and wariness about the power of the media, about what they can do. These fears are not new; every new medium has inspired similar debates. The distribution of information through printing supposedly threatened to corrupt, pervert, and destabilise society by mobilising the working class, uniting them around common concerns and facilitating the formation of trade unions and lobby groups. The emergence of the printing press also decentralised power by enabling widespread communication and distribution of information by organisations other than the state and the church. In the nineteenth century there was worry about how the reading of romantic novels would influence the minds of young women, who were a huge market for such fiction; Thomas Hardy's novel *Jude the Obscure* was banned for its moral dangerousness. We are seeing similar debates today over the advent of satellite communications and the Internet, both of which can cross state boundaries and are therefore difficult to police. These fears are about the political, moral, and cultural damage that the media are capable of.

There are important connections between advances in communication technology and social change, but often our hopes for new technology outstrip their actual impact. It has been common, since the advent of the printing press, for social commentators to see either positive or negative aspects in the perceived possibilities of new media technologies; current debates about the good and bad aspects of the media thus echo earlier arguments. Note the similarity between the following idealistic prediction about the telegraph in the 1840s and more recent predictions about the Internet and the 'global village':

> Universal peace and harmony seem at this time more possible than ever before, as the telegraph binds together by a vital cord all the nations of the earth. It is impossible that old prejudices and hostilities should any longer exist, while such an instrument has been created for an exchange of thought between all nations of the earth (quoted in Czitrom 1982, p. 10).

In contrast, here is the negative view, fearful of the dangers of the new media, from an article in 1889 called 'The Intellectual Effects of Electricity':

> All men are compelled to think of all things at the same time, on imperfect information, and with too little interval for reflection … The constant diffusion of statements in snippets, the constant excitements of feeling unjustified by fact, the constant formation of hasty or erroneous opinions, must in the end, one would think, deteriorate the intelligence of all to whom the telegraph appeals (quoted in Czitrom 1982, p. 19)

Fears about technological developments and the effects they might have on society have also carried through from the nineteenth century to present times.

Fears about political use of the media

The fears about the political ends to which the media can be put relate to the way the media can be used by political parties to control people. While the totalitarian fascist, and communist, states of the 1930s inspired these fears, political uses of the media also occur in democratic societies, where advertising can be seen as a form of propaganda and brainwashing that supports capitalist consumerism, as first shown in Vance Packard's book *The Hidden Persuaders* (Packard 1957). It is often argued that there should be controls placed over the media so they are not misused. Fear that the media may be used for political purposes is one reason why many countries insist that the government should not own and/or control the media; this fear also lies behind many of the debates about who has the right to media ownership.

Note, however, that media practitioners often see themselves as political watch-dogs, and in this respect are referred to as the 'fourth estate'. Used in this way, the term 'estate' derives from the time of the French Revolution, when the judiciary, the parliament, and the Church were referred to as the first, second, and third estates respectively. The media, as the fourth estate, are a body who can comment on, criti-cise, and investigate, through free speech, what these other institutions do. This is why 'freedom of the press' is so important.

Fears about the media's influence on morals

The moral fears arise from the concern that the media will be a corrupting force, particularly in relation to sex and violence. It is argued that people's values can be corrupted by the media they consume. This has led to 'moral panics' and campaigns against 'too much' sex and violence on television. The 'moral panic' tends to focus on the effects of media consumption on young people because they supposedly have less experience on which to base sound judgments and less developed critical faculties with which to position fiction or other media content in relation to exter-nal reality. It has been suggested that the cumulative effects of consuming media that contains violent and/or sexualised content might be particularly harmful for young viewers, due in part to the tendency of young people to learn by mimesis (mimick-ing or imitating what they see and hear). Because interactive media forms, such as video games, require participation in the acts of violence they represent, they are considered to be especially worrying. Another perspective on this issue is that the prevalence of high levels of gratuitous sex and violence in the media naturalises such material, making comparable behaviour in real life seem natural, normal, and acceptable. The danger here is that the media might inadvertently legitimate un-acceptable ethical positions such as the use of violence as a method of conflict resolution, or a lack of respect for one's sexual partners.[4]

Fears about the media's influence on culture

There are those who fear that the media devalue a society's culture because what they produce is so trivial or superficial. This is best illustrated in the debates around the relative importance of so-called 'high' and 'low' culture. High culture is suppos-edly the 'great art' produced by a society—art that is morally uplifting, complex, and serious. It is said to be found in such cultural products as opera, painting, and 'great' literature, the understanding and interpretion of which require training and special-ist instruction. It is elitist because usually only the privileged, educated, and rich have the leisure-time, money, and skills to access and appreciate it. Low or 'popular' culture, on the other hand, is what the 'masses' consume; it is found in magazines, mass-market paperbacks, popular cinema, and television. Critics of low culture deride it as morally degrading and simple.

Traditionally, low culture has been denigrated as inferior and potentially damaging, and the fact that it was a product of mass media was used to disparage it. Educators thought they needed to protect people against the damaging effects of low culture. The first teaching about the media was an 'inoculation' approach.[5] Teachers would analyse mass-media products in class, aiming to show students how corrupt, cheap, worthless, and harmful they were. It was thought that by giving students a little bit of low culture, students could be protected or inoculated, just as you inoculate against disease by administering a small dose of it. The high–low opposition still informs the way a lot of people think about the media.

Such oppositions are partly the product of class-divided societies—high culture is the province of the ruling and middle class, the bourgeoisie; low culture is the province of the working classes. But it's interesting to note politically that both right-wing conservatives and left-wing radicals have disapproved of low culture and the popular mass media: the right wing see the media as offering a diet of cheap, tawdry, corrupt entertainments, the left wing see it as a political sweetener acting to distract the workers from their political grievances.

However, since the 1970s there has been much study of popular culture in media studies. This is mainly due to the need to understand the dynamics of the huge media audiences attracted to popular culture—if so many people are consuming media texts, it is important to understand them—but it is also an attempt to validate popular culture itself and avoid labelling it as something inferior to high culture (p. 24).

APPROACHES

Various approaches have developed different interpretations and methods for analysing the media. Here are some of the most significant.

The Frankfurt School

The Frankfurt School is the name given to a group of Marxist scholars who first analysed the role of the media in Europe and Germany in the 1930s and then moved to consider American media in the 1940s and 1950s. After seeing the political dangers of the media in Nazi Germany, they defined the popular media in the USA as a 'consciousness industry' that helps to control the masses. The Frankfurt School were important in that they produced the first in-depth studies of the media and were the first to see the media as industries.[6]

Effects research

Different strands of research developed in the USA and Europe. In the USA most media research was conducted by sociologists and psychologists who were interested in trying to measure media effects. Effects research has been carried out extensively but its results have been contradictory because the effects of media are so difficult to measure. It seems that the only conclusion reached is that it is not possible to measure direct effects because the media are just one component of an infinitely complex chain of causal factors (such as the audience members' upbringing, social class, education, personal prejudices and experiences, and so forth). Nevertheless, researchers keep trying! However, a major question remains: How do the media, even if they don't have direct measurable effects, influence the way we think, feel, and behave? Contemporary effects researchers are investigating indirect, cumulative and long-term media effects that are important to understand and, if possible, to predict audience responses to media texts. We will return to this central issue since media effects is of interest on so many levels, from gauging the social impact of controversial media content such as stereotyping and pornography, through to more pragmatic, profit-driven questions related to advertising effectiveness.[7]

Communication models

A significant field of media research (predominantly of American origin) is interested in explaining how communication in the media works by focusing on forms of media communication (McQuail and Windahl 1981; Fiske 1990, chs 1, 2). Harold Lasswell's formula (Lasswell 1960) formed the basis for much subsequent work. It is still useful as a starting point for thinking about what communication is. Lasswell showed diagrammatically how the communication chain pointed to different areas of media research:

Areas of media analysis					
question	who?	says what?	in which channel?	to whom?	with what effect?
name of media element	communicator	message	medium	receiver	effect
type of media research	control studies	content analysis	media analysis	audience analysis	effects analysis

Source: adapted from McQuail and Windahl 1981, p. 10

Harold Innis, Marshall McLuhan, and Walter Ong are three important North American thinkers who have further theorised how the mass media work and communicate. They saw the media as significantly changing society. Innis's great contribution was to analyse communication systems in terms of how they change society's use of space and time, including analysing changing modes of transportation as forms of communication. He argued that the means of mediating and transmitting communications shaped history, and this argument was the genesis of the political economy approach to the media. McLuhan's well-known phrase 'the global village' points to the way that media communications unify the world (for further discussion of globalisation see pp. 303–4). Ong, taking a much wider historical view, looked at the way that the print media have changed Western society from a spoken-word culture (an oral culture) to a society based on print and literacy.[8]

Content analysis

Alongside effects research, the method known as 'content analysis' was developed. This aims to measure what the media actually produce: so, for example, research on women and the media could look at how much content is given over to women or what roles women are portrayed as performing. David Rowe has explored the Australian media's coverage of women's sport in this way and has discovered:

> In the period from 1980 to 1988, Australian newspaper coverage of women's sport rose from only 2 per cent of total sports reporting space to only 2.5 per cent, while in space devoted to sports results women's sport actually fell from 12 per cent to 8 per cent of all sports results, and there continued to be 12 times as many photographs of men's sports than of women's sports. Television coverage of women's sport is only 1.3 per cent of total sports time, compared with 56.8 per cent devoted to men's sport, 39.8 per cent shared and 2.1 per cent taken up by animals! (as quoted in Cunningham and Turner 1993, p. 210).

A more recent example is found in the film *Manufacturing Consent* (a significant analysis of media power). In this film the scholar Noam Chomsky looks at American media coverage of East Timor. He does a content analysis in order to support his view that the American media acted politically in the interests of the American government. Thus, in this film he combines content analysis with a political analysis of who controls the media, their bias, and their self-censorship.

He argues that during the 1970s the Indonesian government carried out atrocities on the East Timorese that were equivalent to those perpetrated by Pol Pot's Khmer Rouge forces in Cambodia, but that the American media did not report this equally. His content analysis of *New York Times* coverage of these two events between 1975 and 1979, graphically illustrated in the film, is damning: there were 70 column inches of Index listings in the *New York Times* Index referring to East Timor stories, compared to 1175 inches of Index listings for stories on Cambodia. He links this disparity in coverage to the fact that the USA was involved with the Indonesian government and was implicated in arms sales to Indonesia.

> The church and other sources estimated about two hundred thousand people killed [in the conflict over East Timor]. The US backed it all the way. The US provided 90% of the arms for the conflict. Right after the invasion [Indonesia's invasion of East Timor] arms shipments were stepped up ... There is no Western concern for issues of aggression, atrocities, human rights, abuses and so on if there's a profit to be made from them ... As the atrocities reached their maximum peak in 1978 when it really was becoming genocidal, [media] coverage dropped to zero in the United States and Canada (Achbar 1995, pp. 102–3).

Chomsky's work is very important in demonstrating the way political power can control the media—in this case largely through not reporting events rather than misreporting—and this finding is related to study of the political economy of the media.

Political economy of the media

This approach is concerned with the way the external forces of economics, ownership of the media, and political power impact on media production. The main argument put forward is that the media will serve the interests of whoever owns and controls them—whether this be private individuals interested in profit or governments interested in political control. The political economy approach involves conducting research into who owns and controls the media and what government legislation is in place relating to the media, in order to determine what effects this has on media output.

A simple example is the way in which the production output of the Australian and the British film industries has been determined by the domination in the market of the American industry, a domination felt not just in film production but also in terms of distribution and exhibition. This domination has always had an impact on Australian and British cinema chains, who are more committed to showing American than home-grown products. The varying fortunes of these 'indigenous' industries can be charted in relation to government policies, tax incentives, and investment, rather than in terms of the creative output of film-makers themselves. Similar studies can be made of Australian and British television production, which also engage in an economic struggle with American products.

Major concerns relate to the way media moguls such as Rupert Murdoch and Kerry Packer control more and more media outlets, and what political restrictions there should be on their media ownership. The worry is that their influence on media output is so great that it increasingly limits our information and gives them significant political power. Their companies have control over publishing, print, television, and satellite outlets; and over news, entertainment, sports, and other non-media interests. Australia witnessed the struggle over Rugby League, which was essentially a struggle between these two media giants. Each saw sport as a means to win audiences and market share. One of the ways satellite television has developed is by buying the rights to major sporting occasions: people who want to see these very popular events have to buy into satellite. Public broadcasting channels like the ABC in Australia and the BBC in the United Kingdom have lost out in this fight. Market forces are the all-important determining factor in terms of production and exhibition. These economic issues are also felt in relation to advertising, which is central in media production and threatens, through sponsorship, to exert more control over programming.

George Gerbner, from the University of Pennsylvania, articulates the argument that market forces lead to a standardisation of product:

> It's a paradoxical fact that while channels proliferate, we have many more channels than ever before … at the same time ownership shrinks; so what happens is fewer owners own more channels and therefore can program the same materials across many channels; *therefore instead of more channels creating greater diversity they seem to be creating greater homogeneity, greater uniformity, greater standardisation and greater globalisation* … they can say [to overseas channels] we can sell you an hour's worth of programming for less money than it would cost you to produce your own … this proposition is economically so attractive … it's a standardised, marketing formula [my emphasis] (*The Media Report*, ABC Radio National, 29 August 1996).

There are two major arguments put forward against Gerbner's view that economic control leads to homogenisation. The first is that the market-spread of media actually allows opportunities for many different social groups to be heard. People have the opportunity to use the media to their own advantage, as there is wider and cheaper access to media production and communication. The Internet is regarded as having a huge potential for such democratic and diverse output.

The second relates to audiences: ultimately the audience, the media consumers, have a big say in what gets produced. If they do not like a product it will fail, and this forces the media to produce acceptable material. Additionally, audiences can make their own meanings out of texts. They will not necessarily be brainwashed by what they consume. In relation to the claims that media owners such as Rupert Murdoch have too much control, John Hartley puts forward a contradictory argument:

> As for those who think that we have an evil empire, and it's run by that terrible Uncle Rupert, I'd ask people if they've ever heard of a chap called Panckouke and the answer is 'Probably not'. Nobody's ever heard of him. Panckouke was the most important media identity of the French Revolution. Have we heard of this man who owned lots of Parisian newspapers and French media during the French Revolution, or have we heard of the ideas being promulgated in those media by such as Tom Paine and Marat and all the rest of them? The latter. We hear about the ideas, we're interested in the ideas. Ownership in the long run does not determine what it is that these media are capable of doing, they're … historically outside of the control of the owners, who ride the waves of profitability and legislative opportunity for a while and then disappear. So yes, they're powerful in a business sense but I don't think they're as powerful culturally as people make out (*The Media Report*, ABC Radio National, 21 December 2000).

These debates about control, effects, and response are central to media studies. There is one other aspect of the debate around media power that is worth mentioning here: the idea that the way media products are structurally organised affects the way they present information. Two of the key terms used in this context are 'agenda setting' and 'gate keepers', terms most often used in relation to the spread of news and current affairs.

Agenda setting refers to instances in which media coverage draws attention to an issue or event and 'puts it on the agenda' for public discussion and debate. It can be understood as a form of media management or manipulation in which a public figure (such as a politician) might issue a press release about a particular issue, or include it in a policy statement or speech on more than one occasion, thus encouraging follow-up coverage by the media. This 'sets the agenda' or puts that particular issue on the media agenda, raising its public profile. The media also participates in agenda setting, simply by giving extensive coverage to sensational or spectacular issues and events. A snowball effect can result, as the media coverage of the topic gains momentum and generates the perception that the issue is of great importance (because it is getting so much press coverage!). For example, when cases of anthrax were discovered shortly after the World Trade Center and the Pentagon were attacked in September 2001, the media described it as a 'germ warfare scare that has engulfed Florida and spread to New York' (*Weekend Australian*, p. 1, October 13–14, 2001), despite the fact that there were only four people infected with the disease at the time the newspaper went to print. Extensive media coverage of the threat of biological warfare by terrorists in crop dusters created the perception that an anthrax epidemic was 'engulfing' the population of 'the free world'. When some people purchased gas masks to protect themselves from airborne diseases, the media reported that a wave of panic was spreading in response to the anthrax scare. Rather than *reporting* on a rising incidence of infection or an actual threat of escalating biological warfare, the media was *creating* a wave of panic by putting the issue on the agenda, on the front pages of national newspapers. Four cases of a disease does not constitute a remarkable increase in the risk of contracting the illness. In fact what is increasing is the reporting of the risk.

The notion that the structural organisation of media products affects the way they present information involves showing how the media are often drawn to give more weight to the viewpoints of official institutions than to 'alternative' viewpoints. The news is supposed to be objective and to provide a balanced account of issues and events, airing both sides of a debate and including diverse perspectives. However, the media often privilege certain voices, the agenda setters. This is not a deliberate conspiracy; there are various practical reasons for it: the fact that 'news' is deemed to happen in parliament or the law courts; the reliance on official spokespeople and experts to comment on events; and the use of journalists themselves (who select and present the news). All these are part of the gate-keeping process.

Many broadcasters rely on news-gathering organisations to supply their stories for them in the interests of cheaper journalism. Agendas are also set in advance: news is often 'old' in so far as journalists go to the people and places where they know things are going to happen. People who are skilled in dealing with the media often arrange press conferences in which they attempt to have the media report their point of view, as did Chris Corrigan, the Chief Executive Officer of Patrick Stevedores Company, during the 1998 Maritime Union dispute. Corrigan arranged for press reporters to be transported by helicopter over picket lines into the docks. Election campaigns in the United Kingdom, Australia, and America are now mainly orchestrated by the political parties as media events where politicians no longer meet the 'real' people. Instead, candidates do everything for, and in front of, journalists and cameras.

The way news is organised on a daily basis, with limited time and a need to maintain popular ratings, leads to simplification and sensationalisation of events. Consequently, audiences rarely receive a complex understanding of events with explanations that cover long-term causes: the focus is on what happened 'today' and how the situation changes hour by hour so that each new bulletin will have something more immediate. In this 'sound-byte' era the use of striking headlines and good pictures predominates. There is a stress on individuals to personalise stories,

Figure 1.1 Tom Tomorrow cartoon
Source: Dan Perkins, 1992

which tends to simplify issues. The Tom Tomorrow cartoon (Figure 1.1) illustrates these features of contemporary news reporting.

Perhaps because of the underlying ethos of individualism in Western society, the media place great emphasis on individuals and often make use of the persona or image associated with media personalities (such as celebrities, politicians or news-readers) in order to encourage the audience to 'read something more into the story'. For instance, if a media personality who is perceived to be trustworthy, authoritative, and associated with 'family values' covers a story on juvenile crime, the audience may readily accept that it is a serious issue, and they may even be led to discuss the issue in terms of lack of parental guidance, rather than in terms of broader issues of social justice. By making it easier to categorise and interpret stories in association with the image and values the presenter represents, the use of individual media figures personalises news stories and renders them more accessible. However, this tactic can also lead to over-simplification since the presenter's familiar image and their personal address to the viewer give out messages and impressions that should be substantiated with contextual detail and background information.

Political, economic, and structural power issues are very important. There are numerous books that look at this in detail. From an Australian perspective, Cunningham and Turner's book *Media and Communications in Australia* is particularly good (Cunningham and Turner 2001).[9] This book, however, will focus on how to explore media texts and how to see their connection to society. The approaches used in this book derive mainly from media-study traditions that were first developed in Europe in the 1970s and that can be loosely classified as part of cultural studies.

Cultural studies

Content analysis draws attention to what is being presented in the media. Its limitation is that it doesn't look closely at how events are portrayed, a question that has been explored more in European traditions of media analysis. Whereas American researchers were mainly sociologists and psychologists, European work came from literary, historical, and philosophical studies, and from traditions of textual analysis. In the United Kingdom the most significant research developed at the Centre for Contemporary Cultural Studies (CCCS), the so-called 'Birmingham School'. This brought together literary and historical approaches alongside Marxist, feminist, and structural linguistic theories, combining a body of critical theory with political concerns.

Concurrently with a number of other institutions, it helped develop and spread the growth of cultural studies, which continues to be influential today. Like the political economy approach, it is interested in questions of political power and the social role of the media. A significant area of its work has been in understanding popular culture and issues of representation, alongside examination of the role and position of the audience, and wider contextual studies.[10]

Media education

Since the mid 1960s, media study has grown in Australia, Europe, and America, in schools, colleges, and universities, so that it now stands as an important and popular academic area in its own right. It is possible to find a variety of media courses: mass communications, media studies, cultural studies, film and screen studies, multimedia, journalism, and so on. These are built, to different degrees, on an interdisciplinary method, and present a mixture of critical, practical, and vocational approaches.

CONCLUSION

In trying to define media studies and in thinking about all the approaches mentioned above, it is helpful to include both *sociological* aspects (thinking about the social and political roles of the media) and *aesthetic* aspects (looking at and evaluating texts). So we define media studies as follows: Media studies is the study of media technologies, media texts—their production, circulation, and consumption—and the media institutions in which they are produced.

This definition encompasses social questions about the role of the media, how people use and understand them (their influence) and technical or aesthetic questions about the ways they communicate (that is, the language of the media).

3   *What Do the Media Do to Us?*
Media and Society

The last chapter stated that media studies involves looking at social questions about the role of the media. This chapter looks at society and the media, and explores the relationship between the two.

CONTEMPORARY SOCIETY

We put forward three initial assumptions on which the following discussion is based.

1 Change and crisis

We live in a world that is undergoing huge social and political change and turmoil. Such changes went on throughout the twentieth century, so it is shortsighted to see this as something new. Nevertheless, the rate of change seems to be accelerating. Currently we face the following major issues:

a) an economic crisis of growth, consumption, and production

b) a political crisis in terms of power struggles fuelled by ethnic, national, and religious differences, as well as social inequalities, that are fragmenting individual societies: for example, the conflicts in former Yugoslavia, the former Soviet Union, Rwanda, Northern Ireland, and South Africa; and struggles between countries (for example, East Timor and Indonesia, India and Pakistan, Israel and the Palestinians, China and Tibet, and Iraq and the Western-bloc countries)

c) an ecological crisis of pollution, global warming, and diminishing natural resources. The extent of this crisis is not clear but it hangs over us.

2 Inequality and difference

Looking at the world globally, and at individual Western societies, there are major social inequalities. Societies consist of a complex network of groups with different—sometimes competing, sometimes overlapping—interests. Some of these groups are advantaged (in terms of such social goods as housing, education, and life opportunities) by virtue of their birth, their wealth, their class position, their skin colour, and even their gender. Consequently, there are advantaged and disadvantaged groups in society, or, to put this another way, dominant and subordinate groups. Three major areas of social division are class, gender, and race, although in some contexts religion, age, sexuality, caste, and education can be equally divisive in ways that are often closely related to these three primary categories. Class, race, and gender frequently restrict or create opportunities for individuals and groups to flourish and to attain coveted positions in society.

Global inequality

Since the beginnings of colonial explorations of the rest of the world by Europe in the sixteenth century there have been major differences in wealth between different countries and cultures. However, while we might imagine that the world is becoming more economically equal in the twentieth and twenty-first centuries, the opposite seems to be true, as evidenced by the data from the website of the *New Internationalist* magazine:

> Inequality is on the increase. In 1976 Switzerland was 52 times richer than Mozambique; in 1997, it was 508 times richer. Two hundred and fifty years ago, the richest countries were only five times richer than the poorest, and Europe only twice as rich as China or India. (*New Internationalist*, www.newint.org/index4.html).

3 Maintaining consent in Western democracies

If democratic Western societies are full of social inequalities, why isn't there more social disorder and disruption? Why don't the disadvantaged and underprivileged rebel more often? Why do so many people seem to accept their subordination? There is, of course, some social disruption, particularly crime. However, crime is not usually understood as the actions of oppressed social groups who are struggling to redistribute wealth equally and who have a political agenda. Rather, crime is usually understood as, and presented in the media as, the actions of deviant, psychologically sick (or evil) individuals. In general, Western democratic societies have found ways of maintaining social stability at the same time as maintaining social inequalities. They have succeeded in influencing the perceptions, beliefs, and values of many people, winning their hearts and minds so that they accept the status quo.

How is consent maintained? Here are some initial suggestions regarding this complicated question:

- Western liberal democratic systems give everyone the right to vote (in Australia it's a legal obligation). In effect, voting entails delegating power to the political party that best represents and articulates your priorities, values, and beliefs. Because the politicians 'represent' the views of the citizens who vote for them, this system is termed a 'representative' democracy. Clearly, the media play an important role in the process of representing and communicating political policies, issues, and so forth. But in practice there are limits to democracy: in most democracies there are only two or three significantly powerful parties, so your voting power is limited to the policies and values they are willing to promote. Because of the need to appeal to the majority of voters, the views of the main parties will invariably be relatively conservative, 'mainstream' positions that are often rendered even more general by the media's attempts to cater to the largest possible audience. In the USA only about 50 per cent of eligible voters actually vote at presidential elections. Do we conclude that 50 per cent of people don't think it's worth voting for the candidates? The general belief is that we are given a say in how our society works by being given the right to vote. Thus the consent of the population is won because we have a sense that we have contributed to and participated in the decision-making processes that structure our society.

- The West is built on an *ideology of individualism* that stresses personal rights, freedoms, and equality. Such beliefs are often legally enshrined in statutory rights and freedoms. This is in contrast to the restrictions of communist countries and other societies such as China, who appear to limit individual human rights in the face of collective social good. As individuals, we may appreciate the freedoms that Western democracy offers us, and we are encouraged to believe they make the system just.

- Because Western societies are well developed economically, they are able to offer a relatively high standard of living: most people have access to, or possession of, a phone, a fridge, a television set, a video recorder, and a computer. This is backed up by welfare systems; many people receive benefits (in Australia and the United Kingdom it is possible not to work and still receive some money to live on, although this is getting more difficult) and health support. All these factors keep people relatively content and contribute to a belief that Western democracy is the best system available at present. Even if you do not believe in it, it is relatively easy to survive, and it is easier to go with the system than against it.

Such ideas and beliefs are also maintained through a number of social institutions, one of which is the media. The media are a central arena in which 'consent' is won and maintained by representation, agenda setting, branding, and other mechanisms that position certain values, issues, and attributes as being important, desirable, natural, or normal. This argument informs many of the points made throughout this book and will be illustrated in numerous examples. It is based around theories of ideology, hegemony, and discourse, which are explored in Part 4 of the book and throughout the rest of the text.

HOW THE MEDIA WORK

Here are five starting point positions:

1 The media show us what the world is like; they make sense of the world for us

The processes of representation, interpretation, and evaluation are absolutely central to media studies.

Representation

The media—press, radio, television, cinema, and so on—have become the place through which we receive most of our information (and entertainment) about the world, so they are the primary source for how we see the world. For example, most of us have some idea of what the Himalayas are and even what they look like, but this knowledge is most likely to be gained not from our actual experience of going there, but through reading about them, hearing and watching media stories told about them, and viewing pictures of them.

Interpretation

In their representations, the media give us explanations, ways of understanding the world we live in. They take on an interpretative role by consistently privileging some issues and identities while devaluing others.

Evaluation

In so doing, they teach us how to understand the world, other people and ourselves, how to 'make sense' of the information about the world that we receive.

We can understand these three processes in relation to gender and ethnicity/race. The media 'teach' us about masculinity and femininity, what it means to be a 'normal' man or woman; they 'teach' us about race relations, about non-European and European cultures, about the supposedly typical characteristics of these groups. In the social roles that they assign to men and women, non-Whites and Whites; in the desirable and undesirable stereotypes that they continually present, they give us a structure, framework, and pattern for understanding ethnicity and gender issues. I'm not saying that the media set out with this educational—teaching—agenda in mind, or that they are necessarily even conscious of what they are doing, but that the influence they have on us as we grow up, reading and consuming the media, is to give us these patterns that explain how we will see ourselves and others, how we will understand gender, race, and our own identities as men or women, non-Whites or Whites. This is the politics of representation. As Richard Dyer says, 'How we are seen determines in part how we are treated, how we treat others is based on how we see them; such seeing comes from representation' (Dyer 1993, p. 1).

Of course it is possible for the media to give many different explanations of the world, many contrasting ways of making sense of masculinity/femininity and other aspects of identity, but this book argues that across the major media outlets there is a tendency to give broadly similar views of the world, what we will call later a shared or dominant 'discourse' on masculinity/femininity that outweighs other viewpoints.

2 Media products do not show or present the real world; they construct and represent reality

Many media products re-present the real world but these media products are not the real world itself; they are *re-presentations* or *constructions* of the world. This is also crucial and is explored in depth in chapters 4 and 5. Media studies examines how the media constructs reality, and then explores the values, beliefs, and feelings that these constructions present to us.

3 The media are just one of the ways by which we and society make sense of the world, or construct the world

The media are not the only social forces to 'make sense of the world' for us, nor do they have total control over how we see and think about the world. There are other forces of socialisation that they combine with. Most significant for children will be the socialisation they receive through the family and education systems, which 'teach' them how to understand and act in the world. As we grow up, other views about how to behave, about social morality, are disseminated through a whole set of legal, cultural, and political forces. The media provide just one arena in which these views are presented and popularised. The media generally act to reinforce values that are part of the whole society.

4 The media are owned, controlled, and created by certain groups who make sense of society on behalf of others

Those people who own, control, and create the media are media producers. They are not a totally separate social group, since they are also part of the audience and society as a whole, but they are a small, elite group. They are a complex group of people including:
- owners and business managers, who are concerned primarily with the need for the media to make profits
- creative personnel: writers, directors, camera-people, webmasters and so on
- technicians who run the equipment and machinery.
    Even these categories overlap in a number of ways: for example, many technical jobs are also creative, some managers have creative interests, and most creators are aware of financial needs and constraints. But note that:
- despite the fact that there are a small, limited number of media producers, they speak to, and on behalf of, the whole society (addressing a broad cross-section of the public)
- those people with most media power—particularly financial and creative power—are an even smaller group
- there is limited access to resources required for media production
- those groups who make sense of society on behalf of others are predominantly White, middle-class, and male. Without suggesting any conspiracy here, it seems obvious that they prioritise White, middle-class, masculine values as the norm, since such values are natural to this group. Consequently, the media have a tendency to make sense of the world from this particular point of view.

5 The need for popularity

As an antidote to the notion of a powerful elite in charge of the media, note that the media have to sell themselves successfully to large numbers of the population: they have to win big audiences in order to be economically viable and survive. This need for popularity complicates, and adds a twist to, the power of the White, middle-class males. If people do not like a product, they will look elsewhere for one. So the media must satisfy their popular audience, which is predominantly working-class and is about 50 per cent female. When commercial television was first introduced into Western societies, audiences quickly turned to those channels that offered the most popular entertainment (particularly game shows and soap operas). There was a major move away from public television stations—the ABC in Australia and the BBC in the United Kingdom—that offered many programs with middle-class and highbrow values. These channels have continually struggled with the need to maintain ratings and the need to present programming that satisfies its mass audiences. The ABC is still regarded by many as elitist because it privileges high-cultural texts, although it can also be seen to offer an important alternative to mainstream programming and the predominantly American content offered on commercial channels.

Consequently, there may be an interesting contradiction between the values of media producers and their audiences' desires, a contradiction that is revealed in the course of satisfying the imperative to popularity; there is thus a recognition of the powers of the audience/consumers to determine which media products succeed. We could argue that audiences influence, if not control, media output through their choices over what media products to consume.

To analyse the role and position of popular culture in a way that considers both its products and the way audiences/consumers use them is complex. The media were described by the Frankfurt School as a 'consciousness industry' performing a kind of social control in keeping the masses ordered, but some cultural studies critics see them as a source of potential democracy and empowerment for the people.[11]

This contradiction is illuminated by two different ways of defining popular culture. The first defines popular culture as those cultural pursuits that are *of*, or from, 'the people'; that is they are produced organically, by 'the people' themselves (this definition was most often used when describing earlier folk-culture activities such as songs and dances). In a modern context the notion that popular culture is the culture of the people rests on the idea that ratings and other feedback mechanisms ensure that the content of television and other media forms is at least partly determined by what the people (the consumers) want. The second defines popular culture as *for* 'the people'; this suggests that something is handed down to them that they accept. There is a big difference between that which is of/from and that which is for the people; this difference is useful in thinking about the power of the media and whether it lies mainly with the producers or the users/audience/consumers; whether the content of the media derives from the culture of social elites or from the culture of larger social groups, 'the people'. As usual, there is no simple answer in media studies; we may find elements of both bound together.

THE ACRONYM 'CRASH'

Looking at the social role of the media means being interested in the social values and beliefs of media texts—their ideology. The acronym 'CRASH' foregrounds social issues and social differences. Each letter stands for a way of socially categorising people, and each category usually includes both the socially advantaged and disadvantaged.

'C' stands for class. Modern societies have been described as consisting of three classes: the upper/ruling class, the middle class, and the lower/working class. The upper/ruling group is the smallest in numbers and is the most socially advantaged or privileged, while the lower/working group is the largest in numbers and is socially disadvantaged. Definitions of class are usually framed in terms of either the power (and wealth) or the cultural values of a person. These definitions are complex, and are more difficult to use today than previously, as societies have become much more fluid in terms of social class. In other words, it is less easy to categorise people according to class. Nevertheless, it is worth noting that modern industrial societies, in the wake of increased and continuing high levels of unemployment, now use the term 'underclass' to describe a significant portion of the population, and it is clear that society still has broad divisions both in terms of wealth, money, wages and in terms of what are regarded as acceptable cultural values. So it is still useful to employ this category in understanding society.

'R' stands for race. The world is made up of different ethnic groups and most modern societies are multicultural or multi-ethnic. Historically, however, some races or ethnic groups have dominated and exploited others, in particular through colonialism and imperialism. Racial inequalities and conflict persist, and we can see the existence of dominant and subordinate racial groups, as well as negative attitudes and stereotypes being directed at some ethnic groups.

'A' stands for age. Society is made up of all ages, but many societies have 'ageist' aspects to them in that older and younger people are treated as second-class citizens.

'S' stands for sex and sexual orientation. In comparison to women, men are a socially advantaged group in modern societies. Men have more social power and control than women, and there is discrimination against women. There is also discrimination on the basis of people's sexual preference or sexual orientation—that is, who they are sexually attracted to. Heterosexuality is seen as the norm, while homosexuality, lesbianism, and bisexuality are seen by mainstream culture as deviant, thus making those who are not heterosexual another disadvantaged group.

'H' stands for handicap. Handicapped and disabled people (also known as differently abled people—note how different words and labels, *different discourses*, carry different associations) are another social group who are disadvantaged or discriminated against in various ways.

We could use other categories (height, weight, and hair-colour, for example) as markers of normality or deviancy, but these five (class, race, age, sex, and handicap) are particularly useful for drawing attention to social discrimination. One might also want to consider religion as a category for understanding social groupings. We want to add one more element that provides a broader context in which the key elements in the CRASH acronym are all situated: environment. Our society at present faces a global environmental crisis above and beyond purely human social issues. It's important to see how the media portray the environment today, how they encourage us to make sense of the world globally. It is interesting that the media seem to celebrate the natural and non-human world in many ways—notice how often animals are used positively in advertisements. Yet human growth continues to threaten the planet. You can now contextualise the acronym CRASH within broader environmental considerations, and use it to analyse media texts and to understand how you and others are socially represented, categorised, and positioned.

1 *How are you placed in relation to these six categories? How does it feel to be in these positions, and how well-represented are you in the media?*

2 *How do the media represent the world in relation to these six categories? Ask the following questions of specific media texts/images, using CRASH as an approach:*
   a) *How does each media text/image represent the environment, class, race, age, gender, and (dis)ability?*

Figure 1.2 Advertisement for Levi's jeans

Source: Levi's jeans *circa* 1990

Figure 1.3 Advertisement for Grosby slippers, *circa* 1998

Figure 1.4 Campaign image from the Disability Services Commission

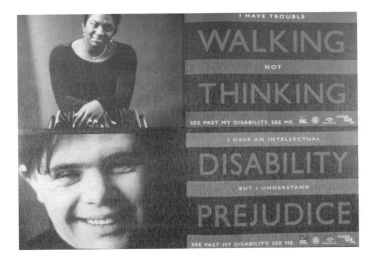

    b) *What would each media text/image look like to a working-class person, a person of non-European descent, an old person, a woman, a homosexual person, a handicapped person, a person concerned with the survival of endangered species?*
    c) *Do the media give a privileged view to some groups over others, showing some groups as advantaged, others as disadvantaged?*
  3 *Look at Figures 1.2, 1.3, and 1.4. What views of age and disability are presented in these three advertisements?*

MEDIA AND SOCIETY

The big question we keep returning to is how, or whether, the media affect and influence us. We like the way the cartoon in Figure 1.5, by Kerry Millard, presents both sides of the argument.

Figure 1.5 Millard cartoon
Source: Kerry Millard 1996;
published in *Australian
Lawyer*, November 1996

Looking at media influence relates to a wider philosophical question that recurs, in various forms and situations, throughout this book: are we automatically affected and controlled by forces outside ourselves (the cogs-in-the-machine view of human beings) or do we have freedom and autonomy (literally the right of self-government or self-determination) to make our own decisions (the free-will view of human beings)?

In relation to the media, are we controlled by the media or do we have freedom and choice over how we use them? In Chapter 13 we explore various theories of social construction that suggest we are unconsciously positioned and determined by forces outside ourselves (pp. 207–8). We argue here that we are programmed and controlled by forces outside our control (including the media), but through our own rationality, our feelings, and consciousness we have the ability to question and change things: we can make choices.

The key to our autonomy is our awareness and understanding, our conscious-ness, of how the world works. Sometimes our awareness of the world may be dormant: 'If it ain't broke, don't fix it' is a well-known adage, so if things seem to be working OK, if people are happy with life, then society can continue as it is, we don't need to think about what's happening, our awareness can be subdued or lie dormant. But when things go wrong, break down, fracture, then we have to look for new ways of living. We have to make an effort to understand what is happening and look for new solutions and systems. Social change occurs at these moments of fracture and crisis.

The Port Arthur massacre in Tasmania (a man shot and killed 35 people) or the Columbine School shootings in America (13 people killed by a high-school student) can be seen as examples of how moments of social fracture, in these cases horrifying and apparently inexplicable massacres, force people to question social rules and norms that were previously accepted as a natural part of life. In the case of the Port Arthur massacre, attempts to answer the question of why one person would go on a random killing spree produced various theories. One course of action was to challenge and change Australia's previously accepted laws of gun control. These events produced shock waves in Australian and American society, forcing people to ask how and why such things happen. The attacks on the Pentagon and the World Trade Center on 11 September 2001 led to an even more widespread sense of shock, leading people to consider what causal factors might have motivated the terrorists. The media played a central role in people's attempts to find explanations, leading to different kinds of reactions.

To open up this issue of free will, ask yourself these two questions. Generally do you see people, and yourself, from a deterministic perspective as 'cogs in the machine' or as self-determining individuals with free-will? In relation to the media, how much do you think the media affect the behaviour of people, or yourself; how much are you free of their influence?

Write down your thoughts on these questions, drawing on your understanding of people and the media, and using examples from your own experience. Ask other people these questions and record their views. Try to include both general views and particular examples to illustrate these general views.

Do the media reflect or affect the world?

Traditionally two models have been suggested as ways of understanding the relationship between media and society. The first suggests that the media reflect the realities, values, and norms of a society. Thus if we want to study a society we could turn to its media—its films, novels, television series, and popular stories. They will reflect to us what people feel and think, how they behave, and so on. The media act as a mirror of society, or a 'window on the world', which can be used as a resource to understand the society. The second model suggests that the media affect how people think, believe, and behave. The media construct our values for us and have a direct effect on our actions. We will examine both models.

The media as a reflection of society
The main arguments against the notion that the media reflect the norms, values and realities of society are that the media construct and change events rather than just reflect them. As an example, think about events that happen in the real world but that are presented extensively in the media—events such as Princess Diana's funeral,

the Academy Awards ceremony, or the Olympics. These events happen independently of the media, but the media build them into something more, into media events, constructing rather than just reflecting them (Wark 1994).

In Australia, the Melbourne Cup horse race is celebrated nationally (and more recently internationally, thanks to worldwide coverage by the media) as 'the race that stops a nation'. This is presented in the present tense, as though it has always and will always be true. Historically, the race only dates back to the nineteenth century; but more importantly 'stopping the nation' only became a real possibility once media communication could transmit this event 'live' across the nation, through the telegraph, then radio, then television. At this point the media allow the possibility of a simultaneously shared, national event (the significance of the Melbourne Cup relates to Australia's search for national identity). Events that bring the nation together into what Benedict Anderson (1983) calls an 'imagined community' help Australians to define themselves and their culture. One national character aspect celebrated in the case of the Melbourne Cup is the triumph of leisure over work.

The media hype up the significance of such events. The newspapers, radio, and television networks start reporting and speculating on the race several weeks in advance. (It fits neatly into the annual sports calendar by coming in early November after the Australian football and rugby seasons have ended, and before the cricket and other summer sports seasons are fully under way, so there is plenty of media space available for it.) It becomes a feature on non-sports media programs, becoming a major news event, so that, for example, Radio National news programs actually broadcast from the race meeting. The speculation about who will win is linked to betting and commercialism: participating in the event means being involved in some form of a bet.

Two points emerge from this 'media event':
- 'Stopping the nation' is only possible via the media, so we can say that the media construct this event rather than reflect it.
- If you are a regular media consumer, you should 'naturally' be interested in this event, particularly if you identify yourself as Australian. Indeed the media suggest that not being interested would mean being un-Australian.

The second point relates to how the media construct and shape our actions, our sense of who we are, our daily and annual routines. This is an example of the way we live in what we call the media-world. The media contribute to the construction of a calendar of annual events. Such constructions are not new; throughout history societies have organised themselves around cyclical events, mainly religious holidays and festivals linked in some way to the change of seasons and the practices and rituals of food gathering. These practices have changed with the process of industrialisation so that holidays and rituals are now organised to suit the needs of an industrial society. The biggest annual media event is Christmas (see Chapter 15), but other times also become media events. Valentine's Day, Mother's Day, and Father's Day are all becoming part of the social and media calendar. These three days are commercialised through the buying and sending of cards and presents; their media promotion is important financially. Gradually, almost every week and every day of the year is designated a particular event or linked to a particular cause, and the media are central transmitters and publicists of these events.

Christmas comes earlier each year; occasions like the Academy Awards—a wonderful piece of media self-promotion and American imperialism—are increasingly big media events. Note how they become part of everyday conversation—'Did you see the Oscars?' people ask us. Knowing who the winners and losers are, what they wore, and who they came with, becomes an important piece of social knowledge, a sort of cultural capital, for social intercourse. Not knowing threatens social exclusion. Increased coverage is facilitated by improved technology (satellite link-ups) that allows the instant and cheap transmission of perfect images and sounds from continent to continent in a way not possible a few years earlier. Note for yourself how particular events have become media events and are developing each year.

There is a process of selection at work here; some events are not promoted—for example in 1998 the African Football Cup of Nations, which is arguably the third most significant soccer competition in the world after the World Cup and the European Cup, received virtually no coverage or news reports in Australia outside SBS, the multicultural television channel. In contrast, American football and world grand-prix motor racing receive extensive and increasing television coverage across the globe. Are these selections made on the basis of audience desires and choice, or on the basis of commercially driven interests? Motor racing, one of the few arenas still available for cigarette advertising and sponsorship, is particularly interesting in this respect. There are big commercial interest groups supporting and lobbying for its media coverage.

While the media thus construct and promote events like the Melbourne Cup, they also change events. The simple act of recording an event will alter it. This is most apparent with the camera. The presence of a camera alters people's behaviour. This may happen in small ways, but it is nevertheless a factor to take note of. It has been a major concern for documentary makers who try to record 'real' events objectively; many now recognise that their presence changes their subjects.

See what happens when you point a camera, whether a photo camera or movie camera, at someone, or they point one at you. It is likely that the person being photographed or filmed will do something in response to the camera, but even if they don't do anything different on the outside you and they will be feeling something different inside, emotionally. The event has thus been changed.

Media recordings have also begun to determine how and when real events will take place. The links between sport and media are significant; each lives off and supports the other, and this relationship means that sports tailor themselves to fit in with and benefit from media coverage. So, for example, when a goal is scored in Australian Rules Football in televised matches, the umpires wait to see a light from the television channel indicating that the television advertisement is finished before restarting the game. Matches are also scheduled over the weekend to fit in with and maximise television viewing times. The Olympics coverage is organised around getting good television coverage and being able to present this across the world for peak-time viewing; because of this imperative, the marathon has been run at times best suited to worldwide television audiences, rather than to athletes.[12]

The media can become an important player in more significant events. One of the most celebrated examples is the media coverage of the Vietnam war. Television pictures of American atrocities and injuries became a major factor in the development of the anti-war movement in the USA and Australia, resulting in popular protests that helped to end the war.

So far the arguments about reflection have considered how the media influence real-life situations; they cannot mirror or reflect them innocently since they become part of the events and change them. When we consider fictions, however, is the reflection model useful? Do fictions show outsiders what life is like in any particular society? Can we gain an understanding of America, Africa, or Australia by looking at their television dramas? The reflection model is unsatisfactory here if it assumes that media products transparently reveal the truth about any society. Using this approach you would assume that the television soap *Neighbours* gives an accurate reflection of Australian daily suburban life! It is clear, however, that while it may reflect some current social attitudes, we need to understand *Neighbours* more fully by locating it in its overall social context, in particular by looking at who produces it and under what constraints. Furthermore, we need to understand the actual social situation of Australia (or the United Kingdom) at the time of the production and consumption of the program to understand how the program fits the popular imagination of its audience. That is, we need to try and understand why Australians and Britons might watch *Neighbours*: how its particular depiction of reality gives these audiences certain pleasures, and how these pleasures relate to the actual reality of the audience. This is particularly significant when trying to understand why *Neighbours* is so popular for a British audience. Is it that its utopian, sunny, and clean lifestyle offers escapist pleasures to an audience living in the stressful environment of a bleak, urban, British landscape?[13] Even the absences or omissions in media texts reveal interesting information about the social issues that were current at the time and in the place where the text was produced, so it is very important to be aware of what is excluded. For example, capable single mothers and people in caring homosexual relationships were rarely represented prior to the mid-1980s.

However, if we were trying to understand British or Australian society in the 1980s and 1990s, *Neighbours*, given its extreme popularity, would be one useful source, amongst many others, to try and get a picture of how those societies worked, what their beliefs and values were. It could, in other words, be partially used as a reflection of this historical period.

The effects model: what sort of influence do the media have on audiences?

Let's now consider the effects model. Part of the problem here is what words to use to describe what the media 'do' to us. 'Effects' is often used scientifically to suggest there is a precise response triggered by the media: we watch something and it makes us do something. The word 'influence' is more useful in that it allows flexibility: we watch something and it encourages us to do or believe something. The term 'affect' is also useful as it can refer to 'change' in a general sense, or can be used specifically to indicate the physiological dimensions of emotional responses (such as hair-raising fear or the hot flush of embarrassment or shame). My argument throughout this book is that the media can and do influence us in many ways. We will therefore prefer that term. Nevertheless, we will sometimes use the term 'effects' to indicate the direct or measurable 'results' of media consumption, and we certainly need to be aware of this term because it is a key concept in the debates about the media's influence and power.

How is the effects issue popularly presented? In 1998, a story in the *West Australian* newspaper with the headline 'Cartoon Triggers Illness' reported that: 'Hundreds of children have been rushed to hospital across Japan after feeling ill while watching a popular television animation program on a nationwide network. The cartoon … triggered convulsions in children … when a bright red explosion flashed for five seconds on television screens' (*West Australian* 1998a).

There seems no doubt that this particular episode of a popular program (*Pokemon*) did produce responses in many viewers but the effects of the media in this instance are not related to the violent subject matter (the content of the television program), but rather to its form (the electronic transmission of light signals). Similar effects to those described in the newspaper report on the *Pokemon* episode are found to occur as a result of stroboscopic flashing lights, which can produce epilepsy in some viewers. This is an example of the way the media can affect audience members on a physiological level. Psychological and direct behavioural effects of media content are much more difficult to measure. Similarly, it is possible to measure immediate, felt reactions like laughter or the tendency to tense up during suspenseful action sequences, but not complex, sustained emotional responses.

The media can also produce effects in our behaviour through their technological forms. Our daily habits and lives have changed radically through the increase of media communication systems. The development of the media has made our lives quicker, more sedentary, and more domestic: telephone and Internet communication allows us to contact each other instantly; mobile phones have given teenagers and business people more geographical freedom, enabling them to easily contact and be contacted by friends, parents, or business associates when they are outside the home or office. We can deal with problems, and communicate feelings, across distances in a moment and people no longer need to be able to do simple arithmetic, as they have learnt how to use calculators. The use of word processors has had a major effect on our own writing practices, making it much easier to produce material that can easily be copied, changed, and rearranged. So the very pattern of our daily lives, in the media–world we live in, is structured differently due to media technologies. This is part of what Marshall McLuhan was getting at when he stated 'The medium is the message' (McLuhan 1987, p. 7). Rather than concentrating on the content of messages, he wanted people to think about the media's technological forms and how these affected people.

But, in relation to the question of effects, affects, and influence, it is the area of media content and the way it is presented that we want to focus on in more detail. This is the area that raises most discussion and controversy. Another newspaper report, with the headline 'Suicide Alert on Film', shows how this argument can be popularly presented: 'The suicide scene in the latest film version of Romeo and Juliet has prompted concerns among psychologists and counsellors that the film romanticises suicide … "Anything that influences suicide [rates] to go up should be a big concern to society"' (*West Australian* 1997).

The implication here is that the film can directly encourage teenage suicide. At the beginning of the twenty-first century Australia has one of the highest teenage suicide rates in the world, with a particularly high rate among young males, and consequently Australian society is sensitive to this issue. However, moves to censor this film because of its portrayal of suicide would be profoundly misplaced. Youth suicide is the product of much wider social conditions, and it is these that need consideration. At the same time the media can still be part of these social conditions. Watching news reports about AIDS, terrorism, refugees, global warming, and famine might conceivably make someone who already feels depressed and disempowered become suicidal for reasons that are easier to understand than being seduced by the glamorous representation of youth suicide in *Romeo and Juliet*. To use a more concrete example, one of the statistics of male teenage suicide in Australia is that many gay youth attempt suicide. It is argued that this is because of their distress over the way society treats homosexuality:

> Between 20 and 35% of gay youth have made suicide attempts, the best available statistics show … Youthful gays often internalise negative stereotypes and images of themselves. And when you have been told that you are 'sick, bad, wrong for being who you are', you begin to believe it (Herdt 1989, p. 31).

Alan McKee (1997) has argued that the media are implicated in this because they present so few positive images of gay youth. He sees the need for popular gay representations as a way of helping raising self-esteem and combating these suicide figures. In relation to this issue, and to most others, the relationship between media and society is complex.

The effects issue is most often raised over questions of sex and violence. The simple hypothesis is that media violence encourages violent behaviour in the audience, and that sex portrayed by the media can corrupt the audience. Even though research about media effects is inconclusive, it is often suggested that criminal acts have been prompted by watching media violence or pornography, an argument that is sometimes used in law courts. The logical answer for many people is to limit what can be seen through censorship. However, as this line from the film *Scream* neatly suggests, the media are not responsible for making people bad: 'Movies don't create psychos, they make psychos more creative'. While accepting that the media can influence us, and that we need some forms of censorship, we make the following points against increased censorship and against the use of the effects model to justify it.

1 We have some autonomy (self-control, and self-determination) in how we behave; while we may imitate some things we learn from the media—what clothes to wear, styles of language and social interaction—we know what it means to be violent to someone and we are careful about such actions. We are rational beings who can think about and reflect on what we see and do. We also know the difference between, on the one hand, media representations, stories, and images of violence—that is, that they are stories/fictions—and the real thing. We can make judgments about what we consume from the media; we do not respond automatically to what we see. We are also adept at distinguishing between media representations, stories, and fictions that might contain images of violence (simulated using pig's blood and prosthetic wounds), and the real thing. Blaming the media is an excuse that denies our responsibilities (and it is often used legally as an argument for a lighter sentence for those charged with violent crimes).

2 It is important that we have access to information about real violence and sexuality in the world because restricting such access and information can be socially and politically repressive. The Vietnam war is a great example of how media coverage can provide society with information that has political consequences. Media coverage of this war was a major influence in turning Americans and Australians against the war. During the Gulf War in 1991 the Western media were much more controlled by the military, and the coverage, likened by many to a video game, was heavily sanitised as part of the propaganda to support the war. We need to have full access to knowledge of events that have a direct public influence on us. Since people rely on the media for information about distant places and events, control of media representations can be remarkably effective in promoting particular beliefs and attitudes: the media shape our perception to a certain extent.

There is also a question about how real violence is presented on television. So-called 'reality TV' programs such as *When Animals Attack*, and shows dealing with footage of actual police business and bad drivers, have been criticised for the way they sensationalise violence.[14] One of the things you will be aware of as media critics is how the language of the media—camera angles, music, editing, slow-motion, and so on—can be used to present and manipulate events in particular ways, and this does need critical analysis.

3 The case around fictional sex and violence raises different questions. Censorship laws in Australia, the United Kingdom, and the USA all underwent extensive liberalisation in the 1960s. Explicit sex and violence have become commonplace in fictional media, helped by improved technology and special effects that have made graphic portrayals, particularly of violence, ever more realistic and detailed. Reactions to this, and campaigns against media sex and violence, have been around since the 1970s, and there is continuous debate about these issues. These developments raise the following questions: Do we need censorship? Are there certain limits to what should be shown? Who should be allowed to see what? What lines and boundaries do we need to draw in order to enable audience members to make informed choices about what they wish to be exposed to, without undercutting the political and artistic advantages of freedom of expression and freedom of choice? How do we define the kind of characteristics or landscape that we want the media-world we occupy to have?

In the debate between libertarianism (autonomy and freedom of choice) and determinism (a more prescriptive, cogs-in-the-machine understanding of human behaviour as being caused, rather than chosen), we are inclined towards libertarianism. In an ideal world we would not need censorship, but this is not an ideal world; we need to protect people, particularly children, against images that abuse and harm them, or encourage such harm—we need some censorship and restrictions. However, I make two arguments against censorship:[15]

- The first relates to the value and importance of fantasy. Fictional stories, like dreams, allow us to explore and indulge in fantasies. Dreaming of attacking someone is not the same as doing it, yet many of us do dream of this at some time. Fictions allow us to explore and understand our sexual and violent feelings (see pp. 168–9). Bruno Bettelheim argues for the value of violent fairy tales for children. Although 'fairy tales underwent severe criticism when the new discoveries of psychoanalysis and child psychology revealed just how violent, anxious, destructive, and even sadistic a child's imagination is', Bettelheim argues that fairy tales allow a space for this imagination and that banning fairy tales, because they are monstrous and scary, would keep 'this monster within the child unspoken of, hidden in the unconscious … Without such fantasies, the child fails to get to know his [sic] monster better, nor is he [sic] given suggestions as to how he [sic] may gain mastery over it' (Bettelheim 1978, p. 120).

- The second suggests that censorship of violence or sexuality won't work. Censorship reflects a belief that if we control media images, we can control human behaviour; if we stop showing violence, people will stop acting violently. However, people act and feel violently to one another for a variety of reasons. If people want to watch a lot of violence/anger in the media it may be because there is a lot of violence/anger felt in the real world (the media are therefore reflecting these feelings). Anger caused by social oppression might be one such reason. The way to deal with such violence is not to censor the media, but to examine what is actually happening in society and try to deal with the deeper causes of anger and violence. Focusing attention on media violence and censorship distracts us from looking at the social problems that determine violence. If the violent feelings are really there, censorship won't make them go away anyway.

The same arguments apply to images of sexuality.

In an ideal world we would spend time understanding what people are feeling sexually and emotionally rather than resorting to censorship of the media. It is disturbing that people want to sexually abuse children or want to watch such representations, but the fact that they do points to the sexual problems in Western society. The media sometimes celebrate sexual feeling, but they also often point to the sexual problems and repression felt by many people. Censorship or fear of media images of sexuality draws attention to the need to look more closely at our sexual feelings, to deal with these openly in the real world. We might argue there is actually too little sex in the media, too few programs (like *Sex/Life*) that attempt to bring aspects of sexuality into more open debate.

The 'media effects' debate is a contentious one because it becomes linked to political agendas. Many of those arguing that television violence has dangerous effects on its viewers are seeking to put forward conservative and restrictive censorship legislation. However, civil liberty supporters are concerned about the possible erosion of democratic freedoms so they wish to argue that there are no clearly proven direct effects that can be measured, that the media do not have a direct effect. The danger of following this second position is that we lose sight of the fact that in some way, media *will* effect/influence their audiences, though it may be hard to measure and quantify in relation to any individual viewer. Music therapy is an obvious example. It is based on the assumption that music (a form of media) can and will affect its listeners. In his book *The Mozart Effect,* Don Campbell explores many examples where music is successfully used to produce different feelings and states of mind (Campbell 1997). If music can change or create different moods and feelings for its listeners, it seems crazy to deny that audiences won't be affected by media in some way. After all why do companies invest such huge amounts of money in advertising or public relations campaigns? We perhaps need to develop more subtle and sophisticated ways of studying and understanding media affects and influences. One analyst has used the concept of 'compassion fatigue' to suggest that there is a cumulative effect of seeing so many news reports of world disasters, famines, and human suffering. We learn to turn off some of our emotional responses—feeling compassion for these people and events—simply because they are too much for us to cope with. I know some people who avoid watching the (bad) news because they feel they are affected negatively by its continual cycle of disturbing events. So I would not deny that the media do affect us in certain ways.

In *The Politics of Pictures*, Hartley notes that 'when judging the merits of candidates for public office, the public must use photographs and talking pictures to decide the issue; acting as a citizen means engaging in the politics of pictures' (Hartley 1992b, p. 35). This quote illustrates just how important the media are in democratic public life, and particularly in informing the public of the different options they face as voters. Political communication is thus one of the key roles that the media play in society.

In an era in which personality and style are deemed to be almost as significant as policy and substance, the way in which a politician's appearance is publicised and reported in the press can have a profound impact on that person's credibility and political standing—and on the credibility of the media. Sadly, the press perpetuates the tendency to judge people, particularly female politicians, by their personal appearance. For example, One Nation leader, Pauline Hanson, has attracted a great deal of media attention over the course of her political career. In an effort to swing public opinion against the racist, right-wing policies she advocates, the Australian press has tended to ridicule her accent, her education, and particularly her appearance. A national newspaper ran a story entirely about Hanson's fashion sense (her image-management strategies) in which leading Australian fashion designers were invited to comment on the politician's personal style. The very personal comments that were printed made the press seem irresponsible and lacking in credibility.

Figure 1.6 Pauline Hanson during the Western Australian election campaign, 2001. 'She's got the right concept but she's missing the beat. Halters are definitely cool, but that print and that fabric ... It's not 21st century dressing.'
Charlie Brown, 'Dressed to Kill or to Distract', *Weekend Australian*, February 17–18, 2001, p. 5.

Figure 1.7 Pauline Hanson during an interview with Sydney radio announcer John Laws. 'She looks like a giant tampon. You just don't wear those dresses at her age. She's trying to be sexy. She's dressing a bit young.' Alannah Hill, 'Dressed to Kill or to Distract', *Weekend Australian*, February 17–18, 2001, p. 5

The resulting controversy raised the politician's public profile. Far from turning people away from One Nation's racist policies, this irresponsible reporting drew attention away from Ms Hanson's political messages and created a surge of sympathy from readers who rightly believed that the attack on personal style was sexist and unprofessional.

List three female politicians that you know of and consider how the media represent them. Are they given the same kind of coverage as male politicians?

Political communication involves far more than televising or reporting election campaigns and interviewing politicians about their policies. It also involves public information campaigns, media management, and image management on behalf of the politicians themselves.

Media management, as described by McNair (1995, p. 114), includes all the strategies that politicians (and their public relations personnel) use to control, manipulate, or influence media organisations in ways that correspond to their political objectives. These strategies include agenda setting and the organisation of media events such as press conferences and official openings of public buildings, complete with photo opportunities and speeches peppered with catchy sound bytes suitable for broadcast media. Since politics is central to the way the nation functions, such material is very important for the press, hence the media and politicians have an interdependent relationship with one another. The role of the media in political communication means that the media have a serious responsibility to the public.

A circular model

We hope you are beginning to see some of the complexities of the media–world relationship. We suggest the following model (Figure 1.8) as a way of showing the media both reflecting and influencing society.

In this model, media producers, media texts, and media audiences are separated from popular common sense. The media producers, in constructing their images

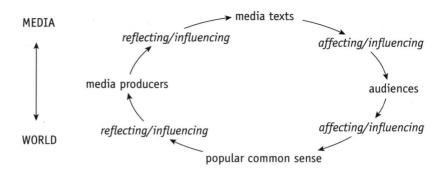

Figure 1.8 Model of the media–world relationship

and stories, are reflecting various social ideas and beliefs, held by different social groups. The audiences consuming these texts are partially influenced and affected by what they see. These influences then contribute to the overall social fabric of popular common-sense ideas.

But media producers, texts, and audiences are all part of the social whole; they are not separate entities. The media are one of the social forces that produce popular common sense, the general social beliefs and feelings of a society.[16] In turn, these social beliefs and values influence the media, who reflect them. Like the chicken and the egg, there is no simple solution as to which comes first, media representations or popular common sense; the two are permanently intertwined. What is more, in today's media–world, media images and reality often blur together: we begin to see real events in relation to familiar media images. For example, the Gulf War could look like a video game, and an observer of a real-life police raid can comment, 'It was just like NYPD Blue on the TV, mate' (*West Australian* 1998b).[17]

CONCLUSION

This chapter has put forward a number of assumptions and arguments about society and the media, and about the relationship between the two. These should form a useful starting point for your analysis and understanding of the media. It may be useful to return to these arguments from time to time, to remind yourself of them and to see how your understanding of them is developing.

4 *What's in a Name? Language and the Social Construction of Reality*

A central argument in this book is that media representations are constructions based on language. This chapter examines the nature of language and relates it to ideas about human societies as a whole and to the 'social construction of reality'.[18] It examines the role language plays in the social construction of reality. What we say about language in general can then be applied specifically to the media.

Here are my arguments in a nutshell:

1 Human societies organise and structure the world in particular ways.
2 In so doing they 'construct' the world and they construct 'reality'.
3 This reality tends to become normalised and naturalised so that it is taken for granted—'that's life'—by the people in that society.
4 We tend to forget that reality has been constructed or that it could be organised differently.
5 We learn about the world primarily through language, and thus language is crucial in this construction and in the transmission of this construction to others.

It's very important to note that this argument means that like the media, reality, the social world we live in, is also a construction. You can get an idea of how this argument works through the following imaginary example. Suppose a group of people who are dissatisfied with the culture and society they live in decide to start a new community on a desert island. Once on the island they organise their times and customs in the following ways: they decide to have an eight-day cycle in which they work for five days and rest for three. The men will all eat and sleep together in one building with the children, while the women eat and sleep in a separate building. Once every 32 days they have festivals where they dance together all night. The women go out and grow the crops while the men do all the cooking!

This may seem rather far-fetched, but it draws our attention to the way any society will organise its time, its rituals, its work practices, and so on. Anyone who travels from one culture to another feels initial surprise at how the new culture organises things differently. Travellers also often notice how the new practices become normal, so that when they return to their original culture it is their home culture that seems unusual.

Imagine the situation of any children born into our imaginary community. For them these 'new' structures would actually be the normal, natural, and everyday structures of the world. As children, we accept the customs of our family and society as normal, and in so doing we lose sight of the fact that they have been socially constructed. This is crucial. The 'naturalisation' of social construction blinds us to the fact of human agency in constructing the realities we inhabit. Throughout this book we ask you to be aware and wary whenever the terms 'natural' or 'normal' are used. These words are often used to naturalise forms of behaviour or social organisation so that we don't question them, but there is nothing natural about the way human societies are organised today. All our actions and behaviour are acted out in social situations and institutions that are the product of human cultures, not of nature. This is not to say that they haven't evolved in relation to natural climatic and geographic conditions, nor is it to say that there is something wrong with these practices, but they are not natural in the sense of being behavioural patterns that inevitably or necessarily arise from human physiology (such as responses to danger or the need for food).

If you have travelled to other cultures you will have experienced the realisation that society can be organised differently and that both the culture that is foreign to you and your own society are constructed by humans.

LANGUAGE AND THE POLITICS OF NAMING

Language, as the primary means of communication, is the central medium used for the understanding, interpretation, and construction of reality.

It is necessary for a moment to consider the nature of language and the relationship it has to the world. There are two theories for thinking about and understanding the relationship between language and the world:

1 **Reflective or mimetic.** This suggests that language simply describes the world, that it is a method used to name and describe what already exists. According to this theory all humans see the world in the same way, sharing the same basic concepts, and language is simply a vehicle for expressing these concepts and the world that exists independently of it.

2 **Constructionist.** This suggests that language doesn't describe a pre-existing world. Rather it constructs the world through naming it, and constructs the concepts through which we understand life and the world. Thus different languages represent the world in different ways, and speakers of one language will understand and experience the world in ways peculiar to that language and differently from the ways of speakers of a different language. This is not to deny the reality of the material world, or that it pre-exists language, but to say that it is only apprehended, only understood, once it has been named, or constructed, through language. All knowledge of reality is mediated by language. Our experiences of the world only take form when presented through language.[19]

Christian mythology illustrates the power of the word, of language, as a means of giving life and structure to the world: 'In the beginning was the word and the word was God'. One of Adam's first tasks was to name all the animals and plants, thus giving them substance or calling them into existence. The Bible tells us that language brings things into being. But there is not just one language, not just one way of describing the world. Anyone who has learnt a second language knows that the two languages do not correspond exactly, word for word. Different languages have different ways of describing or naming the world. For example Inuit language has as many as 27 words for describing forms of snow, whereas English just has two or three (Hall 1997, pp. 21–44). Reality can be named by language in different ways.

Colour is a good example. Although the spectrum of colours is a continuum in which there are countless variations of colour, through language we name it and structure it in a particular way. We simplify the spectrum into seven colours. This enables us to handle it and to describe it, even though we might find it impossible to point precisely to the place where red becomes orange or orange becomes yellow. The seven-colour system we use is just one possibility. We could break the spectrum into six colours, combining indigo and violet into purple, or nine colours, adding turquoise or teal, aqua or ochre, and if our language did this we would even begin to see the spectrum differently. So our words structure the world in particular ways in order to make sense of it.

If the reflective/mimetic method given above was correct then either there would only be one universal language that perfectly described the world, or different languages would correspond exactly so that there would always be exact equivalent words in every language. This is not the case. Not only do different languages carry slightly different meanings, but there are differences in such things as the way tenses are used and the use of verbs or nouns to describe things. Different languages structure the world in quite different ways, for example German is a gendered language with three different words for 'the' (das is the masculine form of 'the', used for phrases such as das Jungen—the boy—whereas die is feminine and der is a neutral term for 'the').

There is an anecdote about a Japanese company that wanted to mount an advertising campaign for selling razors for women to shave their underarm hair. The company used an American advertising agency. This agency devised a cartoon campaign that would feature an octopus shaving under its eight arms. When the commercial was ready the Americans showed it to staff of the Japanese company. These staff were taken aback and shocked, and they refused to accept the campaign. The problem was that in Japanese an octopus does not have eight arms, it has eight legs!

This story illustrates the idea that whatever language we are born into will structure the way we see and understand the world. This is the basis of the Sapir–Whorf hypothesis:[20] 'At the heart of the Sapir–Whorf hypothesis is the claim that the very words we speak and the grammatical structures we use actually influence or determine the way we think. In this light, language is not just a means of communicating ideas, it actually helps fashion them' (Open University 1981, p. 72).

Our view of the world expands as our language capacity expands. We might say that *we don't speak language, language speaks us*. This indeed is one of the main tenets of the work of Sapir and Whorf and of structural linguistics. It suggests that language constructs our identity, that we are a cog in the machine of language. This hypothesis has been interpreted in two ways:

1 our language determines our thinking; or
2 our language merely influences our thinking.

The second interpretation gives us a degree of autonomy. It is worth noting that if we discover new things or new feelings, we have to invent new words in order to describe them, and this gives us further autonomy.

I accept the constructionist position, as opposed to the mimetic position, and argue that language enables us to think and understand. It gives shape to our perceptions and feelings by giving them labels. It is a system of representation, a term discussed below (see pp. 150–2). The whole process of language is a naming or labelling process that carries profound social and political implications.

Imagine two people engaged in sexual activity. How do we describe or name what they are doing?

- They are making love.
- They have gone to bed together.
- They are having sexual intercourse.
- They are fucking.

All of these describe what is happening, but each carries a different set of connotations, associations, and feelings; they construct different discourses. The first description emphasises the romantic feelings involved, while the second is euphemistic, letting us imagine what is actually happening. The third takes a more clinical or medical view, while the last has a cruder, more derogatory feeling associated with slang. None of the descriptions is wrong; they all invite us to view and understand what is happening in different ways. Moreover, there is no way of describing what is happening that does not carry a particular view of the actions. Language is not natural, neutral or static. It is arbitrary, value laden, charged with power relations, and dynamic.

In considering the significance of language we suggest the following guidelines:

1 Language is not natural

It does not simply name the world as it exists, but constructs a view of the world. You may be already thinking that talking or writing about language is a complicated thing, because you have to use language in order to talk about it! As we write this we are aware of the different ways we could express things and the different meanings that would result. We are also aware that you, as reader, may want to take issue with some of the things we write. So we want to qualify what we mean when we say language is not natural. We don't mean that it is not natural for humans to speak. Indeed, it seems that one of the defining qualities of what it means to be human is to have an innate capacity for language.[21] Children have a built-in propensity to learn languages. But there is no normal, right, correct set of words, or way of speaking, that describes the world. Some theorists describe this characteristic of language by saying that all languages are 'arbitrary', meaning that there is no necessary connection between, on the one hand the sounds and symbols that make up any language, and on the other the world itself. For instance, the symbols and sounds in the word 't-h-o-n-g' don't have any real relationship with summer footwear, except by convention. 'Thong' doesn't look like something that goes on a foot; it doesn't sound like the slapping noise a thong makes on your heel as you walk; and the letters t-h-o-n-g certainly don't smell, taste, or feel like the objects with which they are arbitrarily associated. In fact, different cultures use totally different letters, sounds, and words to represent similar forms of footwear (for example, *sandalo* in Italian). In Australia, the thong has a privileged place as a recognised symbol of the relaxed, outdoor Australian lifestyle, to the extent that it featured in the 2000 Olympic Games opening ceremony in Sydney. But some cultures whose peoples don't wear thongs have no word to describe them at all. There are numerous languages that describe the world with their own particular inflections and biases. The idea of bias leads to the next point.

2 Language is not neutral

Language always carries some associations, connotations, or values with it. We have already seen this with the 'making love' example. Even ordinary words like 'up', 'down', 'top', 'bottom', 'left', and 'right' carry significant associations. They may be used simply to describe spatial positions. But 'up', 'top', and 'right' also carry positive connotations that relate to a culture that values right over left and is formulated on a competitive, judgmental ethos that compares us with others and grades us in hierarchical terms such that 'up' and 'top' are viewed positively, but both 'down' and 'bottom' are perceived as negative terms. Even as a named part of the body, 'bottom' carries negative connotations in the way Western culture sees it. In Christian mythology the left hand is considered to be the sinister hand because of its Latin origin in the word *sinistral* (meaning left or left handed), and because the devil is supposedly left handed. The right hand is the superior or dexterous hand (derived from the Latin *dextral*). These words are thus neither innocent nor neutral.

When it comes to more obvious political naming, it is easy to see how the terms 'terrorist', 'guerilla', and 'freedom fighter' have been used by different political groups to refer to the same people. Similarly the terms 'boat people', 'refugees', 'asylum seekers', 'queue jumpers', and 'illegal immigrants' were all used to describe people coming from Asia to Australia in 2001, and each descriptive term refers to a different discourse for understanding who these people are and what 'we', the Australian public, should think about them. (Note how 'boat people' is not a term/discourse normally used to describe the arrival of Captain Cook and his crew in Australia, although it could be.) In the immediate aftermath of the terrorist attacks of September 11, the Western press and some politicians presented the event linguistically in terms of 'good' and 'evil' (see Figure 1.9).

Figure 1.9 Headline from *The West Australian*, 13 September 2001

Note how these words:

- draw on a religious/moral discourse
- construct real events in the same terms as Hollywood adventure films such as *Star Wars*
- tend to negate the possibility of any debate or questioning about the meanings and causes behind such actions by simplifying the issues into good and evil, black and white, terms, thereby sending the message that the only right and logical action is to somehow punish, eradicate, or eliminate that which is 'evil'.

I'm not arguing the political rightness or wrongness of these different labels but noting that the same people can be named in very different ways with very different meanings, and that all such names carry a political position. The critical term 'discourse' is useful to help understand how language works. John Fiske argues that a discourse offers 'ways of thinking about a particular topic, set within a particular context'. He illustrates this:

> You remember what went on in the streets of L.A. after the Rodney King verdict? Was that a riot, or an uprising, or a rebellion? If we call it a riot, that puts it in one discursive frame which suggests that it was criminal, it was social disorder. If we call it an uprising, it suggests that it's another discursive frame, another discourse, there was a point to it, there was some organisation, it was against something and it wasn't just disorder. So the word 'riot' and the word 'uprising' come from quite different discourses, ways of talking about an event. So discourse is extremely important. No social event proscribes what discourse we use to describe it, it's our choice as users of language. And the way we make the choice of which discourse to put a particular event in, is an extremely important thing to understand. (ABC Radio National, *Media Report*, 7 December 2000)

Consider these three ways of describing the area comprising Africa, South America, and much of Asia: the 'Third World', the 'underdeveloped world', the 'majority world'. There is a major difference between the first two and the last. The first two place that world in the negative: if it is 'third' then it comes after the first two worlds—in the language of hierarchy and the language of competition, which structure much of Western thought, it comes below, it is a loser. Similarly, to be underdeveloped is to be less than, or the negative of, developed. So in this context 'underdeveloped' is a negative term indicating that such areas have failed to meet their full potential, to mature or develop.

The point is that while the terms 'Third World' and 'underdeveloped' world are helpful in some ways in pointing out the discrimination against this 'other' world, they remain negative and they give a view from the perspective of the minority world. They don't really challenge the structures of power involved. However, to name this area as the 'majority world' is to give a positive value to it, because in Western democratic thought majorities carry rights and power. Naming this area the majority world places the so-called developed nations in a minority position. Suddenly we see the injustice of a world that is heavily geared towards materially satisfying the minority. When I first heard the term 'majority world' used, it made me see things differently.

3 Language is a changing site of power and struggle

Language meanings and associations can change over time. We need to realise this so that in any language analysis we look at the meanings in a historical and cultural context. Dale Spender has noted how, in relation to gender, language has a tendency to sexualise and denigrate terms used to describe women (Spender 1980, pp. 16–19). She considers the pairings of a number of oppositions: for example, master–mistress, bachelor–spinster, king–queen, courtier–courtesan, lord–lady. Her findings are that either the female terms lose out in terms of their status and value— 'lady' describes ordinary women, whereas 'lord' retains its powerful meanings; 'bachelor' is a social position with more positive values than 'spinster'—or else the terms describe women in terms of their sexuality (for example, over time 'mistress' and 'courtesan' have become words that describe women's sexual position in relation to men).

The label 'queen' has been used to describe and denigrate homosexual men, the implication being that for men to be feminised is a put-down. However, note that in the struggle over language, gay men, who first appropriated and reworked the meaning of 'gay' to validate and celebrate homosexuality, have now also reappropriated 'queen' and 'queer' as positive labels of description. 'Queer theory' is now part of media studies and cultural studies, and fashionable boutiques proudly use the media to advertise 'Queen-sized shoes'.[22] In addition, many women have reclaimed and redefined the diminutive term 'girl' that has in the past been used to refer to mature women in an affectionate way that nevertheless diminished their social standing (by categorising them with children). Now the term 'grrrl power', said with a growl, leaves no doubt about the social standing of the women who use it to refer to themselves, their friends, and to media identities such as Lara Croft, Britney Spears, the Spice Girls, and Buffy. If grown women are being referred to with a word that means 'juvenile female', it seems that the term has literally been 'empowered' and redeployed in an assertive way. The term 'grrrl' has been taken up by groups such as Riot Grrrl and Surfergrrrls. These young feminists, often loosely associated with the punk scene, are media 'hacktivists' who surf the net and/or actively produce media and culture, from 'zines' to music. Such forms of feminist praxis not only recapture linguistic territory, but they also demonstrate that the idea of feminine passivity and technophobia is a fallacy.[23]

This shows that language meanings are not fixed and can be struggled over by different people, and by different social groups. Historically, such struggles have been very important, particularly those that occur between different ethnic groups. These struggles over language are struggles for power and they are very common.

In Britain in the eighteenth century the speaking of Gaelic in Scotland was forbidden and made punishable. The English were seeking to maintain their rule, or hegemony, over the Scots by wiping out Scottish culture and imposing English cultural values through the use of the English language. In Africa, America, and Australia indigenous languages have, at various times in the past, been banned as part of attempts to destroy the indigenous cultures. The English language has been used as a source of establishing European power over indigenous populations. Even now the use of 'Singlish' (Singaporean English) or 'Ebonics' (African–American English) is considered to be improper and accrues penalties in academic institutions in Australia, the United Kingdom, the USA, and elsewhere.

The African writer Ngugi Wa Thiong'o has described how language can be used in struggles for power between different racial or ethnic groups. He talks about how as a child in Kenya he was forced to learn English, on pain of punishment, in a way that alienated him from his own culture and people by depriving him of the use of his native language Gíkúyú:

> English became the language of my formal education. In Kenya, English became more than a language: it was *the* language, and all the others had to bow before it in deference. Thus one of the most humiliating experiences was to be caught speaking Gíkúyú in the vicinity of the school. The culprit was given corporal punishment—three to five strokes of the cane on bare buttocks—or was made to carry a metal plate around the neck with inscriptions such as 'I am Stupid' or 'I am a Donkey' (Ngugi 1986, p. 11).

He shows how the use of English as the official language devalued Gíkúyú and made it inferior in the eyes of those for whom it was a native tongue. As they began to see and think from a European perspective, Africans became alienated from their own culture and came to look down on fellow countrymen and women who had not taken up European ways and words. In this way European economic and political domination—imperialism, the establishment of empire—were supported through language control:

> Economic and political control can never be complete or effective without mental control … For colonialism this involved two aspects of the same process: the destruction or the deliberate undervaluing of a people's culture, their art, dances, religions, history, geography, education, orature and literature, and the conscious elevation of the language of the coloniser. The domination of a people's language by the languages of the colonising nations was crucial to the domination of the mental universe of the colonised (Ngugi 1986, p. 16).

This is not a form of *economic* imperialism, but of *cultural* imperialism. The final irony for Ngugi is that he became a great writer of English whose writing, which has become part of the English literary tradition, is not available to the majority of his own people, who cannot read English. No wonder then that as a successful writer in the 1970s he finally decided to renounce the English language, stating: 'This book … is my farewell to English as a vehicle for any of my writings. From now on it is Gíkúyú and Kiswahili all the way' (Ngugi 1986, p. xiv).

You can look at equivalent struggles over language between Australians of European descent and Aborigines, between non-English-speaking Australian immigrants and English-speaking immigrants, between Afro-Americans and European-Americans, between Native Americans and immigrant Americans. A key question in all these struggles is which language will survive. Even when one language triumphs, as English has done in many situations, there can still be struggles between different kinds of English spoken by different social groups: for example, between cockney English and 'the Queen's English'; between 'Black English' (or 'Ebonics') and 'White English'; between Australian English, Singaporean English, and American English; and between English spoken by Aboriginal Australians and English spoken by non-Aboriginal Australians. These struggles are about having power through language; forms of 'deviant' English are often forms of resistance by oppressed social groups.

In 1995 *The Science Show*, a program on ABC Radio National, broadcast a show about a Canadian conference on indigenous people (ABC Radio National 1995).

The program reported that the contradictions around language were keenly felt. On the one hand, there was an attempt to maintain traditional languages as a way of maintaining traditional culture—once the languages are gone, the culture will be gone. But there was also a recognition that English had become the language of many of those indigenous groups, so that in a sense it could be seen as their language. Moreover, English was the language that made shared communication between the different groups possible at this meeting (ABC Radio National 1995).

A further complication arises when we consider that English is increasingly the language of mass communication across the globe. It is certainly the language that dominates computer-mediated communication, especially the Internet. Therefore, in order to have one's voice heard in an international forum, being able to speak and write publishable and quotable English is becoming a necessity. Does this mean that the media contribute to the formation of a monoculture and that the globalisation of communication networks can only be seen in a negative light? We will return to this complex question in Part 6.

LANGUAGE AND SOCIAL CHANGE

Awareness of the above arguments about language (these arguments are really about the politics of naming) has led social groups to try and change language use in order to change social behaviour, particularly in relation to sexism. This begs the question 'Does changing language lead to social change?' Will, for example, using 'Ms' instead of 'Miss' or 'Mrs', 'differently abled' instead of 'disabled', change how we think, believe, and behave? While changing language will make some difference, several critics have shown that word changes can be accommodated by mainstream culture without social changes taking place.

> 'Ms' was originally intended to be a parallel term to 'Mr'. However there are lots of studies … which suggest that 'Ms' is not being used nor interpreted in this intended way. A study [in Canada] … showed that people had a three way distinction: 'Mrs' was used for married women, 'Miss' was used for single women, and 'Ms' was being used for divorced women … In Britain it's reported that 'Miss' and 'Ms' have sort of coalesced so the distinction now is between 'Mrs' and 'Ms'—'Mrs' signalling a married woman, 'Ms' signalling a single woman … the distinction 'Ms' was intended to eliminate is still getting expressed but in a different way (Susan Ehrlich, quoted in ABC Radio National 1995).

In many cases it is not only language, but also the medium of communication that determines people's choices about how they represent themselves to others. Many forms that have to be filled out (particularly those requiring computerised data entry) either neglect to offer 'Ms' as an option, offer it as a restricted option for females over a certain age, or offer it in conjunction with 'Miss' and 'Mrs', rather than using 'Ms' as the default title to designate females as the term was intended to function (the equivalent of 'Mr', which designates all males who do not have a specific title such as 'Dr').

Additionally, it seems 'Ms' has come to take on feminist connotations. The term 'feminist' has taken on negative connotations for some people, and so some young women do not want to use the term 'Ms' because they do not want to be labelled feminist (although they are clearly the beneficiaries in many ways of the feminist movement).

This example shows that in order to eliminate discrimination against women, there has to be social change as well as language change. Without social change, changing language is like fighting a losing battle. Nevertheless, language change and language awareness are an important part of raising our consciousness about bias and discrimination, and they thus help us move towards social change.

LANGUAGE IN USE

Language always exists in social situations. As such, it is available for different uses. In relation to gender, it is interesting to observe how men and women actually use language, as well as what kind of language they use.

1 *Observe how women and men speak when they are in single-sex groups and how they speak in mixed groups. Early childhood research experiments have observed that two girls, when put together and supplied with toys, spend a lot of time talking with each other, socialising through language. In comparison, two boys in the same situation tend to socialise mainly by playing with the toys, rather than through conversation. Other researchers have argued that men and women talk differently: women tend to talk more supportively than men, who talk more assertively than women; women talk more personally, and defer in conversation more; and men tell more jokes and interrupt more. What general differences do you notice in the ways, men and women speak?*

2 *Sometimes the term 'Miss' is used to communicate the information that the female in question is young. Does this tie in with cultural biases that glorify or privilege youthfulness in ways that might affect the choices women make about what title they use to identify themselves? Think about the names and titles that female celebrities are known by in the media, or ask a selection of women you know whether they choose to be called 'Ms', 'Miss', or 'Mrs' (if all those choices are available) and discuss their reasons with them. You might also like to ask where they stand in relation to the practice of a woman changing her surname if she marries, or passing on the father's surname to children, instead of or as well as the mother's.*

Exercise commentary

The title 'Ms' has not become naturalised in language (due to the backlash against feminism and to institutional resistance to including it as the default option on forms at banks, doctors' surgeries, and so forth). Sometimes women who wish to be called 'Ms' find that it is simply too difficult to get such institutions to change their title. In my experience, fewer female students choose to identify themselves with the title 'Ms' now than was the case a decade ago. When questioned, they explain that either they *don't* want to be identified as feminist or they *do* want to be identified as young and, sometimes, available. This cultural trend in naming may indicate that relationships with men and youthful availability are still defining features of female identity to a certain extent.

CONCLUSION

This chapter has argued that social reality is constructed and that language, as a system of representation, is central in this construction. Language is not natural or neutral but carries certain values. It is also a site of political struggle.

The arguments about language can be applied to the media, even though the media don't always use words—they might use pictures, images, forms of camera movement, editing, or even structural strategies (for example, positioning information that is considered to be most important at the top of a webpage). The media's techniques can be understood as 'the language of the media', and the discussion about language in this chapter is relevant to this language as well. As critics, we can begin to deconstruct the language of the media.

5   *Mediation and Representation*

REPRESENTATION

The last chapter argued that language constructs the world and reality by naming it, and thus by evaluating it, categorising it, defining it, and representing it. The media constitute a language system, so what we say about language applies to the media as well. Language and the media are systems of representation. 'Representation' is a key concept in media studies. It has three meanings:

1 to look like or to resemble
2 to stand in for something or someone
3 to present a second time—to re-present.

Language and media representations do all three.

We know and understand the world through language, through representations. This is not to deny that the real world exists—of course there is reality—but it is to say that all our learning about the world is mediated by language. There is a complex relationship between representation and reality. As Richard Dyer puts it:

> This is difficult territory. I accept that one apprehends reality only through representations of reality, through texts, discourses, images; there is no such thing as unmediated access to reality. But because one can see reality only through representation it does not follow that one does not see reality at all ... Reality is always more extensive and complicated than any system of representation can possibly comprehend and we always sense that this is so—representation never 'gets' reality, which is why human history has produced so many different and changing ways of trying to get it (Dyer 1993, p. 3).

What Dyer is suggesting here is that when we feel that language and representations don't do justice to our sense of reality, we have to find new ways of representing it, and indeed, this has been the history of human culture, constantly developing new modes of representation and discovering new ways of seeing reality. Here is another example of how we are not totally trapped like cogs in systems of representation, but can struggle to redefine language, to invent new languages. But the central point remains that we still only know reality through representations: 'there is no such thing as unmediated access to reality' (Dyer 1993).

Can there be unbiased, objective representations of the world? No. Because all representations come from humans, they come from a particular position. So they are relative; they will carry the bias of that particular person or group of people, just as this book carries our biases and positions. How true can representations be? In the end this is something we have to decide for ourselves. We may decide that one set of representations are true or that they are more true than others—in other words, that they are the best we can do so far. This is my position. As we grow and learn, we find models that best fit how we see and understand the world.

As an example of different and developing ways of looking at the world (very literally in this case) consider these maps (Figures 1.10–1.13). Which map appears most real to you? Which is most familiar and conventional? What are the differences between them?

Figures 1.10–1.12 Traditional world maps
Source: *New Internationalist* 1998

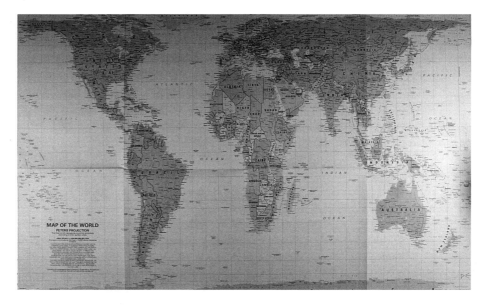

Figure 1.13 Non-traditional world map with countries correctly in proportion
Source: *New Internationalist* 1998; devised by Arno Peters

Exercise commentary

Traditional maps have tended to show countries incorrectly in proportion to one another, to the advantage of the European colonial powers, while the southern continents are shown far too small. Europe with its 9.7 million sq km appears to be larger than South America which is 17.8 million sq km ... North America appears to be considerably larger than Africa which is 30 million sq km. In fact it is smaller, (actually 19 sq km). Scandinavia, 1.1 million sq km seems to be as large as India with 3.3 million sq km.

The new map [Figure 1.13] provides a helpful corrective to the distortions of traditional maps ... No less than our world view is at stake ... By setting forth all countries in their true size and location, this map allows each one its actual position in the world (*New Internationalist* 1998).

The above points are crucial. If you can 'get' these you will be well placed for the rest of the book! Talk them through with other students and try to see how they relate to your own experiences of language, the media, and reality. These ideas lie behind the important statement given earlier (see p. 22): media products do not show or present the real world, they construct and re-present reality.

We will develop this idea by looking specifically at the media apparatus to see how it deals with reality.

THE MEDIA APPARATUS

The word *media* literally means 'middle'. The media are the things that come in the middle of or mediate communication. They are the means through which message senders can communicate to message receivers, or audiences. Anyone wanting to communicate chooses a medium to do this, whether it be spoken or written language, some form of pictorial representation (pictures, diagrams, photographs, films, and so on), or another medium. Figure 1.14 is a modification of Lasswell's formula (see p. 12):

Figure 1.14 Modification of Lasswell's model of communication

In this formula the answers to 'WHAT' and 'by WHAT MEANS', in other words the messages and the modes, constitute today's media. In modern industrialised society, messages are transmitted through the technological means of print, film, video, telephone, computer systems, and so on.

We want to stress the process of mediation. The media stand between us and the world or reality. We can understand our relation to the world and the media according to the model in Figure 1.15.

THE WORLD REALITY ⟷ THE MEDIA ⟷ AUDIENCES

MEDIATORS IN THE MIDDLE
MEANS OF COMMUNICATION
(for example, language, films, photographs)

Figure 1.15 Model of media–world relationship, stressing the process of mediation

Note how the double arrows in this model recognise that the world impacts on the media and that audiences are active in making meanings—they don't just passively receive them.

In relation to the visual media of photography, film, video, and to the sound recording media it has been suggested that they are neutral mechanisms that simply mirror the world, giving us a window or ear on the world. Thus:

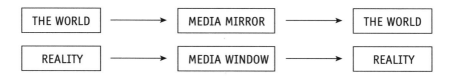

Figure 1.16 Model of the media–world relationship, suggesting that the media are neutral mechanisms that simply mirror the world

Media studies rejects this model, stressing instead media construction, selection and interpretation, to develop the concept of representation (Figure 1.17).

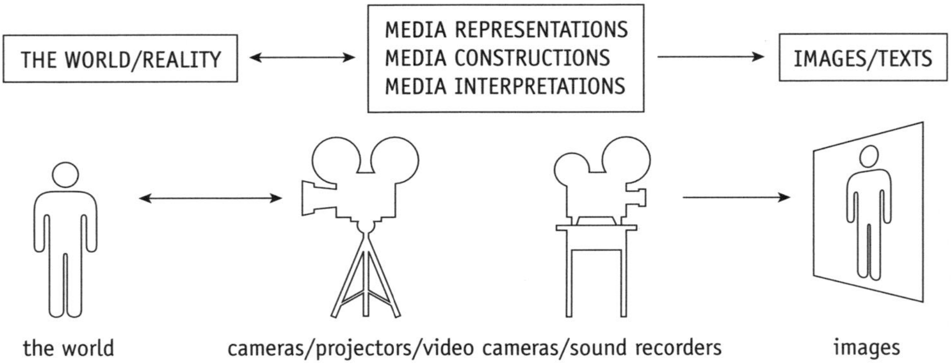

Figure 1.17 Model of the media–world relationship, stressing media construction, selection, and interpretation

We need to reiterate this point strongly in relation to the film-based visual media and sound recording media because of the particular qualities shared by photography, film, video and sound recording.

THE MEDIA AND REALITY

Many media and artistic representations refer to things from the real world. Novels, plays, poetry, painting, sculpture, photography, film, and video all aim to recreate objects and people that are part of the world we live in. But photography, film, video, and sound recording have a different relationship to the real world than other means of representation such as language, painting, and sculpture. They can reproduce reality in a mimetic way, and they therefore appear to show us unmediated reality. These media use actual impressions from the real world, digitising them, or putting them on to film, video, or audio tape, to produce images and sounds. Unlike words, paint, or sculpture, which are produced by the artist's hands and imagination, photography, film, and video actually record the reality that is out there. While these technologies can appear to be objective, human eyes, ears, and hands clearly produce subjective renditions of the world. This has tended to make people believe in the realism of these images; we think we really see/hear the truth when we see photographs, film, and video, or when we listen to recordings. Because these media depend on a connection between the real world (the referent) and the way it impinges on celluloid, light patterns, or sound waves, there is some truth in this belief—but only some. It is crucial to be aware of the fact that these 'realistic' media are constructed as well.

1 For a start we do not actually see three-dimensional reality, we see two-dimensional images of reality in film and television. It was Jean-Luc Godard who remarked: 'This is not a just image. This is just an image'. He meant two things. First, he was making a political point that the dominant media images of Hollywood and mainstream media do not offer a fair or just view of the world in terms of its representation of class and social differences. Second he was saying that images are just that: images—they cannot give us reality, the real thing. He

also commented that 'A photograph is not the reflection of reality, but the reality of that reflection' (Harvey 1978, p. 71). René Magritte drew attention to the illusory nature of images in many of his paintings, including his famous *This is Not a Pipe*. This painting draws our attention to the fact that the image is simply lines and colours that look like a pipe, that it is not the actual thing to which it refers.

2 Second, film, photography, and video images only give us a particular or partial view of what we are seeing. We only see from one angle, with one view and with particular lighting. We cannot encompass the whole of reality on the screen. There are numerous processes of selection and omission in the way we are shown things and the way different shots are put together. Editing selects and omits material. The choices that are made produce a particular viewpoint, give a particular meaning to what we see. Commentary accompanying images also explains what is happening in a particular way. Sound recordings are equally selective.

3 Finally, images are linked together within bigger systems of narrative and genre, which also affect how we see them. In these systems the media have tended to *hide their own processes of construction*. By this, we mean that when they show mediated events they aim to make them flow smoothly without showing the construction that has gone on. All the paraphernalia of representation—the autocue, lights, sound, camera equipment, and so on—are hidden from sight. Events seem to unfold naturally, as if they were happening before our eyes.

The third point is not so true since the 1990s as previously. The media sometimes deliberately reveal their own processes of construction: popular television studio programs show the cameras and behind-the-scenes crew, thus revealing and referring to the recording/constructing processes. Audiences are far more media aware; they enjoy seeing behind the scenes, and they understand that there is a lot of media manipulation and construction. The growth of media studies itself has contributed to this.

The ABC TV series *Frontline* (an Australian fictional series about producing a television current-affairs program) is an excellent example of the way the media are now showing the processes of construction, and exposing behind-the-scenes. Its popularity testifies to the audience's enjoyment at seeing media processes being deconstructed. It illustrates, very humorously, a number of significant things:

- It shows how news does not simply happen: it is gathered and selected. In this way, we can see how what might appear as reality is actually put together (constructed) and framed in various ways that are partly determined by organisational and time constraints.
- It shows that each item is given a particular slant by the way it is filmed, edited, and commented on (the media processes of construction). It shows sequences in the editing suite that, by leaving out important comments, making time seem longer, or even by running events backwards, make events appear in a particular way.
- It shows us that current affairs is actually determined by news ratings and commercial television interests rather than by real concern for the public good. We see this in the way that the motivation for everything the current affairs team portrayed in *Frontline* do is good ratings.
- Of course *Frontline* is itself a construction. It is not necessarily the truth. *Frontline* has its own angle on the media, but it does show us processes of construction.

1 *Watch any episode(s) of* Frontline *and note what examples of media construction it reveals.*

2 *Think of an occasion on which you or your friends/relatives have been represented by the media. Look closely at these representations and consider how you were constructed in this process. These representations may include visual images and words, either spoken as commentary or as printed text.*

Figure 1.18 and the accompanying quote is an example of constructed news: a press photograph and report of Sydney's 1996 Mardi Gras Festival.

Figure 1.18 News story and photograph of the Sydney Mardi Gras
Source: *Sunday Times* 1996

Well, hello sailors

A **RECORD** crowd of 600,000 watched Sydney's eighth annual gay and lesbian mardi gras parade last night.

Police said the massive crowd was generally well behaved.

There were two arrests. One man was charged with offensive conduct and another with four counts of assaulting police.

Fifteen people were taken to hospital and 13 treated for ailments ranging from chest pains to intoxication.

Tons of confetti, bottles and cans awaited council crews on Clean Up Australia Day.

Exercise commentary

We can divide this into three elements: the photograph itself, the caption and the written report. Briefly, the photograph appears to celebrate the event in terms of humour and pleasure. Through the humour associated with men dressing up and dancing, it mediates what might otherwise be, for some, a shocking depiction of homosexuality and male sexuality. Media coverage of the Mardi Gras continually negotiates this risk of offending viewers, using humour to offset this danger. However, while an essential part of the Mardi Gras ethos is to poke fun at male power and authority, this text seems to reveal a very different story. After the humorous caption and the positive opening paragraph, the selection of 'facts' to be reported depict the event in terms of criminality, danger, socially irresponsible behaviour (assaults, littering, drunkenness), and implied public cost (there is no mention of the huge boost to Sydney's economy that this event brings in through tourism). The reference to Clean Up Australia Day in the fourth paragraph (reproduced above) can be read as a veiled moral point suggesting that Australia needs to be cleansed of such events. This report thus becomes increasingly negative about and critical of the event, revealing an interesting example of selection and construction.

If you are having trouble thinking of an instance in which you, your relatives, or your friends have been represented by the media, think of family photos. These too are media representations/constructions, and a fascinating source to examine. It is interesting to note the increasing use of the camera and video camera to document family life—many people are now being videoed from the moment of birth—and to speculate on how this affects people.

Look at photographs of your family. Think about what is being constructed and communicated through these images and how well they fit the reality that you experienced. Consider the following (Figure 1.19) as an example of the family photo.

Figure 1.19
Happy families:
a family snapshot
Source: Author's
private collection

Exercise commentary

Figure 1.19 is a family photograph from 1960. There are two ways of seeing this constructed representation:

1 The image tells an idealised story of the family. It stresses family unity within a patriarchal framework; the five people are working together but are marked out hierarchically in terms of height and age—the male figure, who also has the biggest piece of machinery, is the leader, while the rest of the family are progressively scaled down. The image celebrates not only the family, but also the bourgeois values of property ownership and work: there is evidence of the large garden and the process by which it is cultivated and controlled. The audience is invited to celebrate this process of ownership, to witness and congratulate a successful and happy family. It makes an interesting contrast with John Berger's analysis of Gainsborough's oil painting *Mr and Mrs Andrews* (Figure 1.20) in one of the pioneering studies of media and representation, *Ways of Seeing*.

Figure 1.20 *Mr and Mrs Andrews* by Thomas Gainsborough (1727–88)
Source: National Gallery, London

Berger argued that in the eighteenth century, oil painting, one of the key media of its day, was a way for the property-owning classes to represent and celebrate their power and ownership. The picture of Mr and Mrs Andrews implies a sense of power over the land that they own. It is a land for recreation—Mr Andrews goes hunting (and his gun gives him symbolic phallic power)—and cultivation (we see corn and sheep). But clearly the Andrewses take no part in this rural labour—they simply own and benefit from it. In terms of gender we again see a subordinate female figure in terms of height, but also one who is established through costume as a source of visual pleasure and ornamentation.

Oil painting as a medium was only available to a small elite group who could afford it. However, photography in the twentieth century has set itself up, in contrast, as a democratic medium both in terms of its affordability to all and in terms of its skill—anyone can take pictures: 'You push the button, we do the rest', says one early Kodak advertisement. But it is still being used to celebrate official family and property values, and is one of the key mechanisms for documenting a positive account of the family through snapshots of weddings, christenings, holidays, preserved on the mantelpiece and in the family album.

2 There is an alternative view to the official reading of this family photograph and of the elements that the photographer has chosen to ignore. I am in it, and I know the histories behind the image, the realities that were being hidden. The father was having an affair; within a year the parents had separated; two of the children were extremely unhappy; and there was always a major argument about the children having to do gardening!

What this reveals is the process of construction involved in what we might regard as the most innocent of photographs—the family snapshot. First in the general ways family snapshots are constructed to celebrate family values, presenting a 'discourse' of the family; second in the detail of any particular image. You should be able to see this very clearly when considering how you have been represented and manipulated in any media constructions, since you will be aware of the realities and histories behind the constructions, and of the elements that the camera or the media text has chosen to ignore.

MEDIA FICTIONS

So far, much of the discussion in this chapter has related to media documentation of real events. Where do fictional media texts fit in with this? Most fictions refer to the real world we live in—Sydney, London, Los Angeles, and so on—so we can make connections between the text and the world. The recording techniques of film and video still hide the processes of construction and try to make events unfold smoothly and 'realistically' before us so that we forget about the processes of construction and feel as though we are seeing reality itself. The inherent realism of photography, film, and video (as discussed above) make events look lifelike, and the medium itself, the carrier of the message, becomes invisible or remains unnoticed. This allows certain ideas, values, and viewpoints (what we will later refer to as ideologies or discourses) to emerge naturally from the fictions, in a way that masks construction. Therefore if we wish to understand how we are being manipulated and what values are being presented to us, it is important to deconstruct fictional media as well as factual media.

There are also links between fiction and factual programs, and these links blur the distinction between fact and fiction. Fiction and documentary techniques are increasingly intermingled. For example, documentaries create narratives of suspense, have major characters, and present events with an eye to entertainment value by using exciting pictures and catchy soundtracks. Conversely, fictional film and television use documentary techniques in relation to such matters as camera work and visual style. You may have noticed that contemporary films will often move into black and white footage or use unsteady hand-held camera in sequences that aim to convey a sense of immediacy or authenticity. These documentary film-making techniques, associated with factual representation rather than with fiction, were used extensively in the low-budget horror 'mockumentary' *The Blair Witch Project*. The Blair Witch website, which was used as a powerful and inexpensive means to market the film, cunningly blurred the line between fact and fiction even further, to the extent that the film later suffered a backlash from viewers who felt that they had been tricked into believing it was a true story. This documentary style is also evident in the streetwise look of many advertisements and programs, such as *NYPD Blue*, *Wildside*, and *This Life*. The producers of *Frontline* used documentary styles and technologies to create a realistic effect. The producers felt that recording continuous action as if documenting a real-life situation, and using the Hi-8 cameras that are conventionally used in documentary film-making, would give the program power and realism. This blurring of techniques and styles means that fact and media fiction are not so clearly separated; both need to be critically deconstructed.

SIMULATIONS

Media construction and manipulation have been with us since photography and film began. For example, early film news coverage presented, as real, re-enactments of wars, criminal events, and natural disasters, and audiences accepted them as real. At least three things have happened since the 1980s to change the situation:

1 First, as mentioned above, audiences have become far more media literate and aware, and because they understand many of the media processes, it may be less easy to mislead them. There is a popular cynicism and distrust of the veracity of the media, an awareness of the way the media construct their versions of reality.

2 Second, the technology for constructing reality keeps improving. It is now possible, through computer technology, to compose photographs that appear real but are not. Brian Winston has commented that 'the technology for digital image manipulation is rapidly becoming a fixture in all newspaper and magazine offices'. The consequence is that 'by the summer of 1993, the status of the photographic image as evidence was becoming somewhat tattered' (Winston 1995, p. 5). This technique (known as scitexeing, meaning to retouch digitally) created a stir when the Ford company in the United Kingdom advertised in Eastern Europe. An original British advertisement for the company was 'morphed' to white-out Black faces.

There was an outcry about this from those ethnic groups being misrepresented, who objected to being whitewashed out of the image (not surprisingly, Ford were unwilling to allow the original poster to be reproduced in this book). The consequence of this ability to manipulate photographs is that media reality becomes even more questionable (Figure 1.21).

3 A new term has entered the debate about media constructions: simulation. We are now aware that the media can produce simulations—things that look like real events, but which we know are not—with virtual reality and computer technology. We can understand these simulations as forms of hyper-reality. Simulations are different from representations. Jean Baudrillard makes a distinction between appearance and representation. Representations refer to the real; they are still derived from actual events

beyond the camera; they claim a connection to the real world, and we believe there is some real world out there. In comparison, appearances do not claim to derive from something beyond themselves; they refer merely to other appearances—there is no direct connection to the real world (which we can never know) (Baudrillard 1988, p. 170). This is part of postmodern philosophy (see Chapter 20). Simulations, appearances and the virtual world are thus separate from reality. These terms have become part of the cultural studies debate about what the media do.

Figure 1.21 Digitally manipulated image of American President George Bush, circulated on the Internet in the weeks following the September 11 attacks on the Pentagon and World Trade Center (see also Figures 3.9–3.10, p. 160).

CONCLUSION

As media analysts, it is our job to be aware of the processes of media construction, to ask how images are being constructed and what view of the world we are being invited to see, and to challenge the reality of these productions. We are thus involved in the process of 'deconstructing' the images we look at.

Let's reiterate why this is important:

- As potential media producers—future writers, editors, camera persons, webmasters, and so on—you need to know the tricks or tools of the trade: how you can produce images that will move people to tears, anger, or joy. You deconstruct the media in order to know how to use cameras, lighting, editing, and so on, to produce particular effects and meanings. You are learning the aesthetics and technical methods of the media, the language of the media.
- As critics, you enhance your appreciation of media products through understanding the way they work; you can then communicate this to others.
- Through deconstruction you will be able to see the social and political views that are often implicit but not directly stated in media products. You thus reveal the ideological messages and meanings contained in the media, the ways they make sense of the world for us, through showing the processes of construction. This social, political, and ideological concern is at the heart of this book. Understanding that the media's views of the world are constructions is the key to ideological analysis.

6 *Texts, Meanings, and Audiences*

Having looked at media and society, and at issues of representation, we can now start to look at media texts and how we read them. The term 'read' is being used loosely here to refer to any process of interpretation—viewing, scanning, listening, and other forms of engaging can all be termed 'reading'. By 'text' we mean any media item, such as photographs, advertisements, films, magazines, websites, television programs, newspaper articles, and so on. A text must be capable of being reproduced and subjected to analysis. To read or decode a text is to make sense of it, regardless of whether it has actual writing in it. A central component of media studies is textual analysis. Later chapters present different critical approaches for textual analysis, but first we need a framework to answer the wider question of whether we can determine what texts mean.

There are two issues here:

1 We must question whether there is a definitive answer to questions about what a text means, and whether any text has a single, essential meaning.

2 We also need to consider what factors need to be taken into account in trying to establish what meanings a given text might hold.

Regarding the first issue, it is widely accepted in media studies that texts carry a number of possible meanings. These will depend on who is reading the text, when or where they are reading it, what theoretical approach is being taken, and so on. We suggest, however:

- that there is a dominant or preferred reading for a text (Hall 1980, pp. 128–38).
- that we will see different meanings according to the different critical criteria or personal perspectives we use to approach the text.

The second issue leads us to the different areas that need to be considered in trying to establish a text's meaning. This provides a framework for all textual analysis. There are three overlapping factors to take into account:

- texts—analysis of actual texts and their production
- contexts—the study of texts in their social context of distribution
- audiences—the study of how audiences actually use/make sense of texts.

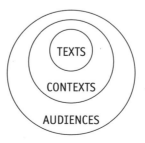

Figure 1.22 Model of the relationship between texts, contexts, and audiences

Each of these contributes to the readings we can make of what a text means. The more we know about all three, the more we will be in a position to establish the different possible meanings of any one text and to give reasons or explanations for these different meanings and readings. Figure 1.22 illustrates this diagrammatically.

TEXTS

To understand the text itself we need to consider two important elements. Both of these lead us beyond the text to extra-textual knowledge, but they remain focused on the text.

1 Background textual knowledge (context of production)

It is helpful to know about the actual processes of the making of a text. This gives us clues as to its meaning, illuminating the text in a number of ways.

a) We can begin by finding out about the acknowledged motivations of those involved in production. Who wrote, filmed, or photographed the text? What did they think they were trying to do? What have they said about it? What other work have they done that is relevant? Where several people are involved, we can ask questions of all of them and find out what interactions went on between them. We can also try to explore their unconscious intentions by finding out important personal details of their lives to see if these illuminate the text. The auteur approach to film study is an example of this way of understanding media products, in that it focuses on the director as the key figure we need to understand in order to understand the film texts (Cook 1985, pp. 137–46; Caughie 1981). A film's director is considered to be the author of the text, and they are assumed to have creative control over the project. Over the course of their career, some directors develop distinctive 'signatures' consisting of characteristic styles, themes, narrative structures, or motifs that brand their films. For instance, complex soundscapes and references to *The Wizard of Oz* can frequently be found in the films of David Lynch, whereas Martin Scorsese's films are often marked by Catholic iconography and an exploration of the discourse of masculinity. The auteur approach to films helps to elaborate on the context of production, but it neglects to acknowledge that film making is a collaborative process involving creative input from many sources including the scriptwriter, cast, and crew.

b) We can look at the conditions of production. What was being aimed for? What financial or political constraints were involved? Who commissioned the work? Where was it made? What social, political, and historical factors influenced the text? All these factors may have determined the outcome of the final text. Political economy approaches stress these elements.

2 The text itself

Some people argue that while background knowledge may be important, what ultimately matters is the text itself. In many instances this is all we have. Anyone looking at a text without background knowledge (which is the case for many audiences) can only determine meaning by looking at the text. Textual analysis focuses solely on the textual content and the textual processes used—the language, the way it was photographed, the kinds of camera movements involved, and so on.

However it is impossible to make full sense of a text (to give it a meaning) in isolation. Texts produce meanings by referring to the world outside themselves and by using pre-existing codes of representation. We, as audience, have to have:

a) knowledge of the real world to which the text refers

b) knowledge of the conventions of the text's medium (its photographic, cinematic, or televisual codes of representation).

For example the film *Dances with Wolves* will not mean much to audiences who don't already know something about the history of North America and the conflicts between Native Americans and the White invaders. Similarly, the film *Priscilla, Queen of the Desert* won't mean much to you if you don't know about the dominant codes of masculinity and heterosexuality in 1990s Australia. Each of these films also communicates by working with the codes and conventions of narrative films in general, such as the use of continuity editing, and of the Western and road-movie genres in particular. You need to know something about these to make good sense of the films.

Interpreting the meaning of the text depends on this understanding. In acknowledging these factors that influence the ways in which a text might be interpreted, we are beginning to refer to the codes and conventions the text is using in its production. Knowing the meaning of the text is dependent on these knowledges. We are beginning to refer to the text's context, but we are still focusing primarily on the text. Semiotic and structuralist approaches work in this way (see Parts 2 and 3).

CONTEXTS

Texts do not just appear on their own. They always exist in a social situation, in a specific context. Because the context of a text influences its meaning, we need to understand this context to do textual analysis. The two main contexts are space and time: where the text is being read and when it is being read.

Space

Every text appears in a specific *media* space and in a wider *social* space. A magazine advertisement appears in a particular magazine and is sold in a particular shop, in a particular location—town, village, city, and so on—in a particular society and country. A television program appears on a particular television channel, and is seen in a particular room—bedroom, hotel room, sitting room, lecture theatre, and so on—all of which are specific social locations. These different spaces can influence the text's meaning: depending on whether a particular advertisement appears in a teenage girls' magazine or a men's soft porn magazine, each of which has a different implied readership and a different social agenda, it will take on a different meaning. The same program screened on SBS, ABC, or Channel 10 in Australia will be affected by the differing ideals of each of these channels: multicultural/experimental broadcasting in the case of SBS, social responsibility in the case of the ABC, and commercial success in the case of Channel 10. In the United Kingdom, the same program shown on BBC, ITV, Channel 4, or Foxtel would also be affected by the differing aims and cultures of these channels.

Intertextuality refers to the relationship of media texts to one another in space and time. Texts are not presented in isolation but are surrounded by other texts—magazine articles, television programs, and so on—that will in turn influence our readings. Popular television texts used in an academic course will be seen and read differently because of the new context they are placed in. You may be watching *South Park* at home with your friends for entertainment and relaxation, while you eat a Big Mac. Alternatively, you may be watching it as part of a study text, in a university lecture theatre, and you may even be taking notes! Programs will even change meanings depending on who we watch them with—on our own, with friends, with parents, or with a group of strangers.

We can easily see the importance of context by thinking of clothes as a kind of text. The meaning of articles of clothing, such as a suit or a dress, will change depending on who is wearing them (man, woman, child) and where they are wearing them (at work, on the beach, at a party). Meanings are affected by and are dependent on their context.

Taking this further, it is important to look at the wider social context any text appears in: images of Madonna, found all over the world, will have different meanings in different countries. Teenage girls in America, Europe, Bali, or Iraq, with different religious, social and moral codes, from different ethnic and racial backgrounds, will make different readings of Madonna's appearance, songs, and performances (Schwichtenberg 1993; Fiske 1989a, pp. 95–113). The social norms and conventions of any culture will engage in an interplay with texts, and will produce different readings and meanings. So, we need to consider the placement of texts within their social and spatial contexts, and their relationship to other texts.

Time

It is useful to notice the time of day that people engage with media texts and consider how that forms part of the context in which texts are interpreted. Many texts are produced to fit specifically with certain times of the day and are consumed or interpreted at these times. Newspapers are focused on mornings (the time associated with going to work). Although there are matinee sessions, movies are usually watched by most people in the evening, in the context of leisure time. Television schedules are organised around what are perceived as normal patterns of work and family life, so that programs aimed at women predominate during weekdays, children's programs are usually shown in the early morning and early evening, adult programs are screened after nine o'clock, sport is shown during the weekends, and radio news bulletins are programmed hourly, on the hour. Thus texts have a specific time context that contributes to their meanings. Note that the Internet is not governed by the usual spatio-temporal conventions. For instance, Internet news bulletins do not focus on local issues as they can be accessed anywhere in the world, at any time. In fact, many Internet users log on at odd times when there is less traffic.

On a wider level, we must locate texts in the specific historical times that they are produced and consumed in. Hitchcock's *Rear Window* was made in 1954 and represents a study of spectatorship at that time. Hitchcock was critiquing the voyeuristic practice of movie-going and comparing it to spying on one's neighbours through the back window: the character in *Rear Window* uses binoculars and a photo-journalist camera equipped with zoom lens to intrude upon the private moments of his neighbours. In this film the medium presented as a powerful source of knowledge, but it is also seen as invasive and problematic. The social concerns in *Rear Window* revolve around privacy, reflecting the paranoia in the USA arising from McCarthyism. (In the late 1940s and early 1950s Senator McCarthy instigated the persecution of anyone suspected of being sympathetic to socialist politics, so the fear of being spied on was very real.)

Kathryn Bigelow's *Strange Days* (made in 1995 but set on New Year's Eve, 1999) also critiques the practice of spectatorship, and questions the ethical implications of the media. In particular, it explores the fear of new technology and social change at the turn of the century. As times change, so does technology. The mode of spectatorship at the centre of *Strange Days* is the SQUID (super-conducting quantum interference device). This device records the experiences of the wearer (not just what they see and hear, as film does, but what they taste, smell, and feel), and allows them to be played back by the media consumer. In this film, the media are compared to an addictive drug, and the social context of the film includes references to the beating of Rodney King by the LAPD, and the resulting race riots.

We must understand how social changes influence the subject matter of films, and also influence the way audiences understand and make sense of these films. When these films are screened again in the twenty-first century, we need to consider how a different historical context leads us to read them in a different way. For instance, we now know that the build-up to Y2K (the New Year's celebrations at the turn of the millennium) were largely anti-climactic and certainly not marked by the expected technological crisis or profound social change. In many ways, *Strange Days* was based on the sense of fear and excitement about the unknown future, and now that that time has come to pass the film is literally dated. In contrast, because so much time has passed since the release of *Rear Window*, the social concerns it showcases and the technology it uses to explore those concerns may seem trivial or clichéd, yet audiences may also derive pleasure and comfort from a sense of nostalgia as the story seems to come from a more secure and easier world than ours (a perception not necessarily based on truth!).

You should by now be realising that study of any media text involves a potentially huge and ever-expanding area of knowledge in relation to understanding terms of the text itself and all the different contexts it might inhabit. Consequently, our readings are never complete; we must be open to finding new factors, such as new background information and different aspects of the social and historical context, that will affect our readings. The more information we have, the closer we get to understanding what a particular text could mean and how it is able to produce such a meaning.

AUDIENCES

All our efforts at finding the meanings of texts may come to grief when we confront the real audience! Theories of the reader or audience suggest that because meanings are only produced by readers and all readers are different, any reading may only hold for particular individuals. Therefore, it is held, any attempt to discover a meaning for a text that holds for more than one reader must rely on generalisations, which runs the risk of becoming overly reductive. While we accept that audiences make different readings, we argue that it is still valid to explore texts through examining their textual codes and social/historical contexts, in a process of textual analysis. In doing so, we can look for a text's 'preferred' reading. While this is a valuable part of studying texts, it doesn't account for how audiences actually read texts, and since, in a way, media texts don't exist unless they are being read by someone, this question must be considered.

A large body of work focusing on media audiences acknowledges that the contexts, practices, and processes of reception are just as important in generating meaning as the context of production, the text itself, and the medium by which the message is communicated. This branch of media studies includes the approaches known as 'reception studies' (such as the 'uses and gratifications' approach, described on the next page), 'hermeneutics' (the theory of interpretation), or 'spectator theory' (of which psychoanalytic models of spectatorship are the most well known).

The inscribed reader

When we look at the way audiences engage with media texts, we need to consider what Paul Willeman has called an 'inscribed reader' (Fiske 1987, p. 62). The inscribed reader is an ideal reader who is constructed by the text, or who is imagined by the producers of the text. The inscribed reader can best be understood as a receptive member of the target market to which the media text is deliberately addressed. When considering the nature of the inscribed reader of a particular text, ask yourself whether the message seems to assume that the receiver is male, female, wealthy, poor, highly educated, image conscious, young, old, a member of a certain nationality, and so forth.

The actual reader

There are a number of ways we can study actual audiences or the actual reader. We can engage in audience research, looking not at texts and the meanings they contain, but at audiences and the meanings they extract from or ascribe to media texts. We need to observe, interview, and interact with audiences as, and after, they read media texts; we need to watch them watching/reading/listening to media texts. We can also develop theories that understand and explain the process of being an audience. These theories examine what is happening when people read texts. You can study your own responses and readings and compare them with other people's as a way to understand this method. Audience research is a crucial part of media study, as it completes the circle of text, production, and consumption.

Audience research and theories about audiences

Audience research has understood the audience in two different ways: in terms of effects and in terms of reception. Effects studies look at how audiences are directly affected by the media—the media are theorised as something that makes them a 'vulnerable' audience (this term is used in Cunningham and Turner 1997). Reception studies, which emerged in the 1970s, looks at how audiences are active: in other words, how they use the media (Cunningham and Turner, 1997, pp. 267–305).

Media scholars are not the only people who conduct studies of audiences. Audience research is very significant for the media industries themselves. For instance, companies such as Nokia invest a great deal in research that indicates how media consumers might use text-message services on their mobile phones, and organisations such as MTV use focus groups, ratings, and other forms of audience research as a way of finding out how successful they are and for testing out new products. In youth media, the advertising executives who undertake effects research are becoming known as 'cool hunters' or 'merchants of cool', such is their investment in the science of defining, packaging, and marketing images that will brand their merchandise as 'cool' in the eyes of young people. Research falls into two areas: quantitative and qualitative.

Quantitative research looks at numbers: for example, how many people watch a particular program? (Ratings research provides this information.) Qualitative research is concerned with how people are actually responding to specific programs: why they like or dislike certain programs, what aspects they respond to positively or negatively, and whether they watch attentively or have media such as television and radio on for the sake of companionship and background noise. Qualitative research falls within the reception studies area.

The media try to perfect techniques for measuring the nature of audience response, which they then use as a guide to improving their products. They use preview audiences to 'test drive' films. In these previews, audiences are asked to give their responses to the film. If some parts of the film don't work, then the producers can change them. The film *Blade Runner* is a well-known example. After initial audience previews it was decided to introduce a voice-over commentary and change the ending to romanticise and simplify the text. At the time the revised version of the movie proved more popular with the preview audiences. Some years later the cult success of the movie prompted the release of the 'director's cut'—the version Ridley Scott preferred to that dictated by the producers. This is a common phenomenon now, but the release of directors' cuts still has to be approved by the producers, and they are only released when it is expected that they will make a profit.

Political parties aim to make party political broadcasts that will win the support of the electorate. The preview process for speeches and broadcasts now measures audience response moment-by-moment, with audiences pressing buttons to indicate their responses. They are asked to choose between such given responses as pleasure/boredom, trust/distrust, and so on. A profile is built up of the most successful kinds of electioneering, and this profile is then built into the finished products. Market research is all about measuring, on the one hand, the numbers of audiences/consumers, and on the other, their likes and dislikes. It is a way of winning markets, and as such we can say that audience research is part of the market economy of the media. Considerable money and effort are put into this work.

In contrast to audience research conducted by commercial interests, audience research conducted as part of scholarly media studies claims to come from a disinterested perspective, and it is certainly less well funded. We have mentioned 'effects' research, which devises experiments to test audience responses to programs, including direct measuring of brain waves and physical reactions, and observation and measurement of actions and behaviour after watching programs. The findings from such research are inconclusive, partly because fear, surprise, and desire can generate similar physiological responses.

Earlier media analysis suggested three ways of understanding the media–audience relationship:

1 **Direct-effects**—the belief that the media are capable of radically affecting people's behaviour and beliefs to such an extent that they can be used for the purposes of political propaganda. The direct-effects model of media audiences assumes that media consumers accept the intended meaning encoded in media messages relatively passively, and that the relationship between media producers and consumers is both predictable and asymmetrical. There is a power imbalance: producers of the media messages have more control over meaning, and the transmission of information is largely one-way, with limited audience feedback or input. This view originated in the 1930s when the media were being used by the Nazis in Germany, by the Communists in the Soviet Union, and by advertisers and political parties in the USA. This view suggests that if you have control of the media, you can control people's minds, beliefs, and actions according to the process represented in Figure 1.23.

all-powerful media ⟶ brainwashing ⟶ audience

Figure 1.23 Direct-effects model of the media–audience relationship

2 **Reinforcement.** This model (represented in Figure 1.24) refines the direct-effects approach by suggesting that the media work in conjunction with other social forces, influencing people when their messages coincide with ideas being produced elsewhere in society—through education, the family, the churches, and so on. Paul Lazarsfeld's influential audience research suggests that the media are most effective when they work to reinforce existing beliefs, values and behaviours (Lazarsfeld 1949). Lazarsfeld's work indicates that people often tend to ignore or resist information that does not reinforce their existing experiences and opinions. However, the media can play a significant role in activating interpersonal channels of communication, especially when messages reinforce the beliefs of opinion leaders, who then pass on the media message to others within their sphere of influence, and so forth.

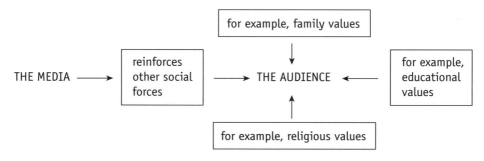

Figure 1.24 Reinforcement model of the media–audience relationship

3 Uses-and-gratifications (Blumler and Katz 1974). This understanding of the media–society dynamic (represented in Figure 1.25) acknowledges that audience members often use television, radio, and other media as a 'background' to other everyday activities such as cooking, domestic tasks, and studying. In such instances the audience might gain pleasure from using the media as a form of companionship, but they are unlikely to experience direct effects in response to media content, as they may only glance or gaze at the television, scan news headlines, or listen attentively to the radio sporadically. The uses-and-gratifications model suggests that direct media effects are impossible to measure due to the infinitely variable, personalised contexts of reception.

This model is significant for bringing the concepts of pleasure and gratification into debate about the media, and it paved the way for more recent research that argues that audiences are not just passive consumers brainwashed by media products, but are active participants, making their own meanings. Such qualitative studies are often carried out through ethnographic work, which explores audience responses through a mixture of direct observation, interviewing, and research.

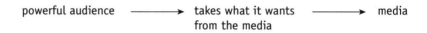

Figure 1.25 Uses-and-gratifications model of the media–audience relationship

Audience research based on an ethnographic model

Hall (1981), and then Morley (1992), worked with Hall's encoding/decoding model of communication.[24] This model suggests that different kinds of decoding or readings of media texts are possible, including:
a) **preferred readings**—readers accept what is being presented without question
b) **negotiated readings**—audiences accept only some of what is being presented to them
c) **alternative/oppositional readings**—audiences read completely against the preferred reading.

While the polysemic nature of media texts does provide the possibility for multiple interpretations, these readings 'correspond to the reader's response to his or her social conditions not to the structure of the text' (O'Sullivan et al. 1994, p. 239). Fiske and O'Sullivan give an example of how these three types of reading might occur in relation to one media text:

> We might take potential readings of a series of advertisements portraying women as sex objects, clothes horses, or mother figures. A preferred reading according to the dominant-hegemonic code is to accept and agree with this portrayal as natural, accurate, and attractive. A negotiated reading may be produced by a middle-class career woman who broadly accepts the preferred reading, but 'for others, not for me!'. She reserves the right to produce her own reading of the ads which corresponds to her social position as an independent woman. An oppositional reading might be produced by a feminist as insulting, degrading, restricting and proof of men's exploitation of women. The first reading could be produced

by women who would buy the products, the second by women who might, if it suited their purposes, and the third by women who would not (O'Sullivan et al. 1994, pp. 239–40).

Morley was interested in seeing how social groups, rather than individuals, make readings so he looked, for example, at trade unionists, young people, and non-White audiences, expecting to see them making readings that would support their own class, ethnic, or youth subcultural values.

The idea of researching audiences as social groups has been productive. Ethnographic research has been developed by Hobson and Brunsdon, who have studied women as audiences of soap operas (Hobson 1982; Brunsdon 1986). A considerable amount of work has been done exploring the way women read popular women's texts (such as magazines, melodramas, and romance novels) in a way that makes these texts meaningful to them (Ang 1985 and 1991; Radway 1987). This work looked closely at the social circumstances in which women consume the media and how they relate media texts and technologies to their real lives. Fiske (1989a) has developed the notion of audiences being able to resist what is presented to them. He argues that audiences have considerable power over the texts they consume. Schwichtenberg (1993) has explored audiences' readings of Madonna, particularly those made by young women, and by non-White and gay audiences. Dyer and others have looked at how gay and lesbian audiences read the media, as in Dyer's analysis of readings of Judy Garland (Dyer 1987, pp. 141–94). Again these studies show how audiences make use of texts from their particular perspectives. An extensive recent audience analysis is found in Henry Jenkins's *Textual Poachers*, in which he looks at a whole range of activities and ways of reading by different groups and people, particularly in relation to the *Star Trek* series (Jenkins 1992; Tulloch and Jenkins 1995). The 'poaching' idea suggests more ways of readers altering the texts and becoming active rather than passive. Turner (1993) adds another element in her book *I Dream of Madonna* in which she gathers records of dreams women have had of Madonna, introducing the level of the unconscious into audience studies.

In their efforts to understand how the media influence/affect us, media industries and social researchers will look for new ways of understanding and researching the text–audience relationship.

Interactivity and audiences

Another way to gain insight into media audiences and the changing role they play in media studies and media industries is to focus on the issue of interactivity. All texts are 'interactive' to a certain extent, in that audiences take an active role in interpretation. However, the term is usually used to refer to forms of communication in which the audience is able to use technology to manipulate the structure, sound, or image of the text itself. In this sense, interactivity is a property of the medium of communication that empowers the audience by offering them more agency and choice.

Interactive television (iTV) is one of the more interesting emergent technologies amongst the various new media forms that are currently developing. Unlike options such as Internet radio, which offer more restricted media consumption options than the parent technologies from which they have emerged, iTV promises to change the media industry landscape as well as potentially revolutionising the role of the humble TV in the lounge room and the relationship audience members have with it. Interactive TV has arisen from convergent changes in two different areas: the technological possibilities associated with digitalisation, and the socio–cultural changes that are broadly associated with the empowerment of media consumers. Over the past decade or so media audience theorists have seen a wave of resistance to the superficial illusions of advertising and commercial television, and a wave of acceptance for the relatively unpolished content of so–called 'reality TV' in which non–actors perform the unscripted dramas of their own lives within the structured environment of a live–in game show.

The tendency to embrace ordinary people, unremarkable stories, and everyday life is not restricted to television programming. It is also a characteristic of Internet content and other media forms as diverse as 'mockumentaries' such as *The Blair Witch Project*, talk–back radio, and the perennially popular biographies of 'average individuals' peppering the features section of newspapers and magazines. As technology becomes increasingly able to enhance and modify appearances using special effects (from 'Photoshopping' family photos, to digitally retouching Cameron Diaz's complexion), what once seemed to be unattainable ideals of perfection have begun to lose their currency. That audiences seem to be developing an appreciation of the value of unglamorous, unembellished 'normality' is evident in the enormous popularity of experiments such as 'Jennicam' (a web camera that films nothing but an 'ordinary' young woman called Jenni, going about her everyday activities in her unspectacular home).

Interactive television is in some ways the next step on from 'reality TV' in that it offers media audiences the capacity to influence the content of the program they are watching. But rather than enjoying the limited freedom of ringing in or logging on to vote for or against a television character, users of iTV in the future may have a degree of control closer to that experienced in a computer game such as *Lara Croft: Tomb Raider*. In television programs, possibilities might include choices among settings, characters, branching narrative pathways, and different camera angles; participation in quiz shows, right down to the detail of clicking on the brand of skateboard a character is riding and deciding to buy it via 'TV commerce'. However, the two most powerful aspects of increased consumer choice resulting from changes to television will certainly relate to escalating control over scheduling and the ability to bypass advertisements. In order to explain these possibilities, we need to understand the technological advances that distinguish iTV (which is currently available only to a limited public in the UK) from ordinary television.

Over-the-air broadcasting, cable, and satellite are the three main modes for transmitting television signals from production studios to private homes (Figure 1.26). Television signals are currently in analog form. The transition to digital television is attractive because digital transmission can offer higher resolution images, takes up less bandwidth (so more channels will be available), and offers more flexibility in terms of storing, locating, and manipulating media content (as anyone familiar with DVDs, Jpeg, and Mpeg images will know). It is possible to transmit digital television by any of these pathways, although the transition will be expensive for both consumers and

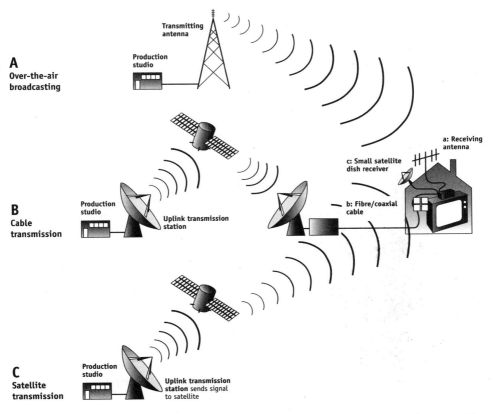

A
Over-the-air broadcasting

Transmitting antenna

Production studio

a: Receiving antenna

c: Small satellite dish receiver

B
Cable transmission

Production studio

Uplink transmission station

b: Fibre/coaxial cable

C
Satellite transmission

Production studio

Uplink transmission station sends signal to satellite

In **A (Over the air broadcasting/transmission)** a transmitting antenna sends a signal to a receiving antenna and the set-top box converts digital broadcasts to analog or pure video signal and decodes pay-TV signals for display on TV.

In **B (Cable transmission)** head-end equipment (in the form of the second large satellite dish) receives, converts and transmits TV signals from the satellite along hybrid fibre/coaxial cable to the set-top box.

In **C (Satellite transmission)** the large satellite dish is a transmission station that sends TV signals to a high powered satellite in geostationary orbit. This satellite sends the signal directly to the small satellite dish located outside a house for set-top box conversion.

Figure 1.26 The main modes for transmitting television to private homes, adapted from 'Unscrambling Digital TV' (Brown Kenyon et al. p. 72)

producers as new transmission and reception technology is required. Even if consumers keep their analog television, they will need 'set-top boxes' to decode the digital signal. Further, technological changes will be necessary to accommodate different digital television formats such as interactive television or high-definition television. Indeed, cable transmission is the only pathway that currently offers a viable conduit for interactive television, as it is the only form that offers a return path for the television user to send signals directly back to the television producer without needing to engage other technologies such as phone lines, modems, and personal computers in the communication. In other words, in order to interact, media consumers need a fast, convenient way of sending information back to the media producers.

Once television is transmitted in digital format, Personal Video Recorders (PVRs) are likely to become desirable additions to the home entertainment system. The PVR has all the functions of a standard VCR, but it has the added advantage of acting like a hard drive on which large quantities of digital media programming and other information can be stored. Once again, this will give the media consumer a greater degree of agency. For instance, users of PVRs are able to record a program and instruct the PVR to play it back without commercials, or they can program personal details and preferences into the hard drive so that the PVR will automatically record favourite shows without having to be reminded. In fact, the PVR is capable of scanning available program selections and using its own initiative to record programs it thinks its user may enjoy, based on previous viewing preferences. For instance, if you watch a science fiction show such as *Stargate* three weeks in a row, your PVR will record it for you on the fourth week whether you program it to or not, and it will also predict that you may be interested in a new science fiction show such as James Cameron's *Dark Angel*, so it will record that too.

The ability of this new technology to collect information about its user and create a consumer profile gives rise to a wide range of possibilities for media users (including the PVR, electronic program guides, and other devices that will be needed to search, navigate though, filter, and reschedule the potentially vast array of choices that will become available via digital media). However, the capacity to create consumer profiles also raises serious concerns (even paranoia) about privacy, since media producers will obviously benefit from obtaining such detailed information about clients in their target markets. Information about who media consumers are, how we make choices, and what our choices are provide ammunition for aggressive marketing strategies, particularly if the gap between participating in an interactive advertisement and following through on purchasing the product is eliminated with online purchasing.

Since the PVR is also likely to hold information such as credit card details in order to facilitate TV commerce and allow users to take advantage of services such as 'video on demand' (which is like an online library/video store, minus the inconvenience of travel or download time), and since interactive media are specifically designed to facilitate a two-way flow of information, these concerns about confidentiality are very real. While many of us enjoy watching *Big Brother*, few like the idea of Big Brother watching us and deciding that—based on our viewing history, online purchasing habits, and PVR profile—we are an ideal target for his latest product.

The concerns about confidentiality and reliability that surround new technology may eventually be neutralised by stringent media regulations and policies that protect consumers. In addition, the same aura of familiarity that surrounds the common household television and insulates it from the threat of change, may well be what eventually makes iTV and TV-commerce successful. As Duane Varan, director of the Interactive Media Research Institute at Murdoch University, has said, 'People fear their computers; they trust their TVs' (Varan, personal correspondence, 2001). This means that people who express concerns about giving out their credit card details online or over the telephone may actually show less hesitation about purchasing things through the television, on which they are used to seeing commercials and trusted media figures. Similarly, those who bemoan the technological glitches that cause their computers to crash rarely even stop to think about the possibility of their television crashing when the transition to digital transmission occurs.

Clearly, the ability to sell filters, video on demand, and electronic program guides, and the capacity to personalise sales through interactive advertising and hone in on marketing targets through profiling and other direct-feedback mechanisms opens up new revenue sources within the media industry. However, the fact that consumers will have the power to skip advertisements will have an enormous impact on current scheduling practices (based on high advertising rates for prime-time slots), and on the whole idea of commercial television.

If iTV becomes a popular, widely used media form, it has the potential to revolutionise the structure of the media industry. However, the obstacles preventing this from happening are not simply economic and technological; they also relate to human pleasures, desires, and habitual patterns of media consumption. For instance, the pleasure of being able to avoid advertisements (or, conversely, the pleasure of being able to shop on television), and all of the other pleasures associated with having a greater degree of choice and power, will have to win out over the pleasure of *not* having to make choices. The familiarity and pleasure associated with existing television has built up a high level of consumer allegiance over time, and since consumers are relatively slow to take to new media, widespread interactivity is not something that we are likely to see for at least another decade. Research also suggests that many people enjoy television because it enables them to *avoid* interacting or making choices: they like being able to relax and 'veg out' and lose themselves in someone else's story without having to lift a finger or say a word. Interactivity (which has been modelled on the one-user–one-machine relationship that most people have with their personal computers or their mobile phones) would also complicate television viewing as a social pastime. In cases where there are multiple users of one television, existing battles over custody of the remote control would inevitably be exacerbated by interactivity, even if multiple personalised remotes were introduced into each household.[25]

Audience projections

We want to introduce a final approach that draws on theories of 'projection'. This is a term that was used by Freud and Jung (see pp. 179–81). The central idea here is that audiences use texts as a mirror for themselves. This relates to the wider concept that everything we see around us is a reflection of ourselves. Of course, this cannot be literally true, but what is being suggested here is the idea that the way we see, interpret, and respond to the external world and to other people is a reflection of our internal state: we see aspects of ourselves reflected back. Another way of putting this is that we project ourselves on to the world and other people. This is a basic tenet of much work in the field of psychology and psychotherapy.

I realised this when I started listening closely to what I and others said when we were interpreting media texts. I understood that I was projecting myself, my view of the world, on to the text. In preparation for a course on melodrama, I watched D.W. Griffith's short film *Mender of Nets* with two friends. Discussing the film afterwards, each of us had a very different reading of the ending, in which the actress Lillian Gish is left on her own. One of us said with optimism, 'Ah well, she's learnt a lot, it will be better next time.' The second said despairingly, 'Of course, relationships never work.' The third reflected that 'All men are bastards!' The three readings (all of which could fit the text) reflected the views on relationships that we held at that time. We had projected ourselves into the text.

I began listening more carefully to students talking and I realised that the same thing was happening: they were using film texts to put forward their own views of the world. This was clearest with students who were dealing with personal issues such as emotional or physical abuse. These students would often see these issues in film texts, and this sensitiveness was often helpful in teasing out the dark aspects of family life and gender relations, which are hinted at in certain films, such as those directed by Jane Campion, Mike Leigh, and Gary Oldman.

Consequently, if you are trying to understand how audiences read texts, you can use the idea of projection and argue that any one person's reading of a text is a reflection of themselves: that is, they project their own ideas and feelings on to the text. Both our conscious and our unconscious feelings and beliefs will be reflected in the way we interpret a text. This is a simple but also quite startling idea. To explore it, try the following two exercises.

1 This exercise draws attention to the different ways audiences make sense of texts, to the fact that, in many ways, we seem to see quite different texts. Select a short film, or television extract, that is about 2 minutes long (preferably with no dialogue). Get a group of people to watch this together and then:
   a) Write down, in as much detail as possible, what you just saw.
   b) Write down your feelings and emotional responses to what you saw.
   c) Write down what you think the film-maker was trying to communicate.

Having done this, read your answers to each other and compare and discuss your responses. The questions are designed to work on levels of simple observation, emotional response, and intellectual reading. Finally, read what you have written and consider in what ways your response is a reflection of you.

2 Make a note of your favourite films. Watch one of them, and while you are watching ask yourself why you like this film. Consider the ways in which you can see yourself, your personality, reflected in the film. Notice the key scenes that most affect you and reflect on them. Can you see this film as a projection of yourself?

This approach takes us into analysis of the mechanisms of cinematic identification as they work for individuals, rather than groups, and it begins to tap into our unconscious readings, which are notoriously difficult to ascertain. For me, it is a very exciting area that takes audience study into a new dimension.[26]

TWO COMMON STUDENT QUESTIONS ABOUT TEXT ANALYSIS

Students analysing texts often ask these two related and significant questions:
- Did the producers consciously intend to create the meanings we see in texts?
- Aren't we reading too much into the text?

Finding out the intentions of the producers of media texts is of some use, particularly because the intention to sell, persuade or entertain is usually profit driven and guided by vested interests on the part of the media producers. It is a good idea to be mindful of who might benefit from a text being interpreted and responded to in a particular manner. However, the following points suggest it doesn't matter that many audience members don't know the specific intentions of media producers because the meanings audiences draw from texts are not necessarily derived from or even related to understandings of the intentions of the texts' producers.

1 Textual analysis focuses mainly on the practices of representation evident in media texts, and on the content of the media images and words. Meaning is inseparable from interpretation; that is, meaning is not activated until it is extracted from a text because meaning is essentially about understanding. The best intentions in the world and the most careful and explicit encoding of meaning will literally mean nothing unless someone reads, views or hears the text and attributes some significance to it. It is the act of interpretation that brings the text to life.

2 A central argument in this book is that much of what motivates people both ideologically and aesthetically exists at an unconscious level (see p. 192). Sexist and racist stereotypes are so deeply embedded in the culture in which we grow up that they may become part of our unconscious, thus influencing both the texts that we produce and our understanding of the texts we consume.

3 Media studies does not just look at the intentions of authors; it takes a wider view. It is concerned with how people read and make sense of the texts, how they explore texts in their overall social context, and because of this it looks at audiences and explores the relationships between production, mediation, consumption, and meaning, rather than focusing on the intentions of the producers of media texts alone.

4 Finally, many media texts are the product not of a single person, but of large groups of people working in the constraints of the media industry. Individual intention is lost in this collective form of production.

In relation to the common student question 'Are we reading too much into texts?', there is a useful distinction between reading things *into* a text (projection) and reading things *out* of a text (exegesis). If the reading comes purely from the reader, then that particular reading may be of little value in determining the meaning, although it tells you interesting things about the reader! You can ensure that a particular reading is coming out of a text by paying close attention to the codes and conventions, structure, and composition of the piece, by acquiring knowledge of its cultural context, and by checking to see if the meaning you derive from the text resonates for other readers.

CONCLUSION

Text, context, and audience need to be taken account of when trying to analyse the meanings of texts. Media meanings are dependent on the text itself, on its context and its audience. As we take more and more aspects into account, we aim to get closer to seeing the potential and actual meanings of a text. There won't be one simple answer as to what a text means, but we argue that some readings and meanings are more complete than others.

This book offers a variety of approaches: semiological analysis, analysis of narrative structure, mythological analysis, and ideological and discourse analysis. In your work you will gradually be able to use all these approaches in the study of any one text. As long as you make clear what aspects of the text you are using—whether it be background information, textual codes, social and historical context, or actual audience research—then you will be able to support the readings of texts you make and the meanings you see in them.

Part 2

PICTURES

'When I use a word', Humpty Dumpty said, in rather a scornful tone, 'it means just what I choose it to mean—neither more nor less.'

'The question is', said Alice, 'whether you can make words mean so many different things.'

Lewis Carroll, *Through the Looking Glass*

OVERVIEW OF PART 2

Chapter 7   Semiology

Chapter 8   Reading Images

Part 2 begins to look at media texts in detail. The focus is on still images, mainly advertising photographs, and the methodology used is semiology or semiotics. After an explanation of semiology, we will illustrate its use as a method of textual analysis by working through a number of examples.

7 *Semiology*

Semiology, also known as semiotics, began as a method for analysing language. It is now used for analysing how all sign systems work. It explores the logic and methodology behind communication, and shows how we can understand systematically, through the semiotic method, what communications mean. It is concerned with meaning and with the ways in which meanings are produced and transmitted.

Semiology is defined as the science of signs, or the study of signs and sign systems. Semiology suggests that all communication is based on sign systems, which work through certain rules and structures. Language (words) is the most important and dominant sign system for humans, but the world is full of other sign systems—traffic lights, road signs, navigation bars in a website, editing and photographic conventions in film and television, mathematical symbols, clothes, hairstyles, hand signals, morse code, and so on. All forms of the media are sign systems. All systems can be analysed using semiology.

Semiology originated at the end of the nineteenth century as a means of understanding language. Its founder was Ferdinand de Saussure (Saussure 1974; Culler 1976; Gordon 1996). From the 1930s onwards, it was developed by, among others, C. S. Peirce, who was seeking to understand non-language sign systems (Peirce 1958). The methodologies of Saussure, Peirce and others have been used since the 1960s as a means of analysing media products (Fiske 1990; Hall 1997; Hawkes 1977 and 1996). Roland Barthes's book *Mythologies* (Barthes 1973) was one of the most significant early applications of semiology in media studies, and despite its age, it is still a readable and relevant text.

The communication model of signs can be understood according to Figure 2.1:

SENDER $\longrightarrow$ MESSAGE/SIGN SYSTEM $\longrightarrow$ RECEIVER

Figure 2.1 Communication model of signs

Any message, any meaning, can only be communicated through signs and a sign system. The sign is the central aspect of semiology. A sign is any signal that communicates something to us. The nature of the sign can be understood in two similar ways:

1 Signs work on the basis that the sign stands in for, or represents, something else—the meaning, concept, or idea to which it refers.
2 Every sign consists of a signifier and a signified, as Figure 2.2 illustrates. The signifier is whatever material form is used as to convey meaning: letters, images, sounds, and so forth. The signified is the concept that the images, sounds, or letters communicate.

Using the first way of understanding the nature of signs (point one, above), we can see that the letters d – o – g make up the word 'dog'. This formation of letters constitutes the sign that stands in for or represents the idea of a four-footed canine mammal. The idea or concept of a dog is what Peirce would call the referent, since it is that to which the sign is referring.

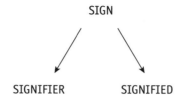

Figure 2.2 Relationship between sign, signifier, and signified

Using the second way of understanding signs (point two), we can illustrate the distinction between signifiers and signifieds by once again thinking of the sign 'dog'. The signifier is the letters d–o–g arranged into the word 'dog' (or the signifier could be a picture of some kind of dog). The signified is the idea or concept of a dog (see Figure 2.3).

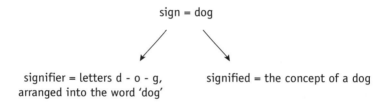

Figure 2.3 The sign 'dog'

An example that shows the distinction between signifier and signified is the situation of a man offering a woman a rose, a gesture that can be understood as a sign. The rose here is the signifier, and what is signified is the man's love or attraction for the woman. Roses do not necessarily signify love, which means that the gesture (sign) is based on a shared code, or convention, that roses can stand in for, or represent, love.

This may seem a slightly complicated way of understanding messages but it is useful for media study because it draws our attention to the processes of re-presentation or signification involved in the actions of the media: all media messages, all their signs, work on the basis of something standing in for something else; all signs include a signifier and a signified. This helps us see the construction involved in media messages, and reminds us that what we are seeing is not 'reality' (although it looks very like it) but signs and signifiers that aim to represent the real world.

There are numerous aspects to semiological analysis. In exploring how signs communicate, how semiology works, we will focus on the following key points, which are explored in more detail below:

- Signs communicate through codes and conventions.
- These signs and conventions are culturally shared—they depend on cultural knowledge.
- Signs communicate through systems of difference.
- Signs communicate through denotations and connotations.

SIGNS COMMUNICATE THROUGH CODES AND CONVENTIONS

All sign systems have a set of elements that are combined according to certain rules, codes, and conventions. The English language is based on 26 letters, which can combine into words and grammatical patterns. We have to learn and understand the correct codes in order to communicate: for example, the letters d – o – g are the code for describing a certain group of four-legged, furry creatures. Sentences are put together according to the conventions of grammar. The words 'code' and 'convention' are key words in media study. All media messages use codes and communicate through conventions.

THESE CODES AND CONVENTIONS ARE CULTURALLY SHARED; THEY DEPEND ON CULTURAL KNOWLEDGE

This is very important. Sign systems will only work successfully with people who know and share the same codes. For example, the Russian language is a sign system with its own codes and conventions; to us, however, it is quite meaningless as we don't speak Russian. Australian Rules football, rugby league, and soccer are all games that depend on knowledge of their rules, codes, and conventions to be played or understood; similarly the tango, the waltz, and the cha–cha are dance steps that must be learnt before they can be enjoyed. These activities will only make sense once we have learnt the code. Different languages are a good example of different sets of codes and conventions used to represent or stand in for the world. The letters d – o – g are signs in the English language code. French uses the letters c – h – i – e – n. All languages have different words. To understand these different signs you have to have learnt the code (the language).

However, cultural knowledge is something more than simply knowing what the code means. It is being aware of all the things that might be suggested by the code. The following points elaborate on this.

SIGNS COMMUNICATE THROUGH 'SYSTEMS OF DIFFERENCE'

One of Saussure's central points in analysing language was the understanding that words don't mean anything on their own. Their meanings depend on the fact that words are part of a system of difference: they only take on meaning in relation to other words. For example 'up' means nothing unless we can relate it to the word and concept 'down'. We can only understand what dogs are in relation to our knowledge of other animals—cats, wolves, horses, and so on—from which we know they are different. The red of a traffic light means nothing in itself; it is only in the context and code of red *as opposed* to green *as opposed* to amber that we begin to make sense of it through a system of difference.

SIGNS COMMUNICATE THROUGH DENOTATIONS AND CONNOTATIONS

Signs work at two levels of meaning: denotation and connotation.

Denotation

To consider what a text denotes is to analyse it on a purely descriptive level, without delving into what it might imply. It is simply to ask 'What is there?' It attempts to *describe* without comment, evaluation, or judgment, the contents of an image. At this level, signs are as close to value-free as possible. For example, on a denotative level the American flag is a rectangular shape consisting of horizontal stripes of red, alternating with white, with a smaller rectangle of blue in the upper left-hand corner. The blue rectangle contains white star shapes, also arranged in horizontal rows.

Connotation

Semiology suggests that all signs carry with them a set of connotations or associations: that is, they will remind the viewer of certain feelings, beliefs, or ideas that are attached to the signifier. It is our task, when analysing images semiologically, to ask what are all the possible connotations associated with any particular sign or element in the image. Objects, colours, clothes, words, print styles, lighting, camera angles, body language, and so on can all carry connotations.

To return to our example of the American flag, we might note that the flag is associated with (has connotations of) liberty and justice (at least for most Americans!). We would also note that stars are associated with excellence, celebrities, heaven, dreams, and so on. The blue rectangle represents the sky. Each star represents an individual state in America, and they are united together instead of being dispersed at random all over the flag.

A similar way of describing this mode of analysis, and an approach you may have come across elsewhere, is symbolism: this suggests that particular objects or images carry symbolic meaning. The colour red symbolises passion, danger and sexuality in Western culture. (Note that symbols are culturally specific: in China red signifies luck and prosperity, and communism.) Note that whereas symbolism tends to suggest something deliberately intended by the image maker, connotations draw our attention to the readings made by audiences, and these connotations may have been unconsciously included by the image makers. Peirce also gives the term 'symbolic' a more specific meaning.

Connotations are something that the viewer or audience perceives in an image. Connotations work on two levels: individual and cultural. For our purposes, we are only interested in the cultural level and the way connotations help us see the interaction between the sign and the values of a culture, but we need to understand both levels.

- **Individual connotations.** The experiences we have in life as individuals shape our ways of seeing the world and our responses. This works in all aspects of our lives, including our responses to images. For example, if the first time a small girl smells a rose is also a time that she has a frightening experience, subsequently the smell or sight of roses may serve to remind her of, or suggest to her, fear. Seeing roses may continue to carry this individual connotation for this girl, so that being given roses would produce fear rather than a feeling of loving appreciation. While it is important to acknowledge the presence of these individual connotations and look out for them when we analyse the meaning of images, they are not useful for a semiotic analysis because they are not connotations normally shared by other people.

- **Cultural connotations**. This second level of connotations points to the way that different objects carry associations and connotations that are shared collectively by many people in a culture. So, for example, a gift of roses is culturally acknowledged as carrying romantic connotations. John Fiske's analysis of the meanings attached to jeans points to the different connotations, such as freedom, youthfulness, and equality, associated by groups of people with jeans (Fiske 1989, pp. 1–21). Being aware of these connotations will make us aware of the cultural meanings in images. Connotations will not be the same for all cultures, which is why it is important for us always to think about an image's context and the cultural knowledge that different audiences will have. Neither will connotations always be shared by all people in a culture, but as long as we can see that they are shared by a significant number of people they will be important in analysing the possible meanings of any texts.

ICONIC, INDEXICAL, AND SYMBOLIC SIGNS

C. S. Peirce's analysis of signs introduces further categories into the analysis of signs by splitting signs into three types: iconic, indexical, and symbolic.

Iconic signs are signs that resemble that which they signify. All photographs or film signs are iconic in that the image literally looks like what it refers to. Similarly, paintings or diagrams that look like what they signify are iconic. Indexical signs are signs that indicate or point to something else. (Note how our index finger is the one we use for pointing, how a book index points us back to a page reference.) So, for example, a knock on the door is a sign that indicates someone is there wanting to come in; smoke indicates fire. Thermometers, speedometers, analog clocks, and graphs are all examples of indexes because they indicate, point to, or measure temperature, speed, time, and so forth. Symbolic signs are signs that stand in for, but have no resemblance to, their signified. The most obvious example is language, which uses symbols, letters, and words to stand in for what is being described. Similarly, road signs and mathematical signs are usually symbolic. The important point here is that there is no necessary connection between sign and symbol; the signs are, in Saussure's words, arbitrary.

An easy way to remember these different kinds of signs is to think of your computer screen. The image of the printer on your tool bar is called an icon because it looks like a printer. The arrow shaped cursor that appears when you use the mouse to pull down a menu and select a file, tool, or function is literally pointing you to further information, so it is an indexical sign. The sound that indicates that you have new email, or the beep that computers make when you hit the wrong key, are also indexes, because they prompt you to check your in-box, or point out that you have made an error. Nearly every key on your computer keyboard has a symbol on it. For instance, the $ sign doesn't resemble money, or indicate that this page has a particular monetary value; it is simply a symbol that stands for money. Depending on the context, $ can also symbolise greed (for example, cartoon characters are often depicted with dollar signs in their eyes when they rob a bank, find buried treasure, or hit the jackpot).

Look around you and identify examples of iconic, indexical, and symbolic signs. It is most like-ly that you will be able to see examples of iconic and symbolic signs in most social situations.

THE LANGUAGE, OR CODES, OF VISUAL IMAGES

When analysing how meaning is constructed in photographs and still images, we must consider the codes of technical representation and the codes of content.

Codes of technical representation

We can analyse any photographic image by asking the question: 'How has it been photographed?' The answer may include any of the following elements: camera angle, framing and cropping, focus, film stock (black and white/colour), and light-ing. All these contribute to the meaning of the image. We can look at each of these and ask what is denoted and what is connoted: for example, a particular camera angle will have certain connotations.

Codes of content

We can also analyse any image by asking the question: 'What has been pho-tographed?' The answer may include any of the following elements: objects, settings, clothing/costumes, body language, body position, and colours. All these elements contribute to the meaning of the image, as they denote and connote something.

Both codes of technical representation and codes of content need to be consid-ered when doing textual analysis of any image. We need to ask how each of these elements contribute, as signs and signifiers, to the meaning of the text.

There is more to semiology and you can explore the topic through further read-ing, but the outline above will give you enough to start engaging in some close textual analysis of images.

8   *Reading Images*

The following examples use mainly photographs, particularly advertisements. Advertisements are a rich source for semiotic analysis: they usually combine images with written text; they are very carefully put together so as to have maximum effect on an audience; they are a form of propaganda, but will only work if they give audiences some form of pleasure; they are ubiquitous in Western culture; they often reveal important ideological attitudes; and because they are fixed, they are often easier to analyse than moving images. However, do not assume that advertisers themselves know or care about semiology. Although some might (particularly advertisers who have studied communication or media studies), they do not need to know the theory of semiology in order to design advertisements. Semiology is a tool of analysis, not of media construction.

What follows is a semiological analysis of a number of different images (Figures 2.4–2.13). These analyses raise questions, discussed in the previous chapter, of how images produce meanings and how we understand them. Each analysis raises questions for you to answer, and is followed by a detailed commentary on the image in question. These comments draw attention to significant points in semiological analysis.[1]

Figure 2.4 Crying child
Source: Werner Bischof

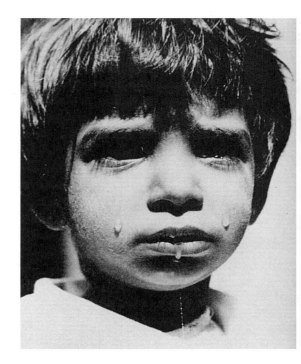

1 Write down quickly what you think the nationality of the child is.
2 Write down quickly why you think the child is crying.

(Do not spend longer than 30 seconds on these two questions. Write down your immediate response.)

Exercise commentary

There is no right answer to these questions. Figure 2.4 draws our attention immediately to the polysemic nature of images. The word 'polysemic' comes from the Greek words *poly* (meaning 'many') and *seme* (which means 'meaning'). 'Polysemic' thus means 'many meanings'. It is possible for an image to be polysemic: thus, the child in this image could be Indian, Australian, Japanese, Italian, English, South American, or any number of other nationalities. The child could also be crying for a number of reasons: because he or she has fallen over, dropped an ice-cream, or lost a parent or a toy; because he or she is hungry; and so on. However, the capacity of images to carry a number of possible meanings does not mean images can mean anything at all. Images and texts are open to an infinite number of possible interpretations, but they have a more limited number of plausible interpretations. The figure in this advertisement is clearly a child, not an adult, and the child is clearly unhappy about something. These things are denoted. Thus, there are limitations to polysemy.

Despite the polysemic potential of the image, many people give similar answers to the two questions posed above. They predominantly suggest the child is from a poor, majority world (Third World) country and that it is crying because of some major disaster such as war, famine, earthquake, or loss of parents. What are the semiological codes and conventions that lead to these readings? What cultural knowledge is required to read the image in this way?

1 We read this image in relation to other images with which we are familiar. It draws on the conventions of the posters and advertisements for charities that call for aid in relation to disasters in the majority world such as famines and earthquakes. These images are familiar to Western audiences, who see them on billboards, in magazines, and on television. Thus our readings are dependent on our cultural knowledge and are constructed intertextually (in conjunction with the meanings produced in related texts). They depend on our position as a Western audience and on our familiarity with such conventionally coded media images.

2 We read the image through its signs and signifiers. There are three points to keep in mind in relation to this:

   a) **The sign/signifier of the child**. Children connote, among other attributes, innocence, vulnerability, need for care, powerlessness, and love. Children are a commonly used signifier in relation to disasters such as famine, as they provide emotive images of innocent victims calling out for our adult care and charity.

   b) **The sign/signifier of tears**. Tears obviously signify pain, unhappiness, and upset, but tears are also significant in photographic terms. We might ask whether this image is a family snapshot. This is possible, but unlikely: the image doesn't conform to the normal conventions of snapshots. Family snapshots are usually taken to record idealised, happy, and amusing moments of family life. Therefore, children in them are usually playing or smiling. Indeed, if a child is crying, family members normally help the child rather than take a picture. So our understanding of the codes or signs of family snapshots suggest that, because of the sign of tears, this is a different kind of photograph.

c) **The use of the photographic code of black and white**. This can signify reality, or it can locate the photo in an era prior to the availability of colour printing. We associate black and white photos with evidence or facts because newspapers have traditionally contained black and white photos, and because they are often used in documentaries (to show evidence of a bygone era). However, as colour printing processes become more accessible, less expensive, and more prevalent in newspapers, black and white photography is more often understood as serious art photography, or a low-budget option when in a newspaper, book, or magazine.

Knowledge of various photographic and cultural codes, and cultural connotations, thus leads people to come up with similar readings of this image. (The photograph is actually of an Eastern European child taken in the late 1940s by Werner Bischof.)

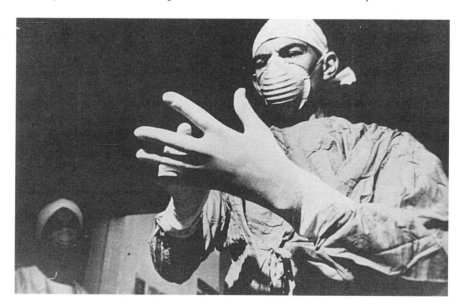

Figure 2.5 Doctor operating
Source: British Film Institute

1 Write down your immediate reaction to this image. How does it make you feel?
2 Write down where you think this image comes from.

Exercise commentary

Figure 2.5 is also potentially polysemic, but commonly supplied answers suggest that people feel uneasy, threatened, or disturbed by it. People also tend to think that the image may be a news image, or a still from a low-budget horror or science-fiction film.

Semiological analysis can explain these answers. The connotations of the image's content are disturbing. We recognise the costume denoted as that of a surgeon/doctor. As a sign, the hospital/operating theatre is a place that connotes sickness and danger—consequently, it is a place of anxiety. Furthermore, the lighting is harsh, and it shows part of the hospital in shadow; it is not a place of light. This plays on the way in which darkness is associated with fear, the unknown, and other such negative connotations. Signifiers such as the doctor's mask and plastic gloves carry a number of connotations. Some of these may be disturbing: the mask, as well as making the doctor anonymous, hidden, and impersonal (and therefore more threatening), connotes danger and warfare. The mask connotes warfare through its similarity to gas-masks and armour. Note the similarity to the mask worn by Darth Vader in *Star Wars*, a likeness that draws on these same disturbing connotations that the environment is not safe and that the wearer needs to be concealed or shielded. The plastic gloves connote the need for protection against germs, and they also make the doctor seem even more impersonal. Doctors put gloves on when they are going to do something to the bodies of patients, so the gloves also signify the threat of invasion of the body!

These signs and signifiers can be thought of with more favourable connotations—the hospital is, after all, potentially a place offering health and protection. But in relation to this image we tend to foreground the unsettling connotations because of the photographic codes—the way the image has been photographed. The most important factors here are the camera angle and the camera lens. The angle does two things: it puts us, as viewers, into a subordinate position because we are looking up at the doctor who dominates us and can therefore threaten us, and it puts us in the position, the point of view, of the patient, and we are thereby invited to identify with the patient. The doctor is looking directly down on us—his hand is going to do something to us. The camera lens is a wide-angle lens. This has the effect of distorting our vision so that the hand is made to appear unnaturally large in relation to the rest of the body. This size of this signifier emphasises its threat to the viewer.

The image takes on further disturbing connotations through cinematic conventions. It is similar to the kind of images we see in black and white horror, and science-fiction, films. A recurrent conventional figure, or sign, in these is the mad scientist/doctor. This figure has featured in movies and popular literature since the days of Mary Shelley's *Frankenstein*, and more recently *Event Horizon* and *Dead Ringers*. The photographic codes complement this: horror and science-fiction films use similar conventions of harsh, shadowy lighting and distorted camera views to create disturbance.

Once again, an image's meaning can be understood in relation to its component signs, connotations, conventions, and an audience's cultural knowledge of these. It is interesting that the photo is actually of Dr Christiaan Barnard, who performed the world's first heart-transplant operations, and the original newspaper caption was 'Hands that Save'. This draws our attention to the way captions and context can give a particular meaning to an image, but also to the way a photograph can convey an attitude to its subject matter. In this case, in contrast to the caption's words of hope, the photograph seems to reflect the unease that some people felt about heart transplants at the time (1969). Heart-transplant operations were new and unsafe, and some people questioned the morality of performing them. Thus, we can see connections between the image and the fictional figure of the 'mad scientist' who is understood to be mad because he or she usurps the powers of God and nature. The caption works as a form of what Barthes calls 'anchorage' (Barthes 1977; O'Sullivan et al. 1994, p. 13): it anchors the meaning for us, reducing the polysemic possibilities and showing us how to view it.

Figure 2.6 Face in front of a wall
Source: British Film Institute

1 *Look at this image for 30 seconds. Then write down all the different things you remember seeing in it.*
2 *Consider whether you think this is a man or a woman. Write down which signifiers in the image support your answer and why.*

Exercise commentary

Answering the first question will draw your attention to the way images are made up of a number of elements. Each of these elements, or signs/signifiers, carries various connotations that contribute to the meaning we make of images. In describing Figure 2.6, you may have written 'A face and a wall', but the face itself is actually made up of numerous elements—black hair, an ear with an earring, a closed mouth, facial hair, staring eyes, and so on.

Being aware of all these elements allows us to start answering the second question: is this a man or a woman? There is no simple answer to this; the image is deliberately ambiguous. Note which elements signify which gender; this is practice in analysing details.

Using systems of difference, can we say that the earring depicted in the photograph signifies a particular gender? Earrings have conventionally been predominantly worn by women, therefore the earring is a signifier of femininity (which is, in this instance, the signified). But, in many countries it is now common for men to wear earrings, so pierced ears do not necessarily signify femininity. Men tend to wear just one earring, so if we could see both ears we would have a further clue as to gender. Women's earrings tend to be bigger and more elaborate than those of men, but then again, women also wear small earrings. All these equivocations make the earring, as sign, gender-ambiguous. We can see it as signifying male or female. If we could date the photograph, this would give us a further clue, as we could determine what earrings signified at the time the photograph was taken.

What can the mouth in this photo signify? It is closed, but has full lips, which look as though they have make-up on. What could this sign signify in terms of gender? Women in full-face photographs conventionally have open and smiling mouths. This relates both to photographic conventions and conventions of real behaviour. As part of their gendered upbringing, women are encouraged to smile at people more than men are. This is related to the way women are encouraged to identify themselves as nurturers, and as people who make others feel good. This, in turn, partly explains the fact that photographic representations of women are presented as pleasurable visual images. It may also connect with the way in which women are socially encouraged to express their feelings more than men. By keeping their mouths closed, men keep their feelings to themselves, and this may well fit in with the gendered image of men as more powerful: we don't know what they are feeling, and therefore we cannot predict their behaviour.

Many women wear make-up, particularly variations of red or pink lipstick, but some young men now also wear make-up, often black or blue lipstick. Full lips are conventionally coded as signifying sexual attractiveness, so photographic images of women wearing lipstick code their subjects as beautiful and sexual.

These comments point to the coded ambiguity of the mouth sign. We can read it as signifier of femininity (full lips, make-up) or masculinity (not smiling, closed-mouth, a street-wise male with black lipstick). We could look further at the whole facial expression and note the furrowed brows and the direct look of the eyes at the camera. The brow, eyes, and mouth all combine to signify a challenge to the viewer. Conventionally, this look of challenge is associated with the male look, whereas women are expected to look inviting and unthreatening. We are not saying that this is how women and men really should behave, nor that it is necessarily true that this is how they do behave. Rather we are pointing to the fact that, traditionally, in photographic representations this is how ideal male and female figures have been coded as behaving. Since the 1990s an increasing number of advertisements feature women with aggressive expressions, showing them as powerful. However, these images often play up sado-masochistic fantasies: the women are coded as sexual at the same time as aggressive. And this sado-masochistic coding means the gender connotations are of a different quality.

We could do a similar analysis about the ambiguity of this person's hair, including facial hair, seeing signs in this of both masculinity and femininity. But there are three other important factors to consider when reading how this image is gendered.

1 **The race or ethnic origin of the person shown**. If we were to read this person as Asian, a number of cultural associations and codings would serve to make the gender ambiguity of the photo even more pronounced. We suggest that to White, European eyes, some Asian males appear feminine, partly because they tend to have less facial and body hair than White males, but also through the way their musculature and bone structure is coded. There is also a generalised coding of Asia as feminine by the West. Thus, those reading this figure as Asian may be

paradoxically inclined to view the signifiers of femininity as indications that the figure is male. However, those who read this figure as Asian may also come to the opposite conclusion by using a different set of cultural assumptions and codings. Non-White women often do not conform to the ideals of femininity of White culture, which suggest blondeness, softness, thinness are ideal feminine attributes. Consequently, for those reading this figure as Asian, the person depicted could be read as female, despite, or indeed because of, the signifiers of masculinity that the photo contains.

This may seem deliberately confusing, but the aim is to draw your attention to the ambiguity of signs and the need to understand how we read them in codes of visual representation and in cultural conventions. These exercises also aim to demonstrate the importance of considering who the audience is. These readings about gender and race will depend on the ethnic position of the readers. Different ethnic groups will make different readings. We have focused more on Western readings.

2 **The setting**. This is an outdoor street scene, and although we can see little of the street, the rough brickwork acts as a sign/signifier connoting an impoverished urban environment. Conventionally, this setting signifies masculinity because it is males, particularly young working-class males, who are understood to be visible in the urban street. Again we are not saying that this is the reality. Rather, we are pointing out that these assumptions are part of the codes and conventions of representation of gender. Consequently, in this photo, the outdoors street scene is a signifier of masculinity. It encourages a reading of this figure as male.

3 **The type of photograph**. Is this photograph coded as a family snapshot, an art portrait, a news photo, or any other type of photograph? The fact that it is in black and white, and the harsh lighting, connote documentary realism, but the framing, pose, and facial expression suggest the 'mug shot', the photograph of surveillance and control used by police and other security agencies as an identification device. In terms of gender this signifies maleness because, once again, males are more conventionally associated with crime and criminality than women.

There is no right answer to the question: 'Is this a male or a female?' The object of this analysis is to make you aware of the possible meanings that can be produced through analysis of signs/signifiers, photographic codes, and cultural codes of understanding. This will equip you with the skills to decode what is signified by the different signifiers, and will enable you to give a detailed argument supporting your findings. In doing so, you are developing your semiological analytic skills.

However, we expect you are still wondering whether this is a man or woman. Why do you want to know? It is interesting to reflect on that question for a moment. We suggest that because we know there is an answer to the question, we want to know if we are right or wrong. But, more interestingly, we think many people do not like to be faced with images that are gender-ambiguous. They feel uncomfortable being unable to classify this person as male or female. Why might this be the case and how do you feel about this? (For your information, it is an Anglo-Indian woman photographed in London in the 1980s for use in semiological analysis such as we have done.)

Figures 2.7 Cropped image
from advertisement for Live clothing

On the basis of the signifiers you can see in the image in Figure 2.7, write down what gender you think this person is and why.

Exercise commentary

The first image (Figure 2.7) is cropped from a larger one. It contains several elements—nipples, chest, white skin, dark clothing—but gives us limited information. Some people see a male here; others a female. The key signifier is the breasts and their semi-developed nature. The development can suggest femininity, coupled with the flowing (signifying feminine) clothing. But the breasts are not so developed that they could not also signify that this is a man.

Figures 2.8 and 2.9 give us more information, more signs and signifiers to build up to our final reading. With the whole image (Figure 2.10) we may easily identify this as a male figure by putting together a number of signs—shorts, chunky jewellery, body type. Although the breasts may signify femininity, the hands, leg position, taut muscular belly, chin, neck, hairstyle, and facial expression all signify masculinity rather than femininity. The similarity of the model to the film actor Leonardo di Caprio (the advertisement from which this image is taken appeared in 1997) also suggests masculinity and desirability.

I chose Figure 2.7 to demonstrate how images are built up from a collection of significant signifiers. You can try a similar process of finding one element in an image, and showing it to people to see how they read it. Then see how they read the whole image. The photo also shows how images of gender and sexuality have been changing since the 1990s. Before I came across this photo, a friend told me that he liked men 'whose tits I can get hold of'. I was struck by this transposition of the stereotypical heterosexual male expression of desirable femininity—large 'tits'—on to homosexual desire for men. I then came across the image, which seemed to portray the kind of body type that my friend would find attractive. The image is from a Perth magazine, *Xpress*, which caters predominantly for a youth market. It is a weekly guide to popular events, cinema, music, fashion, and so on, and its audience would be predominantly heterosexual. I suggest that while the image would have appeal for a female heterosexual audience, particularly di Caprio fans, it also offers pleasures of homoeroticism for a gay male audience, showing how homoerotic images can circulate very easily in popular media with a predominantly heterosexual audience. At the same time, the ambiguity I have pointed to in terms of the depiction of the model's breasts, shows how gender identity is becoming increasingly blurred.

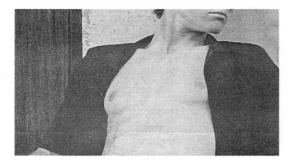

Figures 2.8-2.9 Cropped images from advertisement for Live clothing

Figures 2.9

Figure 2.10 Complete advertisement for Live clothing
Source: *Xpress Magazine*, 18 December 1997

Construct an implied narrative for this cartoon (Figure 2.11) that explains why the woman has her lips zipped. Alternatively, write a one-line caption for the cartoon. Gender is the focus of this exercise.

Exercise commentary

Other than interpretations such as 'zip your lips' or 'my lips are sealed', the kind of captions people write for Figure 2.11 tend to fall into two categories, anti-women and pro-women. The anti-women captions are variants on the theme of 'Women never stop talking, but rarely say anything worth listening to', 'Women need to be

Figure 2.11 Cartoon woman
Source: Wils, *circa* 1980

silenced', and so on. The pro-women captions are variants on the theme of 'Women aren't allowed to speak', 'Women's voices are denied'. Both these types of captions fit the image. We introduced earlier the idea of a preferred or dominant reading (see p. 70). The dominant reading is the reading that takes account of the text itself—how it is coded—its cultural context, and the dominant social values of the audience. In this cartoon, which of the two kinds of captions, anti-women or pro-women, would you say is the dominant/preferred reading? We suggest the answer to this question is the anti-women reading, for two reasons.

1 In terms of the signs and conventions of the cartoon itself: the depiction of the woman is similar to those in cartoons in the popular press about relations between men and women, cartoons that represent women as hen-pecking wives, nagging mothers-in-law, gossiping neighbours, or bossy sisters (as in Peanuts). Such images draw on familiar sexist stereotypes of women. Her rather unpleasant expression is also negative, as opposed to most media images of women, that show women as attractive, happy, and smiling. What is important here is that this relates to popular codes and conventions that embody a negative view of women.

2 The dominant/preferred cultural reading would be anti-women even though the image might also serve to represent women being silenced. This is because the popular reading would fit with popular ideas of gender and the predominant 'common sense' of patriarchal, sexist culture is that women never stop talking. Only if this image were to be placed in a feminist, pro-women context—for example a feminist magazine—would the dominant reading then suggest that women are denied a voice.

We are not supporting a sexist reading. Rather, we are pointing out that the assumptions about gender on which such a reading are based are predominant in our culture at the moment. We use this image to stress the difference between a preferred, or dominant reading and other readings, and to stress that cultural context is crucial in ascertaining the dominant/preferred reading of an image.

ADVERTISEMENTS AND IDEOLOGY

We will take this semiological analysis a stage further. The concept of ideology will be discussed fully in Part 4, but it is also important to introduce it here. What is the ideological meaning of the images you are looking at? By ideology we mean a set of values, beliefs, and feelings that, together, offer a view of the world. Each image contains an implied view of society, of the world, and of our roles in it. You can analyse advertisements with this in mind. Roland Barthes demonstrates this in his essay 'Myth Today' (Barthes 1973, pp. 109–59).

Implied narratives

Consider the two advertisements for Colorbond fencing (Plate 1) and beer (Figure 2.12). Both include a wealth of semiological detail for analysis, but we want to go to the heart of the ideology that they present. Advertisements often work by showing ideal characters in ideal situations. When you are considering these images, ask yourself what is ideal about the two situations depicted.

The Colorbond advertisement (Plate 1) idealises family life and property ownership and, through that, marriage and heterosexuality. 'What is unusual about that?' you might say, for surely these are perfectly normal and healthy ideals. They certainly are 'normal' and this is what we want to explore—the way this image conjures up a whole story, implies and supports a whole lifestyle, and thereby presents an ideological construct. We will show how this is implicit in the image, which is actually concerned with selling fencing!

There is a particularly useful question you can ask about any image, a question that often reveals something of its ideological meanings and ideological work: what is the *implied narrative* of an image? This question involves asking *what has just happened* in the image and *what is going to happen next*: in other words, what story is the image telling?

We can also ask where the viewer or interpreter of the text is positioned in relation to the implied narrative. Are we one of the characters? Are we being invited to enter into the story world in a particular role?

The Colorbond advertisement offers us two images, a past and a present, which together construct a narrative. This narrative is about the positive rewards of following a traditional suburban family lifestyle, a 'normal' or 'ideal' pattern of life. The first image implies the new suburban home of a young family: the fence, lawn, and tree signify a suburban backyard, and this is consolidated by the young puppy (the family pet), clothes on the washing line, and what seems to be a child's sneaker in the puppy's mouth. The tree is a young sapling, newly planted, implying a new garden and, by implication, a new house. The contrast between the established trees over the fence in the second picture and the absence of anything over the fence in the first picture suggests that the first picture is depicting a new housing estate where nothing has grown very tall yet—an estate on which the 'bush' has been removed for a fresh start. This suggests two complementary stories of what has happened in the past. The first is a romance: a young couple met, fell in love, got married, had a child, and bought a house. The second is a story of enterprise and of solid financial investment in property:

a housing estate in an expanding suburb is being sold and occupied by property owners, who are contributing to the prosperity and development of Australia.

The second picture in the Colorbond advertisement expands on these narratives. The passage of time—ten years—brings things to fruition. The garden has grown (witness the tree) and industrious gardening by the owners of the property has produced a much more picturesque setting (although we don't see the labour, just the finished product). Beyond the fence, we see signs that this same process is happening all around, as the gardens of neighbours are also blooming. Humans are out of sight in both images, but the implied stories of marriage and children and of domestic success and modest prosperity allude to the absent characters in these stories. There is also a suggested narrative of the future: a story of continuing prosperity and growth.

These scenes imply that progress and happiness can be found in the domestic lifestyle of the suburban quarter-acre block, in a country that is still young but is growing ever more beautiful and prosperous. The Australian ideological dream of domestic bliss is thus encapsulated in these images. In a sense we have to know this myth before we can read the image in the way it is intended to be read. It does not show us everything. On the contrary, it works by showing us signs or signifiers whose connotations we have to put together in order to see what is implied outside the image ('off screen', we might say). It may be that the advertisement offers its audience the pleasure of putting these connotations together, in the same way as a jigsaw puzzle offers entertainment. It shows us parts of the implied whole. This is a common way for signs to work; a sign suggests something more. This is described as metonymy in semiology (O'Sullivan et al. 1994, pp. 181–2). Metonyms are signs in which one part or element stands in for or represents something larger. If someone says 'I'll take the wheel' they mean that they will drive the car, and in this context one part of the car (the steering wheel) is a metonym for the entire vehicle and the act of driving it. Similarly, an image in the news of a discarded syringe in a public toilet is a metonym for the larger social problems associated with illicit drug use.

Behind this is the assumption that this is the desirable lifestyle. The advertisement suggests that if you can achieve anything in your life, it is through this story of the happy family and the beautiful and prosperous piece of private property. The aspect of private property is crucial. The central sign is the fence. The fence divides up the land, apportioning it out to those who have the money to purchase land. Here, the whole capitalist ideology of Western culture is encapsulated. It is not problematised or questioned; it is normalised. We can see this normalisation process at work by thinking about how else land could be treated. Think about Aboriginal culture's view of the land: it is not to be owned, we are simply the caretakers of what is communally there for all. White and Aboriginal views are two quite different ideologies about land and ownership. This image supports the White view of land as something to be divided and owned. While it could be said that caretaking is going on in relation to this land, it is caretaking within a European garden tradition—the flowers and plants, planted in such an orderly way, are not native to Australia, and they are watered with reticulated water, yet this artificially created culture is shown as normal. Note also the biblical connotations carried by gardens in the Western tradition: the association with the Garden of Eden enables a reading of the domestic garden as a place of paradise, rest, and recreation, an escape from the demands of work. Gardens are idealised spaces of retreat and recreation.

While the fence recedes in terms of visual prominence in the second image, being covered up and masked by the new growth, it is still there as the marker of boundaries. It continues to confirm ownership of property, which is the confirmation of success in White, Western, Australian culture.

Yet there is, in this advertisement, a hint of something that might disturb its domestic paradise. The caption 'Only a Colorbond fence will look as good in ten years time as the day it was put up' draws our attention to the other side of the passage of time—decay. While the garden grows up, the owners are growing old. The Colorbond fence does not age. Aging and decay is the shadow side of the garden's growth. We call it a shadow side because of our culture's refusal to accept decay and aging as part of the processes of nature. Aging is rarely celebrated in our culture. People seek to hold on to youth, and in an ageist culture the elderly are often held up for ridicule. This advertisement raises the spectre of decay and old age but instead of drawing our attention to the problem of an ageist culture, it affirms the ideology of finding ways of avoiding age and decay. It attempts to show we can defeat this in the process of raising a family and owning private property.

The advertisement makes sense to us as an audience because we understand how its signs and signifiers relate to myths of the ideal nuclear family. At the same time, it also confirms these ideological values through its narrative. We are so imbued with these ideals that on seeing this advertisement in our day-to-day lives, we probably would not consciously see all that we have discussed (any more than the advertisers deliberately intended the ideology). Ideology is sometimes difficult to see because it is so obvious to us, which means that you will need to look carefully to discover what ideological assumptions are being confirmed in any advertisement you analyse. You will see many images that link together elements of property-owning, marriage, and by implication, families in similar ideological constructions.

We want to draw attention to just one ideological element that is played on in the advertisement for beer in Figure 2.12. The caption states: 'In 1824 we started brewing pure beer. Nothing's changed'. We could do an ideological analysis of the notion of 'pure' or of beer as a cultural product, but we will focus on the time aspect: '1824 … nothing's changed'.

Ideologically, the stress on time in this advertisement shows a tension about the modern world we live in. The advertisement idealises the past, as though something made in the past would inherently be a superior product because it was produced then: the past is (necessarily) good. It questions the value of change and suggests it is possible to find an element of timelessness, in this case through beer. All these points suggest that the present modern world is one of inferior products, of rapid and disruptive change, and that we are caught up in the rush of time and progress. We are not saying that this is the reality. Rather we are showing how this advertisement wins us over by offering some escape from these perceived problems. It plays on popular common-sense assumptions that progress has brought great benefits but has also denied us our profound, peaceful, human pleasures. The advertisement offers us an image from the past that suggests peace and timelessness, and it offers to make this available to us in the

Figure 2.12 Advertisement for
Cascade Lager
Source: Cascade Brewery, 1993

"In 1824 we started brewing pure beer. Nothing's changed?"

Nothing has really changed at the Cascade brewery for over 160 years. Australia's oldest brewery still produces pure beer. You'd be proud to have resisted change for this long if you brewed with pure water, home-grown hops and your own yeast and malt. Cascade Premium Lager. Pure beer out of the Tasmanian wilderness.

present. It promises that the beer advertised will work to soothe us in the rush and hurly-burly of the present and will be a product made with true workmanship rather than through modern mass-production. It is designed to contrast with fast-food.

Other advertisements can work in an opposite direction, valuing new technologies and the freedoms that progress gives us. This one stresses the uncertainty felt in contemporary society, drawing on the perception that older values and tradition offer us a solution. If you extend this dichotomy between valuing new technologies and harking back to a 'better time' to political and social issues, you will notice that the two sides of the dichotomy correspond with two kinds of solutions often presented to social problems. Suggested solutions to social problems often fall into one of two camps: a move forward into new progressive ways of dealing with these problems; or a return to traditional ways of being, including traditional values and behaviour, and a more conservative view of the world—looking back, in other words, to 'the good old days'. We are not arguing this advertisement deliberately espouses conservative values, but we are arguing that ideologically there are conservative aspects that come through. However, the way in which this advertisement invokes the past has little to do with the actual conditions of production and realities of life in the past (which had its own problems and hardships). It is not a realistic portrayal of history; it draws on romantic and nostalgic images of the past that offer idyllic pastoral comfort and a retreat from the present.[2] Ultimately this retreat into the past is being ideologically used to sell the product.

As a way of extending semiological analysis beyond images and advertisements, try the following exercise. You may find it useful to read Fiske's analysis of the meaning of jeans as preparation for this (Fiske 1989b, pp. 1–21).

The clothes we wear act as sign systems to tell other people and ourselves who we think we are. They don't just keep us warm or comfortable, they give messages about ourselves. Arrange to meet with one or two close friends. Analyse each other's appearance semiologically: that is, look at the clothes you are each wearing as signs and signifiers. What do they signify? What do they connote? You can include hairstyles, make-up and any jewellery in this analysis—they are all sign systems. Try to apply all the relevant concepts: look for iconic, indexical, and symbolic signs in your clothes; understand how systems of difference work by imagining different kinds of clothing, different colours, and each of you wearing the other's clothes. Consider how all these things would change the meaning of the clothes. When you have finished, continue to see your clothing as a sign system. Consider each item of your apparel as a sign and break it down into signifier and signified (for instance, jeans are a signifier, and the idea or meaning that is signified by wearing jeans may be youth or freedom).

WHY USE SEMIOLOGY?

What are the advantages, strengths, and weaknesses of using semiology as a methodology for text analysis?

Advantages of semiological analysis of media texts

1 The first advantage is practicality. Semiology is a helpful method for taking images apart. It gives a set of guidelines, checkpoints of things to do when we face an image, and serves as a guide through the maze of meanings. When we get stuck we can go back to check connotations, or codes, or ask what is being signified. It can also be usefully applied beyond media texts to any cultural sign system, such as the wearing of clothes or the organisation of social space in buildings and architecture.

2 Semiology is a method that stresses the relation of one text to others and to society as a whole. Its insistence on cultural codes and conventions encourages us to make links and comparisons with other texts and other genres, and leads us to see meaning as socially produced. Its insistence on connotations draws attention to the way texts relate to wider social meanings and to the role that readers and audiences play in constructing meanings. In doing so, semiology draws attention away from individual authors and their creative 'genius' and intentions. One of Barthes's famous essays is entitled 'The Death of the Author' (Barthes 1977, pp. 142–8). This movement away from the emphasis on authorial intent and ownership of a text can be seen as a strength or weakness, depending on your point of view. This is one of the distinctive features of the methodology of semiology: it does not focus on the intentions of individual creators. At times, I personally find it useful to return to individual authors, but whatever your viewpoint this is one of the distinctive features of the methodology of semiology: it is not interested in the intentions of individual creators.

3 Semiology's insistence on breaking the sign into signifiers and signifieds, showing how something always 'stands in' for something else, prises texts away from the

notion that they are unproblematic reflections of reality. By continually asking what is being signified by a particular sign, we realise that texts are constructions of meaning rather than transparent reflections of reality. Stuart Hall puts it as follows:

Saussure's great achievement was to force us to focus on ... how language actually works and the role it plays in the production of meaning. In doing so he saved language from the status of a mere transparent medium between things and meanings. He showed instead that representation was a practice (Hall 1997, p. 34).

This is particularly important in relation to photography, film, and video because, as stated before (see pp. 54–5), they can so easily appear real, unmediated, and unconstructed. Semiology helps remind us that they are not, that they are constructions.

4 The way Barthes used semiology, seeing signs as wider systems of social myths, allows us to analyse ideology in media texts.

The limitations of semiological analysis of media texts

1 Semiology is just one approach to texts and the media. It does not cover everything and therefore we need other approaches alongside it.

2 The project or dream of semiology as a 'science of signs' has been productive, but, ironically, it has also led to the main fallibility of semiology. In the end, semiology's acknowledgment of polysemy and its awareness that cultural knowledges, contexts, and audiences are elements that need to be taken into account in understanding meanings, actually leads to the realisation that there are too many variables. We can point to significant probabilities and 'preferred meanings' of texts, but we also have to acknowledge other possible readings. Derrida adds to the semiotic method by introducing the concept of 'difference', an endless chain of signification in which each sign or signifier refers to something else with which it is associated, and so on in a process by which meaning is infinitely deferred. Thus the term *différance* indicates that a sign is meaningful because it differs from other signs (black gets its meaning in relation to other colours because it is distinct from other colours), and because meaning is deferred indefinitely through the process of association (black is associated with darkness, which is associated with mystery, which is associated with suspicion and crime, and so on). Ironically, the 'science of signs' has proven that we can't find the absolute meaning. So we have to go beyond semiology as a way of understanding media.

3 Saussure focuses on the *rules* of language and sign systems (he calls the abstract, formal system of rules and conventions *langue*). While this is useful, it does not take into account the concrete *processes* of language that Saussure calls *parole*. The term 'parole' refers to actual instances of speech and language use, and this is necessarily dynamic, contextual, and transient rather than predictable or rule-bound. Even the sign systems themselves can change over time so it is best to be wary of a cogs-in-the-machine view of communication, whereby language and its rules, and signs and their meanings, are fixed in time. The rules of language do not control language users. Rather, it is the other way around. The reality is that people can break and change codes, struggle over meanings, and exert some autonomy over

and through the systems: we can speak language. Because languages change meanings over time, there is more flexibility than is allowed for in Saussure's approach.

As long as we are aware of these limitations and of other possible approaches, semiology should still be a helpful and ultimately useful means to an end, that end being understanding media texts and, by extension, understanding the place of media in society.

CULTURE JAMMING

Semiotic analysis is very much an analytic process. Can you more actively and creatively engage with the media and media images? 'Culture jamming' is understood as a mode of resistance to the norms and conventions of mass culture that exposes and opposes the media's underlying power structures and ideological messages.[3] Culture jammers use their familiarity with the codes and conventions of advertising and other forms of communication to throw a spanner in the production of meaning by creating spoofs, defacing texts, and subverting the intended meanings of the media texts that they choose to rework. Often they actively try to denaturalise the media images that we see every day, by making us notice and question their underlying messages. What follows is a discussion of three examples of culture jamming:

- an email exchange which developed into an online campaign against Nike's employment policy regarding the manufacture of merchandise in free-trade zones
- graffiti campaigns conducted by feminists and anti-smoking activists
- the work of Barbara Kruger, an artist who uses common media forms, such as the poster and the LED display, to comment on the influences of the media on our lives.

Email and other forms of computer mediated communication (CMC) have been celebrated as being both democratic and empowering mediums of mass communication. This is because they enable individuals and small groups to get their message out to large numbers of people, without having to contend with restrictive policies and regulations or prohibitively expensive equipment and production costs. For instance, the world-famous 'McLibel' case in which a handful of media activists used the Internet to publicise a legal battle with McDonald's was run on a second-hand computer in a rented room. Computer mediated communication is also characterised by a direct feedback loop in which the senders and receivers of messages can exchange views and negotiate meanings.

While there are feedback mechanisms with traditional media such as newspapers, radio, and television, CMC is structured to facilitate a two-way flow of information, rather than the asymmetrical transmission of information in which the sender and receiver are separated by space, time, and an imbalance of communicative resources. In traditional media, audience members lack control over the means of transmitting messages and this gap can only be bridged by initiatives such as phone calls or letters to the editor, or formal processes such as media research, ratings, and opinion polls. Mass media producers have an impersonal relationship with those who receive their messages and media consumers have less power and agency in the communicative exchange: consumers control the interpretation of the message, but they don't have access to the means of constructing their own media products and sending responses straight back to the producers. In online communication, the sender and receiver are connected by the network of phone and cable lines that link their computers to one another, so it is possible for the communicative exchange to retain some interpersonal characteristics. This, in itself, can be empowering because media consumers can make their point of view known, and can communicate it to other individuals with whom they have some personal connection.

An articulate media activist called Jonah Peretti made a statement against Nike's employment policies by putting in a routine request to have his sneakers customised. For a fee of $50 Nike offers to personalise their products by stitching a word or phrase under the Nike 'swoosh' logo. This service, called 'iD', is part of a branding exercise that relates Nike to freedom of choice and freedom of expression by encouraging customers to build their own shoes. Noting the irony of this slogan in light of the conditions that employees who actually do 'build' Nike shoes reportedly endure in free-trade zones, Peretti chose the word 'sweatshop'. In the email exchange that followed, Nike cancelled Peretti's order on the grounds that it contained 'inappropriate slang'. Peretti argued the point, and supported his position by consulting a dictionary. The ensuing email exchange spread spontaneously after Peretti forwarded it to half a dozen friends who were interested in the subject, and they passed it on to their friends. Initially, everyone received the email exchange from someone that they knew. Eventually the exchange circulated around the globe and was widely publicised on the Internet, and became part of a broader media campaign against the negative aspects of globalisation.

In the following correspondence between Peretti and Nike you will note that none of Nike's messages address the issue of whether the company engages in unethical labour practices. For Peretti, Nike's refusal to engage with the issues he was raising was even worse than an admission of guilt because it meant that no headway could be made.

Dear NIKE iD,

Thank you for your quick response to my inquiry about my custom ZOOM XC USA running shoes. Although I commend you for your prompt customer service, I disagree with the claim that my personal iD was inappropriate slang. After consulting Webster's Dictionary, I discovered that 'sweatshop' is in fact part of standard English, and not slang. The word means: 'a shop or factory in which workers are employed for long hours at low wages and under unhealthy conditions' and its origin dates from 1892. So my personal iD does meet the criteria detailed in your first email.

Your web site advertises that the NIKE iD program is 'about freedom to choose and freedom to express who you are'. I share Nike's love of freedom and personal expression. The site also says that 'If you want it done right … build it yourself'. I was thrilled to be able to build my own shoes, and my personal iD was offered as a small token of appreciation for the sweatshop workers poised to help me realize my vision. I hope that you will value my freedom of expression and reconsider your decision to reject my order. Thank you, Jonah Peretti

From: "Personalize, NIKE iD" <nikeid_personalize@nike.com>
To: "'Jonah H. Peretti'" <peretti@ ... .>
Subject: RE: Your NIKE iD order o16468000
Dear NIKE iD Customer

Regarding the rules for personalization it also states on the NIKE iD website that 'Nike reserves the right to cancel any personal iD up to 24 hours after it has been submitted'. In addition, it further explains: 'While we honor most personal iDs, we cannot honor every one. Some may be (or contain) other's trademarks, or the names of certain professional sports teams, athletes or celebrities that Nike does not have the right to use. Others may contain material that we consider inappropriate or simply do not want to place on our products. Unfortunately, at times this obliges us to decline personal iDs that may otherwise seem unobjectionable. In any event, we will let you know if we decline your personal iD, and we will offer you the chance to submit another.='" With these rules in mind, we cannot accept your order as submitted. If you wish to reorder your NIKE iD product with a new personalization please visit us again at www.nike.com

Thank you, NIKE iD

Figure 2.13 Poster promoting a blockade against a NIKE store in Subiaco, Perth
Source: courtesy of April-Jane Flemming, Jacob Black, and the Stop CHOGM Alliance

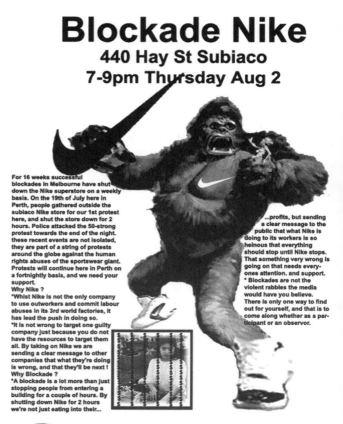

Dear NIKE iD

Thank you for the time and energy you have spent on my request. I have decided to order the shoes with a different iD, but I would like to make one small request. Could you please send me a color snapshot of the ten-year-old Vietnamese girl who makes my shoes? Thanks

Jonah Peretti

<no response> [Sincere thanks to Jonah Peretti for granting permission to reproduce this email exchange.][4]

Figure 2.13 is a flyer produced by an Australian group of media activists who were inspired by Peretti's stand, and by the work of authors such as Naomi Klein.[5] They organised protests against the exploitation of workers in free-trade zones (export-processing zones), which are largely unregulated industrial areas that exist in countries such as Afghanistan, China, Indonesia, the Philippines, and Mexico, where international companies can avoid both tax and trade unions. Like Peretti, Flemming, Black, and their friends studied media and ethics at university and were prompted to make use of the media technologies available to them to communicate their ideas and concerns to the public, and to exert pressure on politicians and corporations.

There is a tradition of media activism, dating back to the 1970s, that addresses images in outdoor advertisements. In the 1970s, feminists, unhappy about the sexual objectification of women, started to paint slogans and captions on images of women in outdoor advertisements. These political graffiti drew attention to the sexism implicit in these images and in so doing challenged patriarchy. Anti-smoking campaigners

Figure 2.14 *Untitled*, 1989,
by Barbara Kruger
Source: Barbara Kruger

adopted similar tactics to point out the harmful effects of smoking, painting captions on cigarette advertisements. Both campaigns appear to have had some effect, in conjunction with political lobbying, in terms of bringing about changes to representations of women in advertising, limitations on cigarette advertising, and harsher regulation around smoking. A recent Australian campaign promoting the value of people learning emergency first aid featured billboards showing a picture of a man who had collapsed. The caption read: 'Your husband's collapsed, what do you do?' The image implied an ideology of family support between husband and wife. Graffiti on one of the billboards read 'Take his wallet', humorously undercutting the family ideal and exposing the possible economic inequalities experienced in marriage.

Barbara Kruger is an artist who has adopted a similar technique to feminist and anti-smoking graffiti campaigners. She places captions on images to produce new and challenging meanings. Her images often deal with women's issues in complex ways.

By portraying the woman as a scientific observer, the image in Figure 2.14 portrays women as powerful and suggests that as the world shrinks with the development of technology, social progress occurs. However the reality of domestic labour is brought out in the punch line of the caption ('but not if you have to clean it'), which draws attention to domestic labour, the economically undervalued, yet essential, work that is still done predominantly by women. Her technique of 'appropriating' and reworking images has been described as postmodernist (see Chapter 20). Its impact is in the juxtaposition of image and caption, and in the way the captions invite critical insight into the image.

The following examples of Kruger's work (Figures 2.15–2.22) are taken from the magazine *Dazed and Confused*. This, as its title signifies, is a youth-oriented popular magazine. It features the latest in photographic style, alongside contemporary cultural articles, and is a magazine concerned primarily with image and style. Kruger was asked to work on photos that had appeared in previous editions of the magazine, which means that the magazine was inviting critical reflection on its own images. The result is a series of images combined with captions that draw attention to the difference between magazine subjects, the people in the images, and the audience/readers. In other words, Kruger's artworks point to the differences between 'them' and 'us'. While the magazines depend on the audience enjoying the images, Kruger's captions suggest that the photographs in magazines despise and belittle their audience. Her work can be seen as a savage criticism of fashion and style magazines.

Consider each image without its caption (Figures 2.15–2.18). Decide what you think each photograph is showing and what caption you would give it. Then look at the image with the caption provided by Kruger (Figures 2.19–2.22). Consider what the combination of the photograph and the caption is saying about the subject of the photo, the audience, and the values of such images.

Exercise commentary

We are struck by the way Kruger's captions critique image. What we mean by this is that the photos, in line with rest of the magazine, seem to show extremely cool, trendy, hip young models, who are defined by their appearance. It is their ability to

Figures 2.15–2.18 Photographs used by Barbara Kruger in artwork in the magazine *Dazed and Confused* (captions provided by Barbara Kruger have been blacked out)
Source: Barbara Kruger

Look at me. Look at me and know you'll never be me. Poor you. Poor unfamous you. Poor unshocking you. You 're almost loved and almost beautiful. You disgust me and you know it. But you still want to be me and who can blame you?

SPECIAL ARTIST'S PROJECT
BARBARA KRUGER
Produced exclusively for Dazed & Confused by Barbara Kruger using photographic images sampled from previous issues.

I'm very serious. I'm brilliant and beautiful. Too beautiful for you. I'm looking into the distance, away from you. I'm thinking important thoughts. Things you can't quite grasp. Someday, you'll understand.

I'm cool. If I wasn't skinny, I couldn't be cool. I'd have to be hot, or even worse, warm. Yuck. I love to look at myself, but I'm way too cool to look at you. And you're too pathetic not to look at me.

I can't believe what's in my pants and I don't give a shit about anything else. Why should I? I mean, you like to look at me and I know it. I know what's on your mind. I can't get over what's in my pants and neither can you.

Figures 2.19–2.22 Artwork by Barbara Kruger
Source: Barbara Kruger: published in *Dazed and Confused*, 21 June 1996

look good that makes them desirable. Kruger's captions expose their glances as looks of scorn that are directed at readers of the magazine. The models despise the people admiring them. Perhaps Kruger is undermining the images as well as this style of photography. Alternatively, she might be suggesting that this feeling of scorn and self-importance is a desirable and admirable state. It is interesting that the magazine, in publishing Kruger's work, promoted this self-criticism. The magazine thus both promoted the desirability of a cool image, through its visual style, and at the same time knowingly critiqued it. This may mirror the way many people both enjoy modern media and are extremely critical and cynical about it.

Criticisms of culture jamming

There are a number of criticisms of adbusting, hacktivism, and related forms of culture jamming. First and foremost, adbusting works within the system that it is attempting to critique. It is still a form of advertising, and it runs the risk of reinforcing brand recognition for the companies it is trying to undermine. In other words, the more clever the graffiti and the more negative publicity that it generates, the more likely people are to remember the brand in question when they walk into a shop—and that is one of the major goals of advertising. Second, the controversy that surrounds a brand or corporation as a result of media activism can end up making the product seem more desirable, particularly to members of the youth market who wish to be identified with controversial and radical positions.

Finally, even culture jamming has been incorporated as an advertising strategy. Once marketing strategists realised that it was perceived as 'cool', they began constructing ad campaigns that appealed to the consumer's awareness of the very process of advertising. 'Sex sells shoes!' Globe skatewear boldly proclaimed in a humorous and provocative ad, and Pepsi created a series of television advertisements that told the viewer that they didn't need some sports star to tell them to drink a softdrink because it was cool. These campaigns made their mark precisely because they were perceived as being honest and up-front instead of trying to seduce the consumer with desirable but unattainable images. In Australia a brand of beer called

Figure 2.23 An example of Internet hacktivism circulated by email during the Bill Clinton–Monica Lewinsky affair, 1999

Piss developed cult status when it launched the no-frills ad campaign 'Buy Piss, Drink Piss, Get Pissed'. This was successful (irrespective of the taste of the beverage itself) because it did not involve inflating the price of the product with expensive advertisements and pricey graphics on the labels and packaging.

The Nike email example raises more subtle questions about the subversive potential of online media activism. For instance, access to online communication is still only available to a cultural elite—the sweatshop workers themselves are not likely to have the facilities to participate in this form of media activism and the Internet itself is largely dominated by the English language and it requires computer literacy which, in turn, requires training and technology. So, despite being a more democratic medium in which more people are able to become media producers, CMC is still exclusive to some degree.

1 *Find some images and see how you can actively challenge their meanings by adding captions or drawing on them.*

2 *Take a television advertisement and make up your own, alternative/subversive soundtrack to replace the original.*

CONCLUSION

In Part 2 we have demonstrated how to use semiological analysis. We have also shown how semiology can be used to do ideological analysis. While the readings of the images used in the exercises are not complete, they provide examples from which you can begin to do your own analyses using these methods. For an example of how to present a semiological analysis, consult the model essay in Appendix 1.

Part 3

STORIES

Dreams give birth to plans and the realising of plans gives birth to further dreams.

Bannister and Fransella 1980, p. 80

'Sex, money, and violence. That's all we ever see.' These are the words of an elderly East European man who commented about cinema at an evening class I once ran. They seemed to me to be the perfect encapsulation of what popular cinema offers us, if you include crime alongside money and violence, and I felt in total agreement with him. However, the tone of his remark was frustration and exasperation. He saw cinema as promoting capitalist ideals, unrealistic escapist fantasies, and immoral violence. In contrast, my assent had a positive element to it: I was saying 'Yes, isn't it wonderful? Can I watch some more, please?' My positive response was based on the pleasure, excitement, and stimulation of these 'fantasies' for me as viewer, but it was also a response that affirmed that popular cinema is interesting and significant because it deals with issues that are central to modern capitalist society. By dealing with sex, money, crime, death, and violence, popular cinema explores the contradictions that lie at the heart of the way we live. Popular films are not simply about promoting the values of Western society; they are not trivial and irrelevant escapism. Rather, they are a place in which we can work out our concerns about these significant issues.

OVERVIEW OF PART 3

Whereas Part 2 focuses on semiology as a method of analysing still images, Part 3 analyses the moving images of film and television fictions. The language of film and television—for example, the techniques of *mise en scène*, cinematography, editing, and sound (Bordwell and Thompson 2001)—is a crucial factor in the way such fictions produce meaning and emotional affect. It is dealt with in Appendix 2, which is a model essay analysing a short piece of film—the opening scenes of *Blue Velvet*. The essay aims to provide a close textual analysis that pays special attention to the techniques of film language. It would be very useful to view the film *Blue Velvet*, particularly the opening sequence, before reading the essay. The essay includes footnotes, references, and bibliography, as should any essay in media studies. It also includes a breakdown of the shots in the film. This is an invaluable tool for detailed analysis, helping you to see the elements that have gone into making the film.

Here, because film and television work predominantly by presenting us with stories or narratives in familiar genres, we demonstrate how to use narrative structures, binary oppositions, and generic conventions as tools of analysis. This work is based on structuralist approaches to the media. In the final section we suggest a different narrative approach derived from the work of Joseph Campbell and Carl Jung.

9   *Genres, Codes, and Conventions*

GENRES

The analysis of *Blue Velvet* in Appendix 2 makes several references to film and television genres. 'Genre' simply means a type of film or program. To say that a film or program is in a particular genre is to say that it shares a set of characteristics, such as story type and visual style, with a group of other films or programs. The similarities mean we can quickly classify any film or program as belonging to a particular genre—horror, musical, sitcom, soap opera, and so on—by recognising its familiar codes and conventions. Genres are useful for:

- producers who make and sell their product by identifying it as part of an already successful, and therefore marketable, generic formula
- film-makers who can communicate easily and quickly through these formulas and can also work creatively within the form
- audiences who use genre as a basis for their choice of films and as a key to understanding them.

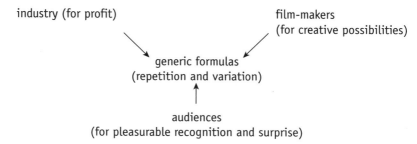

industry (for profit)

film-makers
(for creative possibilities)

generic formulas
(repetition and variation)

audiences
(for pleasurable recognition and surprise)

Figure 3.1 Uses of genres. The constituencies represented in this diagram (the film and television industry, film-makers, and audiences) can use genres and generic formulas beneficially.

We may ask why people watch genre films when the nature of the formulaic plot means that it is generally fairly easy to predict how the story will end. However, this sense of knowingness provides its own pleasures. Those who watch genre films often find a sense of satisfaction in being able to predict what will happen next, and they take pleasure in having these expectations subverted, manipulated, or confirmed. The horror-spoof film *Scream* was a huge success because it made the characteristics of the genre explicit and reworked them playfully. Avid consumers of certain genres like horror and science–fiction also become adept at spotting intertextual references to other films and recognising the familiar iconography and conventions that characterise the genre, and they enjoy this sense of expertise.

Genre study evolved as a way of studying Hollywood films.[1] It showed several things:

- Most genres are immediately identifiable through their familiar iconography, their recurrent use of visual icons: for example, the Western genre is full of cowboys, hats, guns, horses, cattle, wagon trains, saloons, frontier settings, and so on.
- Genre stories work through familiar and repeated plot lines, but many directors, such as John Ford, Howard Hawks, and Sam Peckinpah, have worked within these generic plots (in the case of these directors, in the Western genre) to produce their own deeply crafted and often complex visions of American society.
- Genres continually evolve. Alongside the repetition of familiar codes and conventions, variations on the genre are introduced, which give a new inflection, and often a new direction, to the genre. Thus, for example, the Western was reinvented by Sam Peckinpah, who introduced bleaker and more extreme representations of violence, and again by a type of film known as Spaghetti Westerns (Westerns made by Italian film-makers and often shot in Spain—most notably the Sergio Leone–Clint Eastwood collaborations). Another example of the ability of genres to mutate is the evolution of film noir—those complex and dark thrillers made in black and white in the 1940s and 1950s—which returned in colour in the 1970s, 1980s, and 1990s. A genre can thus continually develop to encompass new elements and produce new meanings.
- Lastly, Steven Neale suggests that some genres focus on a 'core problematic', an issue of social importance that the genre explores (Neale, p. 21). For example, the core problematic of the Western is the conflict between, on the one hand, law and order, and on the other, freedom beyond the law, a conflict that is a major issue for American society. The Western was a space for working out all kinds of scenarios around this issue, and studying the Western provides a chance to see how this social issue has been, and still is being, dealt with.

Genre theory was established for popular cinema at a time when most films were easily placed in a few key genres. Since then, a number of things have happened.

1 First, the advent of television has widened the scope of film culture and has established a whole new set of television forms or genres—game shows, current-affairs programs, situation comedies, soap operas, reality TV, and so on.

2 Second, alongside cinema, television (which recycles older films that would, prior to television, have disappeared from general public viewing after their initial release) has helped to nurture a generation of media watchers who are incredibly knowledgeable and sophisticated as viewers. This generation of media watchers has seen an enormous amount of popular film and television that spans a considerable historical time period. While they may not have studied the media, they know a good deal about media texts, techniques and technologies, and in particular, they know about genres. Program makers need to be aware of the skills of their audience: they must provide novel material that continues to enthrall and entertain them, but they can also rely on the audience being able to appreciate, if not actually analyse, quite complicated variations on genres.

3 Third, the consequence of this has been what is called 'hybridisation', the mixing of different genres or generic crossovers (such as *Blue Velvet*). An example of hybridisation is where elements of a number of genres appear in any one film. The point is that the program makers can rely on the audience understanding

many of these codes; the mixture of genres offers the audience more pleasure and provides program makers with more possibilities and with a broader share of the market. For instance, Jackie Chan's generic hybrid *Shanghai Noon* attracted fans of Westerns, martial arts films, period dramas and comedies. (This postmodern style is discussed in Part 6, pp. 311–13). Key examples on television include *Twin Peaks* (directed by David Lynch), *Ally McBeal*, and *South Park*, which are all ground-breaking series in terms of the way they play across genres.

Thelma and Louise: The Western, the road movie, and the buddy movie

We can see the richness that this hybridisation imparts to films in the film *Thelma and Louise*, an excellent example of generic mixture. It contains elements of at least three different genres: the Western, the road movie, and the buddy movie. What makes this movie interesting, in terms of genres, is the way it takes traditionally male genres and creates new meanings by making women the main characters, placing women in traditionally male scenarios.

The Western

A central theme of the Western is the exploration of the boundaries and differences between civilised society, maintained through the establishment of law and order, and the freedom or disorder found in uncivilised society (the wilderness or paradisical garden that lies beyond the frontier). Stories are often about either the hero's establishment of law and order in this wilderness (the bringing of civilisation to the west) or the hero's escape from the constraints of civilisation to live life more fully outside the law and society (this is often also a journey of self-discovery for the hero).[2] The idea of crossing the frontier, of 'going west' to a 'manifest destiny' is central to American culture. This goes back to the very formation of America by European colonists, who sought freedom from the political and religious constraints of Europe.[3] (Science-fiction films, which portray space or cyberspace as 'the final frontier', continue this tradition.)

the frontier

freedom	vs	restraint
wilderness	vs	civilisation
paradise	vs	law and order

The ideal of the USA as a land of freedom and opportunity is encapsulated in the continual search for new frontiers, new freedoms. The Western explores the historical period when America established its new civilisation beyond the frontier. However, Westerns nearly always present this as a male drama: women are only presented as appendages to the main characters.

Thelma and Louise plays with the generic conventions of the Western. Although it is set in the 1980s, it draws heavily on Western iconography: there are numerous shots of cattle, horses, and cowboys, all of which are irrelevant to the plot but form a background through which the women travel; cowboy-style clothing is worn by the characters, particularly Louise; and the escape to Mexico is a familiar Western storyline, with Mexico representing another frontier and freedom beyond the constraints of the law.

The film also takes place in Western landscapes. The most obvious examples of this are the scenes shot in Monument Valley, a location familiar to film-goers because it appears in numerous other films. Monument Valley is one of the major icons of American culture. It is such a recurring motif in director John Ford's films that it is considered to be one his 'signatures'. Much of the meaning in the scenes in *Thelma and Louise* derives from the fact that they refer back to and develop these film conventions. Some of the scenes at Monument Valley are shot at night and this breaks with the conventional way of filming this place. The night-time shooting defamiliarises the setting, showing it in a new light. What makes it more unconventional is that in this film the women are experiencing and celebrating what have traditionally been male freedoms—the freedom of the road, the freedom of being beyond the law—and they are doing it in this most masculine of places. It as though women are claiming this male space for themselves, and are issuing a challenge to masculinity. It could be argued that there is a similarity between male Western heroes and Thelma and Louise in that they challenge authority, or what is sometimes referred to in psychoanalytic terms as 'the law of the father'.

The heroic 'male' values of the Western are thus turned upside down by combining the conventional Western setting with women as central characters, and by filming this setting at night. The hybridisation is intensified by the soundtrack, which features Marianne Faithfull singing 'The Ballad of Lucy Jordan', a song that is very appropriate for the characters Thelma and Louise, but is not conventionally suited to filming at Monument Valley. For viewers familiar with Marianne Faithfull's own story, there are further connotations at work here. Her original pop success was as an innocent flower-child singer in the 1960s. She then apparently became a victim of drugs and scandal, and she disappeared from the pop world. However, she re-emerged in the 1980s as a mature and gutsy woman whose voice had become powerful and gritty. Her own story of growth could thus be linked to that of *Thelma and Louise* (and would be read as such by those with knowledge of her).

The road movie

The second genre to consider is the road movie.[4] Briefly, the road movie offers its characters a journey of discovery that is both literal, as characters move through a changing landscape, and metaphorical, as they make an inner journey of self-discovery. Such patterns of journeying, character change, and character development are common to many narratives. The act of journeying itself involves embracing change and future possibilities and breaking away from the constraints of tradition, authority, stability, normality and security. These themes also emerge in different ways in other road movies such as *Wild at Heart, Natural Born Killers*, and *Fear and Loathing in Las Vegas*. They are found in theatre, literature, and film. But the road movie has more elements to it. In many ways it is descended from the Western. Once America is fully civilised, tamed, and modernised, the road itself becomes the new frontier: it is 'on the road' that freedom can be found. *On the Road* is a celebrated novel by Jack Kerouac (1958). It describes a moment in 1950s American culture when young people, given a new affluence in the context of post-war prosperity, and faced with the relative affordability of cars, could suddenly leave home and home towns behind to travel across the USA in search of excitement. In *On the Road*, the main character meets up with his friend, Dean Moriarty, and they cross America, from the east coast to the west coast and back again—and again and again. What is important in this book is not the destination but the act of journeying itself.

The road-movie genre evolved in the 1950s and 1960s. The most significant example of this genre is *Easy Rider*, a film that portrays disaffected young people travelling across the USA on motorcycles. There are countless other examples of the genre, some of which you will be familiar with. It is a genre that has particular resonance for Australia, which has its own tradition of journeying through the landscape. Many Australian films—*Mad Max*; *Priscilla, Queen of the Desert*; *Kiss or Kill*—are in the genre.

The road movie has several characteristics.

- First there is the idea and the reality of movement that the road provides: the genre has a dynamic drive inscribed into it. This movement relates both to the idea of escape from a more static and humdrum world (in Thelma and Louise's case, the drudgery and subordination of being either a housewife or a waitress) and to the dynamics of the car chase. Whereas earlier genres tended to save the chase for the final reel, the road movie allows for an extended chase throughout the film. This movement connects with American representations of space: the way to deal with or solve problems is to move; if a crime has been committed you get over the state border to relative safety. Movement also becomes a goal in itself: 'Where we going, man?' someone asks Dean Moriarty in the novel *On the Road*. 'I don't know *but we gotta go*', he replies (my emphasis) (Kerouac 1958, p. 249).

- The road movie explores social mobility and social diversity. Characters who move through the road movie can become someone else: they can discover new identities and can 'find themselves'. It is through such characters, who depart from the fixed social roles they begin with, that social mobility is explored. This relates to the fact that part of the American dream is a belief that it is possible to move up the social ladder. At the same time, the journey through the landscape provides an opportunity to view a whole range of social types and situations: the road movie presents a series of snapshots of American life across the continent. The heroes meet with a diverse range of people, allowing a commentary to be made on the USA as a whole. The static quality of many of these lives is also shown in contrast to the movement of the heroes, who are not so fixed, either geographically or socially. Similar social explorations are found in road movies set in Australia or the United Kingdom.

- The road movie has a typical ending: 'crashing out'. The climax often involves acceleration and a crash. This offers an explosive resolution for the viewer. It is also a climax of death and destruction. As such, it is a challenging genre, since it suggests there is no easy solution to the social problems represented in the film. This is in marked contrast to the happy endings of many Hollywood films.

- Finally, the genre portrays freedom, irresponsibility, lack of social ties, and law-breaking, which are all typically associated with male ways of behaving. Because ideas of home, domesticity, and 'settling down' are anathema to these characters it has traditionally been a male genre and a youth-media form.

The buddy movie

The third genre is the buddy movie, a term used in the 1970s to describe movies such as *Butch Cassidy and the Sundance Kid*. It identifies a common theme across a number of 'male' genres (Westerns, war films, and road movies): male friendship and male bonding. This friendship is often also a competitive rivalry, and buddy movies tend to work through how the male characters can finally bond successfully. The bonding process often involves a degree of misogyny: in order for the male protagonists to bond, women are seen as 'the other'. There is also often repressed homosexuality: while the films show a good deal of affection between the buddies, there is rarely any overt portrayal of homosexual desire. The buddy movie was first identified as a genre by feminist critics interested in constructions of masculinity (Haskell 1974), but it has now become part of everyday ways of talking about films. It is not a classical genre in its own right like the Western, the musical, or the gangster film, and this shows how the term 'genre', first developed in the context of the study of film, is now loosely applied to any group of films showing some basic similarities. By the time *Thelma and Louise* was released, the theme of male bonding and friendship was well established for audiences and producers, and viewers were therefore able to see this theme echoed in the friendship between the two female protagonists.

Summary

Thelma and Louise takes three traditionally male genres and reworks them. This can be seen as a marketing ploy that gives traditional genres a novelty value by changing the gender of the protagonists—it's fun to watch because we haven't seen women do these things—and thus it gives the audience repetition and variation at the same time.

However, this reworking of traditional male genres cannot be dismissed as just a marketing ploy. The film also legitimates male pleasures for women (both the women in the film and those in the audience). Women can and do enjoy the same things that men conventionally enjoy: the freedom of the road, casual sexual liaisons, shooting guns, and breaking the law. This aspect of the film has been read in contradictory ways. Some critics are pleased to see women appropriating the kinds of power traditionally associated with men and patriarchy (violence, guns, and so on). Others who believe that the film suggests that women can only assert themselves by becoming like men are disappointed; they would rather see traditionally feminine qualities (caring, negotiating, communicating, problem-solving through non-violent means, and so on) reasserted as positive and powerful ways for women to assert themselves.[5]

The film raises issues that have been central to feminist studies—rape, the exploitation of women in the workforce, and their subordination in domestic roles, particularly within the institution of marriage—but it does this in a popular genre, which means that the audience is carried along by the pleasures of the genre at the same time as they are absorbing the political content of the film.

The starting points for the film are realistic, everyday issues faced by Thelma and Louise. In the opening scenes of the film, Thelma and Louise are ordinary women living ordinary lives, and particularly because the protagonists are not stereotypically youthful, glamorous, or affluent this gives the film a credibility that some films based on male fantasies lack. This believability makes the film more powerful and effective.

Although the film plays with male genres, some feminine values remain central to the story, and the film celebrates female friendship. Thelma and Louise perform their 'male' roles with ironic humour, compassion, and gentleness, thereby endorsing values that are traditionally feminine. Compared with the portrayal of male bonding in films, female bonding is rarely shown. However, in this film Thelma and Louise's relationship is the most important relationship for the two women. The centrality of this relationship is in contrast to the way that, traditionally, films portray women mainly in terms of their relationship to men.

Thelma and Louise is an excellent example both of the hybridisation of genres and of the ways in which they can be reworked in different frameworks, in this case through an emphasis on women's roles and concerns.

AMERICAN CULTURAL IMPERIALISM

We want to say something here about the significance of Hollywood and the USA in a global context. Film was a new medium at the start of the twentieth century. In the USA, film production was established in Hollywood through the studio system. In this system, the three major stages of film production—making the film, distributing it, and exhibiting it—were centrally controlled by a small group of studios such as Warner Brothers and MGM (Cook 1985, pp. 7–8, 10–25). Films made under this system were set in the USA and were focused on American content. They thus became a form for celebrating, reflecting on, and exploring American society—its ideals, its problems, and its conflicts. Two of the most important film genres, the Western and the gangster film, have been described as genres that reflect on American history and society, genres that have allowed the USA to 'talk to itself' (McArthur, p. 18).

For various reasons, both economic and cultural, the Hollywood studio system came to be the dominant form of film-making worldwide. You could argue that, since then, American culture has become world culture. This raises the whole issue of cultural imperialism. Cultural imperialism describes the process whereby one culture asserts its economic and political control over another culture (or other cultures) not through force of arms, invasion, or political control, but through the invasion of that other culture's values and ideals—in this case, through its films. This is not done deliberately as part of an American political plan. Rather, it is a product of industrial and economic determinations, and of the control of cultural texts, communication, and the dispensation of information via the mass media.

The predominance of American films has an economic basis. The American film and television industries play a significant part in the American economy, and the predominance of American films worldwide brings in enormous profits to the USA from many other countries, partly at the expense of local media industries. The USA can therefore be said to live off other countries economically. There are many struggles about how much American cinema and television should be screened in other countries. In these countries, it is perceived that there are cultural, economic, and moral dangers involved in the predominance of American cinema and television. An influx of American product is seen as a limitation on the expression of a country's own cultural heritage; a limitation on local job creation and on creative opportunities in the local media industries; and a dangerous influence on social values, particularly in relation to young people.

The issue of the USA's relationship with other cultures is central in the twentieth century. The USA was the dominant world power in this century. Its intervention in both world wars led to their resolution; its economy has been the most powerful in the world; and its values have been the most pervasive across the globe. We suggest that it is common to find a love–hate relationship with the USA on the part of people from other countries. This has been my own experience growing up in the United Kingdom in the 1950s and 1960s. During this period, much of British society was disturbed by the influx of American youth culture: milk bars, rock and roll, juke boxes, and so on (Hoggart 1958). Many were also concerned about what were seen as the cheap and sensational depictions of sex and violence in pulp fiction and films from the USA. While British authorities saw the influx of American cultural products as a moral and cultural threat to young people, young people themselves often found them exciting and liberating. American films, novels, and music contrasted with the dull, repressed, and restricted conformity of British life, and so they were eagerly consumed by many British people. In Britain and Europe, American popular culture was part of the liberating movement of the 1960s. Similar struggles over American cultural influence have been apparent in Australia, both then and now. These struggles are often played out over young people, who seem drawn to the excitements of American culture. It is clear from the amount of advertising that American corporations (such as McDonald's, Coca-Cola, and Pepsi) undertake that they are keen to target the youth market. Just consider McDonald's Happy Meals and the way an idealised notion of childhood as a period of innocent happiness filled with fun and games is packaged and sold to consumers as a commodity. Once captured, these consumers offer a lifetime of consumption.

The great positive myths of the USA are that it is a land of opportunity, freedom, prosperity, and equality. It is seen as a melting-pot society in which anyone can succeed, and is thus perceived as a great escape from older, more traditional and restricted societies. Over the years it has invited, and taken in, an influx of immigrants who have created new lives for themselves. My attraction to American culture has developed through popular music, film, television, and literature. These are the aesthetic forms I have most enjoyed, particularly film. But at the same time, I have resisted the influence of American culture because I believe that it glorifies materialist values at the expense of everything else and because the economic interests with which it is allied seem to be taking over and exploiting the rest of the world.

This love–hate relationship seems to be common in Australia, the United Kingdom, and the rest of Europe, not to mention Japan, Asia, and the rest of the globe! American culture promises energy, sexiness, and freedom; American fashions and style are taken up by young people in every continent; and capitalism and competition have become the new ideals of the Soviet Union and of communist countries. But some fear this cultural dominance. They are apprehensive of the way it erodes traditional values and of its competitive harshness. What, for example, is the effect of the influx of American culture on Australian and British culture, sport, music, and the values of young people in Australia and the United Kingdom?

One way of considering this issue is to suggest that television and cinema should aim to tell a culture's own stories, for example that Australia and the United Kingdom should present stories about Australian or British people set in their own countries. The following exchange, on ABC Radio National's *Media Report*, between cultural critics John Hartley and Mick O'Regan addresses this issue in relation to the dominance of American situation comedies on Australian TV.

O'Regan: If television is meant to tell our own story, why is it that so much of the content is about people who, superficially at least, seem to share little with their viewers? Does television impede expression of difference, and present a globalised, uniform televisual product, a sort of electronic McDonald's?

Hartley: There are countries … from Malaysia and Singapore, to France and even Australia … where there is concern … about local content and about preserving national cultures of various kinds … But … one needs to understand how it is that we generally as human beings, watch sitcoms, and we don't watch them as Australians, we watch them as families, and what we're being taught by sitcoms, the American sitcoms are very good at this, is family comportment, how to behave oneself, you know, in relation to one's teenage siblings, or in relation to one's parents or whatever the situation happens to be. Now that is as near as dammit to universal as there is. So I think when you're watching a program [like] *Clarissa Explains it All*, which is on Nickelodeon, you're watching it as an 11 or 12 year old, not as an Australian or a French person or as Malaysian. There is in fact a transparency of the very basic television formats that crosses national boundaries, and does not, in my opinion, although of course this is argued fiercely, does not threaten national cultures but is assimilated into national cultures.

O'Regan: So what about the global appeal of a program like the American sitcom, *Friends*? How would a young South African in Soweto, or an Aboriginal Australian in a remote community like Yuendumu relate to the antics of a group of 30-something New Yorkers?

Hartley: That's a very interesting question, to which I don't have an empirical answer although I do know, in fact I marked a PhD recently of someone who studied sitcoms in South Africa, and the fact is (this is probably going against the argument that I've just put) that they prefer comedies made in South Africa about the particular conditions of that country, possibly because they are so peculiar. So of course there is an interest in one's own condition, and as for Yuendumu or perhaps up in the Kimberleys, I know that there are people up there who are very concerned about which way round young Aboriginal kids are wearing their caps. You know, are they wearing them forwards because they're Australian or backwards because they're identifying with people in New York. Good questions, and these things do need to be thought through in detail. But I still come back to the point I've been making, which is that what's going on in *Friends*, apart from the pleasures of looking at very attractive people with nice teeth for half an hour, is a kind of narration of young heterosexual life. Now are we to say that people in South Africa and people in Central Australia don't have young heterosexual life? Of course not. So if they're interested in those issues, they'll find the show appealing. If not, not. (ABC Radio National, *The Media Report*, 21 December 2000.)

We don't want to prescribe any simple answer to these issues—they are too complex—but we do want to draw attention to them as part of the media landscape. You should be thinking about them, as you also probably have mixed ideas and feelings about American culture and its place in your own society and indeed your own psyche (its place in your identity and subjectivity). Compare the ideals or dreams of American, Australian, and British societies. The USA and Australia, which are young countries from the perspective of their mutual coloniser, England, have established dreams of what future life could be like. These are dreams of social equality and opportunity. But while the American dream is one of success—think of the goals of 'making it to the top' and the saying 'anyone can become President'—the Australian dream is less ambitious. The Australian dream is much more modest: owning your own quarter-acre block and having a good job and a family. In other words, it is more about survival, contentment, and fulfilment, than about spectacular success.

Returning to *Thelma and Louise*, we can see that because the genres it works with (the Western, the road movie, and the buddy movie) are essentially American genres— they derive from American culture, society, and history—they are a useful commentary on that society. In this respect the crash that is the end of this movie may well be a suitable response to and comment on the state of American society. But are the values of the Western, the road movie, and the buddy movie universal? Are they useful for Australian, Asian, African, or British audiences? As we are caught up in American genres, are we drawn more towards American society and its values? Or can we watch such genres without being significantly influenced by these values? Again, these are big questions and they are presented here for you to give them further thought.

Note your own feelings and ideas about American culture. Note how often you can see evidence of it in your cultural surroundings and list the cultural products from the USA that have been popularised by the media. Your list may include films, television shows, magazines, fashion, celebrities, and food chains that you love, or that you hate, or that you hardly notice because they are so much a part of the fabric of everyday life. Consider how you feel about this influence and ask yourself why this is so. How do the events of 11 September influence your thinking and feeling about American cultural imperialism? Record some interviews with young and old people asking them about their attitudes to the USA and to American culture. Do your interviewees give similar answers?

CODES AND CONVENTIONS

Genres work on the basis of codes and conventions that are easily recognised by the audience. How do filmic conventions produce meaning? Can the meanings of film codes and conventions change through time and be reworked so that they are not necessarily fixed to one meaning? When considering these questions, it is interesting to note that James Dean and Judy Garland are now widely recognised as gay icons, though they would not have been understood as such by mainstream audiences at the time their films were released. In this case the cultural context has changed radically, and this has resulted in a re-reading of classic texts in light of discoveries about the private lives of the stars, and public perceptions of what forms of sexuality are deemed acceptable or even cool.

The history of art and aesthetic production is a history of people finding new styles and new means of representation and expression. It is also replete with examples of people rediscovering and reworking old styles into something new—neo-classicism, neo-realism, and so on. Each new style is initially seen as an aesthetic breakthrough, as unconventional and challenging. Such innovations that supplant more traditional, conservative styles, are often rejected by some people because they are too radical. However, in time, the new style becomes familiar and conventional, so that eventually it does not have the same impact and its meaning changes. It becomes traditional and clichéd, and in time new styles and conventions emerge that offer further breakthroughs.

In relation to film language, a convention that means one thing when it is first used may take on other meanings later on. A good example of this is the evolution of the film-making style known as 'montage'. In the 1920s, Russian film-makers such as Sergei Eisenstein and Dziga Vertov developed a stylistic form of editing known as Soviet montage. Montage is the practice of joining or editing short pieces of film together as the basis for telling stories. As first used in the 1920s, it was designed to complement the revolutionary ideals of the communist revolution, and it was theorised as a film style that was radically different from the conventional techniques of the capitalist Hollywood film-making system. Today the aesthetic techniques of Soviet montage continue to thrive, but they are no longer the exclusive province of radical film-making. On the contrary, montage has been taken over by mainstream film-makers, and today the best place to see montage in action is in advertising or on MTV (which is really an extended advertisement for the music industry)—the most potent forms of capitalist film-making!

What we can see from this is that a particular film language or film convention does not guarantee particular kinds of political or social use or meaning. Forms and conventions can be used in different contexts to give them different meanings. This is very important in film and video because many new techniques are often developed for radical and innovative purposes. Like Soviet montage, they may be used originally to challenge the dominant system but can be appropriated by the dominant system, which then uses the same technique in a non-challenging way. The most innovative television advertisements often borrow techniques, style, and conventions from experimental, radical film-makers. For example, the surrealist films of Jan Swankmajer challenged the conventions of his society but his techniques and he himself have been used by advertisers selling commodities.[6]

The film-maker Godfrey Reggio is an interesting case of someone who was very aware of conventions and how to use them. He was the major force behind the films *Koyaanisqatsi* and *Powaqqatsi* (similar to *Baraka*). In his previous work, which aimed to raise public awareness about the abuse of young people, he used advertising billboards. In that work he used 'conventional techniques in an unconventional way' (Reggio 1990). In other words, he took the apparatus of capitalist advertising to promote radical, socialist ideas. In the 1990s, some of the advertising campaigns for the Benetton clothing company were similar to Reggio's work in that they used unusual, shocking images such as portraits of convicted murderers and serial rapists on death row. This form of campaign aims to raise awareness of issues such as the death penalty at the same time as heightening consumer recognition and awareness of the Benetton brand.

The tension between these two objectives (one humanitarian, the other profit driven) has led to accusations that Benetton is guilty of the commodification of social issues.

Reggio (1990) has stated that in *Koyaanisqatsi* and *Powaqqatsi* he was 'trying to let people see from another point of view things that we see every day—looking for things people have seen zillions of times to see them afresh, from another point of view'. He hoped that his images would shock and disturb viewers, making them question where modern society is going. He wanted to do this as spectacularly as possible, partly to attract the audience, but also to draw attention to the way our society is becoming increasingly fascinated by spectacle and images. He used the techniques of time-lapse photography to critique modern-day industrial societies. By speeding up the action, the humans who are portrayed appear as insects or robots, functioning unthinkingly, automatically. This technique also shows the city as an animated live creature, whose arteries pulsate with the red and white corpuscles of speeding car lights replayed in fast-motion. *Koyaanisqatsi* has achieved a cult following.

Paradoxically it has now become somewhat conventional to use unconventional images to try to create audience interest. *Juice* magazine caused a stir when they featured photos of supposedly murdered corpses in clothes advertisements (Figures 3.2 and 3.3). These styles and the images associated with them were attempts to break taboos of what is acceptable.

Figures 3.2–3.3 Fashion spreads in *Juice*. These are examples of heroin chic.
Source: *Juice*, June 1996, pp. 62–3, 66

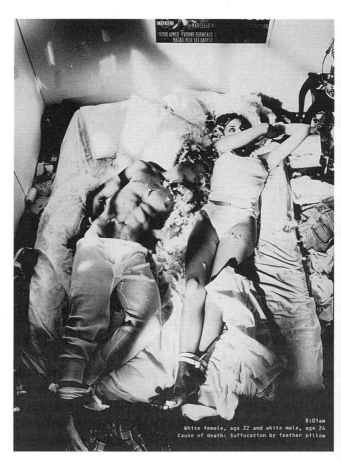

Figure 3.3
Source: *Juice*,
June 1996

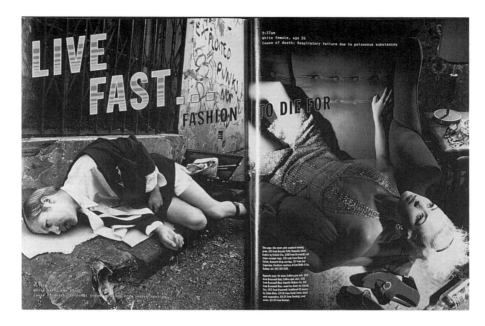

When it was first released *Koyaanisqatsi* was an unusual film to watch. However, since then the very techniques that Reggio used to critique society have been used by advertisers to celebrate modern societies! For example, accelerated images of urban societies have been used as trailers to promote commercial television shows such as *Angel*, and to sell gas and electricity in the United Kingdom.

As analysts, we have to be aware that the formal style of any images, the convention or codes used, do not guarantee particular meanings: meaning is dependent on content and context (both geographic and historical). Because film conventions are continually changing and being reworked, radical form does not guarantee radical meaning. The credit sequences of *Melrose Place* use techniques similar to those of avant-garde, radical film-makers of the 1960s and 1970s. The opening shows the actual 'frames' of a piece of film, and the very final credit of the fourth series shows the end of a piece of Super 8 film as it would appear going through the film projector. These techniques were originally used by radical film-makers in the 1970s who wanted to draw spectators' attention to the fact that film is a construction. They deconstructed film by showing the film-making process, and in so doing mounted a critique of film's claim to realism. These once radical, alternative techniques are now part of the mainstream, and they no longer carry their original critical meanings.

The ending of the film *Basic Instinct* demonstrates how mainstream film-makers play with film conventions to generate audience interest. This ending is effective because of the audience's awareness of the conventions of Hollywood film endings. Towards the end of the film, the two main characters, played by Michael Douglas and Sharon Stone, finally go to bed together; under the bed is an ice-pick that has been used earlier to kill men. Stone reaches for the ice-pick and the film ends. We do not see Sharon Stone use the ice-pick, but the film leaves us with an unresolved question—was she really the killer?—and excited and disturbed—what will she do now? The full effect of the ending is built on, and depends on, our awareness of other conventional Hollywood endings. Traditionally, Hollywood film endings have been 'closed': everything is resolved, usually happily. The horror film in the 1970s began to use open-ended endings, in order to suggest that evil was still alive, that questions remained unanswered. These endings, for example the ending in *Carrie*, were initially very shocking, but as they were repeated (for example, in the *Nightmare on Elm Street* series of films) and became more familiar to audiences, their shock value decreased.

However, in a different genre, the family melodrama, we would still expect conventionally closed endings. The power of the ending of *Fatal Attraction* lies partly in the fact that it combines melodramatic content—a family story of adultery—with horror conventions. The final sequence, in which Glenn Close, who has been attacked by the man she has been stalking, refuses to die, is presented like a horror movie. This is shocking because up until that point in the film, the conventions of melodrama predominate. This is an excellent example of mixing generic conventions to rouse audience interest.

The trick of a good film ending is to give us a final surprise, a final twist. The audiences of *Basic Instinct* are aware of the possible inclusion of 'horror' endings in other genres; many of them are aware that Michael Douglas appears in *Fatal Attraction*, a story about a dangerous, psychotic woman. *Basic Instinct* thus sets the scene for a similar final violent act. The effectiveness of *Basic Instinct*'s ending lies in its refusal to give us what is, by now, the conventional violent ending. It ends quite peacefully—Sharon Stone does not use the ice-pick—but leaves us with an unresolved question.

To see the relevance of codes and conventions in relation to television and film, try the following experiment. Switch on the television at random: flick from channel to channel, watching each for about five seconds. Note what type or genre of program you think you are watching and why. If you are uncertain about any programs, keep switching channels and watching until you can make up your mind. Think about how you identify each program as belonging to a particular type/genre. Repeat this experiment on a regular basis, over a week. You will realise that you are a skilled reader of codes.

CONCLUSION

It is important for us to recognise and identify the use of film genres, codes, and conventions; to be aware of their history and development; and to understand that genres, codes and conventions can change their meanings in different contexts (and that film-makers will often mix genres knowing that audiences are aware of them). This knowledge gives us greater insight into the uses of the language of the moving image.

10 Narrative Structure and Binary Oppositions

THE IMPORTANCE OF NARRATIVE

Narratives or stories are a basic way of making sense of our experience. This seems to be a cultural process shared by all societies; humans tend to understand and relate experiences through stories. In Western culture, when people talk about things that happen, both in fiction and real life, they put these experiences into a story or narrative structure—a sequence of events linked through cause and effect, with a beginning, a middle, and an end. We have fictional stories but we also have feature stories about current affairs in the newspaper, documentary stories, and even sports stories. When we relate our own daily experiences—'How was your day at work?'—our accounts often come out as stories.

But stories and narratives do something more than this. It is very normal to ask about a story: 'What's the point of the story?' or 'What's the moral of the story?' This idea of stories having a moral, a point, or a lesson to teach goes back to stories such as Aesop's Fables, biblical stories, myths, and legends, but is just as relevant today in film and television narratives. All these 'stories' can be considered as means by which societies 'talk to themselves'. They look at certain human issues and questions and by the end of the narrative, a solution, resolution, or overall message about the problem has been presented. As discussed in the conversations between John Hartley and Mick Regan extracted above (pp. 121–2), family sitcoms show us how to relate to teenage siblings or deal with parents. Others such as *Friends* and *Dawson's Creek* show us how to live out young adult heterosexuality and explore relationship issues. The point is that stories have a point to make—they are trying to communicate something, send a message to audiences. This message is often not fully realised until the ending of the story—in comedy it is with the delivery of the punch line. We wait in anticipation for this final delivery, which usually resolves the preceding conflicts and questions that have been set up but which also provides us with a position to make some kind of judgment or evaluation of all that has gone before: we thus 'get the message'. The logic of storytelling is to communicate some message, some point, and any good analysis or reading of that story will aim to try and understand what those messages are.

The aim of this chapter is to analyse how stories work as another way of analysing texts. The first stage will be simply to identify the components of a story. The second and more significant stage is to see how the narrative structure determines the meaning of the story. The argument we're making here is that the way a story is told or structured will affect how we understand it.

NARRATIVE STRUCTURE AND STRUCTURALISM

The approach offered here is based on structuralism. Structuralism was developed by anthropologists, particularly Lévi-Strauss (1978), for analysing many aspects of human society, such as kinship patterns and cooking practices. It has also been used to study myths, and has been applied in many other academic areas. In media studies, structuralism has been used to analyse narrative.[7] Its broad aim is to go beneath the surface of any media text to see how the story structure contributes to meaning.

The importance of narrative structure is made clearer if we distinguish structure from content. A useful example is to look at how gay characters have been represented in films. This is well documented in Vito Russo's book *The Celluloid Closet*, which has also provided the basis for an excellent documentary film. He argues that most early representations of gay characters were negative in that they laughed at and demeaned homosexuality or showed gay characters as deviant and criminal. He argues that from the 1970s on, films sympathetic to or supportive of gay characters began to appear, but he draws attention to the way these characters are positioned or structured in the narrative. He finds that however 'sympathetically' the gay characters may be portrayed, more often than not the story provides an unhappy ending for them. At the end of his book, he includes, alongside a bibliography and filmography, a 'necrology' that charts the various endings assigned to gay characters, drawing attention to the predominance of unhappy endings for them: suicides, madness, solitude, imprisonment, death. The crucial point is that the narrative structure shows that gay characters will end up unhappy however sympathetically they are portrayed. This is a damning conclusion. We can still see this tendency in films such as *The Sum of Us* or *Priscilla, Queen of the Desert*, which, while being very affirmative, celebratory gay films, do not have classic happy endings.

HOW ARE NARRATIVES STRUCTURED, AND HOW DOES THIS STRUCTURE DETERMINE MEANINGS?

Narrative pattern

There is a basic structural pattern to narratives. According to Todorov all narrative is a movement between two equilibriums:

> At the start of the narrative there is always a stable situation ... something occurs which introduces a disequilibrium, a disturbance to this situation ... At the end of the story, the equilibrium is then re-established but is no longer that of the beginning (Todorov 1975, p. 163).

The 'equilibrium' established at the end is a form of resolution of the questions, enigmas, and desires that have been introduced by the disturbance. We can express this diagrammatically:

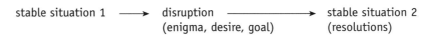

stable situation 1 ⟶ disruption ⟶ stable situation 2
                                 (enigma, desire, goal)   (resolutions)

Figure 3.4 Basic structural pattern of narratives

The disturbing incident at the beginning of the story catalyses changes for the main characters and often also sets up a goal or objective that the protagonist strives to attain. This creates a narrative question in the reader's or audience's mind that draws us through the story: we continually wonder how the protagonists will deal with the trials and tribulations they face. Of course, the central narrative question is only answered at the end of the story when the major crisis is finally resolved, but before that point we are seduced further into the narrative world as the main characters encounter obstacles, turning points, complications, and conflicts that threaten to prevent them from attaining their objectives. These dramas need to be overcome before a new equilibrium can be attained, and before the audience feels a sense of narrative closure.

In *Thelma and Louise*, both women are initially in stable situations—work and marriage respectively—but these are quickly shown as unsatisfactory. The disruption comes when they decide to leave for the weekend. This produces disequilibrium as their goals and desires come into play: they desire a happier life. Uncertainty and anticipation ensue: will they achieve this goal? In almost every narrative, a variation of this central narrative question drives the plot and maintains the audience's interest. An even greater disruption occurs when they kill a man, at which point the uncertainty becomes the question of whether they will escape or be caught. The disruption also raises the question of how Thelma and Louise will relate to each other. Another question also demands resolution: What has happened to Louise in the past? All these questions reach a resolution at the end. The ending—whether happy or unhappy—finishes off the story, providing a new stability and an answer to the central narrative question.

There are several important consequences of the basic narrative structure. First, it suggests that all problems and disruptions will have a resolution, an answer. This means that narrative as a formal structure is a reassuring and comforting structure: even if the ending is unhappy, at least it is resolved. This does not fit with our experience of real life: we know that the resolution to a problem often raises new problems, choices, or questions, and that there is rarely a definitive ending to situations or disruptions. Narrative serves to put a reassuring frame on the way we see and structure life.

Second, because there is closure to the story, audiences are invited to do nothing more than emotionally react. The closure suggests finality, which means that the audience is not invited to act, to do something in response, even if it is a challenging story.

Third, the way stories are told suggests an inevitability about the outcome—there are no other possible solutions. It is possible to produce narratives that suggest a range of different outcomes, as in the film *Run Lola Run*. *Bill and Ted's Excellent Adventure* provides a humorous example of this, with three possible endings. While such narratives are rare in film and television, a branching narrative structure that invites audience interaction and participation by offering choices among multiple pathways, settings, and character traits is increasingly common in computer games, interactive television, and other variants of computer-mediated communication.

Questions and answers

Narratives are essentially driven by questions and answers, which 'hook' the audience into the narrative—we want to know what happens next. All narratives set up key puzzles or questions. There tend to be one or two major questions and a host of smaller ones, and each one is answered at some stage. This is what Roland Barthes has called the 'hermeneutic code' because the word 'hermeneutic' refers to inquiry and interpretation (Barthes 1974). The British Film Institute has described the way that audiences are involved in film narrative as follows:

a) The viewer is prompted to ask questions—e.g. 'who-dunnit', 'who is this mysterious stranger?', 'will they fall in love?'
b) He/she watches on confident of getting an answer eventually.
c) The film, meanwhile, lays down in the viewer's path a series of false trails, dead ends and delays, keeping us from the answer—just yet.
d) The film introduces smaller questions which get answered quicker.
e) The film also leaves 'lying around' certain clues, hints and tantalising revelations about the original 'big' question. These lure the viewer onwards.
f) The viewer predicts, from time to time, answers to questions and then adjusts these predictions according to new evidence and re-predicts again until he/she reaches the conclusion with a start of surprise or satisfaction of expectations fulfilled (British Film Institute, Notes on Narrative).

Write down the ways in which Thelma and Louise *illustrates this pattern described by the British Film Institute.*

Exercise commentary

As discussed previously (p. 129), the obvious 'big' question that drives the narrative is 'Will Thelma and Louise survive, get caught, or die?' Alongside this are numerous other, smaller questions: Is the policeman played by Harvey Keitel a good guy? Will Thelma and JD get together? What happened in Louise's past? How will they get more money?—and so on. Note how the narrative often works by setting up a suspenseful question—for example, 'Will Thelma get raped?'—that it then answers quickly—in this case 'No'—but in a way that sets up new questions (for example, 'What will happen now that Louise has shot the rapist?'). This ongoing process of asking and answering questions leaves us both satisfied and wanting more: we become involved viewers, emotionally, imaginatively, and intellectually engaged with the story world rather than distanced from it as we might be while watching an avant garde film that encourages us to question the institution of cinema and the dream-like stories it offers. We can see here that film audiences are active participants in the process of making meaning. Our imaginations, intellect, and other faculties are constantly stretching to find answers to the questions raised over the course of the narrative, and to relate what is happening in the story to our own experiences and knowledge of the world. However, we must also consider the possibility that media audiences are passive to the extent that we tend to become immersed in the narrative world and are not encouraged to question the capitalist, consumerist values that underlie many mainstream cinema texts and the versions of reality they construct.

The structural position of characters

How are characters structurally positioned in narratives, and how does this positioning contribute to meaning? There are six useful questions to ask about any narrative:

1 Who and/or what makes things happen in the narrative?
2 What structural roles do people have in the narrative?
3 Whose point of view do we see things from and whose voice narrates the action or dominates the dialogue?
4 What is the dominant discourse or the hierarchy of discourses?
5 Are women positioned differently from men in the narrative?
6 What does the ending tell you about the ideology of the film?

The answers to all these questions carry consequences in terms of the text's meanings.

1 Who and/or what makes things happen? Social and psychological determination

Events may be driven by the actions of impersonal forces, such as tornadoes and earthquakes; by social forces, such as poverty and war; and by humans, either in groups or as individuals. Whichever of these determines events, most mainstream film narratives focus on individual humans and how they respond to these events. In *Twister*, for example, we are most interested in how the main characters deal with the tornado and what will happen to them in this situation. In most films, we are encouraged, by the way events are filmed and the way the story is presented, to take up a position of identification with the main characters, or to empathise with them. Furthermore, we are usually invited to understand these characters psychologically rather than socially: that is, we are encouraged to ask what makes them tick as individuals. Instead of being given a larger social, political, and economic context from which to make sense of their lives, we are given psychological reasons, from their past and present lives, for the way they feel and act.

This point leads us to the question of social and psychological determination. The question we want to ask is: 'What makes us, as individuals, act the way we do; what determines our actions?' We can split determining causes into two broad areas: external forces (social forces brought to bear on us) and internal forces (how we psychologically respond to events). Clearly these two forms of causal factors are linked to each other. For instance, the psychological character of an individual is not given at birth. While we have different inherent qualities and abilities, these are influenced by outside forces that are specific to each individual person, such as the treatment we receive from our parents and the kind of places, people, opportunities, and experiences we encounter as we grow up.

Social forces as a determining cause take us back to our social categories of class, gender, race (see pp. 24–5). The social situation we are born into will determine many of our life opportunities: an Aboriginal child, or a British child of West Indian descent, or a black South African born in an inner-city location in the year 2000 will have particular health, education, and employment possibilities. As we grow up we are all subject to social forces such as recessions, wars, ethnic disputes, and gender roles.

Popular narratives tend to privilege, or at least show more interest in, the psychological over the social. This relates to the whole ideology of individualism that permeates Western society. We can see this at work in the type of history that we are taught. Traditionally, history has been presented in terms of key historical figures, personalities who 'made history' (the 'kings and queens' version of history). We have learnt about individuals—Queen Elizabeth, Columbus, Joan of Arc, Yagan (nineteenth-century

Aboriginal leader of the Nyungar people of Western Australia), Captain Cook, Hitler, and so on—rather than major economic shifts and changes.

Film and television narratives have this same interest in individuals. This may be because it is easier to represent and understand individuals—for example, they can be made memorable by being endowed with interesting characteristics—than it is to represent and understand social forces, which are more complex and abstract. In the case of film, it became clear early on that audiences were interested in individual actors (stars). This may be related to the size of the screen and the use of close-ups, which enlarged the human face to huge proportions. The interest in individuals crosses most areas of media and the industry has actively constructed this fascination with individual stars, directors, and media personalities as a marketing device. For example, news stories are often structured around key individuals, and sports coverage focuses on stars and personalities. I myself often find it easy to think of film history in terms of individual directors rather than in terms of movements in film.

Most film narratives focus on one or two major characters, inviting us to be interested in these characters. Our interest is held by making them interesting characters—attractive, witty, cruel, loving, and so on—and by having stars, who are themselves often charismatic, fascinating people, play these parts. But more important than this is the general pattern of narrative that shows main characters going through an individual process of change, growth, and development.

Paralleling the narrative pattern of stable situation–disruption–new stable situation, there is usually a pattern of character change. Major characters are initially presented in narratives as having some kind of flaw in their character or an emotional problem. The film then provides a situation that tests them out: they have to work through a series of problems and in so doing they resolve their own character flaw—they go through a process of moral development and character growth. (This does not always happen, some characters remain fixed in their flawed situation and end up unhappy—Citizen Kane, for example, never learns from his situation.) The narrative focuses more on the character's growth than the social problems that provoke this. So in Thelma and Louise's case, what matters to us is that through the course of events they have 'discovered' themselves: they are liberated from their previous roles and have found their own power, strength, and feelings. In the end, it is this process of individual growth that is the focus of the story—more so than their oppression as women, which prompted the series of events traced by the movie. This stress on individual growth and resolution relegates social issues to second place in mainstream narratives.

So film and television tend to privilege the psychological over the social. They may include both, but our interest as spectators focuses on the individual. Narratives do not have to work like this. The Soviet Montage film movement of the 1920s–30s concentrated on social groups and issues, rather than heroic individuals with whom audience members could identify on a personal level. These films often used untrained actors to play nameless characters who embodied or typified a particular social class or identity.

Thelma and Louise provides an interesting example of the balance between social and psychological issues, in terms of gender. The film does raise social issues that are particularly significant for women, such as rape, domestic drudgery, male oppression, and the law's unequal treatment of women. But does it locate its two characters in these structures in such a way that the film raises our awareness about the position of women in society? Or does its focus on the desires, problems, and motivations of two individual women who are going through a process of change and development obscure this wider social picture? Angela Martin (1979) asks the following question of feminist film studies: 'Are we looking for images of real women or films which are really about women?' With this question she is distinguishing between films that show individual women understood in psychological terms and films about the general social conditions that women endure, as women. Both sorts of films might be important for feminists, but the latter put more stress on the social problems experienced by women and on the need for these to be changed if women's lives are to be improved.

We think *Thelma and Louise* does both. But, while it signals several important social gender issues, the following two characteristics of the film take the edge off its critical possibilities:

- The stress on the individual growth of the two characters becomes more important than the broader gender issues (although it could be argued that this growth represents a kind of feminist 'consciousness raising'—Thelma and Louise's growth stands as an example for all women of the kind of freedom they can achieve).
- Looking at the film generically, we see that the kinds of pleasure offered spectators are typical film-viewing pleasures: for example, the thrill of a good guys–bad guys chase. It is possible to watch the film purely for the excitement of the narrative without being concerned about the social issues at all.

The final point we want to make is that if you stress social causes and problems in a narrative, then the narrative's answer to these will be in terms of social issues and contexts; if you stress psychological causes and problems, then the narrative's answers will be to work on people's individual characters, and the social problems will thus become a background to the psychological problems. This is particularly significant in relation to how we are invited to understand texts that represent crime and criminality. If the narrative presents criminals as produced by social forces, and if the narrative focuses primarily on these forces, then the logic of the story is that we must change society to solve the crime problem. If, however, crimes are committed by psychologically deviant individuals who need to change their characters, then the solution suggested by the narrative is that we must change the individuals. The social issues again recede into the background as the individual issues are foregrounded.

Ask yourself how crime is usually presented in film and television narratives. Is it portrayed in social or psychological terms? Think, for example, about the criminal characters in Hannibal, Chopper, Face/Off, *and* Lock, Stock and Two Smoking Barrels.

2 What structural roles do people have in the narrative?

The way characters are positioned in the narrative tells us something about how we are expected to understand them. Consider, for instance, how many mainstream films and television programs consistently portray non-White characters in minor roles, or cast characters with accented English as villains or petty criminals rather than placing them in positive positions of power. Later in this chapter we discuss the different kinds of structural roles assigned to men and women in narratives. For example, many films invite us to be interested in the male hero's search for knowledge by providing us with information about what he thinks and feels: we are invited to identify with him. In contrast, we are often invited to watch female characters without knowing their personalities: they tend to be more objects of visual pleasure whose structural role might be to sing songs or perform strip routines: the audience is encouraged to 'objectify' them. Similarly, male characters are often set at the centre of a film while women serve secondary support functions such as wife, mother, or mistress. In this way women are structured as supports or appendages of men.

In this chapter we also examine the way characters are structurally positioned at the end of narratives. This positioning also encourages us to understand the character in a particular way. Analysing the structural position of characters requires us to think not so much about what characters do as about their positions in the narrative. These issues are central to understanding *Thelma and Louise* which, through a structural role-reversal, puts women into typically male roles.

3 Whose point of view do we see things from?

'Point of view' is an important cinematic term that raises questions about where the viewer is positioned in relation to the screen characters and the narrative world, and about how the text addresses its audience. It stresses the way we are invited to view events. Often films encourage identification with a character, particularly through the device of first-person, voice-over narration, or by point-of-view shots that encourage us to see things from the perspective of that character. Close-ups are another technique that literally bring us into intimate proximity with screen characters and can invite a sense of identification. (Note how rare it is for minor characters to be filmed in close-up, and how rarely the camera will position the audience in line with their audiovisual or subjective point of view.) In these ways we may be invited to sympathise with the characters even if they are murderers or criminals. *Psycho* is a film that uses certain techniques to encourage the audience to sympathise with the character of Marion Crane, who has stolen $40 000, and to see events from her point of view. Her murder in the film shocks audiences because a strong identification has been established with her, but the film then goes on to establish sympathy with her murderer by showing many events from his point of view. In *Thelma and Louise*, we are continually invited to identify with the two women characters, to see things from their point of view. A very different story would emerge if the film were told from, for example, the policeman's point of view or Thelma's husband's point of view.

Most narratives invite viewers to identify with characters and to be emotionally involved with the events shown. Emotional involvement comes about because audiences are encouraged to enjoy being close to (simulated) exciting events. In the cinema we can almost feel what it is like to go on a roller-coaster ride, to fly in an aeroplane, to be part of a bank robbery, to make love, to be in a fight or a car crash, and so on. These 'virtual' experiences are dependent on camera work, editing choices, and sound techniques, all of which draw us into the action, making us feel part of the events being portrayed. This encourages a viewing experience based on both emotional responsiveness and rational thought, and such emotional viewing experiences are often more stimulating than a detached intellectual appraisal of the same issues and events.

However, it is possible to present events in different ways. Some narratives invite detachment rather than identification. In order to facilitate detachment, these films may use long shots (to encourage the audience to distance themselves from the action) and slower editing. They may also avoid presenting events from the point of view of any particular character. All these techniques are designed to encourage the audience to be critical and detached in their viewing, and to make them aware of the construction of the film itself, unlike the techniques of traditional Hollywood cinema, which try to convince the audience of the realism of the story. While this may be less conventionally exciting, in the sense that the emotions are not so immediately engaged, it has the advantage of encouraging critical thought about what is being portrayed. You can find excellent examples of this detached style of viewing in several of Peter Greenaway's films or in the documentaries of Peter Watkins.[8] Can you think of other examples?

These kinds of structural positionings are crucial in constructing our responses to any narrative, and it is important to be aware of this process of construction, which is, in effect, a process of manipulation of the audience's response.

4 What is the dominant discourse or the hierarchy of discourses?

To develop the idea that characters' structural positions in narratives contribute to meaning let us consider the terms 'dominant discourse' and 'hierarchy of discourses', as used by Colin MacCabe (1974). Discourse is discussed in more detail below. The simplest definition defines it as a voice or speaking position. In a film/television narrative we are presented with a number of different voices that explain or comment on the situation. Most obviously there are characters' voices. Thus in *Thelma and Louise* we have the voices of Thelma, Louise, Thelma's husband, Louise's boyfriend, the murdered man, the detective, JD, the Afro-American cyclist, and so on. On their own, each of these characters might have quite different ways of seeing and making sense of the world. The film allows these voices to coexist. MacCabe argues that a narrative will organise these voices into a particular hierarchy, such that one voice is more important, more truthful than another. This explains how we know that the view of sex and women held by Harlan, the man who attempts to rape Thelma, is unacceptable, whereas Louise's is correct. Her voice, or her speaking position, is privileged over his. In watching a film, our job as analysts is to work out whose voice, whose discourse the film thinks is right: we must determine the hierarchy of voices.

The popular daytime Australian TV chat show *Beauty and the Beast* illustrates the hierarchy of discourses well. It features an opinionated, heavy-set older man (the Beast) in the middle of a panel of female speakers (the Beauties). Topics discussed range from political issues such as the oppression of women under Taliban rule to what to do when your boyfriend 'pervs' on other women. While each participant is entitled to speak about the issues featured on the program, the Beast has the most screen time and the most dialogue, and he controls the discourse, interrupting the other speakers freely, speaking over them and calling for advertisement breaks; the Beast's discourse is thus the dominant discourse; the Beauties' discourses are subordinate.

Note how, in this film, minor characters or discourses can be important in directing us how to think about people and events: at the scene of the murder there is a waitress who has only a few lines. She knew the murdered man, Harlan; she knows the detective; and she has seen Thelma and Louise. She is, moreover, a blonde, attractive, humorous, female character (who does the same job as Louise). These character attributes make her a convincing and potentially reliable witness. She remarks to the detective 'They're [Thelma and Louise] not murderers'. Although we have seen Louise shoot Harlan and we know there is a question about whether they should be tried for murder, the waitress's discourse confirms their innocence. She is allied with them.

Later in the film, another voice makes an alliance with the discourse of Thelma and Louise. Thelma and Louise have locked a White policeman in the trunk of his car in the middle of the desert. An Afro-American cyclist rides past and hears the policeman calling for help. He blows the policeman some marijuana smoke but does not release him. This character is on screen for no more than a minute and does not speak at all. The Afro-American discourse consists of the character's appearance, his actions, and the music soundtrack (an excerpt from Jimmy Cliff's reggae hit *I Can See Clearly Now*). This humorous moment introduces an Afro-American discourse into a film that has so far been almost exclusively focused on White Americans. The peaceful refusal to help the police; the celebratory Afro-American song about a 'sun-shiny day'; and the pleasure-taking, law-breaking smoking of marijuana by a man who is, like Thelma and Louise, 'on the road', together forge an alliance between this cyclist and Thelma and Louise (neither of whom he has seen). This alliance can be seen as linking two discourses: that of oppressed Afro-American men and that of oppressed White women. Thus, in a single moment, Thelma and Louise's discourse, their struggle, is widened to include the discourse of other disaffected social groups. The use of cycling is interesting: it connotes an ecologically aware, peaceful, anti-urban subculture, which may invite audience members sympathetic to the concerns of this subculture to identify with the cyclist, and therefore, by extension, with Thelma and Louise.

MacCabe suggests that in addition to the discourses of the characters we must pay attention to the discourse of film language. By this he means that the things that comprise film discourse—camera style, lighting, editing, and so on—invite us to see things in a particular way. Thus:

- The camera shows JD as sexy in the way it frames his body. The way his body is lit also invites the audience to see him as attractive. (His similarities to James Dean in initials and appearance also construct him as desirable.)
- The detective, played by Harvey Keitel, is portrayed as potentially sinister by the way that he is filmed in dark and shadowy spaces.

Along with the film discourse, which is a visual discourse, *Thelma and Louise* includes aural dimensions of discourse. The dialogue, the music, and the sound effects also articulate a particular way of thinking and feeling about the events and characters in the film.

Other discourses, from outside the film, can also influence our readings. Let's consider the discourse surrounding celebrities and the values and viewpoints stars bring to a film. The idea of 'star image' or 'interpretive drift' relates to the ways in which the audience's knowledge of other roles played by a star and the other publicity that surrounds celebrities can influence interpretations of a film narrative. The role of the detective, played by Harvey Keitel, is interesting in this regard. The detective trails Thelma and Louise and he is vital in leading the FBI to them. His motives are not immediately clear: he seems to be offering them friendship but we don't know if this is genuine or just a ploy to catch them. In terms of the discourse surrounding an actor or star, what effect is produced by this role being played by the actor Harvey Keitel? The fact that the detective is played by a star makes him significant in the plot. At the time he was the only other actor in the film who was equal, in terms of star status, to Geena Davis and Susan Sarandon. Although they have all now been eclipsed to a certain extent by Brad Pitt's celebrity status, at the time Pitt played JD he was relatively unknown. Audiences therefore take note of Keitel as more significant than any other male characters, and potentially as important as Thelma and Louise. Our hierarchy of discourses is thus influenced by star hierarchy.

Theorists who study stars have argued that a star's image is built not only from their roles in films, but also from the publicity that surrounds them—interviews, press reports, photographs, and so on. Many stars play similar roles across a variety of films, thereby developing a consistent image that can either fit with their latest role or contrast with it.[9] Harvey Keitel has played the roles of numerous gangsters, petty criminals, and corrupt officials in films such as *Mean Streets* and *Taxi Driver*, and most of the films in which he appears are quite 'dark'. Does this star image influence our reading of him in this film? We are not saying that he can only play corrupt characters, but given his tendency to play such roles, will audiences faced with an ambiguity about his character tend to read his motives as suspect? In other words will audiences be more likely to read him as a 'bad guy' than a 'good guy'? In the end, this possibility is pleasurably confounded. If Robin Williams had played the role, his star image would have made the character much less morally ambiguous and there would not have been the same element of surprise at the end of the film when Keitel is revealed to be a character with 'heart' who is trying to help Thelma and Louise.

MacCabe's argument is that viewers make sense of all these competing voices, linking and comparing them until they are arranged into a hierarchy that finally produces a dominant discourse. This is the discourse that will ultimately give us the 'truth' about events. Normally, the discourses of film language and the film itself give us a fuller and more complete view of events and how we should understand them than do the individual, contradictory voices/discourses of the characters involved.

It is important to remember that different audiences may make different readings. A sexist, violent man may regard Harlan's view as the best way of understanding the world. Although the film puts his discourse way down the hierarchy, an audience member could put him at the top. That is why it is also useful to make a distinction in textual analysis between looking at what 'the film thinks' about any situation and what we, as audience, might think. We are not suggesting that the film is really a conscious being that literally thinks. Rather, we argue that it is possible to look at the film's arrangement of the different discourses and, from that, deduce what we are being invited to think and feel. Viewed in this manner, it makes sense to ask 'What does the film think about what it is showing us?' or 'What is its project?' (What does it project to us on the screen?)[10] Looking at the film's hierarchy of discourses and seeking out its dominant discourse becomes a way of understanding what the overall film is presenting, what the film thinks about what it is showing, and how this is inscribed into its narrative structure. These are useful questions that will shift our attention away from our own personal reactions. Asking these questions is similar to looking for a film's 'preferred reading' (see Part 2, p. 70). You can investigate the dominant discourse of any text by asking:

1 What/whose different voices/discourses are presented?

2 What order do you put them in, in a hierarchy (which is most persuasive)?

3 What is the dominant discourse?

It would be easy at this point to fall into the 'intentionalist' position and argue that the dominant discourse is that held by the director (what the film thinks is what the director thinks). While the view of the director is significant, we argue that there is a dominant discourse in the text that is the product of not only the director's intention, but also a host of factors beyond this (Scott 1991, pp. 18–19).

5 Are women positioned differently from men in the narrative?

Are there major differences in the way men and women are positioned in narratives? Many critics have suggested that recurrent patterns are apparent in the structural roles normally given to men and women.[11] The following table of oppositions suggests some of the main roles, characteristics, and functions that men and women tend to have/fulfil in narratives, as well as some of the gender lines that transect different genres.

Male hero	Female heroine
Identification	Objectification
Narrative movement and control	Narrative stasis and spectacle
Primary characters	Secondary characters
Active	Passive
Feelings expressed by external actions	Feelings expressed by displays of emotion
Strong	Weak
Work/public world	Home/private world
Investigators	Investigated
Known	Unknown
Westerns, thrillers	Melodramas, musicals

These are generalisations and do not apply to all narratives but they show interesting tendencies in the representation of men and women. We briefly mentioned above the difference between identification with men and objectification of women. This is a useful distinction and draws our attention to how we watch films. I sometimes ask students to list their favourite male and female stars. I then suggest that for heterosexuals favourite same-sex stars represent the kinds of women/men they themselves would like to be, the kinds of women/men they identify with; favourite opposite-sex stars represent the kinds of women/men they desire, the kinds of women/men they objectify. This points to two major viewing pleasures we are offered and experience as film-watchers—the opportunity to imagine oneself as an all-powerful fantasy figure (the character we most identify with) and the opportunity to gaze erotically on a beautiful fantasy figure whom we desire and objectify.

Laura Mulvey notes these two different kinds of viewing pleasure, and in one of the most influential pieces of feminist criticism she describes the way men and women are presented in films as follows:

Woman as Image, Man as Bearer of the Look: In a world ordered by sexual imbalance, pleasure in looking has been split between active/male and passive/female. The determining male gaze projects its phantasy on to the female figure which is styled accordingly. In their traditional exhibitionist role women are simultaneously looked at and displayed, with their appearance coded for strong visual and erotic impact so that they can be said to connote *to-be-looked-at-ness*. Woman displayed as sexual object is the *leit-motif* of erotic spectacle: from pin-ups to striptease, from Ziegfeld to Busby Berkeley, she holds the look, plays to and signifies male desire (Mulvey 1985, p. 304).

She continues, arguing that in many mainstream films audiences are invited to identify with men and objectify women, regardless of whether they are male or female. Thus female audiences are asked to look through a male perspective, to see things through men's eyes. Mulvey demonstrates that identification with male heroes is produced primarily through narrative position and editing techniques: in the narrative men are often the major characters—they are introduced at the beginning of the story, we know the most about them, and they are involved in unravelling the enigma in the story. Through editing and camera position we are often encouraged to see the things they see and thus we are stitched into their point of view. All these elements create a position of identification.

Women, on the other hand, are seen from the outside: we rarely know their thoughts or hear their voices as narrative voice-overs, they are often part of the enigma to be investigated, and we don't see things from their point of view. Furthermore, in the kinds of narratives Mulvey critiques, women often play disempowered characters who are punished, persecuted, or endangered within the narrative world. Such character positions do not invite identification. They become the object of the look (or gaze) of both the male characters in the movie, who we see looking, and of us, the audience. The camera delights in shots of women that use lighting, soft focus, framing, music, and erotic costuming to create an erotic spectacle. Often these techniques will be employed to full effect while female characters perform actions—dancing, singing, and so on—that invite the camera, the male characters, and the audience to take pleasure in looking at them. John Berger sums up the differences between the portrayal of men and women:

> One might simplify this by saying: *men act* and *women appear*. Men look at women. Women watch themselves being looked at. This determines not only most relations between men and women but also the relation of women to themselves. The surveyor of women in herself is male: the surveyed female. Thus she turns herself into an object— and most particularly an object of vision: a sight (Berger 1972, p. 47).

This explains the uncomfortable relationship between female subjectivity and personal appearance, and it foregrounds the point that being looked at is a passive subject position. This relates to the idea of narrative stasis: the narrative pausing to enable spectators to dwell on the spectacle of the female form. While female characters may function to provide visual pleasure and create desire in film narratives, the male actor's deeds and actions are usually what drive the plot forward.

Mulvey's work, along with the work of other feminists, draws attention to the 'politics of looking' and the stress on visual appearance that is associated with women in film. *Thelma and Louise* shows an awareness and reversal of this 'looking' when Thelma uses her car-mirror to look at JD (Brad Pitt) erotically.

Here he becomes the object of the gaze, he is unknown and we are identifying with her in the narrative.

The table on p. 138 also suggests that women are often secondary or subordinate characters in films; men are more important. This is certainly true for genres such as Westerns, thrillers, science-fiction films, and crime movies. Content analysis reveals that, on the whole, there are more major roles in film narratives for men than for women. However, there are genres where women take the primary roles—notably musicals, melodramas, and soap operas—but as the table suggests, these roles tend to operate differently from male roles. Often the women playing such roles are being 'reactive' (they respond to events rather than initiate actions); the focus is on feelings rather than action; and the settings tend to be the private, domestic world of home rather than the professional, public world of work. These are not necessarily negative aspects, but they tend to portray women as less powerful and by suggesting almost mutually exclusive male and female spheres, they can be seen to be excluding women from meaningful public life.

You may think that these observations refer to the kinds of media texts produced in the past, and that the situation is now different because there are television shows such as *Buffy*, *Sex and the City*, *Dark Angel*, and *Ally McBeal*, and films such as *Legally Blonde*, *Lara Croft*, *GI Jane*, *Erin Brockovich*, and *Jackie Brown*. However, it is still worth considering how our attitudes (and the attitudes of established media producers who are currently in positions of power and making decisions about media content) have been and are still being influenced by the cumulative impressions of masculinity and femininity that we have acquired throughout our viewing histories. Most of the changes in the way race and gender are represented are very recent and figure in only a small proportion of media texts produced globally. Note also that the emergent trend to include strong female characters is a marketing device, and it still frequently positions the value of these characters in relation to their physical appearance. Even in texts such as *Charlie's Angels*, the women are not the most powerful characters in the narrative: they all defer to their boss Charlie, and their appearances are still of central importance.

In the light of this table we can see why *Thelma and Louise* generated interest. It did not conform to typical gender positioning but offered a role reversal. How progressive is this for women? By portraying women assuming male power through playing male roles, the film attributes strength to women. But does it thereby suggest that in order to be successful, women must act like men, become masculine in order to be successful? Does it, in other words, condemn femininity and assert masculine values as dominant? Some critics have even suggested that the images of strong, assertive, and still conventionally attractive women in the film fulfil male viewers' sexual fantasies about dominant women!

This raises the question of why men might enjoy *Thelma and Louise*. At a generic level the film offers the typically male pleasures of the Western, the road movie, and the buddy movie. You could watch the film taking on these pleasures and disregarding gender as an issue. However, the film is also about men's oppression of women, and in raising these issues it certainly includes several male characters who are made ridiculous, objectionable, or weak, and are narratively humiliated (notably Thelma's husband, Harlan, the potential rapist, the truck driver, the policeman and, to a lesser extent, Louise's boyfriend). In this context, the inclusion of the JD character, the detective (played by a star), and even the Afro-American cyclist are all significant. At one level the film is anti-men, but the inclusion of a few positive men provides male viewers with positions of identification. On a typically competitive level, male viewers can even place themselves above the ridiculous men but enjoy the roles of these other three (it is interesting to note, in this context, that JD has sex with Thelma and steals the money belonging to Thelma and Louise). These three roles become central in giving male viewers a position of identification, and in so doing the film recognises that only some men are bad.

6 What does the ending tell you about the ideology of the film?

Finally, consider the importance of narrative endings and resolutions. These are an essential part of the narrative pattern. Endings are significant in determining a narrative's ideological meaning. There are different ways of ending stories. Let's explore this further.

First, note three different possible types of ending:

1 closed/circular

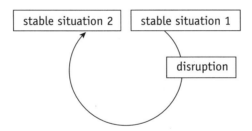

Figure 3.5 Closed/circular ending

2 closed/progress

Figure 3.6 Closed/progress ending

3 open/unresolved

Figure 3.7 Open/unresolved ending

Most narratives are closed in that they answer all the questions set up in the narrative and they resolve any problems that the film sets up. The closed/circular ending (possibility number 1 in the list above) is one that ends where it started. This seems to be a very common cinematic device (much more so than in novels) where shots at the end echo or directly repeat the opening shots. *American Beauty* is a good example of a film in which the opening shots show the ending of the film. This convention signals to the audience that the end is coming. It may have some connection with the way in the past cinema goers would pay a single entry fee which would allow them to stay in the cinema and watch the movie being screened again. Audiences could enter at any time and stay for as long as they wanted. The normal point of exit would be when you reached the 'this is where we came in' moment, indicated by the repetition of images that occurred at the moment of arrival.

The circular characteristic is found particularly in flashback films, which start at one point in time, go into the past, and then return to the original point for the ending. *Citizen Kane*, *The Virgin Suicides*, and *The Usual Suspects* are good examples. The ideological point about such narratives is that, in a sense, they don't go anywhere, they don't progress, they just bring you back to where you started. This suggests that progress is impossible, that it is impossible to change things. The status quo is thereby reinforced. This view of society is fatalistic and conservative. However, the cyclical, flashback narrative structure can also indicate other things. The structure of a film can make a statement that the issue at the heart of the film is unresolvable, or that it is a problem that tends to resurface; a pattern that repeats itself over and over again in families, in individuals, or in society. For example, *Nil by Mouth* and *The War Zone* are both narratives that deal with the cycle of domestic violence and family abuse, and they are both structured to avoid closure and progress. An open or unresolved ending can leave the audience with the responsibility for defining their own ideas and positions, and can even encourage us to take action. Few films have a truly cyclical narrative structure that denies the audience a satisfying sense of closure. *Lost Highway* and *Memento* are both films that leave the audience at the beginning of the narrative, freshly engaged with exactly the same questions that we began with. But in each case we have more knowledge about the characters and their situations, and consequently we move on to a deeper level of questioning. In such films the narrative structure is indicative of the philosophical enormity of the unanswerable questions about identity and memory with which they grapple.

The flashback form was popular in so-called *film noir*. *Film noir* are dark and threatening thrillers, initially made in the 1940s and 1950s, that show humans trapped in a hostile universe. These films suggest that whatever humans do, they are doomed to their pre-ordained ending. Similar circular patterns can be seen in many cartoons or situation comedies today.

In contrast closed/progress endings (possibility number 2 in the above list) allow for progress and change. Things are not as they were at the beginning (whether happy or unhappy). This suggests that humans can change their life situations. This relates to the process of moral change and growth that main characters go through. This pattern is usually positive—characters learn and become better people during the narrative—and it suggests that we can move on from the status quo.

When watching a film/television program, try to determine whether or not, and how, it reproduces these closed/circular and closed/progress patterns. Consider how Thelma and Louise *fits these patterns.*

Exercise commentary

Note that *Thelma and Louise* includes elements of both closed/circular and closed/progress patterns. (Many narratives have aspects of both.) The film starts with images of the road and of the mountains at which Thelma and Louise will finally arrive at the end of the film. We don't know why this is there at the beginning but it is like a fatalistic portent of the destiny they are inevitably approaching. However, the film does move on beyond this point in time and, more significantly, it shows the progression and change of Thelma and Louise (how they have left behind their dominated, domestic, downtrodden personas). This is positive in that it shows the possibility of change for the better, even if the ending may seem tragic.

Mainstream Hollywood cinema tends towards closed endings. However, films can be open/unresolved and this is sometimes the case in relation to mainstream cinema. The horror genre has traditionally had open endings (this has been briefly discussed in relation to codes and conventions—see pp. 125–6) such as in the *Nightmare on Elm Street* series of films. This is not only so that there will be room for a sequel (though this is commercially sensible) but more because the horror genre is meant to disturb us. Part of the power and the pleasure of horror films is that they allow us to experience fear and confront things that frighten and fascinate us in a safe cinematic setting. But the nature of fear is about being unsafe, and it is important for the success of the genre that the endings of the stories leave open the possibility for the horror to return. Thus we leave the cinema with the beginnings of the sequel already taking root in the shadowy corners of our minds, waiting to haunt our nightmares and surface in our thoughts when we are alone and the lights are out. Refusing the comfort of a closed ending allows the narrative structure to create disturbance. Critics have suggested that at times of moral and social uncertainty, commercial films may not offer clearly resolved endings (Wood 1986). However, non-mainstream narratives are the normal place to find more open endings.

Non-mainstream narratives with open/unresolved endings are often found in so-called 'art films', a type of film that is more intellectually oriented than commercial cinema. Art films frequently present a challenge to the audience, and a challenge to the dominant order and the accepted norms of society. They often aim to say something meaningful and many have a slower editing pace and a more consciously artistic approach. Endings can be deliberately ambiguous, inviting spectators to think reflectively about what they have seen, to puzzle out the meanings, and to explore the moral and social dilemmas raised. These films may thus reflect more of the uncertainties of real life; they certainly don't offer us easy answers and are not so comfortable and reassuring. *Happiness*, *Requiem for a Dream*, and *Dancer in the Dark* are good examples of films that unsettle and challenge the audience because they deal with disturbing subject matter in complex ways, without presenting characters to whom the audience can easily relate.

Open/unresolved endings are also found in avant-garde, experimental, and independent films. We don't discuss these films in this book, but it is important to recognise that they exist as alternatives to mainstream cinema. Such films work with different narrative patterns or even with no narrative at all. To see examples of such work, watch programs such as SBS's *Eat Carpet*, or experimental and independent films on the UK's Channel 4.

In relation to endings, consider now the question of how characters are positioned at the end of narratives. Most obviously, consider whether they receive rewards or punishments, happy or unhappy endings. This gives a good indication as to whether their actions and behaviour are legitimated or not. For example, ask about a character: is he/she dead or alive, married or single, alone or with someone, rewarded or punished, and so on? These structural positions show us what to think about a character, as demonstrated earlier in relation to gay characters in films (p. 128).

Coupling endings

It has been suggested that cinema is a machine for making couples. This is because film endings tend to lead to or suggest a potential marriage or sexual union. The final result of all the narrative drama, tests, tension, and suspense is for a man and woman to get together as a heterosexual pair. While this is obviously not true of all films it is common. The predominance of successful coupling as the desirable end-product of narratives reproduces an ideology of heterosexual marriage. This goes back before cinema to other story-telling traditions, and to plays and novels. For example, it is encapsulated in fairy tales, which invariably begin with the introduction 'Once upon time there was a …' and end with the phrase 'and they lived happily ever after' (suggesting a heterosexual couple who have just married).

Consider the ending of Thelma and Louise *and note down what view of the characters and issues the ending gives you in the light of the above remarks.*

Exercise commentary

The ending of *Thelma and Louise* has been the source of much debate (*Film Quarterly* 1992). Note that this film does 'make' a couple, but that this couple is made up of two women. Audiences can view this coupling in many different ways: as similar to a friendship between male buddies, as an example of sisterhood, as a demonstration of the fact that women do not need men, and as a celebration of lesbian love. Here we have a good example of a polysemic text whose meaning depends on its audience. But however it is read, it is not the conventional heterosexual male–female bonding: the film is doing something different.

Some audience members may take issue with the death of Thelma and Louise. Some may feel that the final freeze-frame denies the reality of what happens to them after they go over the lip of the canyon: we should be shown their death below, as they crash on to the rocks. This more violent ending would really bring home to audiences the oppression and suffering women go through. Not showing the crash at the bottom of the canyon is a cop-out that reduces the film to fantasy. Others may feel that such an ending would be too depressing and negative: the freeze-frame allows the audience to celebrate the couple. When I am teaching about *Thelma and Louise*, I always point out (to people who say that the ending is sad because Thelma and Louise die) that Thelma and Louise actually don't die. The film finishes with them alive. Indeed it holds them alive eternally in the freeze-frame in a way that makes me feel very differently from the way I would if the film had shown them crashing. In a sense they are immortal and, for me, this is a very positive ending.

In fact the freeze-frame is not quite the end of the film. As the credits begin to roll we see a number of short clips showing Thelma and Louise together during the course of the film. This draws our attention back to, and celebrates, their friendship. Not seeing the car crash deprives us of the spectacular explosive climax that so many action films give us. But note how the narrative provides such a moment about ten minutes before the end when Thelma and Louise blow up the truck in spectacular fashion. We don't need another explosion! How would you like the film to end?

While the statement that 'cinema is a machine for making couples' was initially directed at film texts, it also says something useful about the cinema as an institution, as a place that audiences visit. The cinema is a place that has a special significance for (hetero)sexual couples. When sexual expression was more repressed, the cinema offered couples a traditional space of darkness, privacy, and eroticism, a place where they could experiment with physical intimacy. Eroticism and romance, the focus on sexuality and love, have always been a major part of the cinematic output, complementing or encouraging the feelings of couples in the audience. Cinema has traditionally been a space to which you invite a partner. Today you can still see many couples attending the cinema as part of their romantic connection. Many advertisements screened in the cinema before the main film are addressed to couples; they focus on such activities as eating out together and buying furniture for the family home. I am often struck by the contrast between advertisements in local cinemas, which tend to portray a normal, family-oriented, routine lifestyle, and the actual stories of drama, fantasy, and excitement that the audiences come to see. This contradiction is beautifully expressed in the film *Brief Encounter*, which includes a scene in which a couple in a cinema watch a trailer for a film entitled *Flames of Passion*—clearly an exotic, erotic, over-the-top fantasy—followed immediately by an advertisement for prams! The two aspects of sexuality for couples—eroticism and the mundanity of bringing up children, the latter being a potential result of the former—are ironically juxtaposed in this scene.

Happy endings with successful coupling were the norm for Hollywood films from the 1930s to the 1950s. Movies with happy endings are still being made and they are now often referred to as feel-good movies, but since the 1960s there have also been more unhappy, unresolved endings. This change can be seen as a reflection, initially, of the optimism of American society and the durability of the family unit from the 1930s to the 1950s, and then, since the 1960s, as a reflection of the increasing instability and uncertainty of social values and of the fact that the family unit has been under considerable pressure in the past three decades.

Couple endings can have many variations: for example, tragic endings of the death of the couple or the failure of the couple to come together. Many Westerns end with the male hero walking away alone into the sunset, continuing on his journey/quest and remaining outside society and marriage. Non-heterosexual couples are another possibility: male buddies, female buddies, and gay and lesbian couples. The coupling of women at the end of a narrative is increasing. For example, *The Stepfather* concludes with a mother and daughter together after the evil male presence has been dispatched. *Desperately Seeking Susan* features two female leads. While it ensures that each of them has found a suitable male partner by the end of the film, it does not close with these couplings. Instead it shows an image of the two women bonded together. In the final shot of the film they are photographed together in a freeze frame triumphantly holding upraised hands, and this shot has the caption 'What a pair'. While happy heterosexuality is promoted by the film, the ending attributes more significance to female friendship and solidarity. A similar bonding, but without the promotion of happy heterosexuality, can be seen in *Thelma and Louise*.

My Best Friend's Wedding, directed by P. J. Hogan, is an interesting variation on the couple ending. The title of the film draws attention to the fact that a wedding is the central narrative action (the title is similar to *Muriel's Wedding*, an earlier film of Hogan's, and another film that concludes with a female friendship). We might thus expect a wedding to be the happy conclusion. The film is based around four characters. Julianne Potter (Julia Roberts) has a best friend, Michael O'Neal (Dermot Mulroney) who is engaged to be married to Kimmy Wallace (Cameron Diaz). Julianne has another friend, George Downey (Rupert Everett), who is gay. Julianne is clearly marked out as the central character of the film: she is the protagonist whose eyes we view things from, she is the audience's main figure for identification, and of all the actors in the film, Julia Roberts has the most star status.

Julianne, having learned of the impending marriage, realises that she really loves Michael and wants him herself. She hopes to sabotage the marriage and win him back, and her attempts to do this form the body of the film's narrative. At the end of the film she fails: Kimmy and Michael are happily married and she is left on her own, although she still has her career and her gay friend George (her new 'best friend'?). The film concludes with a shot of Roberts and Everett dancing happily together at the wedding, although neither of them has sexual or life partners. Does this constitute a happy ending? In traditional storytelling, getting married is a happy ending and not getting married is an unhappy ending. From this perspective, since the unmarried characters are the main stars of this film, it would appear that overall the film is presenting an unhappy ending. The ending of the film may also be suggesting that strong-willed, career women who take an active role in determining their own destiny don't get rewarded by the conventional pleasures of marriage with a desirable partner (whereas the ditzy, devoted, affluent, girly type played by Diaz does). However, we think there are a number of elements here that demonstrate that non-marriage and strong friendship are as good as if not preferable to heterosexual marriage, that the 'outsiders' (unmarried career-oriented woman and gay man) are the ones who find the happier ending. What leads us to this reading?

1 The film is a comedy. Comedies traditionally end happily for the main characters. Therefore, reading generically, because the main characters are unmarried at the end of the film, non-marriage becomes a happy ending, and is therefore validated over and above the ending assigned to the subsidiary characters.

2 The desires of characters played by stars usually outweigh those of characters played by actors who are less famous. Characters played by stars also usually end up happier than characters played by less famous actors. Therefore, reading through star analysis, being unmarried will be read as more desirable than being married. (Mulroney is virtually unknown as a star and Everett, at the time the film was made, was more well known than Diaz.)

3 The characters played by Julia Roberts and Rupert Everett are funnier, more knowing, and more attractive than those played by Diaz and Mulroney. We are invited to like Roberts and Everett, and to laugh at the other two. Mulroney's character is something of a non-entity: marriage to him could be far less fun than freedom and friendship with Everett's character, George!

4 The comic tone of the film is satirical of American manners, particularly in relation to marriage and the family. As in *Muriel's Wedding*, Hogan uses a 'camp' music soundtrack, thereby sending up the ideals of marriage and family.

We may have overstated this argument that the film denigrates marriage. The final shots of Kimmy's wedding invite the audience to take pleasure in the spectacle of the wedding, and it may be that the film presents the argument that there are happy possibilities both *within* and *without* marriage: after all, the film concludes with two different kinds of successful coupling. It is, however, the image of Julianne and George together that is the final shot in the film.

Where does this leave the statement that the cinema is 'a machine for making couples'? The central concern of the film is intimate human relationships and how these can work for the best. This topic, especially in relation to heterosexual bonding, marriage, and the family, is the central issue of many films and television shows, particularly melodramas, soap operas, and situation comedies. It is interesting to explore this further.

Whereas endings used to point to happiness through the establishment of the heterosexual couple and the family, at the beginning of the twenty-first century this has become problematic in many cases. The increasing ambivalence about happy-coupling endings can be seen as a reflection of the changing state of marriage, sexuality, and the family in the West over the past 30 years. There is a crisis in these institutions, an uncertainty about how to live out sexual desire and relationships. The narratives reflect this and also give some commentary, some answers or suggestions, as to how these problems can be resolved. We can look at narratives as positing different solutions to these issues. *My Best Friend's Wedding* posits a happy buddy ending outside the norms of marriage and heterosexuality as one possibility.

The Next Best Thing, another film starring Rupert Everett, works strongly to reinforce the dominant discourse of the family and warn against or undermine possibilities for happiness to be found in alternative couplings. *The Next Best Thing* takes up precisely where *My Best Friend's Wedding* left off. This time Madonna, not Julia Roberts, is Everett's best friend. Because Everett is essentially playing the same character in both films, and because Roberts and Madonna are both extremely powerful, independent career women, the notion that our interpretations of films are subject to 'interpretive drift' about a star's persona, and the fact that cinematic narratives often work strongly to reinforce dominant ideologies, have particular relevance here. If this 'interpretive drift' about the stars and the characters they play leads us to see *The Next Best Thing* as a kind of follow up to *My Best Friend's Wedding*, then we can no longer read the friendship between a gay man and a career-oriented woman as being a viable alternative to marriage—at least not if that relationship involves children. As *The Next Best Thing* unfolds, Madonna's and Everett's characters form an alternative family unit that is later destroyed when Madonna enters into a conventional heterosexual marriage with Benjamin Bratt's character and subsequently restricts her former 'best friend's' access to the child they had raised together. (Ironically, at the time the film was made Bratt was Roberts's real-life partner, so the forces of interpretive drift and the relationship between the fantasy world of cinema and the real world become stronger still.) This example is a powerful illustration of the way audiences read films intertextually, and of the way the institution of cinema tends to reinforce dominant ideologies.

Many films reconstruct the family unit despite its crisis. *Parenthood* is a good example of this. In this movie, despite all the problems of divorce, separation, problem children, absent fathers, and sexual needs, at the end there is a celebration of family values. Overall, film and television narratives tackle this central issue, coming up with a range of possible solutions.

Television narratives

Most of what we have said about narrative applies to film and cinema but only partially applies to television dramas, which are equally important media texts. It is possible to apply all the above concepts to television but there are some major differences.[12]

In contrast to the private, darkened space of cinema, suitable for couples, note how the television was initially introduced for domestic and family viewing. Its original location was normally in the collective family space of the living room, to be viewed by all members of the family, often together. This togetherness is now fragmented, partly by programming schedules, which mean that different family members can watch at different times of the day, but also by the increased manufacture of televisions and their correspondingly cheaper prices. We now find television sets in rooms other than communal family rooms, such as bedrooms where television can be watched more privately.

There is also a difference between television and film in relation to narrative structure. Television's predominant form is episodic or serial in structure. The continuous form of the series leads it towards more open endings, particularly in the soap opera, which is a never-ending narrative structure. The series includes some story lines that are resolved each week and others that are carried over from week to week. In contrast, cinema favours the closed ending.

Film narratives tend to focus on one or two characters at the centre of the story and a plot-line that involves one major question such as 'What will happen to Thelma and Louise?' Television fictions are often organised around multiple stories and groups of characters in a community. The multiple story was originally the province of soap operas, which keep a group of stories going over many episodes. This approach has been adopted in many television series: for example, consider the way in which the television series *Northern Exposure*, *Ally McBeal*, *Hamish Macbeth*, and *Ballykissangel* feature three separate but inter-related stories in each episode. These self-contained stories usually relate to the ongoing narrative concerns of the series. Multi-story lines are suited to representing communities and groups of characters.

Television also tends to be more dialogue-driven and fragmented into short, self-contained segments so that the story lines can be followed by someone who is not giving the screen their undivided attention. The structure of televisual narratives invite a different kind of engagement, and different interpretive practices arise from the context of reception. Often, instead of gazing intently at the screen as we do in the cinema, television audience members glance at the set while they are going about other everyday activities such as studying, ironing clothes, making lunch, and talking on the phone.

Are these narrative structures of television also geared towards 'couple-making'? Many television series are built around one central couple who are slightly more important than the rest of the community—this is true of three of the four series just mentioned. But, a major question in these series' is 'Will the couple actually get together?' This question is also found in *The X-Files*, and in comedy series such as *The Nanny* and *Men Behaving Badly*, while other comedies such as *Seinfeld* constantly explore whether and how couples can get together. If a couple finally does get together or get married then the series spends many episodes exploring how this is working out and seems to take great pleasure in the uncertainty of any simple 'they lived happily ever after' resolution. Melodramas such as *Melrose Place* focus on the constant making and breaking of couples. Whereas cinema tends to concentrate on the problematic of relationships and marriage for individuals, many television series have a wider social concern: how can communities work effectively and supportively?

What we see in television, as in film, are stories fascinated by questions of sexuality and sexual desire, by 'the couple', and by implication, the family (the basic social unit that Western society is built on). But in television these concerns are linked to a focus on how members of the wider community relate to one another and to the economic and social problems this community faces at the end of the twentieth century and beyond. *Sex and the City* is an interesting series that explores some of the issues and dilemmas faced primarily by women (but also by men), and predominantly from a heterosexual perspective, attempting to establish and enjoy sexual/emotional couplings.

The result is a continual exploration of how men and women relate in a post-feminist, post-nuclear world, an exploration that is well aware of power struggles, oppression, abuse, exploitation, and sexual desire. Television narratives are, in part, attempts to work out how we can live in ways that satisfy our social and individual needs and desires; how we can live in a society undergoing economic and social crisis. In this respect, film and television narratives are a wonderful place to observe how society understands itself, and this explains audience pleasure and fascination in these media-world dramas.

Binary oppositions

We can develop narrative analysis further through the application of binary oppositions. These are used by many critics (Turner 1993, pp. 72–6; Kitses 1969). You can see them at work in the table on p. 152. You may well have encountered them elsewhere.

The concept of opposition or duality is fundamental in the organisation of language, and in Western philosophical thinking as a whole. Aristotle expressed this when he stated 'Everything is either A or not A'. He used opposition or negation as a means of definition. This use is apparent in language: as discussed in relation to semiology, words don't mean anything on their own—they mean in relation to other words (through systems of difference). Each word or concept is defined by its opposite and only makes sense if we understand its opposite as well. For example, 'yes' is understood in relation to 'no'; 'right' in relation to 'left'; 'up' to 'down'; 'light' to 'dark'; 'good' to 'bad'; 'black' to 'white'; 'masculine' to 'feminine'; and so on. We make sense of the world through oppositions. As John Hartley puts it , 'Such binaries are a feature of *culture* not *nature*; they are products of signifying systems, and function to structure our perceptions of the natural and social world into order and meaning' (O'Sullivan et al. 1994, p. 30).

So we, as humans, create these categories. 'Binary' is derived from the Greek word *bio*, meaning 'two'. It is about splitting or pairing things into twos: positive and negative, yes and no, and so on. It is the basic numerical system used in computers. All computer decisions are based on asking and answering yes/no questions. Whichever answer is chosen will lead automatically to the next stage of computation.

This system of duality has been challenged by those who argue that it creates distance and separation and does not adequately represent reality. It also implicitly condones adversarial or oppositional ways of thinking in which there are rigid, mutually exclusive discursive positions and winners and losers of debates, instead of negotiated compromises and flexible positions that entail mutual incorporation of different perspectives. There is also the fact that biologically, the opposition male/female may not adequately describe reality. First, there is no absolutely clear dividing line, since it is possible to be hermaphrodite (both male and female). There are also numerous gradations or variations of what is male and what is female. The chromosomal and hormonal differences used to biologically define male/female difference show that nearly all men have some female chromosomal/hormonal elements, while nearly all women similarly have male elements. Few people are 100 per cent male or female in these terms. Thus, biologically the categories of male and female are more fluid than Western culture has traditionally recognised. The lines of difference are not clear cut. New thinking seeks a blending of oppositions and an end to duality. Such an approach perceives difference as a continuum of possibilities with greater concentrations at either end of the spectrum, or in the middle. In the case of gender and sexual difference, hermaphrodites and transvestites might occupy the more sparsely populated middle regions of the continuum.

Note that binary oppositions such as male/female and right/wrong are hierarchical: one term is often privileged over the other and the devalued or negative term tends to be defined in relation to the dominant category. For instance, the male/female opposition has been objected to because male is taken as the primary category against which female is defined. As Turner puts it:

> Assuming male and female are opposites means that, automatically, women are what men are not; if the male is strong, then the female must be weak, and on it goes … we can see the accretion of negatives on the female side as a necessary product of the assumption that male and female are opposites. To continue the chain is to end up with good (male) versus bad (female) (Turner 1988, p. 74).

In Chinese culture we see a way of thinking oppositions in the ancient yin/yang symbol (Figure 3.8), which again splits male and female.

This symbol is an image of opposites. The yin stands for the passive principle of the universe, characterised as female, dark, passive, yielding, negative, and absorbing; yang stands for the active principle of the universe, characterised as masculine, light,

Figure 3.8 Yin/yang symbol

active, firm, positive, and expansionary. This is not unlike Western oppositions around gender, which similarly link a whole set of attributes to each position (male or female). These sets of oppositions around gender have come under attack from feminists who argue that women should not be positioned as one set of characteristics, particularly if these are negative and less powerful than the set assigned to men. We will consider this when looking at Jung's ideas below, but the major point we want to make here is that while yin/yang is a system of opposites, it is also a system and symbol of equality and complementarity. The two sides take up equal space in the overall circle, which represents the world and the universe, so the feminine/yin is of equal importance to the masculine/yang (incidentally, circles are often seen as a feminine symbol, perhaps because they are linked to ovulation cycles, seasonal cycles, and the shape of eggs—thus the feminine is the defining structure here). Moreover, yin and yang are complementary since each includes an aspect of the other, an internal feminine in the masculine and vice-versa (the black and white dots), that is an essential aspect of them. Even the separation between the two principles is not a rigid straight line but a flowing curved line that allows a blending of the two. They depend on each other to form a complete whole. So this Chinese system of difference is not about two elements opposing each other, but about working together.

Let's return to the use of binary oppositions in narrative analysis, as it is useful and productive for our purposes. Narratives are organised around conflict and opposition, which are fundamental to narrative interest. We have to have some kind of struggle, some disruption that sets up conflict. The conflict is most obviously between individual characters but this will also indicate conflict between different value systems. Indeed, we can think of the overall structure of all narratives as involving the resolution of conflict between two opposing forces. The term 'dialectical synthesis' refers to a discussion or argument between two competing or opposing sides. In a philosophical argument or an academic essay, these two sides are called the thesis (what is being argued for) and the antithesis (the counter-claims or alternative points, perspectives, views and voices that are being argued against). In a narrative, the thesis and the antithesis relate to whatever binary opposition structures the story and, just as in an argument or essay, each side must engage with the other and be able to explain or understand the opposing point or perspective in order to be able to refute or incorporate it. When the two sides come to terms with each other, the dialectical synthesis or narrative resolution is reached.

We can often discern many different oppositions within the structure of a single narrative. You should find a clear and fairly obvious set of oppositions in almost every mainstream narrative you analyse. These oppositions give the narrative a pattern. In compiling sets of oppositions in a story it is important that all the elements on one side have some links between them, so that collectively they add up to a particular viewpoint or value system. You can see this opposition process at work by comparing the characters of Luke Skywalker and Darth Vader in the *Star Wars* films. The two individual characters are clearly opposed through the films. For example, their names have opposing connotations: 'sky' in 'Skywalker' connotes light and 'Luke' is close to the Latin word for light (*luce*), whereas 'Darth' in 'Darth Vader' connotes the darkness and death; and 'walker' appears peaceful beside 'Vader', which connotes the word 'invader'. Luke is often dressed in light colours, in contrast with Darth Vader who is always in black. The individual character struggle becomes a major mythical struggle between the abstract competing forces of light and dark, life and death, good and evil.

We can observe oppositions between particular characters, between different human characteristics, between different settings or colours, and so on. These then cohere to provide a central opposition between two different value systems. Analysis of this opposition leads us to a deeper understanding of what the film is essentially concerned with. Jim Kitses uses oppositions illuminatingly in his analysis of the Western. He suggests that the Western is replete with the following oppositions:

the West	vs	the East
Wilderness	vs	civilisation
Individual	vs	community
Freedom	vs	restriction
Nature	vs	culture
Disorder	vs	law and order
Innocence	vs	corruption

Source: adapted from Kitses 1969

Kitses's list of binary oppositions (which can be considerably extended) is enormously helpful in relation to the Western genre. He shows how this pattern relates to America's movement westward, searching for and crossing new frontiers between the East and the West, between civilisation and the wilderness or Garden of Eden that lay across the frontier, between restriction and freedom. We have already discussed this in relation to *Thelma and Louise* (pp. 115–16), but it is worth noting again because it is such a powerful mythical structure for us. As a general method, using binary oppositions will illuminate other genres and individual narratives.

The richness of this system of oppositions is that there is no clear-cut 'good' and 'bad'. The conflicting oppositions have to be resolved by the end of the narrative, and this is where the system gets interesting. Once again, the idea of dialectical synthesis can help us to understand how resolution is reached. Just as the thesis and the antithesis must be brought together into a synthesis, the protagonist and the antagonist in a story typically need to take on aspects of each other's value systems and character traits in order for the conflict between them to be resolved. For example, Western cowboy heroes often bring civilisation and community to the wild Western frontier, but paradoxically, their ability to enforce law and order is dependent on the strength of their individualism, and they themselves remain free (outside or beyond the law) in the wilderness. In order for a cowboy hero to defeat the Indians, he frequently needs to acquire traditional Indian skills such as tracking and hunting, and often he understands Indian culture and language better than characters such as the settler or the merchant, who are totally aligned with civilisation and the East.

If you analyse a narrative, making a list of binary oppositions like the one above, you will see that the protagonist is fighting for the side that is generally considered to be 'good', but in order to win the battle he or she may become associated with some elements from the opposite column. This strategy is also enormously helpful in analysing media texts outside the Western genre. For instance, *Face/Off* provides a great example of the mutual incorporation of good and bad that happens in the process of dialectical synthesis. John Travolta and Nicholas Cage's characters literally have to get inside each other's skin in order to resolve their conflict.

The attempted resolution of oppositions is central to the meanings of film narratives. It can also be seen as a search for an end to dualism and opposition. It often reveals that the opposites are linked. For example, in the *Star Wars* films, it is finally revealed that Darth Vader and Luke Skywalker are actually father and son: they are like two sides of the same coin.

Draw up a list of oppositions in the film Thelma *and* Louise *and consider how these are resolved at the end of the film.*

Exercise commentary

The following table gives some suggestions as to how you could apply binary oppositions to *Thelma and Louise*:

	oppositions		
characters	Thelma	vs	her husband
	Louise	vs	rapist
characteristics	scatty	vs	organised
	smoker	vs	non-smoker
	dress	vs	jeans
	jewellery	vs	hat
	static	vs	moving
settings	home	vs	away
	restaurant	vs	mountains
	America	vs	Mexico
value systems	female	vs	male
	lawful	vs	outlaw
	trapped	vs	free
	oppressed	vs	liberated

These are just some of the oppositions in the film. You may find many more. Note how the first three sets of oppositions—characters, characteristics, and settings—lead us towards the abstract value systems. In looking at the resolutions, one of the most interesting features is that while we are clearly invited to identify and sympathise with the females (Thelma and Louise), their journey to fulfilment and maturity is one that involves them crossing over from the female side of the central opposition male vs female to the male side (Thelma even remarks at one stage that something has 'crossed over' in her). They leave behind (female) dress and jewellery and adopt (male) jeans and cowboy-hats; they leave the (female) static life of home and restaurant for the (male) mobile life away on the road. Ultimately they become liberated by incorporating some characteristics of male outlaws in order to resolve the problems associated with their initial position.

In analysing the film's overall views of masculinity and femininity, note that, in the final pro-female resolution, Thelma and Louise have actually adopted male characteristics and are following a male way of life. This could be grounds for critique of the film since at the very moment it seeks to support women it is endorsing male values (see p. 118). Alternatively, it could be seen as showing that male privileges and ways of life should be available to women and should not be seen as exclusively masculine. The film is an affirmation of the close bonds of friendship, solidarity, support, and mutual understanding, indicating that these traits (which are traditionally associated with women) are among the most valuable in life. The fact that they kiss before they plunge over the edge of the canyon in the final scenes of the movie can be seen as retaining their femininity, since most Western men do not kiss each other. Whatever line you take, you will begin to see how oppositions are central to the pattern of a narrative and how analysis of these will lead you to a further understanding of the whole piece.

Applying structural approaches to non-narrative texts

The approaches in this section on the structures of narrative have all related to fiction. Structural analysis and the awareness of binary oppositions can be used for analysis of non-fiction texts such as news, sports, quiz shows, and chat shows. We have already mentioned how fiction and factual media texts share a number of characteristics (p. 59). Documentaries, in particular, present themselves as stories—narratives with a beginning, a middle, an end, and major characters. All the analytic tools discussed in this section on narrative structure so far can be used to analyse them.

News programs, quiz and game shows, and sports programs are also carefully and conventionally structured, and analysis of these structures begins to reveal some of their underlying meanings. The news is a non-fiction media text that does not follow a narrative structure with a beginning, a middle, and an end. Instead, news articles typically begin at the 'climax' of the story and then present information in decreasing order of priority, ending with the background details that set the scene, introduce the characters, and form the foundation of most narratives. Because news texts 'get to the point first', they are said to be structured like an inverted pyramid. Thus, news articles tend to privilege controversy over context, the climax over the exposition, and impact over emotional or intellectual engagement and understanding. Yet the structure—

headlines, then a series of stories that recede in importance, ending with feel-good stories about animals or children, sport, and finally a friendly closure by a familiar team of newsreaders—is one that, in the end, leads us to reassurance, closure, and acceptance, a state that requires us to do nothing. Peter Watkins draws attention to the similar structure of news presentations, what he calls its monoform, that treats all stories in the same way:

> This same method of story-telling is used night after night, year after year, no matter what *the emotional demand of the theme or subject being presented*. The repetitive, split-second similarity in the way that it organises sounds and images blurs the distinctions between different themes and subjects, and between what might otherwise be entirely different emotional responses to them. There is no allowance for differentiation of information, whether about a terrible air-crash, or a man who has painted his pet elephant pink. Both stories are presented via the same grid-lock and narrative structure … This repetitious story-telling pattern, linked with the fact that it is closed (has no space for the audience to reflect or intervene), and that it usually consists of a dense, non-stop bombardment of violent juxtapositions of image, sound and conflicting themes, has had a devastating effect on society (Watkins 1997, p. 6).

Watkins sees this sameness in the manner of representation as extending beyond news coverage to all areas of the audio-visual media.

Bill Nichols, looking at the form and structure of news coverage, suggests that the point of view constructed for audiences is a position of 'viewer-observer'. This position means we are detached from the news coverage. Consequently: 'News reportage urges us to look but not care, see but not act, know but not change. The news exists less to orient us towards action than to perpetuate itself as commodity, something to be fetishised and consumed' (Nichols 1991, p.194).

Analysis of discourses on television is very revealing. Amongst the myriad voices and discourses presented, certain voices are privileged. They are privileged or dominant because they use direct address: they speak directly to us, bidding us good morning or good night and wishing us a safe weekend on Fridays. These voices are thus more intimate and connected than other voices. They are the voices of television professionals: newsreaders, weather announcers, quiz- and chat-show hosts, sports commentators, and so on. These people are the mediators, the gatekeepers of our access to the world; everything and everybody else has to pass through their privileged discourses. They are allowed to look at the camera and hence directly at us; they are the mediators for other people whom they introduce, frame, question, and say goodbye to; and they comment on what we have just seen or heard. The faceless voice-overs that announce programs are also privileged discourses. Like the voice of God, they emerge out of nowhere, speaking with authority and certainty.

However, since its inception, television has allowed increased access to ordinary people's voices. Television quiz shows and talkback radio are major examples. But the ordinary discourses of participants are mediated and controlled. Quiz-show participants are shepherded through their paces by the all-controlling discourse of the host. Every call to talkback radio is policed by the presenters, whose voices come across more clearly because they are not on the phone and who have the power to cut off callers whenever they want. Ordinary discourses are either secondary or, as in *Funniest Home Videos*, they are a source of humour. Nevertheless, there is room for change. The most interesting developments in relation to ordinary discourse have been 'access' series such as *Video Diaries* (BBC), *First Person* (SBS), and *Home Truths* (ABC), where cameras are given to ordinary people to record and relate their own stories. In such ventures, ordinary discourses can gain greater prominence and participants are left to speak for themselves, relatively unmediated by television experts (Dovey 1995, pp. 26–9; O'Shaughnessy 1997, pp. 84–99). More recently, 'reality' shows like *Big Brother, Survivor, Temptation Island*, and *Popstars* have given a new space for 'ordinary' people to appear on television. It is certainly interesting the way these programs focus on aspects of competition and elimination, which might be seen as a chance to reflect on aspects of capitalist society; they also seem to demonstrate a fascination with the 'private' that can be revealed. However, it should be noted that these 'ordinary' people are, themselves, often looking for media exposure and they are very much controlled by the guiding TV 'big brothers' who put the shows together.

·1 Make a call to talkback radio and record the result. How does this experience feel? Analyse the exchange between you and the media presenters.

2 If possible, arrange a trip to a live television recording at a television studio. Note the level of structure and preparation that goes into putting on such a seemingly spontaneous show.

CONCLUSION

In this analysis of narrative structure we have described narrative as a pattern of dialectical synthesis structured around the resolution of binary oppositions and we have shown that this pattern affects meanings. Understanding these structures is another way of seeing how texts work and ascertaining their possible meanings. Close examination of endings (where characters are positioned at the ends of texts) and of what narrative structure 'does' to people can reveal the ideological meanings and social values of a text.

11 Joseph Campbell and Carl Jung

WHY WATCH NARRATIVES?

Before looking at the work of Joseph Campbell, we want to raise a wider question: Why do we watch film and television narratives in the first place? What do we get out of this experience? This question could be broadened to ask why we read books or watch plays, or why we look at paintings. Like the questions raised in Part 1—Do we have free will? Are our actions and choices psychologically determined, or are they a product of social forces?—this is another 'big' question that has produced volumes of theoretical work and it is worth spending a short time considering it here.

The simplest overall answer to this question is that we get pleasure from watching and reading narratives. But how do we define this pleasure and what different kinds of pleasure are involved? Film and television produce at least two types of responses: emotional and intellectual. They provide us with an affect: laughter, sadness, fear, excitement, and so on. Cinema is a particularly visceral medium: it literally works on the organs of our body, making our hair stand on end with fear, making us weep tears, producing belly laughs, gut reactions, or even sexual arousal, and these translate into emotional feelings.

Feelings of pleasure are compounded by the aesthetic forms of stories: in other words, the way things are presented provides pleasure. The simple narrative form, the process and structure described above, can be an intensely satisfying viewing experience: lives unfold and cohere, and conflicts are resolved. While our physical and emotional responses are based on story content, our understanding of stories and the pleasure we derive from this understanding depend on our intellectual response.

Stories allow us to see a wide range of human characters and experiences from across the globe. They also allow us to exercise our imaginations. The range of stories enriches our own experiences. At the same time, they are always connected to, and have something to say about, our world; like fables they have a moral or a point. This suggests that part of the pleasure we take in these stories derives from the fact that we learn from them.

FICTIONS AND REALITY

Fictions—imaginary characters, invented places, and constructed stories—are about real concerns over issues as diverse as relationships, history, social conditions, and emotional states. However fictional and fantastical the content is, however near or far away in space or time from the present the story is, every fiction deals with concerns that relate to the real world. Fictions are ways of exploring issues that concern people in real life. How are fictions, unrealities, connected to our real world? First, nearly all stories are about characters. Usually these characters are humans, but sometimes they are mythical beings, animals, or other fictional creatures. Second, many fictions are also about place. Some are actually situated in real places (London, San Francisco, Sydney); others are set in fictional spaces within real spaces (*Northern Exposure*'s Sicily in Alaska); and others may be set outside the world we know (in science-fiction, dream, or fantasy worlds).

Narratives are always related to the historical and social moment of their production. For example, Australian films made in the 1970s and 1990s that look back at Australia's past are the product of 1970s or 1990s concerns, and in some way they reflect these concerns. The film *My Brilliant Career*, ostensibly about feminist issues in 1900, arose out of and reflects the concerns of Australian feminists in the 1970s.

Fictions can be compared to dreams. According to Freud and other psychoanalytic thinkers (Freud 1976; Ullman and Zimmerman 1979), dreams are messages about our real-life selves. Fictions are also messages about our world (or about the world of the authors of the fiction). Creators use fiction as a way of talking about issues that concern them in real life. In this way, fictional texts and the real world are inextricably linked. We call this link the 'media–world connection'. Our pleasure in watching, reading, or listening to fictions derives partly from the fact that we learn something from so doing; we gain insight and understanding into how people and society work. There is thus an important relationship between the fictional and the real, between texts and society.

We have shown this already in discussions of the Western and the road movie as genres that explore American culture. These genres work through the oppositions between freedom and law and order, and between the wilderness and civilisation, allowing the USA to 'talk to itself' about itself (see p. 119). We have shown this in the discussion of representations of coupling, the family, and sexual expression (pp. 144–8), subjects that feature in many narratives, particularly the melodrama, which repeatedly explores the dilemma of whether people should follow their individual desires or conform to the demands of familial and social responsibility. Even when we turn to stories which are in some sense fantastic and 'unreal'—for example myths, legends, fairy-tales, science-fiction—we can connect these to an internal or psychic reality. Robert Johnson reports on a schoolboy giving a definition of 'myths' as: ' "Something that is true on the inside, but not true on the outside" (Johnson 1987, p. 2). A myth *is* true: it is not true in the outer, physical sense, but it is an accurate expression of a psychological situation, of the inner condition of the psyche.' Similarly Bruno Bettelheim argues that children know that fairy tales are not real, but recognise on some level that these stories have internal, human truths they need to learn to help them grow up happily: 'The child intuitively comprehends that although these stories are *unreal*, they are not *untrue*; that while what these stories tell about does not happen in fact, it must happen as inner experience and personal development' (Bettelheim 1978, p. 73).

Let us further explore how fictions work by looking at theories that aim to understand what happens in the viewing/reading/listening process.

ARISTOTLE AND CATHARSIS

The classic model of what is going on when someone consumes a fictional text is found in Aristotle's analysis of Greek tragedy. He suggested that the experience allows people to feel extreme emotions, particularly fear and terror, provoked by the story, and then at the end to experience a purging of these emotions in a moment of catharsis or emotional release (Wellek and Warren 1976, p. 36; Benjamin 1977, p. 38). Audiences experience the feelings and dilemmas of the characters through identification with them. They can understand extreme situations that they might never experience in their own lives. As audience members experience and therefore begin to understand the world inhabited by the characters, they empathise with them, and this empathy makes them develop as people. 'The function of literature ... is to relieve us ... from the pressure of emotions' (Wellek and Warren 1976, p. 36).

Notions that texts serve to release pent-up emotions have been applied to comedy. Some theorists argue that in letting out air, laughter acts as a release valve, and is therefore a form of relaxation. Laughter is increasingly being seen as therapeutic (Koestler 1975; Powell and Paton 1988), as an activity that makes us healthier, and generating laughter is a common aim of media fictions. The notion that laughter is healthy release partly explains the popularity of comedy.

There are other ways in which comedy is a release or safety valve. Freud suggested that comedy allows us to speak about social taboos and repressed topics, particularly sexuality. It is a way of speaking the unspeakable (Freud 1976).

There is debate over whether the function of comedy as a safety valve is socially progressive or reactionary. It can be progressive (that is, it can contribute to social change and development) by raising issues that would otherwise not be dealt with. But it can also be reactionary (that is, it can help to maintain the social status quo) because once there has been a release of tension, there is no need to deal with the social problem that produced the tension. The prominence of comedy in the modern media can often be seen as a similarly safe form of criticism and satire. On the other hand it can also be argued that some comedy shows extend the boundaries of what is socially acceptable and break social taboos: when shows such as *The Young Ones*, *Absolutely Fabulous*, and *South Park* first appear audiences are divided on whether these are funny or unacceptable. A key question is 'Does humour contribute to social change, or do people continue to accept the things that they laugh about, enjoying the release of tension rather than taking social action?'

We think that, at its best, comedy can raise our awareness of social ills and can thereby contribute to social change. Because comedic texts are 'not meant to be taken seriously' they can provide a space to poke fun at and criticise authority without fear of retribution. For example, the film *Three Kings* pokes fun at the self-interest of the USA's involvement in the Gulf War without posing an explicit challenge to authority. It certainly creates a space to laugh and release tension about a serious conflict. However, as media analysts we also need to consider whether such films have the potential to change society, or whether they simply encourage audience members to think about American foreign policy up to the point of resolution in the media text, and then forget about the issues as the laughter dies and the lights go up in the cinema. Since the Gulf War and the release of *Three Kings*, there have been few changes in the way the

USA relates to the Middle East except that the situation has worsened and conflict has escalated. For example, Americans have long been uninterested in exploring the reasons for the animosity towards the USA felt by many in the Middle East. This has not changed. After the destruction of the World Trade Center, President George W. Bush expressed amazement at how deeply the USA was hated in the Middle East. Laughter makes serious material seem harmless, which is why comedy can be a subversive agent of social change, or a mechanism for trivialising significant issues.

Figures 3.9–3.10 Joke images circulated by email after the September 11 attacks on the World Trade Center and the Pentagon

in true architectural style *arquitectonica* have submitted their proposals for the new World Trade Center

The New World Trade Center, 2005
Fuck You, Bin Laden

It is interesting to note how soon after a 'serious' event it is acceptable to make jokes about it. Can you remember when you first heard a joke about the September 11 attacks and what your reaction to this comedy was?

However, although comedy, which invariably laughs at someone, can satirise those in power and authority, it has often turned on minority or oppressed social groups— Irish, Poles, Aborigines, Jews, non-Whites, women—in a racist and sexist fashion. A useful question to ask about comedy and jokes is 'Who is the joke against?' Answering this will begin to reveal its progressive or reactionary tendencies.

MARXISM AND BRECHT

Thinking about comedy and catharsis as emotional release leads to the question of whether media texts should provoke us to social action or not. Marxist ideas are relevant here. There are many Marxist interpretations of literature and film.[13] These endeavour to show how narratives reveal the struggle between social groups and classes, and how the stories of individual characters are part of these struggles and of the changing economic forces that determine our actions. It is possible to carry out Marxist analyses of films and literature produced by non-Marxists or writers who lived before Marx: Marxist interpretations exist of the works of Shakespeare, the Brontë sisters, Balzac, and other writers. There are also Marxist analyses of various films: for example Frederic Jameson's examination of *Dog Day Afternoon* (Jameson 1977).

Marxism's answer to the question 'Why do we need stories?' is that they show us what is wrong with our society and they point us to a better world. Viewed in this light, they are part of the revolutionary movement; they contribute to social understanding and social change. According to Marxists, in a classless society we might actually no longer need stories or art, because life would be perfect! There would be no more fictions. Ernst Fischer writes of the painter Mondrian, who held Marxist views: 'Reality would, he believed, increasingly displace the work of art, which was essentially a substitute for an equilibrium that reality lacked at present. "Art will disappear as life gains more equilibrium"' (Fischer 1963, p. 7). According to Marxism then, stories are signs that things are not perfect.

One of the most influential Marxist practitioners and theorists was the playwright and poet Bertolt Brecht. He challenged the worth of theatre as catharsis, arguing that this form of emotional involvement and release:
- encourages acceptance of life as it is
- privileges emotional response over intellectual insight and understanding
- contributes to maintaining the status quo rather than provoking social change (Willett 1964; Benjamin 1977).

In Brecht's view, a narrative might explore social problems, but if it works through emotionally involving its audience the final result is the banality of 'a good cry', or a comment such as 'How terrible, how terrible things are, but that's life'. According to Brecht, theatre that works through emotions fails to provoke audiences to action: the only thing such texts might prompt audiences to do is go for a drink after the show!

Brecht argued that it is the way stories are told, their form and structure (the final narrative closure, the level of suspense, and so on), that produces these affects, and therefore viewing pleasure. He argued for a different kind of story-telling, 'epic theatre', that would produce 'pleasurable learning' (Willett 1964, pp. 72–3). This learning would allow us to see the world in a new way, revealing new truths. I first came across this kind of learning when I saw the 7.84 Theatre Company in the United Kingdom. Their name referred to the statistical distribution of wealth in Britain in the 1970s: 7 per cent of the population owned 84 per cent of the wealth in the country. My view of the United Kingdom as a basically egalitarian, democratic society (which is how it is often presented in the media) was shaken by this wider social truth. The current figures for wealth ownership in Australia (which is often referred to as a classless society) and the United Kingdom have remained virtually the same. Learning the following facts was a similarly shocking revelation for me: 'In some states in Australia, between 50 and 60 per cent of all children in custody are aboriginal, although they represent less than 4 per cent of the juvenile population'; and 'The United States consumes 33% of the world's resources' (*New Internationalist* 97, p. 6). What would be important to Brecht about these statistics would be that rather than focusing on individual, psychological concerns, they reveal certain deep-seated political truths about society, uncovering the inequality of social structures. He sought a theatrical form that could encompass such teachings while still involving the audience.

His most famous technique for achieving this aim was the use of '*verfremden*', which has been translated as 'alienation' or 'distanciation'. *Verfremden* techniques are theatrical devices, now sometimes called Brechtian devices, that interrupt the realistic flow of the narrative in such a way that the audience is jolted out of their emotional involvement with the exciting narrative, or out of their identification with the main characters. Such techniques aim to make audiences think critically about what is happening by putting them in a distant or alienated position. Advocates of this technique argue that such reflection leads to insight, understanding, and ultimately to acceptance of the need to act. Moreover, it is argued that this learning process is pleasurable for oppressed audiences since it contributes to their liberation. Whereas catharsis produces a pleasurable emotional release that occurs while the audience is watching the play, the release that is provoked by a Brecht play comes afterwards, from doing something about problems raised in the text.

These revolutionary ideas were very influential on a group of film and television makers in the 1960s and 1970s. The most famous of these was the French film director Jean-Luc Godard. Godard tried to incorporate these Brechtian devices into his films in order to make spectators think critically, come to new understandings of society, and be provoked into social action—rather than having them just go off for a post-film drink. Film-making and film-going became an actively political pastime rather than purely pleasurable recreation.[14]

This begs the question of whether narratives should encourage social action or contemplation. Can you think of any examples of film or television narratives that have shocked or surprised you? Why and how did they do this? Describe the reactions they produced in you. Did they prompt you to act?

LÉVI-STRAUSS AND MYTH

Another approach to narrative is found in the structuralist work of Lévi-Strauss. He examined the role of myths (the earliest forms of stories) in 'primitive' cultures (Turner 1993, pp. 72–4; Lévi-Strauss 1978). He argued that they served an important function for these societies. Myths dealt with the central problems and contradictions felt by a culture; in story-form (they were often stories about gods or heroes) they played these conflicts out to a resolution that gave societies some sort of framework for how to live. Graeme Turner explains it as follows:

> Within myths, contradictions and inequities which could not be resolved in the real world were resolved symbolically. The function of myth was to place those contradictions—between man and his natural environment, for instance, or between life and death—as part of natural existence. Myths negotiated a peace between men and women and their environment so that they could live in it without agonising over its frustrations and cruelties (Turner 1988, p. 72).

Lévi-Strauss's theory stressed the play of binary oppositions as structures that set up and resolve contradictions. The result here is not social action, but social peace and acceptance of the status quo. Our discussion of contemporary media narratives and their resolution of oppositions relating to contemporary social concerns—for example, marriage and family vs friendship and multiple partners—suggest that media narratives can be seen, using Lévi-Strauss's terms, as forms of contemporary myths.

Myths will be looked at more with Jung and Campbell but the idea of 'rites of passage' is worth mentioning here. Rites of passage are traditional points or periods of significant change in a person's life—birth, marriage, and death are the most obvious, but most societies also have traditional rites that help mark the transition of young adults · from childhood to adulthood. They are often described as death/rebirth rituals or as initiation ceremonies—a symbolic death is experienced that allows new life to come forward at the same time as another stage of life is left behind. Modern and postmodern Western culture has lost many of these traditions, athough we can see remnants of them in many of the adolescent activities of teenagers involving sex and drugs, for example the celebrations that Australian school leavers indulge in (known as 'schoolies'), traditionally a week of relatively excessive holidaying after they have left school, a kind of initiation into, as well as a challenge to, adult life.

While there may be an absence of formal rituals in real life we can see how film, television, and fiction narratives fill some of this gap by providing us with numerous examples of 'rites of passage' and 'initiation' stories. For example *Yolngu Boy* is a 'rites of passage film' and *The Princess Diaries* is a 'coming of age film'. Many stories show characters going through ordeals that can be understood in this light and thus offer readers examples of how to undergo these rites and ordeals successfully. Mircea Eliade (cited in Bettelheim 1978) expresses this well in writing about the appeal of fairy tales:

> It is impossible to deny that the ordeals and adventures of the heroes and heroines of fairy tales are almost always translated into initiatory terms. … initiatory scenarios … are the expression of a psychodrama that answers a deep need in the human being. Every man

wants to experience certain perilous situations, to confront exceptional ordeals, to make his way into the Other World—and he experiences all this, on the level of his imaginative life, by hearing or reading fairy tales. (Eliade 1963, as quoted in Bettelheim 1978, p. 35)

We would suggest this holds true for many other film, television, and written narratives—and (note the gendered language in the quoted extract) for every woman!

ENTERTAINMENT, ESCAPISM, AND UTOPIA

The pleasures we get from media products are often described as escapist, and the texts we consume are often belittled as 'just entertainment'. Saying something is escapist or 'just entertainment' is a way of dismissing it. These disparaging terms are presented as self-evident—it is assumed that they don't need explanation, that we know what they mean. This does not do justice to the terms. Richard Dyer has written most illuminatingly about the term 'entertainment', analysing its history, development, and meanings (Dyer 1992). He has also written about popular genres that are often dismissed as escapist, particularly musicals and soap operas (Dyer 1981).

To describe a media text as escapist is to suggest that people watching it are avoiding reality, that they are not facing up to the real world. It suggests that the text is unrealistic, that it promotes irresponsible avoidance of social problems. Escapist entertainment is often contrasted with realistic stories that explore the grim realities of life and are therefore deemed to be more worthy and valuable. We don't agree with this characterisation of popular entertainment as escapist. Dyer has suggested that many cultural products have a utopian element to them: they point to the possibilities of a better world (as suggested by Marxist analysis of media texts—see p. 161). There is a long and respectable tradition of utopian writing and visions. The utopian vision of a perfect world can inspire us with hope and optimism and can give us a blueprint for how we would like to live. It is something to work towards; it suggests the possibility of social change (in contrast to many realist stories that simply confirm how terrible life is rather than positing an alternative). These escapist visions involve both an escape to something and an escape from something.

Dyer suggests that the musical and soap opera can present ideal values and ideal ways of living that are in direct contrast to the realities of everyday life. The musical offers the following ideal qualities as a response to their mundane, everyday opposites:
- abundance vs scarcity
- energy vs tiredness and exhaustion
- community vs isolation and alienation
- transparency in human relations vs human deviousness
- intensity of experience vs lacklustre lives and boredom (Dyer 1981).

In classic films such as *Singin' in the Rain*, and modern versions of the musical such as *O Brother Where Art Thou* and *Moulin Rouge*, the musical provides all five elements of contrast between the ideal world that we escape into and the everyday world. Particularly in spontaneous song and dance numbers, musicals offer the open and simple expression of intense and exciting feeling (often love, joy, and friendship), and there is a great outpouring of energy and movement. Even in Lars Von Trier's *Dancer in the Dark*, a bleak film that undermines the conventions of the musical genre, these contrasts between social realism and the transcendent, uplifting possibilities of music are apparent. Typical musicals show people brought together in a sharing, caring community and there is plenty of material and emotional sustenance for everyone (in fact there is often an abundance of these things). This contrasts with the dull, daily grind of everyday life, where people work hard for a living but often don't have enough, either materially or emotionally; where human relations are often unclear and conducted with ulterior motives; where people are often stressed, tired, or bored; and where many live isolated and alienated lives.

We realise that we are painting a grim picture of reality here, one that does not do justice to life in the Western world, which is actually very well-off in material terms, particularly compared with the majority (Third) world. Australia, which is often called the lucky country and whose motto is 'no worries', is in many ways a wonderful place to live. Yet despite its seeming wealth and health, it too is a culture beset by stresses and strains, internal ethnic struggle, high youth suicide rates, and so on. The myth of Australia's equitable social structure and multicultural harmony may have negative ramifications. For instance, it may have made it possible for the politician Pauline Hanson, leader of the controversial One Nation party, to critique the social systems that attempt to help disadvantaged members of the population both inside and outside Australia. If everything is perceived to be fine and dandy in a world where everyone has a 'fair go', then some people become resentful that certain groups get extra help. The 'lucky country' image perpetuated in media representations of Australia may also encourage some people to hide their problems until it is too late: if the message is that everything should be OK, they may feel ashamed if they can't 'make a go of it'.

All this is to illustrate that so-called 'escapist' entertainments have a connection to our real lives and can offer something positive. There can of course be a negative side to entertainment. Some game shows and gambling (especially as presented in lottery advertisements) offer magical fixes to our scarcity problems, but these fixes promote the same consumerist values on which much of our culture is built. (Interestingly, research has shown that most lottery winners actually end up losing friends and fighting with their families, ending up little better off than before.) These operate like the circuses provided by Roman emperors, as devices to keep people happy and distracted from social and political problems. We may therefore want to question these forms of entertainment. But entertainment that is simple and easy to watch, and therefore accessible to many people, should not be denigrated as a whole for these reasons. We need to examine each example to see what is being presented. In so doing, we will often find valuable elements, as Dyer has pointed out.

The utopian visions provided by the media thus provide us with pleasure and are sources of aspiration and inspiration. The flipside to this is the media's presentation of dystopias or dystopic views of the world, stories of social breakdown, decay, and apocalypse (for example, the films *Blade Runner*, *The Matrix*, and *Delicatessen*). These dystopic texts also relate to our present world. They provide us with warnings of what could happen to us.

The critic Roland Barthes adds another dimension to thinking about audiences and our responses to fictions when he discusses the pleasures of reading fictions. He uses the French word *jouissance* (bliss) and distinguishes this from *plaisir* (pleasure). *Jouissance* is a difficult word to translate, but he is aiming to convey a difference between pleasure, which is straightforward enjoyment of fictions that don't really have a deep impact on us, and *jouissance*, a disturbing pleasure that produces an extremely heightened response. These are the kinds of fictions that have a potentially life-changing impact on us, making us see the world anew.

To clarify this try to make a list of fictions that you have simply enjoyed and fictions that have 'blown you away' with jouissance. *Compare these with a friend and try to explain to each other what the nature of the* jouissance *impact was on you.*

REALISMS

The aesthetic tradition that is closest to real life is the mimetic or realist tradition. In contrast with escapist entertainment, mimetic cultural productions aim to imitate reality, to produce narratives and stories that are recognised as realistic. This mimetic tradition started with Greek culture and the history of mimetic art is a history of continually evolving styles and methods used to reproduce reality.[15] The styles evolve partly because reality is, in the final analysis, impossible to capture. 'Realism' is an important critical term in relation to nineteenth-century painting and literature, and twentieth-century film and television. Raymond Williams has explained the different elements that make up realist texts: ordinary people, particularly the working classes, as subject matter; serious treatment of their lives; and lives situated in contemporary social contexts (Williams 1977a, pp. 61–74). Roy Armes makes the important distinction between realism as an aim/attitude (aiming to tell the truth, to show things with verisimilitude so that they look very similar to what we see) and realism as a method/style (a set of artistic/stylistic conventions that try to achieve this aim) (Armes 1971). Films with a high degree of verisimilitude are perceived to be more accurate representations of society, and they are therefore often interpreted as offering productive, instructive social commentary. Mike Leigh's films are good examples of media texts that use realism. As a director he encourages improvisation and spontaneity in the actors, and tends to shoot in long takes in order to sustain the energy and intensity of performances.

Because there are numerous, changing ways of seeing the world there are also many realist styles or sets of conventions (realisms). Neo-realism, Soviet realism, naturalism, kitchen-sink realism, social realism, magic realism, and dirty realism are all terms used to describe styles or tendencies in literature and in film and television products. The connections these styles forge with real-life issues, and the seriousness this imparts to the particular media product mean that media products using these styles have tended to be given more cultural weight than 'escapist entertainment'. Because they appear realistic it is sometimes easy to forget the construction involved in these representations. The pleasure we derive from them is connected to the way we recognise our own lives and society being presented.

FANTASY AND PSYCHOANALYSIS

Fantasy

In contrast with an understanding of fictions that sees them as imitations of real life, the use of the term 'fantasy' to describe and analyse fictions draws attention to dreams, imagination, the subconscious, and story worlds that differ significantly from everyday experience. Links have traditionally been made between films and dreams. The description of Hollywood as a 'dream factory' points to both the desirable aspects of Hollywood films (they provide wish-fulfilment, as do dreams) and their unrealistic nature (the unattainability of these dreams).

Psychoanalytic approaches to film and television explore what is involved in looking at images on screens. Freud argued that one of the key human drives or desires is the desire to look (Mulvey 1989). This desire is called scopophilia (it derives from the Greek expression for love of looking). It is a source of great pleasure and satisfaction. One aspect of scopophilia is voyeurism, the desire to look secretly at events, to spy on people. This can be seen as one of the pleasures offered by film and television texts. Audiences indulge in the fantasy that the actors on screen are real people acting out their lives before cameras, seemingly without realising those cameras are there. Audiences watch these events unfold, often from a darkened auditorium. We choose to believe that we are being permitted to see the most intimate aspects of these lives, beyond what we experience in relation to most people we actually know. A film such as *Blue Velvet* consciously explores these pleasures. Voyeuristic vision is characterised by distance (the observer is separated or concealed from the observed in some manner) and secrecy (the observed is not aware that they are being watched, and does not consent to it). The combination of distance and deception leads to a sense of control and objectification.

The pleasures of identification and objectification (see pp. 138–9) can also be said to be built on scopophilia. Fetishistic scopophilia is more to do with being absorbed in the pleasures of looking, rather than controlling or objectifying what the viewer is looking at. Often the object that is being fetishised (frequently this is a part of the body or clothing) takes on huge proportions and is fragmented, so it fills the screen in close-up and overwhelms the viewer with its beauty. This is a different experience from the scopophilic pleasure derived from voyeurism. Freud reminds us that a fetish object is a substitute, it fills the gap in a reassuring way and takes on disproportionate importance because it is taking the place of something that is deeply desired. For instance, a fetish for silk, velvet, or fur may be a reassuring substitute for the feeling of skin or hair. The film *There's Something About Mary* depicts the villain as having a fetish for the shoes that Cameron Diaz's character slips her feet into. A shoe fetish is often explained as an analogy between the action of a foot slipping into a shoe and sexual intercourse.

The use of the term 'fantasy' to analyse media texts has another dimension to it. Fantasies are essentially unreal, the product of our dreams and imaginations. One of the most exciting things about film and television stories is that they give film-makers and audiences a chance to live out their wildest and most extreme fantasies. This has been the source of some controversy, particularly in relation to representations of sex and violence. Some people argue that these representations are dangerous and have the potential to corrupt us or lead us to commit violent acts (see p. 33). Others reject this, saying:

1 that we are capable of recognising that we are not seeing real events
2 that these stories allow us to work through difficult aspects of ourselves, and our society, safely.

The second point is an argument that it is important to allow violent representations because they give us a chance to explore and understand our own violent tendencies. Very few people are murderers, but many of us, at some point in our lives, dream of killing or attacking someone. Looking at and understanding these dark and repressed sides of ourselves allows us to cope with them. Denying us the opportunity to explore them will repress them further, and that could be harmful. Stories allow us to play out, in our imaginations, a whole set of possible actions, to test them out, to see what happens if . . .

Rosemary Jackson describes fantasy as 'the literature of subversion'. According to Jackson, this literature of subversion 'attempts to compensate for a lack resulting from cultural constraints; it is a literature of desire, which seeks that which is experienced as absence or loss' (Jackson 1981, p. 3). This is similar, in some ways, to Dyer's view of the utopian musical. Jackson sees media texts that portray extreme human behaviour as explorations of areas and desires that society normally represses.

Illuminating what happens when our fantasies are played out on screen, Victor Perkins describes audiences as 'participant observers' (Perkins 1990, ch. 7). He notes that the language of film, the way stories are told, allows the audience to feel as if it is participating in the events on screen. We are thus involved in extreme actions and intense emotions—killing, being killed, making love, chariot racing, and so on. However, at the same time, we still know we are in the cinema; part of us remains detached and we can observe what is happening both on the screen and in ourselves as we experience these situations. We are simultaneously participants and observers. The cinema becomes a playground where we experience all sorts of emotions and actions and at the same time reflect critically and rationally on how it feels and on what the consequences are for ourselves and others. This testing ground provides a significant arena of pleasure and learning.

We have already referred to Bruno Bettelheim's argument that 'violent' fairy tales are actually good for children as a way of letting them face and explore their own violent capacities (see p. 35). On ABC Radio National's *Media Report*, Robert Kee, a noted Hollywood scriptwriter, discussed the social role of dark media fantasies with interviewer Donna McLachlan.

McLachlan: What is your feeling about the kind of depth and strength of some of these monsters that are appearing on screen, *American Psycho*, and Hannibal Lecter and so on? Is it disturbing do you think that there is that portrayal of the monster, or is it healthy?

Kee: Oh, it's very healthy. Human beings are angel and devil, and a perfect balance of the two. And the fascinating thing about human beings is you never know from one day to the next which you're going to get. I mean, on Monday they build Notre Dame cathedral and on Tuesday, Auschwitz, and which is it going to be? And you only need to pick up a newspaper from one day to the next, and you see this constant manifestation of the deep evil in human beings. And what all of us try to do, of course, is deny it exists in us. It's that backpack serial killer over there, it's not me. But every time you cut somebody off in traffic, every time you slam a door in somebody's face, every time you're rude to a clerk, every time you take advantage of somebody, there's a little bit of evil seeping out of you, and you enjoyed cutting that guy off in traffic, and don't deny it. And so if we turn our backs on the dark side of our nature, if we just try to avoid it and insist it doesn't exist, it's going to sneak up from behind us and swallow us whole.

And art, which has the power to illuminate these dark corners of human nature, can make us understand that it's us, and it's in our nature. It doesn't mean that we're evil ourselves, that we're going to be overcome by our own evil nature, but it's always there, and the power is there, and as long as we understand that and are aware of it, then we can keep ourselves in balance and go round being a decent human being. (ABC Radio National, *The Media Report*, 28 June 2001)

Stories that go beyond everyday realism—horror movies, the surreal explorations of film directors David Lynch and David Cronenberg, and so on—allow us an even wider testing-out of human feelings and experiences. For us, this aspect of storytelling is part of the exciting potential of fictional narratives in film and television. Finally we might note the role of films showing seemingly unrealistic possibilities. Films such as *Fight Club*, *The Matrix*, *Crouching Tiger Hidden Dragon*, and *Groundhog Day* can be understood (like myths discussed above, p. 158) as allowing audiences to explore their inner world, their psychic processes, or as symbolic of external social situations. The fantasies they portray—for example living in a computer-generated reality (*The Matrix*), having a real-life double (*Fight Club*), being able to fly (*Crouching Tiger*), living the same day over and over (*Groundhog Day*)—allow the main characters to explore internal psychological states and allow the audience a space to consider what it is to be human.

Psychoanalysis

Mention of Freud and scopophilia leads us to psychoanalysis as a general approach for understanding art, literature, film, and television. Psychoanalytic theories suggest there are certain innate drives in human beings. Two such drives posited by Freud are the pleasure principle and the reality principle, which lead us to seek pleasurable satisfaction or protective safety respectively. These are sometimes in conflict, since pursuing pleasure can be dangerous. We have to decide which principle is more important to follow and how much risk we should take in following our desires. Psychoanalysis also suggests that humans go through patterns and stages of development as they grow up, develop, and mature. Negotiating these stages, it argues, is crucial to our health and growth. The most well-known stage is that of the Oedipus complex. It is held that at this stage male children negotiate their antagonism towards their father and their desire for their mother. Stories are seen as places where these drives and stages of development are played out in various ways, sometimes successfully, sometimes with tragic consequences. Oedipus and Hamlet are the two most famous literary examples, but many contemporary media narratives, such as *Blue Velvet*, can also be seen in this way. The application of psychoanalytic theory, mainly deriving from Freud and the subsequent work of Jacques Lacan, to media studies is too complex to pursue here, but there is a body of reading and research you can follow up (Kaplan 1990; Lapsley and Westlake 1989, ch. 3; Leader and Groves 1995).

READING AS A MYSTICAL EXPERIENCE

We have given a brief summary of some approaches to what happens when people view fiction. We want to conclude by reflecting on what the viewing experience is like and how this compares to real, everyday experiences. My brother has asked me at times why I watch so many films, and he suggests that part of me is missing out on real life. His comments suggest that I am having surrogate experiences through these films rather than actually doing the things myself, as though reading about or watching real life is not the same as actually living it. Similarly, I am surprised at how many people watch sports events rather than participating in the sports themselves—it seems to make sense to say that participation is more pleasurable than observation. Part of me agrees with my brother, and as I get older it seems more important to experience many things for myself rather than read about or watch them.

But the experience of viewing fictions is not just surrogate experience. We suggest that it is itself an intense form of human experience, a part of real life that yields profound pleasures. These pleasures can be compared to those found in meditation, ritual, and mysticism. The origins of fiction and stories lie in myths and religious rites; stories serve direct spiritual ends. The 'fiction experience' invites us into an altered state of consciousness, a different way of being. This can be more intense than many real-life experiences. It may be deeply spiritual, filling us with wonder and revelation, thereby helping us in our everyday lives; it gives space and time for contemplation, allowing us to put our lives in perspective; and it may help to re-create us, as suggested by the word 'recreation'. Just as our dreams are sometimes more intense than our daily experiences, so being immersed in fictions can stimulate our hearts, minds, and emotions in extraordinarily fulfilling ways. While the fiction experience seems to be about external events—it comprises stories happening to other people—it actually allows us to go on an inward journey. As we consume fictions, we leave behind the mundane practicalities of everyday life to travel deep into the heart of ourselves, discovering our core beliefs, feelings, and desires.

These thoughts are a good introduction to the work of Joseph Campbell, who shows how fictions and real life can be wonderfully intertwined.

NARRATIVE STRUCTURE AND MYTH: JOSEPH CAMPBELL AND CARL JUNG

The final approach to narrative structure that we will explore is the work of Joseph Campbell, who describes general, recurring patterns in all forms of story-telling. Campbell is not the only one to have sought out such general patterns. The structuralist work of Vladimir Propp, who analysed the common characteristics of fairy tales is most well-known in media studies (Propp 1975; Turner 1993, pp. 68–71). He looked at fairy tales and concluded that a recurrent pattern involving set characters and plot actions forms the basis of all fairy tales.

According to Propp, the characters are the villain, the donor (the provider), the helper, the princess (or the person who is being sought), the princess's father, the dispatcher, the hero (or the victim), and the false hero. Film narratives have been subjected to Propp's analysis and have revealed similar set characters. For example, the main characters in *Star Wars* fit Propp's character types neatly:

the villain	Darth Vader
the donor	Ben Kenobi
the helper	Han Solo
the princess	Princess Leah
the dispatcher	R2D2
the hero	Luke Skywalker
the false hero	Darth Vader (Turner 1988, p. 71).

Propp's structure comprises six stages:
1 preparation
2 complication
3 transference
4 struggle
5 return
6 recognition.

Such a structure can be fruitfully applied to many film texts. However, Propp's work does not go much beyond discovering and describing these patterns. Campbell's approach is similar in that he too looks for structural patterns in myths, fairy tales, and stories from all over the world, but he progresses beyond this to explain what this structure means for human beings. In this way, his work has a similar aim to the work of Lévi-Strauss. Campbell, Jung, and Lévi-Strauss all aimed to understand the role and meanings of myths and stories in human society.

Campbell gives a very different view of the media to the approaches that we have presented so far. Much of our analysis has stressed the social construction of representations. We have presented methods for deconstructing texts, a process that makes us aware of the ideological and social meanings inscribed in them and reveals that the media are produced by dominant social groups in such a way as to reproduce the dominant values of society. This deconstructive approach is a critical one that gives you tools to challenge the media.

Campbell, however, draws on a quite different theoretical framework. In particular, his theories are greatly influenced by the work of the psychologist Carl Jung, and his aim is much more a celebration of media texts than a warning critique. He is not concerned with issues of social construction or the politics of representation.

Whereas we stress the social construction of reality, Campbell stresses the universal aspects of human nature and societies. He suggest that we can see universal human patterns and truths in myths, legends, and religious beliefs. Campbell's work is accessible in his books, in texts that comment on his work, and in video interviews

(Campbell 1972, 1988a, 1988b, 1991; Golden 1992). Here is a brief summary of the central aspects of his work.

Joseph Campbell and the hero's journey

Campbell's work explores myths, legends, and religious beliefs found throughout the world in different societies. He shows that there are essential similarities to be found in all these stories and that these stories can be seen as a blueprint showing us how to act in the world to find enlightenment, fulfilment, and achieve our human potential. He argues that they have a dominant pattern or structure.

This structure follows what he calls the hero's journey. It involves a hero who goes through tests, struggles, and problems on the way to achieving his/her goal. This is similar to Propp's analysis, but whereas Propp merely notes the fact that there is such a structure (and in his later work, explores the socio-historical context in which the stories arose), Campbell suggests that this structure provides a framework whereby stories can teach us how to act as humans if we are to realise our heroic potential. According to Campbell, we are all (men and women) heroes with the potential to find our heroic fulfilment. In order to do this, we have to undertake a hero's journey by 'following our bliss'. This idea of 'following your bliss' is crucial to Campbell's work. He suggests that each of us can find something that truly moves and touches us. Our culture should encourage people to find this and then to follow it. Only by following our bliss can we realise our potential, our happiness. He also notes that many pressures of contemporary society, such as the exigencies of surviving in particular economic systems and pressures on us to conform socially, do not encourage this. We are thus faced with the challenge of deciding whether to do what society pressures us to do or following our own spirit. He argues that earlier, so-called 'primitive' societies were more able to encourage people to do this than modern industrial, secular, capitalist societies, which have lost this capacity.

Campbell is interested in the power of dreams. What does the phrase 'follow your bliss' mean to you? As a way of getting in touch with your unconscious (your bliss), do the following exercise. Just before you go to bed write the question 'What is my bliss?' on a blank sheet of paper 30–50 times, and then place the paper under your pillow. Having the question fresh in your thoughts before you sleep may make it seep into your unconscious, and hopefully the answer will manifest itself in your dreams of that night. Have a pen and paper beside you so that as soon as you wake up, you can write down your dreams. In the morning, once you have written down your dreams, read over what you have written and ask yourself whether your dreams show you what your bliss is. How much have you followed your bliss in your life?

Campbell's theories on dreams can be described as universal for two reasons (as can Jung's theories of the collective unconscious):

1 They posit similarities across different cultures and their myths and religions, such that Aboriginal, Christian, and Islamic cultures, for example, are said to share the same basic stories.
2 People's dreams, as uncovered through Freudian and Jungian psychoanalysis, seem to reflect these same universal stories, icons, and images, but at an individual level. Consequently, Campbell holds that a developmental path is built into the human

psyche like a genetic blueprint. This links all humans across societies, and as something we have in common it has the potential to bring us together. His theories are based on the collection of a body of supportive evidence from around the world.

The stages of the hero's journey outlined by Campbell in his book *The Hero with a Thousand Faces* (Campbell 1972, pp. ix–x) are:

1 departure
the call to adventure
refusal of the call
supernatural aid
the crossing of the first threshold
the belly of the whale
2 initiation
the road of trials
the meeting with the goddess
woman as the temptress
atonement with the father
apotheosis
the ultimate boon
3 return
refusal of the return
the magic flight
rescue from without
the crossing of the return threshold
master of the two worlds
freedom to live.

In *The Hero with a Thousand Faces* he elaborates on each of these stages (which parallel Propp's work), finding examples of them in a multitude of stories. He suggests that, like ancient myths and stories, film and television narratives are our modern myths in that they include and illustrate these same heroic structures. According to Campbell, analysis of them will reveal the same truths about human nature, about heroism, and about the paths to enlightenment and maturity. This is graphically illustrated in films such as *Star Wars* (directed by George Lucas) and *The Matrix*.

Here is an extract of Campbell talking with Bill Moyers, an American television interviewer, about *Star Wars* and the hero's journey. He explains one aspect of the adventure, the belly of the whale, in some detail. This will give you an idea of how the whole pattern can be looked at in depth.

Moyers:	The first time I saw *Star Wars*, I thought 'This is a very old story in a very new costume'. The story of the young man called to adventure, the hero going out facing the trials and ordeals, and coming back after his victory with a boon for the community …
Campbell:	Certainly Lucas was using standard mythological figures. The old man as the adviser made me think of a Japanese sword master. I've known some of those people, and Ben Kenobi has a bit of their character.
Moyers:	What does the sword master do?

Campbell:	He is a total expert in swordsmanship. The Oriental cultivation of the martial arts goes beyond anything I've ever encountered in American gymnasiums. There is a psychological as well as a physiological technique that go together there. This character in *Star Wars* has that quality.
Moyers:	There's something mythological, too, in that the hero is helped by a stranger who shows up and gives him some instrument …
Campbell:	He gives him not only a physical instrument but a psychological commitment and a psychological centre. The commitment goes past your mere intention system. You are one with the event.
Moyers:	My favourite scene was when they were in the garbage compactor, and the walls were closing in, and I thought, 'That's like the belly of the whale that swallowed Jonah'.
Campbell:	That's where they were, down in the belly of the whale.
Moyers:	What's the mythological significance of the belly?
Campbell:	The belly is the dark place where digestion takes place and new energy is created. The story of Jonah in the whale is an example of a mythic theme that is practically universal, of the hero going into a fish's belly and ultimately coming out again, transformed.
Moyers:	Why must the hero do that?
Campbell:	It's a descent into the dark. Psychologically, the whale represents the power of life locked in the unconscious. Metaphorically, water is the unconscious, and the creature in the water is the life or energy of the unconscious, which has overwhelmed the conscious personality, and must be disempowered, overcome and controlled.

In the first stage of this kind of adventure, the hero leaves the realm of the familiar, over which he has some measure of control, and comes to a threshold, let us say the edge of a lake or sea, where a monster of the abyss comes to meet him. There are then two possibilities. In a story of the Jonah type, the hero is swallowed and taken into the abyss to be later resurrected —a variant of the death-and-resurrection theme. The conscious personality here has come in touch with a charge of unconscious energy, which it is unable to handle and must now suffer all the trials and revelations of a terrifying night-sea journey, while learning how to come to terms with this power of the dark and emerge, at last, to a new way of life.

The other possibility is that the hero, on encountering the power of the dark, may overcome and kill it, as did Siegfried and St George when they killed the dragon. But as Siegfried learned, he must then taste the dragon blood, in order to take to himself something of that dragon power. When Siegfried has killed the dragon and tasted the blood, he hears the song of nature. He has transcended his humanity and reassociated himself with the powers of nature, which are the powers of our life, and from which our minds remove us.

You see, consciousness thinks it's running the shop. But it's a secondary organ of a total human being, and it must not put itself in control. It must submit and serve the humanity of the body. When it does put itself in control, you get a man like Darth Vader in *Star Wars*, the man who goes over to the consciously intentional side (Campbell 1988, pp. 178–81).

Star Wars and George Miller's *Mad Max* films are directly based on and inspired by Campbell's theories. The popular success of the films suggests that they resonate deeply with the beliefs and feelings of audiences. Originally, Campbell built his theories on analysis of pre-existing myths and stories. Now there has been an interesting reversal. Lucas and Miller know about Campbell's work and used it in constructing their stories. Script writers now learn and use Campbell as a basis for writing their stories (Vogler 1992).

Campbell has been criticised for his Jungian position and the way that his theories can be aligned with an ideology of individualism. The universalist aspects of his theories are seen by some as deriving from a Western perspective that fails to see and acknowledge the differences between cultures. The focus on the hero supports a typical American ideology of individual power rather than acknowledging the importance of society as a whole. I don't agree with these criticisms. I find Campbell's work insightful and inspiring; his ideas certainly connect with the ideas of many people today and interestingly we can see their presence in various advertising campaigns on television that celebrate ordinary people as 'heroes' or even in slogans such as Nike's 'Just do it'. We can see this as encouraging us to follow our bliss.

Whichever approach to media analysis you find most convincing, it is important to train yourself to look for patterns in media texts, whether they take the form of structural patterns (such as dialectical synthesis and cyclical narratives), generic codes and conventions, the director or auteur's signature, transcultural symbols and character functions, or universal fears, desires, and developmental phases.

Watch the scene near the beginning of The Matrix *when Morpheus offers Neo the choice to accept reality as he knows it, or to question it and be released from the matrix. How does this scene relate to Joseph Campbell's structure of the hero's journey?*

Exercise commentary

When Neo faces the choice between the red and the blue pill, between awakening to reality or remaining in the dream world in which his fate is technologically determined, he chooses to 'leave the realm of the familiar ... enter the dark place where new energy is created (the belly of the whale) and emerge, transformed'. After Neo chooses the red pill, he faces what can be interpreted as a rebirth (or even a resurrection), during which he emerges from a membrane like an amniotic sack and is separated from the umbilical-like cord that connects his vital energy to the matrix. He then travels down a narrow tunnel to emerge from an enclosed, watery space into the light. Do you think that the makers of *The Matrix* were familiar with Campbell's work and knowingly drew upon it as they structured the narrative, or do you think that variations of Neo's story are told over and over again in different media texts because they narrate the kind of awakening with which we all need to come to terms?

JUNGIAN CONCEPTS AND THE MEDIA

Since Jungian theory lies behind much of Campbell's work, it is useful to give some overview of key Jungian concepts. Jung's psychology is also illuminating in relation to understanding media texts. While Freud and other psychoanalytic approaches are often cited in media studies, Jung is not, which is one of the reasons I want to address his approach here. I will outline some key Jungian concepts and suggest ways they relate to narratives and the media (Jung 1978; Platania 1997).

Individuation

Jung argues that as each person grows older they go through a process of individuation. This is like a maturing of the soul or the psyche. He suggests that there are stages people go through in order to grow successfully. These stages involve the person confronting his or her 'shadow' side and his or her 'anima' or 'animus', both of which are difficult and testing processes. Successful individuation involves the person finding his or her 'real inner self' and fulfilment in life.

This description of individuation closely parallels the individual narrative progression that characters go through in stories—the processes of testing and change undergone by characters as they find their successful selves. Thus the growth and transformation of fictional characters reflect Jung's notion of 'individuation'. We can analyse narrative growth as an individuation process.

Archetypes

Jung describes archetypes as genetic blueprints for ideal types of behaviour. These archetypes, transmitted from generation to generation, help us to act in appropriate ways in various circumstances. He argues that archetypal figures and behaviours are inscribed in mythological figures, who are guides teaching us to act in certain ways. The hero who journeys successfully through his or her tests and trials is the most obvious archetype. The systems of gods and goddesses found in many cultures, such as the Greek and Roman gods, point us to different facets of behaviour, different archetypes. As Jean Shinoda Bolen puts it, 'Gods and Goddesses represent different qualities in the human psyche' (Bolen 1989, p. x). Seeing how such fictional characters act in various situations can teach us how we can reach our best potential.

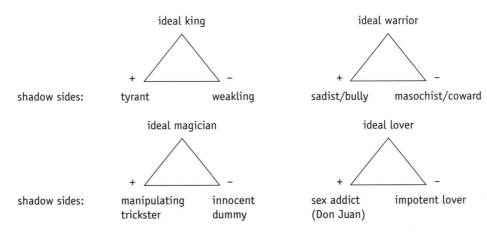

Figure 3.11 Archetypes of masculinity
Source: adapted from Moore and Gillette 1991, pp. 16–17

Moore and Gillette (1991) use this pattern in their exploration of contemporary masculine behaviour and images of masculinity. They focus on four archetypes: the king, the warrior, the magician, and the lover (equivalent to the Greek gods, Zeus, Ares, Hermes, and Dionysius). Each of these represents some aspect of masculinity that can be explored and developed by individual men as they grow to their maturity. A key point is that these different qualities can be successfully realised or not: too little or too much of a particular aspect throws things out of balance, leading to the shadow sides of the archetype. Narratives built on resolving conflicts are an ideal ground for exploring these archetypes and their positive and shadow aspects. What follows is a brief summary of what these four archetypes represent, with examples of fictional characters and real people to illustrate both the ideal and the shadow side. The following discussion of masculine archetypes is based on the work of Moore and Gillette (1991).

The king

The archetype of the king provides what Moore and Gillette refer to as 'father energy'. The king provides order through laws; he brings fertility and blessings; and he holds the key to peace, calm, and order. The shadow sides of the king figure are the kings whose performance of these functions becomes obsessive (the tyrant) and those who fail resoundingly at all of them (the weakling).

King Arthur is an obvious positive king figure, but it is easier to think of shadow kings—Darth Vader, Citizen Kane, Harvey Keitel in the film *The Bad Lieutenant*, and the head teacher (not the character played by Robin Williams) in the film *Dead Poets' Society* are all tyrants. Homer Simpson of the television series *The Simpsons* shifts between the weakling—selfishly indulging himself, lacking power and authority, and easily manipulated by Bart, Lisa, and Marge, who are all cleverer than him—and the tyrant (in that he holds ultimate power in the household and abuses this by mistreating Marge and the kids). But occasionally he is the good father, protecting, helping, and loving his wife and children. Male news readers and current-affairs presenters such as Ray Martin (presenter of a national Australian current affairs show) and John Humphries (his BBC equivalent) often try to adopt the position of fair adjudicator (the balanced, good father). Gandhi is a figure who has been seen (and presented on film) as an ideal king archetype, while figures such as Hitler, Pol Pot, and Stalin are obviously shadow kings.

The warrior

The warrior has aggressive energy and clarity of thought and action; he knows what he wants and how to get it; he is trained, like a samurai, in the way of the warrior; he has 'transpersonal commitment' (he is committed to an ideal or code that takes precedence over his commitment to any specific individual in his life); and he is emotionally distant. The shadow sides of the warrior figure are the bully (or sadist) and the coward (or masochist).

This is one of the central archetypes found in media narratives and it is perhaps the most problematic, since it seems to teach boys to be aggressive as a way of dealing with the world. Many stories are about men needing to fight to achieve their aims. They have the moral 'might is right'. Yet while this archetype encourages fighting and the negation of emotions (so that the warrior can fight successfully), the fact that the warrior has 'transpersonal commitment' can be seen as a positive attribute because he fights for causes for the good of others (for humanity) rather than for himself or for those with whom he is personally connected (which could lead to tyranny or bias). Think, for instance, of the difference between Maximus and Commodus in Ridley Scott's film *Gladiator*: one warrior is motivated by transpersonal commitment and the other by dysfunctional emotions and greed. The need to be emotionally distant is also not so problematic if we keep in mind that this emotional distance is only needed for a specific purpose—to fight successfully—and that after this purpose has been achieved the warrior can let his emotions in. King Arthur's knights of the round table in the Arthurian legends exhibit these characteristics. Good warriors are also found in the television series *Hercules* and *Xena: Warrior Princess* (the latter shows that despite the fact that Moore and Gillette use them to analyse male behaviour, archetypes, in general, are not gender exclusive—women can be warriors too). The young boys in the film *Stand by Me* are warriors (demonstrating that archetypes are also not limited to adults) as are a host of male stars (Clint Eastwood, Arnold Schwarzenegger, Mel Gibson, Bruce Willis, Bruce Lee, Brandon Lee, and so on). Luke Skywalker and Han Solo in *Star Wars* are warriors fighting for good causes. Heroes are the good warriors, villains are the bad warriors. *Ghost Dog: Way of the Samurai* (Jim Jarmusch, 1999) is a film that explores Japanese warrior codes, placing them in a contemporary American situation with a Black hero who also mentors a young White girl. It thus uses the theme of warrior behaviour to explore race and gender issues.

Perhaps the most interesting warrior stories are those that explore characters whose virtue is ambiguous and who are struggling with different aspects of the warrior archetype. Robert de Niro, in films such as *Raging Bull*, often portrays both the positive and negative aspects of the warrior. The film *Face/Off*, which is mentioned earlier (p. 153) in relation to dialectical synthesis and the process of mutual incorporation that often takes place to resolve a binary opposition, can also be seen as an interesting examination of the struggle between different aspects of the warrior. Male heroes in the films of the directors Quentin Tarantino and John Woo are characters exploring the codes of the warrior and trying to find out how to live successfully, and the tragic endings they meet suggest how difficult it is for men to find 'the way' in contemporary society. Real figures such as Ned Kelly and the Anzac soldiers are good warrior figures, and this ideal type is built into the Australian figure of 'the Aussie battler'.

The magician

The magician has shamanic energy and he is the master of technology, magic, and science. He is the teacher and initiator; the seer and prophet; knower of secret knowledge; the Healer who understands and regulates internal energies. The magician is often engaged in reflection rather than action. The shadow sides of the figure of the magician are the bad wizard, the trickster, and the dummy.

Morpheus in *The Matrix*, Merlin the Magician and Prospero from Shakespeare's *The Tempest* are obvious examples. Robin Williams has played various magician figures, notably the teacher in *Dead Poets' Society* and the therapist in *Good Will Hunting*. In both of these it is his job to heal, liberate, and mentor the young men who are struggling to grow into adulthood, so that they can find their own warrior and king

ONLY A COLORBOND FENCE WILL LOOK AS GOOD IN TEN YEARS' TIME AS THE DAY IT WAS PUT UP.

A COLORBOND* steel fence won't rot, warp, flake, peel or be eaten by termites. Which makes it reassuredly maintenance free: a simple hose-down will do. And because it's easy to install, you can do-it-yourself if you like. For more information and the name of your local contractor, call 008 022 999. **BHP** Colorbond

Plate 1   Advertisement for Colorbond fencing

ONLY ONE GIVES YOU TOTALLY GUILT-FREE SATISFACTION.

Hot, tasty and fibre-enriched. (No, we're not talking about the guy.) Made with the finest natural ingredients and with less than 54 calories a cup, Continental Slim-a-Soup is the treat you can enjoy every day. And because size really does matter, there's a generous four tasty sachets inside every pack.

Plate 2   Advertisement for Continental soup

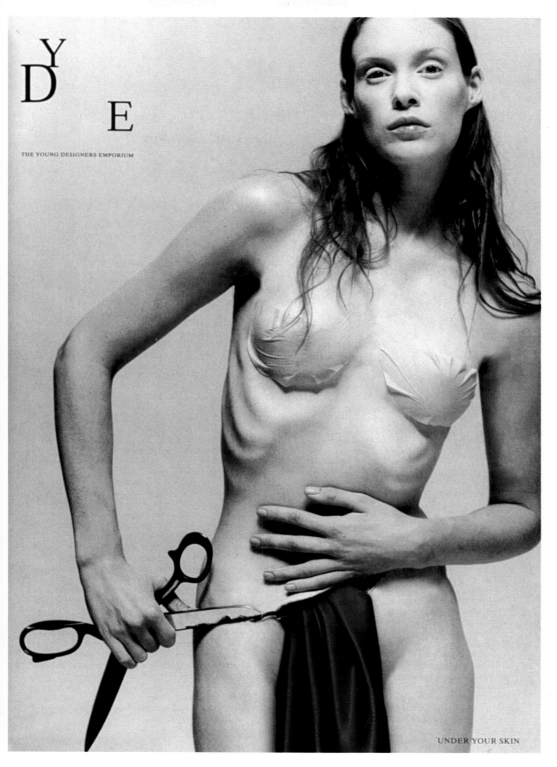

Plate 3 Advertisement for South African clothing company Young Designers Emporium

Plate 4 Advertisement for Levi's jeans

Plate 5 Advertisement for Ella Baché sunscreen (no. 1)

Plate 6 Advertisement for Ella Baché sunscreen (no. 2)

Plate 7 Gordon Bennett's *Altered Body Print (Shadow Figure Howling at the Moon)*

Plate 8 Advertisement for CAT boots

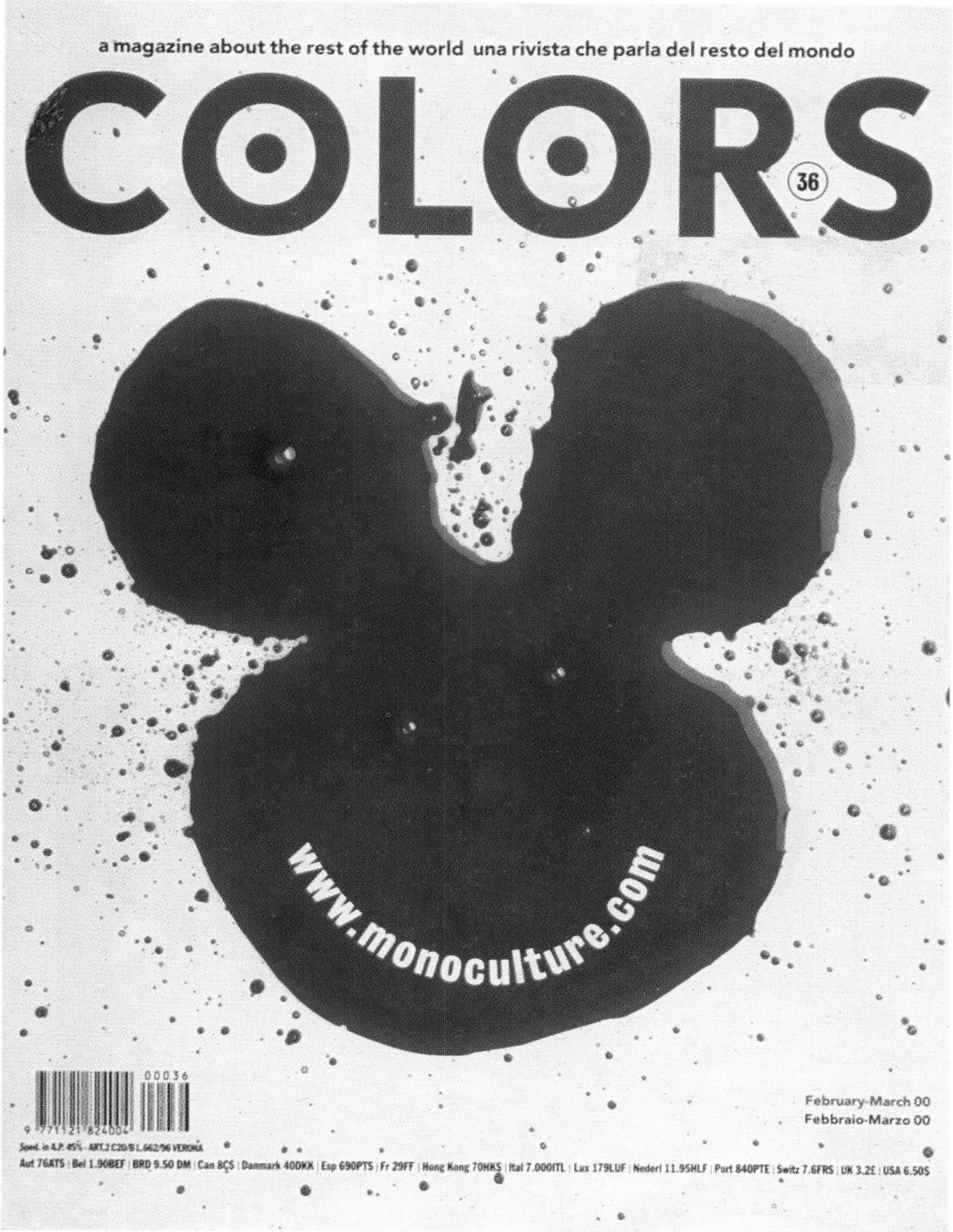

Plate 9 Cover of *Colors*—Benetton magazine

Plate 10   Banned advertisement for Chiko roll

Plate 11   Accepted advertisement for Chiko roll

qualities. Ben Kenobi is such a mentor figure for Luke Skywalker. *The Wizard of Oz* is a good example of a magician who changes from bad to good, from, in Moore and Gillette's terms, manipulating trickster to ideal magician. Bad magicians are found in the mad-scientist figures of science-fiction films: for example, Dr Jekyll. People such as Albert Einstein, Freud, even Jung himself can be seen as magician types.

The lover

The lover has the following attributes: passionate energy, sensual appetite, empathy, connection to others, compassion, spiritual energy, and aesthetic vision. The lover wants to touch and be touched, seeks oneness and unity, and seeks to break down boundaries between people. Psychics and artists are often lover figures. The shadow sides are the addicted lover, the sex addict, and the impotent lover.

A number of film stars play out various aspects of the lover: Leonardo di Caprio, Hugh Grant, Jack Nicholson, Woody Allen, Brad Pitt, Johnny Depp, and Richard Gere all specialise in romantic roles or roles that centre on relationships between men and women. These roles permit exploration of the 'feminine' side of men: openness, emotional honesty, caring, and so on. They also provide examples of loving behaviour: the successful lover acts out of openness, compassion, and connection with other people. But too little or too much of a particular pattern of behaviour throws things out of balance. The lover can become a Don Juan figure, overly self-indulgent and fixated on sensuality and seduction. The lover can become so concerned with 'winning' women over that he becomes cold, cut off from his feelings, and unable to connect lovingly. Stories of love are about negotiating these different patterns. In *Star Wars* Luke Skywalker is sometimes the warrior, sometimes the lover. He needs to fit into these archetypes at appropriate moments.

These are just four archetypes, but there are many others. I have explored only masculine ones, but I will address this imbalance below (pp. 182–3). Archetypes show us that there are many spheres of action we can be involved in at different times, many possible personas we can adopt in different situations. Media heroes and villains are like contemporary archetypal figures. Jungian analysis of media stories sees the characters acting out archetypal patterns of behaviour.

The shadow and projection

Jung's concept of the shadow can best be understood in conjunction with the idea of projection. The shadow side is our dark, negative side. It includes aspects of ourself that we have denied and repressed, that exist only in our unconscious and that we tend to project negatively on to others. Negative projection occurs when we see our dark qualities in other people. Individuation involves recognising our shadow self and embracing it in order to integrate it into our personality rather than projecting it on to others. Jung explains projection as follows:

> Projection is an unconscious, automatic process whereby a content that is unconscious to the subject transfers itself to an object, so that it seems to belong to that object. The projection ceases the moment it becomes conscious, that is to say when it is seen as belonging to the subject (Jung 1978, p. 121).

Societies often find social groups who become scapegoats. Jews, non-Whites, and homosexuals have been subject to discrimination from Christian, White, heterosexist societies. These minority groups are held to engage in antisocial forms of behaviour and be the cause of social problems. A Jungian analysis sees that the 'bad' tendencies that members of these minorities are accused of—greed, uncleanliness, homosexual desires, and so on—are repressed and denied aspects of those who accuse them of such sins (Christian, White, heterosexuals). Jung argues that people need to look into their own darkness rather than project it on to others, and in this sense they are involved in the process of becoming conscious of their own unconsciousness.

Figure 3.12 Cartoon illustrating the consequences of denial of our shadow sides
Source: Ron Pyatt, 1990

"One does not become enlightened by imagining figures of light, but by making the darkness conscious." C.G.JUNG.

Jung argues that we need to look at the negative aspects in ourselves in order to reach any kind of maturity. Ron Pyatt's cartoon (Figure 3.12) suggests that denial of our shadow side can be dangerous for ourselves as well as others; if we ignore our shadow it will become more monstrous and threaten to destroy us. It needs to be acknowledged, not ignored.

Work about the notions of shadow selves and projection is very useful in exploring film and television narratives. Robin Robertson, commenting on the shadow figure in dreams says: 'Shadow figures usually appear first as non-human: aliens from another planet, vampires, zombies, half-animal/half-human creatures, etc. They confront us with their unwanted, though unavoidable, presence' (Robertson 1992, p. 113).

This is the language of many films. Genres such as film noir, horror, and science fiction deal explicitly with the shadow and monstrous aspects of ourselves. In Jungian terms, they are explorations of these dark aspects of ourselves. (Films are also literally projections of light so the two concepts are neatly linked.) Horror films can express the shadow side of our unconscious. Exploration and analysis that employ a Jungian awareness of what the shadow represents allow us to understand films as ways of dealing with our shadow selves. This can help us to own and integrate our shadow selves as part of ourselves, instead of projecting them on to others. In this way we can begin to defuse the dangerous and destructive potential of our shadow selves. The film *Fight Club* explores the idea of the alter-ego. The shadow side of the main character (played by Edward Norton) is represented in the form of Brad Pitt's character, Tyler Durden. The film's resolution comes when in some sense Norton is able to become conscious of his shadow side and thus integrate it. (*Fight Club* is also interesting as a film that seems to anticipate some of the events of 11 September 2001. It could be seen as expressing the collective unconscious.) The final coupling with the Helena Bonham-Carter character could also be seen as an integration of Norton's anima figure (see below, p. 182).

This notion of projection works on several levels. In addition to analysing how the characters in a story project aspects of themselves outwards and perceive the world through that distorted lens of awareness, we can also argue that media texts are projections of different aspects of the society that produces the text. Similarly, it can be argued that the characters with which we identify or to whom we relate are projections of certain aspects of ourselves (villains can often be read as projections of negative aspects of society, of the creators of the story, or of the interpreters of the story).

Much contemporary Western film and television focuses on the shadow side of humanity. Many film and television texts look at crime and warfare, and at sexual violence. A Jungian perspective would see these films as a reflection of the way contemporary society is living out its shadow side and as constituting a demand that we fully face this shadow. A Jungian appreciation of the level of violence and sexuality in contemporary films is a completely different approach to that of censorship. It links with Freud's idea of 'the return of the repressed', another psychoanalytic term that is relevant to censorship issues. Freud argued that anything that is repressed doesn't disappear or go away. On the contrary, it will return, but in a more disturbing or violent form. This is the basis for Robin Wood's readings of horror films as explorations of the 'return of the repressed' (Wood 1986). Repressed desire or sexuality, for example (a common enough feature of Western society!) may return in some more violent form.

In the film *American History X* the protagonist, Derek, has violent, criminal impulses that he does not acknowledge, understand, or own up to. Instead he projects his hatred and fear of this disturbing, poorly understood part of himself outward on to others. He sees non-Whites as violent criminals and he hates and fears them. Only after facing and taking responsibility for his own violence and criminality and developing an understanding of the traumatic circumstances in which it arose, is Derek able to see others as individuals and judge them on their own merits without projecting his fear, rage, and prejudice outwards on to them. In seeing himself clearly, he becomes able to see others as they really are, rather than perceiving them as the sum of his projections.

The anima and animus

The above concepts (individuation, archetypes, the shadow, and projection) are helpful for analysing narratives, but the major criticism of Jung's theories is that his system uses a male-dominated, heterosexist, and essentialist framework. Essentialist theories are theories that hold that people are defined by their biology. Jungian theory is called essentialist because the biological sex of people (whether they are men or women) is said to define who they are: it determines their characteristics (masculine or feminine) and hence their social roles (see p. 241).

Jung deals with gender issues through his concept of the anima/animus. These terms are used to describe the feminine (anima) or masculine (animus) soul or spirit that we each possess. Men have an anima, women an animus. Everybody's unconscious contains their opposite gender aspect. In Jung's model of psychic development, the stage that continues the process of individuation after incorporation of the shadow involves men discovering their anima, their inner-feminine, and women discovering their animus, their inner-masculine. Jung notes that this process tends to take place after middle age. This contrasts with the process that occurs before middle age, during which time men and women seek their opposite and absent gender attributes outside themselves in a complementary partner. After middle age men and women begin to seek these attributes within themselves.

The insistence on the uniting of masculine and feminine elements can be seen as prescriptively heterosexist in that it is based on essential differences between men and women. It is true that Jung posits masculine and feminine attributes, but:

- These are complementary, not antagonistic, and union between the two is desirable—they balance each other and one without the other would constitute an imbalance. Indeed this is what the process of integrating the anima/animus is about.
- More importantly, men and women have both masculine and feminine attributes within themselves, an internal masculine or feminine side. Thus men can be very feminine and women can be very masculine. Consequently, the balancing of masculine and feminine is not about union with another person (heterosexual coupling) but an internal balance that is achieved by individuals. If we consider once again film and television's continual focus on 'making couples' at the end of narratives we can consider this in Jungian terms as symbolic of the internal union of one individual's masculine and feminine. This relates also to the resolution of opposites (see p. 150).
- These characteristics are thus not gender exclusive; it could be argued that labelling them as 'masculine' or 'feminine' is simply a system and that this does not necessarily link them to real men and women.

A further criticism against archetypes is that they favour male types. However, it is worth noting that these types are also not exclusively for men. Jean Shinoda Bolen, exploring the notion of god and goddess archetypes, writes, 'The pantheon of Greek deities together, male and female, *exist as archetypes in us all*, although the gods are usually the strongest and most influential determinants of a man's personality, as the goddesses are for women' [my emphasis] (Bolen 1989). Bolen is arguing that while male and female archetypes are most strongly linked to their same sex, all the archetypes exist in both men and women. So women have their kingly and warrior archetypes for exploration, just as men have their feminine archetypal qualities of nurturing and caring.

Using the idea of the anima/animus may reveal interesting aspects of the media. Most media representations are male projections produced by men for men, and many of these focus on representations of women and the feminine. If we accept Jung's position, it would seem that representations of, for example, Marilyn Monroe—who seems to be the essence of femininity and the antithesis of masculinity—are actually representations of aspects of the male psyche, outward projections of the inner-feminine. Individuation may entail men accepting these feminine characteristics as part of themselves. This is clearly a step forward from thinking of women as 'the other', as always in opposition to masculinity. Media analysis can ask men to be self-reflexive when they look at representations of women, to see these representations as projections of aspects of themselves, and to develop the question of how they deal with their inner-feminine. Similarly, media analysis can involve asking women to be self-reflexive when they view representations of men. However, the former may be more important today, since it will help deconstruct forms of masculinity that predominate in the current patriarchal system.

An important part of critical thinking is to become aware of the premises or assumptions that underpin different approaches. In Jung's model of the psyche, we might note that it is assumed that a form of heterosexual complementarity is the natural, healthy state towards which we all progress. For example, an individual with predominantly masculine traits will seek to balance that out over the course of a lifetime, first by seeking a feminine partner (not necessarily a female), then by developing the anima within themselves.

Finally, it is worth noting that Jung himself recognised the negation of the feminine within patriarchy, the over-valuing of the masculine. But he also saw as positive the emergence of the feminine archetype in the cult around the Virgin Mary, which evolved out of the Catholic Church, an institution that has been central to patriarchy. The work of the women's movement and of gay and lesbian groups, and the shifting patterns of contemporary male/female roles and representations, can be seen as part of the re-emergence of the feminine. Armed with the insights of theories of anima/animus, we are able to see this not as a battle against masculinity (although it is part of the battle against patriarchy), but as part of the integration of masculine and feminine, both externally, in terms of equality between the sexes, and internally in the psyches of men and women.

Kay Turner has researched the dreams that women have about the singer and actress Madonna. Turner cites psychologist Karen Signell: 'Signell suggests that women are currently showing new archetypes in their dreams. Signell finds that one such archetype is the sisterly companion, who serves as a helper from the unconscious' (Turner 1993, p. 15). Turner sees Madonna as filling this sisterly archetypal role for women.

Reconciling/balancing opposites, and binary oppositions

One of Jung's fundamental ideas about the way human nature operates is to argue that we all contain opposing qualities, drives or desires, for example the opposition between extravert and introvert tendencies. He suggests that opposite characteristics may be found in a person's conscious and unconscious attitudes, often represented in the differences between persona and shadow. The Dr Jekyll/ Mr Hyde duo—the good doctor versus the evil monster—perfectly illustrates this idea of opposites, whereby one set of character traits are hidden or denied. A central part of the process of individuation and psychic growth is becoming conscious of these oppositions and then beginning to reconcile or balance them. So, for example, a very mild-mannered person may have dreams of violence and anger and gradually begin to allow this more dynamic energy to become part of their conscious personality and life.

The Jungian Daryl Sharp put it as follows:

> The conscious mind is on top, the shadow underneath, and just as high always longs for low and hot for cold, so all consciousness, perhaps without being aware of it, seeks its unconscious opposite, lacking which it is doomed to stagnation, congestion and ossification. Life is born only of the spark of opposites (Sharp 1996, p. 32).

Joseph Campbell suggests that 'We always think in terms of opposites. But God, the ultimate, is beyond the pairs of opposites, that is all there is to it'. And when asked why we think in terms of opposites he says 'because we can't think otherwise ... That's the nature of our experience of reality. [Man–woman, life–death, good–evil] I and you, this and that, true and untrue—every one of them has its opposite. But mythology suggests that behind that duality there is a singularity over which this plays like a shadow game' (Campbell 1988a, p. 49). So Campbell sees the final resolution or balancing of opposites as a desired transcendence of duality.

This concept of psychic opposites and the need to balance them neatly parallels the concept of binary oppositions in stories. The first aim of a story is to set up a conflict between opposing characters and sets of values and then to see if these can be reconciled and resolved by the end of the story. We can see this aspect of fiction and stories from a Jungian perspective: the narrative drive towards resolution is the necessary development of psychic growth as it seeks the reconciliation of opposites.

As a final comment on Jungian analysis of narratives it is useful to consider how Jung would analyse dreams. In a dream every aspect of the dream—characters, animals, objects, settings, and so on—can all be considered as different parts of the dreamer's own psyche or character. A Jungian interpretation would invite the dreamer to see these different things as potential parts of themselves and then to reflect on what this might mean for them. Clarissa Pinkola Estes, a critic who has applied Jungian theory to studying fairy tales, argues that: 'In Jungian psychology when we tell a fairy tale we consider that all the parts, all the characters in the fairytale, are one single individual psyche' (Pinkola Estes 1997). A similar approach may offer some insight into film and television fictions. It may be possible to see the film elements surrounding the protagonist—scenery, other characters, and so on—as aspects of the character requiring integration and reconciliation. Such an approach would illuminate the film *Fight Club*: the characters Tyler Durden and Marla can be seen as Edward Norton's shadow and anima figures. Similarly, the other characters and settings can be seen as various parts of his initially confused character. The whole film can then be read as a dream expressing the psychic conflicts that allow Norton to explore these issues. Such an approach can be applied to many other films—*The Matrix, Blade Runner, The Mask, Dead Poets' Society*—whereby we understand the stories as psychic representations of the inner turmoil of the main characters, turmoil that is worked through in the course of the narrative. As audiences we may also identify with those concerns of the main characters that parallel our psychic concerns: the successful resolution of these in the film helping us understand ourselves and our own psychic issues. This may be one of the central pleasures to be found in watching and reading stories.

CONCLUSION

Campbell's work is very different from the approaches to media analysis put forward in Parts 1, 2, and most of 3. All these approaches are useful in different ways. Whether they can be reconciled is an interesting question. The approaches discussed prior to the treatment of Campbell's work see human nature as a construction and argue that the ways in which the media make sense of the world act to socialise us and determine our views and beliefs. The other approach sees human nature as universally the same throughout culture and throughout history—an essentialist view—and the media are thought to be reflecting this essential nature. How would you reconcile these two approaches?

Campbell's framework, combined with analysis of narrative structure and binary oppositions, completes a range of methodologies for analysing media texts. Figure 3.13 sets these out in relation to *Thelma and Louise*. This should be a useful guide and checklist for any text analysis you are doing. It also points to the importance of ideological and hegemonic analysis, which is dealt with in Part 4.

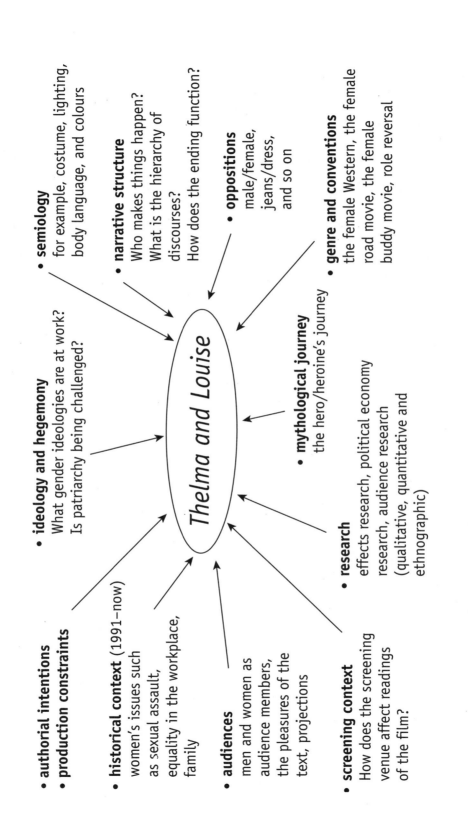

Figure 3.13 Media studies methodologies, as applied to *Thelma and Louise*

Source: Michael O'Shaughnessy, 1998

Part 4

MAKING SENSE:

IDEOLOGY, DISCOURSE, AND HEGEMONY

To me what makes the world tolerable is that it's going insane—

that's what keeps me going.

Errol Morris (film-maker) 1997, p. 54

OVERVIEW OF PART 4

Part 4 extends the process of textual analysis by exploring in detail the concepts of ideology, discourse, and hegemony. After reading this chapter, you should be able to use all three concepts in your analysis of the media, media texts, and the relationship between the media and society.

These three terms—'ideology', 'discourse', and 'hegemony'— relate to the work of three important theorists: Louis Althusser, Michel Foucault, and Antonio Gramsci. Like the work of these thinkers, these terms are all concerned with issues of social power and with the question of how power and knowledge are constructed and communicated in societies. The work of these theorists demonstrates that power is unequally distributed in society—that is, there are dominant and subordinate groups— and these three terms help to explain and describe how that power is maintained and reproduced. We choose to use the term 'ideology' as the main way of discussing issues of social power and the media, but there are many occasions on which you could substitute the term 'discourse', and there are also parallels between ideology and hegemony.

Media studies has sometimes been criticised for its use of complex jargon, and there is probably more jargon in this section than anywhere else in the book. In defence of this, it should be noted that society itself is complex and we need complex tools to understand it—complexity is not a valid reason for rejecting the jargon. We have found the concepts of ideology, discourse, and hegemony illuminating in relation to understanding both media and society. Our aim is to try and make the terms easily understandable so that you too can benefit from their insights.

12 Defining Discourse and Ideology

The terms 'discourse' and 'ideology' have been enormously influential in the development of media and cultural studies. They are complex: they contain various possible meanings and can be interpreted in many ways. Alongside their use in the work of Foucault and Althusser, they have been the subject matter of numerous essays, articles, and books and have formed the theoretical basis for much media analysis. The more reading you do about these concepts, the better. We will give a brief definition of 'discourse' first, as used by Foucault, and then we will focus on 'ideology'.

DISCOURSE

You have already come across the term 'discourse' in this book in relation to language as demonstrated by John Fiske (p. 44), and in relation to narrative using Colin MacCabe's concepts of 'hierarchy of discourses' and 'dominant discourse' (pp. 135–7). Its simplest meaning is the articulation, voicing or putting forward of a point of view. This act of articulation is usually part of a conversation or exchange of ideas amongst several speakers or groups. Thus 'discourse' is a social process of constructing meaning. Note that discourses find expression in texts and other communicative practices as well as in speech. The term 'discourse' typically refers to the collective discussion or interplay of meanings and ideas circulating around a particular subject, incorporating these different modes of expression and instances of communication. Foucault's theory of discourse is that societies tend to bring together a range of voices, ideas, and beliefs into overall discourses that offer ways of understanding the world (Fiske 1987, pp. 14–15). Any society has a number of discourses by which it makes sense of the world. Foucault has used the notion of discourse to examine how societies understand and make sense of sexuality, madness, and criminality (Rabinow 1984; Foucault 1981; Fillingham 1995).

He argues that a range of ways of thinking (discourses) are brought together to make sense of these areas, and that these discourses can and do change over time. In relation to crime and criminality, for instance, he sees how medical, legal, religious, and moral discourses define criminality and criminals and suggest ways of dealing with them. Medical discourses define criminals in terms of being sick or healthy, and if they are deemed sick then they need curing and rehabilitation; religious and moral discourses define criminals in terms of being good or evil, deserving rewards or punishment; and legal discourses define criminals as a danger to other people and, being concerned with the preservation of other people's safety and property, decide what courses of action to take to prevent further crimes. Thus we can see three kinds of possible treatment for criminals, based on three discourses for understanding their actions: *rehabilitation* or cure for their sickness, *punishment* (which could take various forms) for their evil deeds, and some form of *restriction* (for example, the removal of limbs or imprisonment) to prevent future crimes.

You are probably aware that elements of all three of these discourses—medical, religious, and legal—are present in the way societies construct prisons and use imprisonment today. Prisons are simultaneously supposed to be instruments of rehabilitation, punishment, and crime prevention. You might ask which of these predominates in practice. For Foucault, discourses are always linked to what he calls 'disciplinary power' in that they are 'concerned with the regulation, surveillance, and government of, first, the human species or whole populations, and second, the individual and the body' (Hall 1994, p. 123). They are, in other words, the means of organising and transmitting social control.

Foucault suggests that at different historical moments these discourses cohere in different ways: religious and moral discourses used to be the dominant ways of understanding criminality. Now legal and medical discourses carry more weight. There is a continuous struggle between competing discourses, each of which attempts to instate itself as the overall discourse for making sense of criminality. Because this model understands that the dominant discourse changes over time, it incorporates the possibility of social change. This is the major difference between discourse theories and theories of ideology, which seem to suggest a much more fixed view of how society works.

The second major difference between discourse and ideology is that discourses tend to be modes of thought, speech, or expression whereas ideologies can also be *material* in the sense that they can be found in buildings or activities. For example, rosary beads and crucifixes are part of the ideology of Catholicism, but not part of the discourse of Catholicism, whereas Scorsese's films, in which these material objects frequently appear, are part of that discourse because film is a mode of expression. Discourses do, of course, result in material practices—the kind of prison that a society builds will depend on its discourse of crime and criminality—but discourses remain modes of thinking and speaking, modes of expression.

Think of films that explore incarceration such as The Green Mile, The Shawshank Redemption, Chopper, *or* Dead Man Walking. *What discourses surround the issue of imprisonment in each of these?*

Exercise commentary

In the film *Dead Man Walking*, Sean Penn plays a convicted criminal sentenced to death by lethal injection as a punishment for rape and murder. Susan Sarandon is cast as a nun who acts as his spiritual adviser and seeks to rehabilitate him and redeem his soul. In this film the religious discourse is linked to rehabilitation, the medical discourse is linked with administering the punishment, and the legal discourse is bound up with the restrictive aspects of prison policy and politics. Each of these discourses can be conceptualised as a set of discussions in which ideas linking medicine, law, and religion to prison are articulated and circulate in society. These ideas find expression in interpersonal conversations (such as those between

Sarandon and Penn's characters, and between audience members after they see the film), in mediated communication such as the film text itself, and in the written laws that condone or prohibit capital punishment.

IDEOLOGY

Let's start by giving two definitions. The first one is a 'common-sense' definition that you will be familiar with from newspapers, television news reports, and current affairs. But, for the reasons outlined below, it is not one that we adhere to.

1 The common-sense definition of ideology

Ideology is a set of deliberately formulated, coherent, rational, usually political ideas that is used as a way of defining and understanding how society can be organised.

When used in this way 'ideology' is usually being used pejoratively, to denigrate and put down the people whose ideas are being referred to. Such a use of the term assumes that ideologies are always in some sense inherently false and flawed because they are not realistic (that is, they are unattainable) or because they do not reflect reality. For example, it is common for people to describe the political philosophies and beliefs of a political party as the ideology of that party—liberal ideology, 'new labour' ideology, socialist ideology, fascist ideology, and so on. This can be person-alised into 'Howard ideology', 'Blairite ideology', 'Thatcherite ideology', and so on. These political, economic, and social beliefs are seen as flawed in that they don't fit with reality. In this context, describing someone as following an ideology suggests that their views are unrealistic, rigid, and dogmatic, that that person is always trying to make reality fit their ideological beliefs.

Because this definition is so widespread, it is likely that you will already have a negative view of what ideologies are. You probably see them as false, dogmatic, rigid idea systems that politicians attempt to impose on people. This definition is not help-ful for media studies because it dismisses ideologies without bothering to ask how they work. In contrast, the second definition provided below does not use the term pejoratively; it does not see ideological beliefs as false. Rather, it defines ideology in such a way that allows it to yield insights into how we and our society work.

2 A more useful definition of ideology

Ideology is a set of social values, ideas, beliefs, feelings, representations, and institutions by which people collectively make sense of the world they live in.

There are several things to say about this definition (by the way, it also functions as a serviceable definition of 'discourse'). The term 'ideology' relates to a body of knowledge and a set of texts and practices that are naturalised to the extent that they form a 'taken for granted' view about the way the world works.

What do we mean by 'making sense of the world'?

Every person has a set of values, beliefs, and feelings that make sense to them and enable them to function in the world (see the quotation from Errol Morris that opens this Part, p. 187). Whatever we do—whether it is donating money to a charity, angling for a promotion at work, inviting someone to go to a concert, or watching television—it not only has to make sense to us in some way but it also *enacts* the way that we make sense of our world. Our actions arise from our view of the world and they act out our values, beliefs, and feelings, fleshing out the fact that we believe it makes sense to help those less fortunate than ourselves, or to compete with others in order to become successful, or to initiate a relationship by 'going on a date' rather than by means of arranged marriage. Since the way we conduct our lives is an interconnected social practice, this stresses that people make sense of the world collectively. In all societies there are shared values, beliefs, and feelings that govern how people act and live together. Institutions such as schools and television contribute to this, since they provide forums for a wide range of individuals to receive the same message. If an ideology is to have a significant social impact, it must be shared and agreed upon by a large group of people. This is why the mass media are so important in communicating and reinforcing ideologies.

At times of stress and turmoil, our personal ideology may be challenged and may change, as we find that it no longer makes sense for us to carry on in the same way. If a loved one dies, or we have a child, or we lose our job, or get divorced, or a major disaster befalls our community, we may find it no longer makes sense to conduct our lives in the way we have been. At that point, our ideology is challenged. If we do change our behaviour, we will simply have found a new form of social action that once again makes sense for us; we will have found a new set of values, beliefs, and feelings, a new ideology.

Beliefs and feelings are important in ideologies

This second definition is similar to the first in that both suggest that ideologies are a set of ideas that explain how society works, that make sense of the world. But this second definition adds much more. It stresses that beliefs and feelings are important to any ideology. This takes us out of the realm of the purely rational and conscious. Whereas the first definition stresses deliberate rationality, the second definition suggests that people's ideologies are connected to their hearts as well as their heads and that these ideologies are not consciously thought out. It suggests that they operate at the level of what Louis Althusser called 'unconscious consciousness'.

This is a very useful concept. We perform many human actions without being conscious of our motives. We do not always think carefully about what we are doing; we act through learned habits. This is obvious in terms of motor skills, such as walking and driving a car, which are learned and which we do without thinking about what we are doing. But actions performed with unconscious motives don't operate just at this physical level of unconscious motor skills. Many of our social actions are imbued with beliefs, feelings, and values, and are performed with unconscious motives.

A couple of simple examples illustrate this. What happens when you and a person of the opposite sex approach a door together? Who goes through first? Does either of you hold the door for the other or invite the other to go first? Does either of you immediately go in front of the other? Watch other people and yourself in this situation. We suggest that normally you would do whatever you do without much conscious thought, but that behind the choices you make lies an ideology of gender relations. There are a number of different possibilities: first, the man holds the door open for the woman, who goes through; second, the man holds the door open for the woman, who then invites the man to go through; third, the man almost imperceptibly slows his pace, allowing the woman, who has maintained or quickened her pace, to arrive at and go through the door first; fourth, the woman holds the door open for the man; and so on.

The traditional method has women going first. Any sequence that produces this result fits into traditional ideology. The following are different interpretations of what this means in terms of gender relations: it shows male respect and deference for women and constitutes a recognition that women are superior; it shows men treating women as inferior and weak, as needing male help for this activity; it suggests that although women go first, men control the action through opening the door, thus demonstrating male power; men who open doors for women are sending women into environments first so that the women will ease the way socially for them, thus allaying male fears about their own social skills; the custom is related to medieval codes of chivalric behaviour.

Most of these views suggest that men control what happens. While these explanations allow for the possibility that women might take positive action in advancing towards the door first and might even enjoy being shown 'respect', they can still all be seen as sexist in that they accept the notion of male power. People wanting to challenge such behaviour might deliberately break the convention by having women wait for men to pass through first.

This may seem a trivial incident, yet it is an aspect of day-to-day gender relations. Our point is that in relation to many areas of life, people act at the level of unconscious consciousness; they do things without thinking about their motives. Yet their actions still imply an attitude to gender relations, an ideological position. The next time you come to a door with someone of the opposite sex you will be conscious of what is happening. This will illustrate to you the concept of the unconscious consciousness and will encourage you to reflect on what gender ideologies and relations are implicit in such actions. It may also make you wonder what to do next!

As a second example, consider how students occupy space in lecture theatres. I suggest that people choose where to sit in lecture theatres at the level of unconscious consciousness, and that certain patterns emerge that relate to gendered ideologies of space and education.

I observed students attending my lectures over a period of time and noticed that women tended to seat themselves in the following positions: near the front, next to one or two people, and in the middle of rows. In contrast, men tended to sit in the following positions: at the back, on their own, next to just one other person, and on the ends of rows. Why might these differences have existed and how do they relate to gendered ideologies of space and education?

Note first that the results might have been different had I been observing lectures given by a female lecturer. The gender of the lecturer may be an important variable in such a situation, alongside other factors such as how amusing, interesting, boring, or attractive the lecturer is. I think the following points apply. By sitting at the back men can see everything that is going on, thereby gaining overall knowledge of (and therefore power over) the situation. Sitting at the back also enables them to be distant from the authority figure (the teacher), such that they are less likely to be surveyed by the teacher and thus have more freedom to do what they want.

In these ways they are winning a space of freedom and autonomy within an authoritarian and controlling system. They are thus resisting power and authority. They are also conforming to typical male desires to have a degree of control over situations, possibly because men are often socialised to compete. They are using seating as a way of protecting themselves. By sitting at the front women can: learn better by being closer to the knowledge givers, be supportive of the teachers, be conformist and win points for being good.

In these contrasting patterns, we see men and women fitting in with learnt gender behaviour: boys are encouraged to be rebels, to challenge authority, and to work independently of it; girls are encouraged to see themselves as conformist, gregarious, helpful, and conventionally good. This good/bad opposition goes way back. Think of the following popular nursery rhyme that contrasts 'ideal' gender characteristics:

> Sugar and spice and all things nice, that's what little girls are made of.
> Slugs and snails and puppy dogs' tails, that's what little boys are made of.

Both girls and boys learn at an early age what is correct male/female behaviour and also what are correct male/female spaces. In order to avoid direct conflict and so as not to compromise their own gender identity, they will tend to avoid occupying the space of the other gender and will refrain from behaviour that fits the patterns expected of the opposite sex.

In relation to space, in terms of who sits close to others and who sits apart, I see that men often keep physical distance from other people. This is because they are protective of their independence and because they may be less tolerant of close physical contact than are women. Boys are normally given less physical affection than girls and they may associate touch more with sexuality and conflict (fighting) than with comfort and closeness. Women often find close physical contact easier, more comfortable, and less focused on sex. In addition, there is less of a sexual taboo on close same-sex female friendship than there is in relation to same-sex male friendship. Finally, the safety factor may encourage women to group together. Being isolated and on their own in public places may make them a target for sexual harassment; being together brings safety through numbers.

I am suggesting, through this example of gendered space in lecture theatres, that learnt behaviour, past experience, and sexual stereotyping form patterns that are internalised by people. Our choices about where to sit reflect aspects of our ideologies of education and space. The choices we make about where to sit will be made at an unconscious level, as part of our ideology, our way of making sense of the world.

Please note that the points I have made about male and female socialisation and ideologies do not apply to everyone. They are also not fixed for all time. Ideologies of masculinity and femininity are currently changing; younger generations may be more fluid in how they deal with educational and spatial ideologies. As an experiment, observe the 'spatial decisions' made by men and women in such spaces as theatres, cinemas, the street, public transport, and so on.

I also noted two other seating trends. First, mature students, whether men or women, tend to sit near the front. My reading of this is that they have come to university very motivated to learn and they want to get as much out of it as they can—consequently, they get close to the lecturers, where it is easier to hear and where they can feel more involved and, being closer in age, may also feel more equal to the lecturers. Second, many Asian male students also tend to sit close to the front. I understand this as reflecting an ideology that values education and conformity more than White Australian male culture and sees educational success as a relatively more important stage in social success.

The consequence of our living and behaving through unconscious consciousness is that certain patterns of behaviour become naturalised, defined as part of human nature, regarded as 'the way things are'. These behaviour patterns are not seen as ideological by those who practise them. Indeed they are not even thought about much. This relates back to our ideas about language and the social construction of reality (pp. 39–40): neither language nor social organisations are natural; both are constructed. However, both are often regarded by people as natural and normal. We have already suggested that you should think carefully whenever anyone suggests that the way humans act is normal or natural. If someone says to you that something is 'just human nature', look for the ideological implications in the action they are describing. Remember that the consequence of naturalising behaviour is to naturalise and thereby hide ideology. In this way ideology is capable of reinforcing existing power relations and social structures in a manner that inevitably works to the advantage of one group (the dominant group in that context), and disadvantages others by making them seem abnormal, different, or deviant.

Are we always in ideology?

Finally, in relation to the second definition, we can ask 'Are we always in ideology?' We can never fully escape the framework of our own perceptions of the world. Ideology is both constituted by and concealed in our world-view, and in language. Trying to see ideology and step outside it or look around it is like trying to see contact lenses when we are looking through them. As Levinas says, we see the world as we are, not as it is. We will always have a set of values, beliefs, and feelings that guide our behaviour, determining how we think, feel, and act. These may change over time, and you will probably be aware of changes you have gone through in your own life. But in losing one ideology or world-view, we replace it with another. This is not a bad or a good thing; it is just the way things are. Although you may think that some ideologies are better than others, ideology, as understood in our second definition, is not used judgmentally; it simply describes the state we live in.

13   *Where is Ideology Found?*

To try and make the concept easier to understand we can ask 'Where is ideology?' Can we see it? What examples will illustrate it? There are three places to look for and find ideologies:

1 in language, texts, and representations
2 in material institutions and in our methodologies and practices
3 in our heads and hearts (our subjectivities and our identities).

IDEOLOGIES IN LANGUAGE, TEXTS, AND REPRESENTATIONS

These ideological sites—language, texts, and representations—are the most significant for media studies concerned with ideologies. In our analysis of language, advertisements, and narratives (pp. 95–9), we mentioned ideological meanings. As media students, you should ask the following questions of any text you analyse: 'What are the values, beliefs, and feelings that inform the way this text makes sense of the world?'

Children's early readers: ideology at work

Look at children's early readers as an example. The books children use to learn to read are a fascinating repository of ideological meanings and are particularly interesting because they are one of the early media sources that socialise children. The Key Words Reading Scheme, better known as the Ladybird Peter and Jane books, is a readily accessible example. Try to locate copies of these books to look at. They were first published in 1964. The early editions now seem out of date and have been superseded by a new series, Learn to Play: Tom and Kate (first published 1990), but the Peter and Jane series was still being published in 1990 and may well be familiar to you. This series corresponds closely to the Happy Venture Readers series featuring Dick and Dora, first used in Australia in the early 1960s.

The Peter and Jane series

A close look at the illustrations and text from these books reveals a number of significant ideological aspects in relation to gender, class, and the family.

The first point to make is that these books present one family—Peter and Jane and their parents—as the ideal family. While this family is presented as the norm, as the natural state of a family, the representations of the family are imbued with a particular set of ideologies. The most obvious are its ideologies of class, ethnicity, and gender. Peter and Jane's family is the nuclear family: mum, dad, and kids. The home is middle-class and suburban. The illustrations show a detached home (which signifies middle-class in the United Kingdom) and a sizeable garden, and combined with the storylines, the series depicts a family with enough money to buy good toys and go on regular holidays. The family members are White (later editions of the series included some non-White characters as background characters).

The values of the children are conformist in relation to two institutions: the police and schools. In *Boys and Girls* (a title that seems interested in setting up difference and delineating acceptable behaviour for the two genders) the text reads: 'They go on to the school. Here it is, says Peter, here's the school. *Peter and Jane like the school*' (my emphasis). In *Things We Like* the text reads: 'Look, Jane, that is a Police car. It says POLICE on it. That is the Police Station. *I like the Police, says Peter. They help you. Yes, says Jane. The Police help you*' (my emphasis).

Without wishing to denigrate the institutions of the police and education, it is clear from the perspectives of class and ethnicity that the police and schools may have very different meanings for Aboriginal children, Black South Africans, Afro-Americans, or Black Britons living in inner-city areas. The police may not be seen so simply as 'good' but as agents of social control.

It is in the gender area that the stereotyped ideology is most apparent. It is significant that in these children's readers the boy is always older than the girl, thus validating male power through age. Jane also looks up to Peter. This is literally so in a number of illustrations that depict Jane in physically lower positions, often sitting rather than standing. This age hierarchy continues in the narrative, in which Peter is the main character. He is given more actions to do and Jane is often given a supportive role, praising and validating Peter's behaviour. He controls actions: 'Peter likes to play with toys. He plays with a toy station and a toy train. Jane says, Please can I play? Please can I play with you? Yes, says Peter. I have the train. You play with the station.' Peter gets to play with the most important (and mechanical) part of the toy while Jane plays with the more static background parts of the toy, although this does allow her to play with the toy people on the station rather than the machinery.

Jane also tends to serve Peter: 'I want a cake, please, says Peter. A cake for me, please, he says. Here you are, says Jane. Here are some cakes.' She acts as cheerleader for his football exploits: 'Peter has the red ball. He plays with the boys with the red ball. Jane looks on. That was good, Peter, says Jane. That was good.'

Both children are socialised into helping with domestic chores, encouraging ideals of pride in property and reinforcing the notion that good behaviour is rewarded. But these chores are clearly divided on the basis of gender: boys do work outside the house, while girls work inside. 'Here we are at home, says Daddy. Peter helps Daddy with the car, and Jane helps Mummy get the tea. Good girl, says Mummy to Jane. You are a good girl to help me like this.'

Jane is given more positive reinforcement for doing chores than Peter, and is thereby encouraged to take on the traditionally feminine role of doing domestic chores: Mother keeps telling her, not Peter, that she is good for helping. This suggests that women are encouraged to take on supportive and nurturing roles, while boys are encouraged to express themselves through play. The book depicts Mother talking more than Father, suggesting that she has the primary role in rearing the children, and possibly also suggesting that women talk more than men (who are held to be more inclined to do things). Mother is depicted in the home more than Father, who goes out more: 'Peter and Jane are in the car with Daddy. They like it in the car. Mummy is at home.'

All of these gendered differences are presented as normal, and thus ideologies of gender, class, and ethnicity are naturalised. Children do not necessarily internalise these values when they read the books, but if they do not they will not find themselves reflected in these stories. And children whose families are different from this normal, ideal family may perceive themselves as different, as not fitting within the norm. Children who are not White, middle-class, and living with happily married parents are not being addressed. Either you take on these values as normal, or there is no space for you in the narrative.

The Tom and Kate series

The more recent Tom and Kate series shows significant changes. But there is an interesting comment about language in the introduction, which includes an acknowledgment that the books use the pronoun 'he' to refer to boys and girls in general: 'To avoid the clumsy he/she, him/her, we have referred to the child as "he". All the books are of course equally suited to both boys and girls' (Murray 1990, p. i).

The stereotyped views in these children's readers are very obvious to us today (this is not a reason to dismiss them). It is often easier to see ideologies from a distance. To follow this up, look back at children's readers you grew up with and see what ideologies of class, ethnicity, and gender are embedded in them. Do the same with some current children's readers.

The education activist Paulo Freire showed how important the ideological content of readers can be when he was trying to increase literacy in South America. He argued that many peasants failed to learn to read because the subject matter of their readers—stories such as Peter and Jane—was too remote from their experience. They could not connect with these experiences, and they did not see themselves reflected in the stories. Freire instituted readers for illiterate adults with topics, situations, and people that related to their experiences: stories of farming and tractors, of everyday peasant life, and of social oppression and how to challenge this. Freire described his educational processes as a form of 'conscientisation'. This seems very similar to the term 'consciousness raising'. Because the readers focused on their experiences and their troubles, the peasants could use literacy as a political tool. While Freire's work achieved great results, it also disturbed the authorities because as the peasants became capable of articulating their experiences and concerns, they became more politically powerful. Freire's work demonstrated that illiteracy had been a useful tool of social control (Freire 1972).

Roland Barthes has analysed childhood by considering children's toys. He saw that these were also instruments of socialisation, determining how children would see and understand the world. Toys, like media texts, are socialising agents. They help children to learn what their role in society might entail, and they allow them to practise playing that role. Dolls, trucks, tea sets, and toy doctor's instruments enable children to imitate adult behaviour and practise adult roles, while children's media texts model adult roles and enable children to explore these possibilities via the mechanisms of identification and fantasy. As Barthes says, 'The fact that French toys *literally* prefigure the world of adult functions obviously cannot but prepare the child to accept them, constituting for him, even before he can think about it the alibi of a Nature which has at all times created soldiers, postmen and Vespas' (Barthes 1973, p. 53). This leads us directly into more material areas of ideology.

IDEOLOGIES IN MATERIAL INSTITUTIONS

So far in this chapter, we have spoken of ideology in terms of representations. However, we can also see ideology in actual material institutions and human activities. Most obviously, we can see this in the buildings that structure our lives, marking out our territory, determining how we can behave and act in the world. In Australia the idealised quarter-acre suburban block is a space for families to grow up and socialise in; in the United Kingdom, flats or terraced houses do the same. These architectural arrangements confirm that we live in family-based spaces. Our houses structure some space as communal and social, for the whole family; other spaces in houses (bedrooms, toilets, bathrooms, and so on) are defined as more personal and private. Many Western cultures structure their buildings around the culture and ideology of the family, so that it seems perfectly normal and natural to live in these separate spaces rather than in more communal forms of living. Visit any new housing estate and you will see how the structure of rooms is built around adults' and children's spaces. Familial ideology is embodied and naturalised through architecture.

These architectures do change. Feminists have noted how, with the gradual emancipation of women since the nineteenth century, kitchen and cooking areas, which were once separated and placed at the back of houses, in inferior positions, have become bigger, more central, more comfortable, and more communal, showing the increased status of the activities conducted in them and the sharing of domestic activities with men.[1]

Educational buildings as an example of ideology in material institutions

As a more extended example, it is interesting to look at educational buildings to see how the organisation of interior spaces has a built-in ideology of education.

Write down your thoughts on what ideology of education is built into lecture theatres and then read the commentary below.

Exercise commentary

The first thing I notice about lecture theatres is that they are built for one-way transmission: knowledge is given out from one person, one source, to many people. Those seated are invited to look at and interact with the lecturer, not each other. They are invited, by the trays attached to the seats, to take notes, thus validating what the lecturer is saying. Apart from the taking of notes, the theatre is essentially a passive learning place—you remain seated and don't talk—and one in which you absorb information and knowledge from the lecturer, the overheads, the screen, and the whiteboard. Education is focused on the mind and rationality rather than the body and feelings.

First, this suggests that knowledge is not to be gained experientially but by accepting views from authority. It sees knowledge as rational rather than emotional. It suggests that knowledge is there to be transmitted to students, rather like pouring knowledge from a jug into the upturned mouths of the students. In this process, the lecturer is given power and a voice. He/she speaks and students listen; he/she can stand and move about, whereas students remain in their seats; he/she can survey all of them at once.

Second, lecture-theatre education is like mass production in factories. Many students are dealt with at one sitting and are regulated through the timing of lectures. No attention is paid to whether the time of the lecture is a good time for learning—education is controlled by the demands of time-and-space-management, as in a factory, only here the product is student bodies, not cars or televisions.[2] My observations in Western Australia suggest that in Australia there are fewer clocks in public spaces than in many other Western countries, and that many Australians do not wear wrist watches regularly.

You could argue that what education and the lecture theatre teach, what the ideology of education is, is that students have nothing worth saying. Education teaches you to be silent, to respect your elders, to keep still, and to ignore your body, your emotions, and your experiences!

Imagine for a moment a round building in which students sit on cushions arranged in a circle, all on one level; where before students start learning, they tune into their inner feelings through meditation. You can see how such a building and its organisation of space would embody a different ideology of what knowledge, learning, and education are. (Note the dominance of four-walled rectangular buildings in Western architecture. Is this a reflection of an architectural culture that thinks predominantly in terms of squares and rectangles? Western culture often structures the world using the number four—the four points of the compass, the four seasons, the predominant 4/4 beat of Western music. Such a structure has a different feeling to 6/8 music, which is structured in threes, giving a more lilting, lyrical beat to the music.)

I have painted a somewhat one-sided view of the lecture theatre. It does have an element of performance and pleasure built into it: like a theatre for plays, it is an auditorium (literally a place for hearing), with fairly comfortable seats and a kind of stage for the lecturer to perform on. In addition, music, videos, and films can be transmitted. There are ways of using the space that challenge some of the aspects I have described. However, inviting student response and interaction, while possible within the space, is not what it has been constructed for. It does not reflect the ideology of education that has informed its architecture.

Our argument is that the way the material institutions we live in organise us in terms of space and time reflects the ideology and the discourses of our culture. We are not suggesting that there is a conspiracy to socialise us. Rather, these architectural patterns have evolved as a way of fitting in with the dominant trends of a society. They become so much part of our everyday landscape that they seem quite normal to us. We lose sight of the process of social construction—until we see another way of doing things and realise that 'our way' is not the only or the natural way.

1 *You can play with this concept by asking what ideological values are embedded in any human activity or way of living. As one example, consider dancing. What ideologies are embedded in different venues for dancing and in different types of dance (such as ballroom dancing, folk dancing, disco, and rave dancing)?*

2 You can also develop this through experiential learning. Arrange to meet with at least one other media student (even better, get together a group of up to five or six friends) and visit one of the following spaces: a dance venue; a multi-screen cinema; a public 'media space' such as Timezone, Qasar, and venues in which virtual reality games can be played; an Internet café, or a shopping mall. Go as a group, to have fun and experience the activity offered in that particular space. While you are there, remember to 'be in' the experience yourself: that is, try to act as you normally would in this situation. At the same time, observe your own feelings and behaviour, and try to observe the behaviour of other people around you: What are they doing? What kinds of people are there? How are they behaving and interacting? After the visit, take time to discuss and analyse how this experience felt for each of you—what gave you pleasure or displeasure. Then do a media studies analysis of the activities you participated in and observed: How was the space constructed? How were the activities constructed? What values seemed to be embedded in the signs and signifiers of the space? How did it appeal across gender, ethnicity, and class? Then try to determine what ideologies are built into the space and the experience. Remember that everyone's experience is valid: there is no right or wrong way to experience events, and hearing other people's experiences will help you understand the wider processes at work. As background reading, try looking at John Fiske's essay on shopping, 'Shopping for Pleasure', and video games, 'Video Pleasures', both of which are in Reading the Popular *(Fiske 1989a).*

IDEOLOGIES IN OUR HEADS, HEARTS, SUBJECTIVITIES, AND IDENTITIES

While texts exist outside us, ideology is also carried internally by us. If we accept and internalise the values of Peter and Jane then we carry those ideologies as part of who we are. The idea here is that our identities (our concepts of who we are) are, like language and ideologies, constructed. This is quite a challenging belief because it causes us to question ourselves. What we are suggesting is that our personality, our individuality, and our subjectivity have been produced by a number of external factors. Our ethnicity, class, and gender are once again the most obvious. Ask yourself 'Would I be a different person if I were of a different nationality, or if I were from a different class, or if I were of the opposite sex?' Would you be different if you had been born in a different century? How would you be different? By asking these questions, you may begin to get a sense of the constructedness of your own subjectivity. Identity can also be formed by things such as height, weight, attractiveness, religion, and so on. All these factors go towards who we are and how we think of ourselves. Would being fatter, thinner, or more attractive change how you feel and how you are perceived by other people?

Names as an example of ideologies in our identities

You can see this clearly in the case of names. It may seem obvious to you that your name is part of yourself, but names are given quite arbitrarily, and different names may cause us to think differently about ourselves, to see ourselves in a particular way. I was born in London, England and most of the kids at my school were White and

English. My name, Michael O'Shaughnessy, marked me as an outsider because both my Christian/given name and my surname are particularly Irish. (Note that calling a first name a 'Christian name' places you in a particular cultural and religious tradition while your 'surname' probably identifies you with your father rather than your mother, thus structuring you into patriarchy.) At school I was called a 'wild Irishman' (in a friendly way). This label, given to me by my English teachers and classmates, reinforced a stereotype of Irish wildness and Irish savagery, and it gave me a sense of who I was. I saw myself as having a wild streak, and I came to see myself as different, as an outsider. Such an identity allowed me to adopt a critical view of England and Englishness at the same time as being a part of that culture. Had I grown up in the same place but been named John Smith or Sebastian Courteney-Smythe, I suspect my character and my values would have been markedly different, and in many ways I am pleased with my non-English identity: because the Irish aren't seen as 'Pommies' it feels easier to be an Irish-Australian than an English-Australian!

People often have a number of different names: first names, diminutives, surnames, nicknames, and so on. All of these construct us differently and are used by other people to construct our identity in their eyes. They also allow us a number of different personalities for each name. In work situations, hierarchical positions can be reinforced by the use of names. Because using someone's surname indicates formality and respect, those in junior positions tend to address those in senior positions by their surnames (although this is, of course, dependent on the culture of the organisation). Conversely, because using someone's first name is a sign of familiarity and informality, those in senior positions tend to address those in junior positions by their first names. For example, secretaries are often referred to by their first names. Consider how different names bring out different aspects of your personality.

Sometimes people change their names. Some immigrants to Australia from non-English-speaking countries change their names or adopt different names to fit in more easily. My own experiences with Asian students in Australia has demonstrated that some adopt a new or Anglicised first name partly because non-Asians have difficulty pronouncing and remembering Asian names. In changing their names, they may also take on new personas, and may discard some of their traditional cultural practices. People who adopt a religious group or cult sometimes change their names to give themselves a different identity that marks them as part of their adopted group.

1 *Ask yourself how many different names you have. In what ways do your names affect your personality? Think of other names you could have. How would these give you a different personality?*

2 *Think of four prominent media personalities and reflect on how their names construct their public personas or identities. Some may have altered their given names or adopted a stage name. For instance, John Wayne managed to transcend the feminine connotations of his original name, Marion Morrison, without ever legally changing it. He did act under the stage name of Duke Morrison at one point, and became known as 'the Duke', which carries aristocratic connotations. It remains to be seen how Heavenly Hiraani Tiger Lily Hutchence Yates, the daughter of (deceased) INXS lead singer Michael Hutchence and Paula Yates, will manage to weather her exotic name. What do you think she will want to be known as when she grows up, and why?*

Consider why Norma Jean became Marilyn, why Madonna does not use her surname Ciccione, why Jennifer Lopez wishes to be known as J. Lo, and what the underlying ideological story behind Sean Combs (also known as Puff Daddy and P. Diddy) and the Artist Formerly Known as Prince might be.

We argue that our subjectivity, who we think we are, is constructed by the way we are positioned through class, ethnicity, gender, national identity, religion, naming, and so on. In this process we take on, we internalise, particular ways of thinking, feeling, and believing; we take on particular ideologies.

Interpellation

The term used by Louis Althusser to describe this process of internalising ideologies is 'interpellation' (Althusser 1977b, pp. 162–70; O'Sullivan 1994, pp. 155–6). To interpellate means to call someone by a name, to hail someone. This 'hailing' has the effect of putting us in our place or positioning the addressee in relation to the addresser. For instance, the Nintendo game *Joanna Dark*, released to rival *Lara Croft: Tomb Raider*, was advertised with the tag line: 'Are you man enough for Joanna Dark?' This question is hailing or addressing the audience as male, as though only men would play the computer game. The audience is also positioned within the discourse of sexuality and is assumed to be not just male, but also heterosexual. There is a good reason for this: the game *Joanna Dark* is in '3D first person shooter' format which means that those who play the game have to 'be' Joanna Dark. In other words, male players have to transvest themselves, in a virtual sense, and 'occupy' a female body in order to participate in the game. In order to overcome any discomfort that this act of virtual transvestism might cause, the marketing strategy interpellates audience members into a position of sexual conquest. Joanna Dark's character is code named 'Perfect Dark'; thus the fantasy of conquering the 'perfect' woman fuses with the fantasy of inhabiting a body that is a 'perfect' combat machine. Instead of threatening the player's masculinity by asking him to pretend to be a woman, the text interpellates audience members into a subject position in which they willingly take on Joanna Dark as a challenge. This communicative strategy works because competitiveness and a sexually predatory attitude is an accepted (though not necessarily acceptable) part of the dominant discourse of masculinity.

Gender and interpellation

Gender is central to identity, and gender socialisation is one of the earliest processes of interpellation. Try to remember, or imagine, how people talked to you when you were an infant and how much they encouraged you to see yourself as either a boy or a girl. ('It's a boy' or 'It's a girl' may have been the first words ever spoken in your presence.) To confirm this gender identity you probably adopted certain kinds of appropriate male or female behaviour. Simply being labelled as boy or girl tends to determine your behaviour to a large extent.

Pick up a copy of any newspaper and note how it interpellates its readership into particular subject positions. Do you notice that different sections of the newspaper seem to be addressing different social subjects? The sports section hails the reader as male, the social pages hail the reader as female, the finance section positions readers as anonymous but tends to locate them within a privileged, well-educated class. What are the specific differences in these modes of address? Do journalists speak to the public differently, depending on whether they assume that they are addressing a male or a female, a professional, or a tradesperson? You might also notice that the local news section and the world news section locate the reader within a particular national identity, assuming allegiance to and interest in that nation's celebrities, issues, and events. For world news, the same event will be reported differently in different countries, in a manner that is geared to position the audience to respond in certain ways, depending on whose interests are at stake.

Nationality and interpellation

National identity is also crucial in our understanding of who we are. Because the history of White settlement is relatively short, many Australians feel that establishing a national identity is a crucial task. Phrases such as 'un–Australian' (used to describe certain activities, such as snobbishness, being pretentious, cheating, or betraying the code of mateship) and 'a fair go' are typically Australian. They mark out the territory of what 'we', as Australians, understand as acceptable behaviour; when we are spoken to using these terms, we are interpellated as Australians. Different national identities are constructed in similar ways. Britain, for example, draws on its traditions and history as an independent 'island nation' in the construction of its identity.

The media work as a hailing system. Through the way they address us (their modes of address), they constantly interpellate us—as family, as Australian, as children, and so on. This is particularly true of television and radio, where there is often a direct address by announcers to 'you', the listener. Such modes of address give us our identities and subjectivities.

In 2001 the Australian Government launched a big public-information media campaign called the National Illicit Drugs Campaign. This used a variety of media forms to communicate its message, including a series of disturbing television commercials depicting the effects of drugs on young people's lives. At the same time, a sizeable booklet was distributed to households across the nation via the postal service. On the front cover of the booklet these words appear in block capitals: OUR STRONGEST DEFENCE AGAINST THE DRUG PROBLEM. Opening the booklet, the reader finds the word FAMILIES spread across the first two inside pages. The contents page includes the following headings:

- What families can do about illicit drugs
- What to do if you think your teenager is trying drugs
- The reasons teenagers give for taking illicit drugs and what you can say
- The Tough on Drugs plan.

In addition to this, the first page of text features a letter to the nation written by the Prime Minister, John Howard. The letter, which appears next to a picture of his smiling face, opens with the words: 'I believe that the best drug prevention programme in the world is a responsible parent sitting down with their children and talking to them about drugs'. Howard goes on to warn that 'if we don't talk to our sons and daughters about drugs, you can be sure that our children will hear the wrong message from someone else'. This places the responsibility for dealing with 'the drug problem' squarely on the shoulders of parents rather than on members of the public service such as educators, police, health care professionals, and politicians.

This campaign provides a very clear example of the process of interpellation at work. The reader is being addressed or hailed as a personal friend of John Howard. Linguistic strategies such as the use of personal forms of address ('I' and 'you', 'we' and 'our') create a sense of inclusiveness and interrelatedness, diminishing the difference in power relations and opinions that might otherwise exist between a prime minister and members of the voting public. On another level, the Australian public is assumed to consist of family units living together in households. It is not only the process of interpellation that ensures this (the writer assumes that the reader has children and is a member of a family), but also the means by which the message is being communicated. The fact that the campaign booklet was distributed in letterboxes was based on the assumption that young people who use illicit drugs live at home and are members of a family that lives together, rather than being homeless street kids, or occupying share houses with other young people.

The process of interpellation also works to construct the Australian public as one big, extended family with the Prime Minister as the father figure offering helpful advice about raising healthy, prosperous children. Howard is using mass communication to have a chat with parents, instructing them how to communicate with their children about drugs. In one sense, readers are being interpellated into the subject position of responsible parent, but in relation to the Prime Minister they also occupy the position of child, student, or friend in need of advice from a more knowledgeable fellow parent.

Examining the process of interpellation at work in the National Illicit Drug Campaign tells us a great deal about the role mass communication plays in public life in this instance. The National Illicit Drugs Campaign is informing or educating the public, but it is also acting as a mechanism of social control: it is working to unify the nation, and to reduce the government expenditure on crime and health care costs associated with illicit drug use. The campaign can also be understood as an instance of political communication that is functioning to promote John Howard's image as a leader who supports 'family values' (despite the fact that his government has been responsible for significant cuts to health, education, and social security that have affected families adversely).

It is useful to examine how the pronouns 'us' and 'we' and the possessive 'our' are used in the media as forms of interpellation. During the Sydney Olympics the *Sydney Morning Herald* headline on the day of Cathy Freeman's 400-metre final was 'Race of *Our* Lives'; when Australia recorded an amazing Test Match cricket win over Pakistan in 1999 the *West Australian* headline was '*We* Did It' (Figure 4.1, my italics). We can ask about these headlines: Who is being interpellated? Who is being included within 'our' and 'we'? Who is being excluded (since any notion of an inclusive we/us always implies an excluded them/other)? And what ideologies and discourses of identity are being constructed and circulated here?

The Freeman caption occurs in the context of the Olympics. As this competition is held between nations, Freeman's race is Australia's race and the 'our' of the caption assumes all readers to be Australians (although many non-Australians would have been in Sydney at the time). What is significant here in the construction of Australian

Figure 4.1 Front page coverage of an Australian Test Match win over Pakistan
Source: *West Australian*

national identity is that an Aboriginal woman becomes the leading symbol and representative of Australia. It thus includes and unites Aboriginals and non-Aboriginals, men and women, together as 'us', as Australian. It could be argued that the reverence and adulation shown by the Australian media and people to Cathy Freeman goes against the norms of discrimination against Aboriginal people and was part of a public-relations campaign attempting to show the rest of the world that Australia was a well-integrated, non-discriminatory, multicultural society. Alternatively, it may be seen as a powerful symbol and example of reconciliation and a challenge to discrimination.

The cricket headline example, in the context of the other words and photographs of the front page, has further complexities. The 'we' here could again be seen as referring to all Australians but as it is a picture of two White men it could be seen as interpellating just White, male Australians or even just White, male, cricket-loving Australians. There is a further complexity in that the 'we' may only refer to Adam Gilchrist and Justin Langer and since these men both play for Western Australia the 'we' comes to mean Western Australians in opposition to other Australians. The headline can thus be read within a context and history of interstate rivalry within Australia. The implied and excluded 'them' is most obviously the

Pakistani cricket team, but this could be widened to be all Pakistanis, all non-Australians, or all non-Western Australians. The headline is thus not as inclusive of all Australians in its interpellation as the Freeman headline. The other words and images are interesting in the way they provide further narrative threads and inter-pellated positions:

- The reference to the players' wives seeks to interpellate and include female readers (though within a heterosexual and competitive discourse).
- The image of mateship and teamwork draws on earlier digger ideologies of Australian warriors (the two sporting heroes may be viewed as similar to the young male heroes of the film *Gallipolli*) that naturalises the idea of inter-nation conflicts between 'us' and 'them'. This is supported by the caption 'How the Test was Won', which is a wordplay on 'How the West was Won', a celebration of the subjugation of the indigenous native Americans.
- Finally the caption, 'The Match that Stopped the Nation' refers us to the Melbourne Cup horse race, making this event equally significant and nationally inclusive. The words 'we', 'us' and 'our' thus become rich interpellative mecha-nisms worthy of detailed analysis.

We hope you can come to an understanding of this process of interpellation and can see how it may relate to your own identity as male/female, White Australian/Aboriginal Australian, White British/Black British, of a particular ethnic group, and so on. (Issues relating to ideologies about gender and ethnicity in the media are developed more in Part 5.) If you have never been in a situation in which your identity has been challenged, for example by moving to a new society or by changing your name (or even by going through a body-building course, which tends to change body image), the process of interpellation may be difficult to see. While your national identity, your personal name, and your body shape may seem to be a natural part of you, you should try to see these as parts of your constructed subjectivity and be aware of how the media will address messages to specific aspects of your identity for marketing purposes or to serve other vested interests.

Notions of identity and subjectivity: are we cogs in the machine, or do we have free will?

'Identity' and 'subjectivity' are terms often used in media studies. They are partly inter-changeable: both refer to the way we understand who we are—our identity—and the position from which we look at and understand the world—our subjectivity.

We would again like to raise the question of whether we are cogs in the machine or self-determining, autonomous individuals with free will. We live in a culture that stresses individuality, encourages us to believe that every person has unique quali-ties, and puts forward the view that we have control over who we are, what we do, and how others see us, but this is questionable.

On the one hand Western culture glorifies the individual and understands much of what happens to the world in terms of individual actions. News stories and political events are presented to us as the stories of individual people—politicians, business people, army leaders, criminals, and so on—and what they do. Entertainment, sports coverage, films, and television programs focus on individual stars and personalities. These media products are often also packaged in terms of the individual stars they feature. Magazines gossip about the private lives of individuals. History is often presented and taught in terms of key individuals. Even media studies sometimes stresses the individual role of film directors, for example. These characteristics of the media relate to the *ideology of individualism* that permeates Western culture.

On the other hand, the nineteenth and twentieth centuries have also produced numerous academic and theoretical perspectives that show the opposite—that individuals are not in control of their own destinies, that we are subject to forces beyond our individual, conscious control. Challenges to the view that individuals have control over their own destiny have come from seven major sources:

1 Darwinian theories of evolution and 'survival of the fittest' suggest that we are determined by our genetic evolution, which determines what we do and who will survive.

2 Marxist theory sees class struggle and economics as the motor and determinant of history (it holds that we act in accordance with these impersonal forces). According to Marxism, it is the actions of whole groups or classes, not the actions of individuals, that change the world. The following famous quotation from Marx illustrates Marx's view that humans have only a limited degree of autonomy: 'Men make history, but only on the basis of conditions which are not of their own making'.

3 Freud and other psychologists have argued that we are determined by our unconscious, driven by our basic drives towards survival and pleasure. We act on the basis of these unconscious desires and the fears associated with them, rather than on our conscious choices.

4 B. F. Skinner and other behaviourist psychologists have suggested that all human activities are simply determined responses to external stimuli: in other words, we do not act, we react.

5 Saussure and other linguists have suggested that language determines who we are, what we think, and how we understand the world; rather than saying 'we speak language', we could say 'language speaks us'.

6 Most recently, feminists have put forward the view that gender is the key factor determining who we are and how we behave.

7 Those working on the problem of racism have proposed that ethnic origins are the most important factor dictating behaviour and identity.

So we have two polarised positions. The first sees humans as possessing individual autonomy and free will—the ability to make our own choices and determine our own destiny. The second sees humans as cogs in the machinery of biology, psychology, history, and culture. This opposition is not new. For centuries religions have posited the question of whether humans have free will or whether our fate is preordained.

The term 'subjectivity' draws attention to both our autonomy and to the fact that our actions are predetermined (Fiske 1987, pp. 48–61). On the one hand, the word 'subject' is about us having power: in grammatical terms, sentences are built around the structure subject–verb–object: someone/something (subject) does something (verb) to someone/something (object). Similarly, to 'subject someone to something' is to have power over them. On the other hand, we talk of people being subjects of kings and queens: as subjects we are under the power of other people and other forces ('subject' comes from a Latin word that means 'thrown under'). When we think of our own subjectivities it is helpful to see both the autonomous power we have (the fact that we have our own way of seeing and operating in the world) and the determined quality of our identity or subjectivity (the way it has been shaped by outside forces).

We do not have a final answer to the question 'Do humans have free will or are we cogs in the machine?' (although we hope you noticed that we presented most of the nineteenth- and twentieth-century theories that challenged human autonomy in terms of the individuals who pioneered them). But we do question the notion that our individuality is something existing outside culture. It is useful to see the ways in which our individuality is actually a social construct. Discussing this, Kathryn Woodward states:

> Identity can be seen as the interface between subjective positions and social and cultural situations … Identity gives us an idea of who we are and of how we relate to others and to the world in which we live. Identity marks the ways in which we are the same as others who share that position, and the ways in which we are different from those who do not (Woodward 1997, pp. 1–2).

She stresses the role of the media, images, and language—of ideology—in contributing to our identities: 'Representation as a cultural process establishes individual and collective identities, and symbolic systems provide possible answers to the questions: Who am I? What could I be? Who do I want to be?' (Woodward 1997, p. 14). Understanding this is a form of consciousness-raising that can give us more power and awareness in terms of understanding ourselves and others, and can help us to decide how we would like to act in future. Seeing how we are determined by the ideology we were born into, seeing how our behaviour has been shaped since birth (when people first start telling us who we are and how we should act) can give us a broader set of social choices about who we want to be and what we can do in the future. We can break out of earlier ideological constrictions.

An essential self?

Another big question in relation to identity is whether there is such a thing as a 'real you' (whether you have an essential character), or whether all identities are constructions. In looking at this I want to use and compare two approaches: a cultural studies approach and a psychological/psychotherapeutic approach (with an emphasis on Jungian theory). I suggest that there are some interesting similarities in the ways these approaches understand subjectivity, identity, and character, and that both approaches are useful.

Both argue that our identity, our character, is constructed, and both aim to facilitate a deconstruction of that character. Cultural studies sees identity as constructed and determined by external social forces. Psychology and psychotherapy see our character as constructed by the behaviour of our parents, and of other people in our lives, and in particular by the attitudes these people have towards us.

Cultural studies aims to deconstruct subjectivity. It shows that who we think we are is a result of a series of interpellations, discourses, and social structures into which we are born: ethnicity, class, and gender position, alongside nationality and language system, structure people's identities and subjectivities. Through intellectual analysis these identities are questioned, destabilised, and undermined. Successful cultural studies teaching challenges students' 'common-sense' assumptions of normality and naturalness, assumptions on which their identities were founded. This leads them to ask 'Who am I?' or more radically 'Is there such a thing as an "I" at all?'

Psychotherapy and psychology also see identity as a construction (the term 'character' is used more often than 'identity'). It suggests that, as children, we learn a series of behaviour patterns and defence mechanisms that allow us to cope with, and survive, the traumas of growing up that are inherent in every childhood. These mechanisms coalesce into the structure or 'character' through which we live our lives and through which we are recognised by others and ourselves. We see this character as our identity (Reich 1990). Many people come to therapy because these defence mechanisms, which have served their purpose in helping them survive their own traumas of childhood and growing up, have become counter-productive and are preventing them from finding and fulfilling their true potential. Character mechanisms are not static parts of ourselves; they can be changed or discarded. Ideally, psychotherapy leads to awareness of this and facilitates some basic shifts in a patient's character, allowing for new forms of behaviour and experience.

Interestingly, many psychotherapeutic approaches hold that these characters are materially located—they are actually in the body. Wilhelm Reich's work and all subsequent 'bodywork psychotherapy' sees emotions and feelings as related to our breathing patterns and the way we learn to hold, use, and discipline our bodies. 'Body armouring' is a term used to describe the 'holding in' of what society deems to be socially undesirable emotions: for example, traditional methods of raising children, and codes of behaviour applicable to certain situations, encourage us to restrain our anger, our sexual feelings, and our love for others. According to bodywork psychotherapy, body armouring leads literally to 'tight-arsed', 'stiff-necked', 'stuck-up', physically rigid people (Totten and Edmondson 1988). Bodywork works directly on the body, using deep-breathing techniques and massage to loosen up and soften the body, with the aim of releasing pent-up emotions. For Reich, this was also a political activity, as he believed that sexual repression was a central aspect of fascist, communist, and other forms of authoritarian government. The political dimension of Reich's thought did not go unrecognised by those in authority. Various political parties and governments saw him as a substantial threat and he was deported and jailed (his books were also burnt). He was a cultural activist, and the materiality and social politics behind his theory link him with the project of cultural studies today.

Cultural studies and psychotherapeutic processes are similar in that they both aim to deconstruct character. The social questions of identity raised by cultural studies are crucial, but so too are the psychological issues relating to individual situations dealt with through psychotherapy. It may make it easier to think of subjectivity and character as structured on two levels—the social and the psychological. I argue that uncovering the way in which subjectivity is constructed through social categories (class, gender, ethnicity, and so on) is important, but that underneath this process of construction lie psychological structures. Theoretical work in the area of cultural studies is a form of consciousness raising; psychotherapy and psychoanalysis go beyond this, making us aware of how our unconscious natures determine our behaviours and our identities—they perform what we might call 'unconsciousness raising'. Psychological structures can be incredibly powerful in determining how we feel, act, and behave, and psychotherapy is capable of producing deep shifts in personality and character. I would argue that this work is potentially revolutionary. Cultural studies has aimed to explore ways in which people are socially controlled and constructed through political and ideological mechanisms. Psychotherapy explores the ways in which people are controlled and dominated emotionally, and thus can be seen as taking the cultural studies approach a stage further.

Despite this compatibility, there seems to be a fundamental difference between the two approaches. Psychotherapy, as described above, seems to suggest that underneath your learned character or identity there is a real you to be discovered. The idea of finding your real self is not exclusive to psychotherapy; it is a common desire permeating Western culture. Cultural studies challenges this notion, arguing that all identities are constructions. Postmodern (see Part 6) and 'queer theories' develop this position, suggesting that we can move fluidly from one identity to another, as appropriate. They hold that there is no one true position—all identities are performances.

However, it is possible to challenge the view that this notion of fluid identity is foreign to psychotherapy. A similar notion of fluidity in identity can be seen in the Jungian and psychotherapeutic models. Jung postulates the existence of a system of archetypes—models of ideal behaviour—that we have the potential to use as a guide to our actions in the world. Because there are many archetypes, we are not limited, as individuals, to one mode of being, to a single core identity; we can move around the identities. New-age thinking about identity is just as fluid as postmodern or queer-theory positions.

I find that this notion of multiple possible identities is best explained by an analogy with radio. Radios broadcast through many potential frequencies, but each radio station has its own particular frequency—101.9, 102.7, Triple J, Radio 1, Radio 3, and so on—with its own style of music or information. Paul Lowe suggests that like radio stations, most of us, in our dealings with the world, adopt a particular 'frequency' (identity, archetype, character) from which to 'broadcast' or interact with other people, a style that reflects who we think we are. However, we could, if we wanted, broadcast from any or all frequencies, at any time—these frequencies offer us the potential to be jazzy, sedately classical, funky, into hip-hop, reggae, and so on, according to what we feel is appropriate (Lowe 1989).

The aim of psychotherapeutic work is not to find the one true frequency (the real self) from which to broadcast. Rather, it aims to give us the ability to tune into whatever frequency is appropriate for the moment, and to be available to be any of these styles at any time. The real self is simply the self that has the flexibility and fluidity to move and act appropriately, according to what makes us feel good and what does not harm others.

In this section on the notion of the essential self, we have pointed to links between cultural studies and Jungian and psychotherapeutic approaches to understanding identity. These links show how these approaches can complement each other in analysing human beings and society.

Take time to reflect on what this section has said about identity and subjectivity. Can you think of any film or novel in which the protagonist undergoes major changes to their identity to which you can relate through personal experience? How did the narrative structure (particularly the binary oppositions, the archetypal character functions, and the nature of the ending) support or undermine that process of transformation? What might this indicate about the dominant ideology of the society in which the text was produced? (For instance, if you were thinking of the film Thelma and Louise, *you might wonder whether American society was resistant to or supportive of women's liberation, because Thelma and Louise met both misfortune and adventure when they moved away from their socially constructed identities.) Next, consider how the story you have in mind interpellated its audience: did it align the audience with or against the character with whom you identified? Was it assumed that the audience shared the same position in terms of gender, race, class, or age as the protagonist, or were these chatacteristics used to mark the character as different? Finally you might like to consider how your personal experience of major change differed from that of the character with whom you identified.*

14 Dominant Ideology, RSAs, and ISAs

DOMINANT IDEOLOGY

So far we have talked about ideology and ideologies, and this may have prompted you to ask, 'Is there just one ideology or are there many ideologies?' There are numerous ideologies. Each social group has its own way of thinking, feeling, believing, and making sense of the world. We can talk about ideologies (or discourses) of masculinity and femininity; of Australianness, Britishness, or Asianness; of blackness or whiteness; of teenagers or senior citizens; of middle and working classes; and so on. However, we want to consider the idea of a 'dominant' or 'ruling' ideology, as suggested by Louis Althusser (Althusser 1977b, pp. 147–8). His work is useful in providing a framework for understanding how ideology works in society.

Althusser, following on from Marx, suggested that each society has a dominant ideology (Marx, in an earlier version of this idea, talked of the 'ruling ideas' of a culture). This ideology—comprising a set of shared feelings, values, beliefs, and so on—is shared by the majority of people in a society. It is thus dominant in two senses. First, it is dominant in numerical terms. Second, it is dominant in the sense that it tends to support the interests of the dominant, ruling groups. We are interested in the way dominant ideas, beliefs, and values, which support particular groups in society (Whites, the middle classes, men), come to be accepted and believed by many people in society. We are also interested in the way the media contribute to this acceptance.

Below are some relevant extracts from the works of Marx and Althusser. These extracts give a flavour of the ideas of these writers. You may not understand them at first because they are complex and densely packed with concepts and ideas, but this density means they are rich with meaning and import. Read them through a couple of times and try to write, in your own words, what you think they are saying.

First, here is Marx discussing ruling ideas:

The ideas of the ruling class are in every epoch the ruling ideas: i.e., the class which is the ruling *material* force in society is at the same time its ruling *intellectual* force. The class which has the means of material production at its disposal, has control at the same time over the means of mental production, so that in consequence the ideas of those who lack the means of mental production are, in general, subject to it. The dominant ideas are nothing more than the ideal expression of the dominant material relationships grasped as ideas and thus of the relationships which make one class the ruling one; they are consequently the ideas of its dominance. The individuals composing the ruling class possess, among other things, consciousness, and therefore think. In so far, therefore, as they rule as a class and determine the whole extent of an epoch, it is self-evident that they do this in their whole range and thus, among other things, rule also as thinkers, as producers of ideas, and regulate the production and distribution of the ideas of their age: thus their ideas are the ruling ideas of the epoch (Marx 1846, 1974, p. 64).

Marx, as you can see, stresses ideas, but sees these as determined by 'material forces'—that is, the forces of economic ownership and production. Althusser's wider concept of ideology takes us a stage further in the argument about how societies adhere to values and ideas supporting the dominant groups and how ideology is not worked out consciously or conspiratorially.

It is customary to suggest that ideology belongs to the region of 'consciousness' ... In truth ideology has very little to do with 'consciousness', even supposing this term to have an unambiguous meaning. It is profoundly unconscious ... Ideology is indeed a system of representations, but in the majority of cases these representations have nothing to do with consciousness ... they are perceived/accepted/suffered cultural objects and they act functionally on men via a process that escapes them. Men 'live' their ideologies ... *not as a form of consciousness, but as an object of their 'world'*—as their 'world' itself ... The ruling ideology is then the ideology of the ruling class. But the ruling class does not maintain with the ruling ideology, which is its own ideology, an external and lucid relation of pure utility and cunning ... the bourgeoisie has to believe its own myth before it can convince others (Althusser 1977, pp. 233–4).

Althusser's concept of ideology thus goes beyond pure ideas and consciousness to *the way in which people believe* in ideology. He sees ideology as an unconscious force that people live rather than see: it is lived 'as their "world" itself'. Both these extracts argue that ruling ideas or ideology are so deeply embedded in our society that they are shared by almost everyone and seem totally normal.

As an example, think how we unproblematically accept the basic notion of private property, the notion that individuals can claim exclusive ownership over all kinds of goods and land. Private property is so taken-for-granted in Western society that it may seem ludicrous to challenge it, and indeed it may seem as though we all benefit from it because we all own something. I certainly do not want my precious possessions taken away from me! But private property has evolved in societies where ownership of property is predominantly in the hands of a minority. Remember the 7.84 statistic (p. 162): 7 per cent of the population own 84 per cent of the wealth. Who really benefits from the system of private property, which is well maintained by laws and law-enforcement bodies? (Note how some offences against private property in Western cultures are traditionally subject to punishments greater than those meted out for some assault offences; for example, fraud attracts a harsher penalty than rape.)

What happens to this common-sense ideology when we say 'All property is theft'? This saying, attributed to the French philosopher Proudhon, and taken up by Marx, asks us to rethink and re-evaluate the social conditions of property. To say I own something is to deny others the right to share it: it is to steal it from them. How much of our own property have we actually made ourselves? Have we really stolen it from someone else? Compare this ideology with Aboriginal ways of relating to material things. Ideas of land guardianship and communal ownership offer a very different possibility, a different way of organising how we live in the world and with its resources.

We are not saying that private property is wrong. Rather, we are suggesting that this ideology, which is shared by most people in the West, may actually be most beneficial to those who traditionally have owned the most. This dominant ideology (dominant because it is supported by most people) supports the dominant (socially powerful) groups. We also want to shake up your common-sense, accepted values, just to show that there are other points of view.

As the world's resources are depleted, questions relating to the desirability of our system of private property may be particularly urgent in these times. The ultimate aim of our consumerist society seems to be for everyone to possess their own car, fridge, electrical goods, and so on. The economic growth of our society is built on this provision of an ideal and comfortable style of living. If this were achievable it would be wonderful, but I, for one, question the possibility of planetary survival given the continuing explosion of private ownership of consumer goods. The ecological crisis may reach a point at which society will have to find some new way of living, some new ideology, in order to survive. Note that the Latin word from which the term 'consume' derives—*consumo*—means to destroy, implying that consumers are destroyers!

RSAs AND ISAs

Althusser wanted to understand how ideology was transmitted socially, how it was that people took and accepted the values of the dominant groups even if these views might not be in everyone's interests. He suggested two sets of mechanisms that achieved this: repressive state apparatuses (RSAs) and ideological state apparatuses (ISAs) (Althusser 1977b, pp. 133–48).

RSAs

RSAs are mechanisms that are called into play to force people to conform to the dominant ideology. They are used deliberately, to control, punish, and coerce people who attempt to challenge the system. They are primarily the institutions of the law, the law courts, the police, the prison system, and the army, all of which are used to deal with people who trouble and disrupt society. RSAs do not work ideologically on people's feelings and beliefs; they work directly through force (including force of law) and, when necessary, through punishment. They are only deployed for extreme forms of social disorder such as crime or mass protest. In the media, censorship laws provide this form of control.

ISAs

ISAs are of much more interest to media studies. These are the institutions through which we are socialised into accepting the dominant ideology. ISAs do not force people; they work more like hypnosis, convincing people or winning their consent to the dominant ideology. Althusser again identified key institutions that carry out this socialisation process: the Church, the family, the education system, and the media.

The media are now very important; in many ways they have taken over the role of the Church, which has declined considerably since the nineteenth century. Together with the family and the education system, they offer us ways of understanding and making sense of the world and of ourselves. They explain how we should think, act, and feel. It is important to note that these institutions may not always agree. Church and family ideologies may at times conflict with the ideologies of the media.

The media as an ISA

How do the media work ideologically? What values and beliefs do they construct as normal, natural, and desirable? How do the media work in relation to the dominant ideology? These are major questions in media studies.

Our basic argument is that the media tend to support the dominant ideology; if you use this as the starting point for your study of the media and ideology, later on you will be able to develop a more complex and sophisticated reading of the relationship between the media and the dominant ideology. The media support the dominant ideology by producing programs and products that support the values of White, patriarchal, capitalist culture. There are two important things that tend to militate against, or undermine, this relationship:

1 In order to win support for the dominant ideology through media products, the media must win the support of subordinate and minority groups in society (women, indigenous people, the working class, and so on). They must come up with products that give these groups pleasure, since these groups comprise the bulk of the audience.

2 The media are often drawn to addressing social tension, focusing on social conflict and on contradictions in society. For example, news and current affairs focus on moments of social disruption and conflict. Drama, fiction, and films are nearly always based on conflict: conflict between characters and between value systems is the very stuff of drama. The police drama, one of the major prime-time genres of popular television, always focuses on moments of, and places associated with, social breakdown. Police dramas choose to explore crime, and consequently, at some level, they consider the social causes of crime, touching on poverty, inequality, unemployment, drugs, and so on—major social issues that threaten to disrupt society. Situation comedies focusing on the family and gender relations draw attention to the battle of the sexes and the breakdown of the family unit. This is the staple content of these programs. Similarly, a significant proportion of narratives look at issues associated with families (such as family breakdowns) and sexuality.

Thus we can see that despite the fact that the media support the dominant ideology, they also draw our attention to social problems. However, merely because they draw our attention to these problems does not mean that they do so in ways that call the ultimate desirability of the current system into question. In this respect, what is crucial is the conventions used by these programs to deal with and resolve the social issues raised. In many cases, these conventions are in fact a source of pleasure for viewers. For example, television news, which provides a forum and mouthpiece for dominant institutional voices, ultimately reassures and normalises every disruptive act, thereby allaying our fears about the stability of our world. Police dramas, while they depict poverty and crime, raising them as potential problems, tend to turn criminals into psychopaths (thereby reassuring us that we are not like criminals) and the police into figures that we identify with. Situation comedies, while they raise issues relating to the family and gender relations, relieve our tension through the safety-valve of humour. In these examples, we can say that the ways the media deal with the problems constitute ideological work. Their resolutions will not ultimately disturb society. Rather, they allow the predominant ideology to be maintained. (This over-states the case a little; the idea that dominant ideology easily maintains its position is questionable. Many narratives offer alternative ideological ways of thinking.)

How do the media do ideological work?

We will now explore two ways in which the media do this ideological work.[3]

1 The media function to support the dominant ideology by 'masking and displacing' social issues and problems.

As discussed above, the media can hide or avoid social problems. This happens in a number of ways:

- Some issues are simply avoided or rendered invisible. These are the issues that do not get media coverage at all. Some social groups are notably absent from certain types of media representations: for example, in Australia popular drama rarely features Aboriginal culture, handicapped and differently-abled groups, gay culture, and so on. Such groups are often marginalised through their exclusion.

- Social difference is masked or displaced by interpellations that address all social groups under a unifying label. The three most common interpellations or forms of address used by the media are to address the audience as 'family members', 'Australians'/'Britons' (or some other nationality), and as 'members of the public'. Sometimes we are addressed as all three at the same time (the National Illicit Drugs Campaign, discussed on pp. 204–5, is a good example of this). These labels and interpellations are not false. We are all family members, citizens of Australia, the United Kingdom, or some other nation, and members of the public. But these labels—which are used to unite us, to bring us together as equals, and to suggest that we share the same aims, needs, desires, and the same views about the ideal family and about national goals—also mask and displace differences: for example, differences between White Australians and indigenous Australians, between rich and poor, between two- and one-parent families, between men and women, and so on. These interpellations focus on some parts of our identity rather than others: for example, 'family member' focuses on our family and domestic identities rather than on our working identities as trade unionists, factory workers, office cleaners, company managers, and so on. Social differences, particularly those relating to class and ethnicity, are dissolved into the unities of domestic and national identity. The media thus favour interpellations that unite us rather than those that highlight social difference. The common 'family' address heard on television—'You and your family'—assumes all viewers watch as parts of families, thus excluding viewers who are not 'family viewers'.

How often do you notice the media addressing or interpellating its audience—you—with these or other labels? Collect examples of these interpellations.

- Social problems and contradictions are often masked or displaced by being understood in personal or psychological terms or within a moral framework of good and evil, rather than in social terms. Police dramas are a good example of this. A criminal's behaviour is often understood as the result of individual personality disorders: he or she has a psychological problem. The social causes of crime, such as unemployment and drug trafficking, which have the potential to portray this criminal as typical of a social group, are displaced in favour of personal, psychological explanations. Similarly, struggles between heroes and villains in films often focus on the villain not as a representative of a social group, but as a particularly bad, cruel, evil individual. When you next watch television, listen to the radio, or read a newspaper article, see how the social problems being raised are addressed. Are they explained as the result of social causes or are they personalised in terms of individuals with particular personal problems? The film *Traffic* is a good example of a film that focuses on individuals caught up in the problems of drugs, and drug trafficking (including us, the audience) but then places them in a wider social context and draws attention to these social problems.

- Another way of thinking about society is to argue that we live in a 'pluralist' society. A pluralist society has many different social groups, and therefore exhibits a plurality of many different voices. These may have different social perspectives and positions, but within a democracy all are allowed to speak and will have some access to the media. This suggests that social positions are not displaced or masked, but simply coexist alongside others, in the same way that, for example, people of different ethnic backgrounds coexist. According to this view of society, audiences are free to accept the views they agree with. This pluralist position avoids social conflict, and hence masks it, by saying that we all have the right and opportunity to speak if we wish. It suggests that we are all equal within the society.

2 The media support dominant ideology by incorporating or containing other ideological positions.

Rather than attempting to disallow or even censor dissident ideological voices the media sometimes neutralise these voices by allowing them space but containing them within the overall system. For example, since the end of World War II, youth cultures in Western societies have threatened to disrupt ideologies of how youths should behave. Popular artists such as the rappers Eminem and P. Diddy and the comedian Ali G, have managed to amass a huge fan base because they actively resist the dominant order. These prominent figures in youth culture undermine political correctness and set out to alienate members of 'nice', 'responsible', 'mature' social groups. As Nick Hornby (author of the novel *High Fidelity*) argues, by contrast with the violent misogyny of Eminem's rap collective D12, whose bestselling album *Devils Night* contains lyrics such as 'Independent women in the house/show us your tits and shut your mother f—ing mouth', the 'sonic ferocity', obscenity, and nihilism of groups such as the Sex Pistols and Nirvana seems 'thoughtful and politically engaged' (*Weekend Australian*, November 3–4, 2001, pp. 4–6). But all these figures are allowed some space in the media and are thus accepted.

Some attempts are made to curtail youth movements through legal and police action focused on drugs and youth gatherings, but the movements are often better contained by allowing them to continue within the confines of the society: in other words they are accommodated or incorporated within society in such a way as to defuse their radical potential ('incorporated' means 'taken into the main body'). The challenges thrown out by youth cultures are incorporated into an ideology that sees teenage years as a natural time of rebellion—this is what it means to be a teenager so it is acceptable. For example, popular music is incorporated into the music industry and radio station playlists (radio announcers provide the music with a context and accompanying commentary that gives it a safe, socially acceptable interpretation). Similarly, the initially shocking clothing style of punks in the 1970s was incorporated into mainstream fashion. The commercialisation and popularisation of elements of youth culture defuse them of their radical challenge. Young people are also given some spaces and times—nightclubs and weekends—in which to indulge themselves as they wish without disturbing others. Attempts are even being made to organise 'official' events as part of Schoolies Week, to control the potential disruptions.

In relation to who has the right to speak on the media, democratic societies have actually encouraged 'other' voices: for example, television channels such as Australia's SBS and the United Kingdom's Channel 4 are understood as forums for the articulation of non-majority positions. However, it can be argued that these forums again function to incorporate these different voices (rather than allowing them to fulfil their radical potential) by including them as a minority part of the mainstream, thereby preventing the social groups represented from feeling left out and causing social disruption. Similarly, while mainstream television channels occasionally present challenging programs that question the dominant ideology, their very positioning within normal television schedules—surrounded by advertisements, trailers, and other non-challenging programs—functions so as to neutralise their messages, which get lost both by being incorporated into the overall output of television, and by the way in which audiences have been encouraged to be passive spectators.

We can even see incorporation at work in narrative structures. Many popular fictions are drawn to social problems. What can happen is that initially a narrative may give support to a radical point of view, but then the way that the narrative is structured and resolved neutralises this point of view. Thus, as a whole, the narrative contains radical positions. This is why we stress the importance of narrative structure in relation to ideological meanings.

When feminist ideas were gaining popular currency in the 1980s, women's magazines and magazines aimed at teenage girls reflected this interest in feminist ideas. A story in the British magazine *True Romance*, called 'I Followed My Dream', is a typical example of incorporation (*True Romance* 1980). The initial stages of the story include many feminist ideas: the first-person narrator discovers early on that there is a popular conception that 'Girls … were just around to help in the house'; she rejects love and marriage: 'No one's going to walk all over me … I am going to be somebody, Anna. I am not going to marry some male chauvinist who thinks a woman is just a servant'; she knows what men can be like: 'Having a brother like John convinced me that men are just big, selfish babies'; she knows that housework is hard, poorly paid, and is unrecognised labour, and that being a wife and mother is hard work: 'Men haven't had the burdens of bearing children and running homes. Most men take clean houses, clothes, meals on time, babies fed and burped, as a matter of course'; and she recognises the contemporary possibilities for women: 'It's a woman's world today, you know. A woman can do whatever she wants, be whatever she wants.'

Yet as the story develops, the narrator falls in love with her boss, an older man, whom she nurses back to health after he is injured, and who proposes marriage to her after this! Under the weight of romantic love, all the earlier ideals are forgotten (incorporated) as she happily accepts marriage and children: 'I have been thinking about it. Jason, I'd like to be your wife ... I'd like to have your children ... Marriage? It's wonderful! There's no reason why a woman can't use all her abilities and still know the joys of home and children. Jason was right. Lots of women are doing it all the time' (*True Romance*, 1980).

There is a transition here: women's domestic labour is magically transformed from hard, unrewarded work into 'the *joys* of home and children' (my emphasis). It is worth making one final point about this ending. The narrator's voice, the woman's discourse, is finally subsumed into the male voice: 'Jason was right'. This voice is also the discourse of an older value system, as opposed to the younger narrator's (initial) values. Jason says to her at one point: 'I'm quite old fashioned. I expect to get married some day when I find the right woman. I want her to be a home-maker ... Funny I guess men haven't changed as much as women in their attitudes'. This story thus allows two ideologies or discourses about marriage and gender roles to meet. Raymond Williams describes the way that 'residual', 'dominant', and 'emergent' cultural aspects, or discourses, can be present in texts at the same time (Williams 1977a, pp. 121–7). By this, he means that old ideologies and discourses from the past, present ideologies and discourses (that are part of the dominant ideology), and new, emerging ideologies and discourses (that relate to new ideas and social groups seeking a change of ideology) can all coexist. In this story, the emergent discourse of women's liberation meets the dominant discourse of patriarchal marriage (which is also perhaps slowly on its way to becoming a residual discourse) and the latter wins out. This is another case of incorporation. In the movie *My Best Friend's Wedding* (discussed on pp. 145–7) it may be argued that the emergent values of being single and unattached to family win out over the dominant values of marriage and family or, as we suggested earlier, that the emergent values (strong, career-oriented femininity and alternative sexualities) are only given a place in society to the extent that they exist outside the privileged space of the married couple and family unit. Again, it sends the message that it is OK for young single people to rebel against the dominant order, but they need to 'outgrow that phase' if they are to attain romantic and domestic happiness.

In this example the emergent, radical ideology of feminism is incorporated into popular culture and given a position inside the dominant discourse of femininity and the family. Indeed, it is legitimated—but only to an extent. The text suggests that feminism is OK for young, single women, but mature women must conform to older models of femininity. If they want to continue to lead a 'feminist lifestyle', women must find a way to fit independence and a career around 'the joys of home and children'. Presumably Jason was not volunteering to stay at home and raise his children and manage the household after he got married so that his wife could pursue her personal aspirations and further her career.

The argument about incorporation is two-sided. While you can argue that democratic societies are able to neutralise any dissident voices through incorporation, you can also argue that rather than being neutralised, radical ideas are actually being popularised and are thus beginning to shift the overall ideology of society. We think there is truth in both arguments and the discussion of hegemony below pursues this.

This chapter has presented a lot of complex material. Get out a large piece of blank paper and draw an illustrated picture, mind map, or flow chart depicting ideology. The act of producing images that represent ideas not only helps to work through and develop understanding of concepts such as ideology; it also offers insight into the process of media production itself, and thus into the ways in which ideology is communicated and shared. This exercise will be an antidote to the heavy intellectual work you have done in coming to terms with the ideas presented in this Part. More importantly, this exercise will free you from the structured forms of thought required in essays and verbal expression. You may be surprised at what you come up with. Share your pictures or mind map with others and then interpret what you see in each other's pictures.

15 Christmas and Hegemony

PLEASURE

If the media can provide us with pleasure, we will be very likely to consume their products. The following section examines how the media hype around Christmas functions to promote the ideologies of materialism and consumerism, amongst other values.

The primary aim of most media is to provide audiences with pleasure. As consumers, our feelings of pleasure (our emotional responses) may be deeper than our ideological understandings of the media—if I enjoy a program, who cares what its ideology is! Ultimately this is crucial for the media to 'win our support'. If the media can provide us with pleasure, we will very likely consume them. Try telling a child with a sweet tooth that hamburgers and milk-shakes are unhealthy and ideologically unsound!

THE IDEOLOGY OF CHRISTMAS

We hope you are beginning to see the complexity of ideology and its potential richness as a way of understanding how societies work. One more example will illustrate how ideology is rarely simple, how it usually contains many different and sometimes contradictory aspects.

Most societies are based on a number of different value systems and on a set of contrasting and competing ideologies or discourses. Some of these will be very old, others more recent; some will be current and others will relate to the emerging values of new groups in society (as Williams suggests with his categorisation of discourse as residual, dominant, or emergent—see p. 220). In this chapter, we use Christmas as an example of this complexity. While Christmas is not a media text, it can be considered a media event and it is certainly a social and cultural phenomenon that creates a great deal of media attention—including advertising blitzes, special cinema releases and television programming, and carols on the radio. (For instance, the release schedule of the *Lord of the Rings* trilogy of films is promoted on the website as 'coming Christmas 2001, 2002, 2003'.) A media event is something that, like the Olympics, or an election, overshadows and disrupts normal programming and that involves a bevy of special features and interviews across a number of media forms.

Christmas has become the most important calendar event in Western cultures. Linked as it is to New Year celebrations, it is a time that signals the end and beginning of our annual cycle. What is the ideology of Christmas? What are the discourses of Christmas? There is no simple answer to these questions. Christmas contains a variety of ideological positions, a variety of discourses.

What does Christmas mean to you and what do you think the ideology of Christmas is where you live? Can you find examples of residual, dominant, and emergent discourses within the way Christmas is experienced in Western cultures?

Exercise commentary

It is worth noting that the establishment of Christmas as a major festival in the West was developed in the nineteenth century, particularly in Victorian England. Many of the traditions and rituals of Christmas were encouraged then and have persisted and developed since then. We want to identify four distinct ideological strands or discourses that converge in Christmas as a cultural experience:

1 Christmas is of course a religious celebration of the Christian faith. It celebrates the birth of the central figure of Christian religion, Jesus, and it honours a more minor figure, Saint Nicholas (Santa Claus). As such, it emphasises love, spirituality, and the giving of presents to express our love and care for one another.

2 Christmas is founded on and related to older religious festivals—for example, Greek and Roman festivals of Saturnalia (a winter celebration for Saturn, the Roman god of agriculture, and a time for wild revelry) and pagan celebrations—that celebrate death and rebirth in the depth of winter and the move towards spring. The natural symbols of these festivals—trees, holly, mistletoe, and so on—connect with the fact that the religions associated with these older festivals involved worship of the earth and nature. Historically Christianity incorporated these symbols partly to help establish itself as a successor to pagan religions. The Roman Saturnalias were orgiastic festivals. The dark times of winter meant some months of deprivation before spring. Saturnalia was the 'final fling' before the period of frugality and cold. It was a celebration involving indulgence in hedonistic pleasures. (Note that 'festival' derives from the Latin word *vale*, which means farewell; 'fest' derives from the Latin word for feasting; and 'carnival' derives from the Latin for farewell (*vale*) to the flesh (*carne*), meaning that there will be less meat to eat until new animals are born in spring.)

- Saturnalia allowed great indulgence, as do many holidays, which today are seen as pleasurable breaks from work rather than as times of religious contemplation (holy days). Saturnalia also involved a social 'topsy-turviness'—the turning upside down of normal cultural values and conventions. This occurred in the depiction of social values that are not 'normal' in such practices as pantomimes and role-reversal games (such as the rich serving and feeding the poor). Christianity 'won' its audience over to the Christian story partly through maintaining and incorporating these other traditions, which clearly gave people a lot of pleasure.

- Saturnalia and other pagan traditions are still fundamental to Christmas. They have been blended in with the religious story, even though they contradict the religious meaning of Christmas in some ways, and they have found their own patterns of expression in late twentieth-century Christmas. The holiday period allows for excessive partying, drinking, and merry-making, alongside observance of Christian religious ceremonies. While the contradictory nature of these may involve clashes between religious observance and general celebration, they tend to coexist reasonably well. Both the pagan-derived traditions and the religious aspects of Christmas are linked to two more ideologies or discourses.

3 Christmas has become a time for celebrating and honouring the family, which is one of the cornerstones of modern society. The ideal is for everyone to spend Christmas Day with their families. This ideal is lived out by many, but of course it breaks down for those people who do not have a family. In reality it also often provokes major stress among families. Christmas is a time when there is a rise in marital and family breakdowns as well as a rise in suicides. Thus, as the holiday attempts to cement the ideology of the family in place, it also makes the cracks in the structure all too visible.

4 While all three aspects—Saturnalia, Christianity, and the ideal of the family—are still central to Christmas, it has now become primarily a celebration of capitalism and materialism. Christmas is the time for a mass celebration and frenzy of consumerism, a mass spending of money. Christmas has become progressively more commercialised, such that the spending of money and the selling of goods is now the predominant feature of Christmas. It is often said that Christmas begins earlier each year, which is a reflection of the fact that the success of Christmas is measured, to a large extent, by shop sales.

These four ideological aspects blend together. It is difficult to take any one position on how to judge Christmas because all four contradictory aspects are in play at once. Presents, for example, are inscribed into all four discourses: they can be seen as an expression of our Christian love and charity to one another; they offer great pleasure, indulgence, and enjoyment; the biggest presents are usually given to family members, and present-giving rituals are focused on family gatherings; and presents cost money—the more expensive the present the better it is deemed to be. Nearly everyone can find something positive in the present-giving aspect of Christmas, which accounts for its popularity. Those who decry Christmas—for example, because it is too commercial, or because they are disgusted by the waste of money involved, or because they are atheists and disagree with its promotion of religion, or because they are Christian and disapprove of the orgy of indulgence that occurs— risk being labelled 'scrooges' and being seen as outsiders.

Australia still holds on to old traditions that are linked to its British heritage, some of which, particularly the tradition of roast turkey, and the emphasis on winter, are clearly out of place in our climate. The move towards champagne breakfasts on the beach, however, is an attempt to construct new traditions, new ways of celebrating that take Christmas into another dimension. Some clever entrepreneurs are encouraging the celebration of 'Christmas in July' as a way of connecting Christmas with winter and getting people to spend even more money on celebrations. It will be interesting to see how multicultural Australia develops Christmas rituals.

In this example of Christmas as a repository of different ideologies (residual, dominant, and emergent), contradictory ideological aspects are at work, but they can exist relatively comfortably side by side. Similar contradictions can be found in media texts. In analysing media texts ideologically, you should be able to show various contradictory ideological aspects at work. The idea of contradictory ideological aspects and the attempt to understand how they work together is central to this book. You may well find traces of new and old ideological positions, and traces of progressive and conservative discourses, within the same media text. You will begin to see how different ideological elements interact, how they are linked, and how they are often cemented over (or sugar-coated, as is Christmas) with the promise of pleasure.

To see how different ideological strands exist in popular texts, look at the news item and Christmas card (Figures 4.2 and 4.3). The news item is taken from the local newspaper of the Perth suburb of Claremont, Western Australia. See if you can find evidence of all four ideological strands mentioned above. Is there evidence of people feeling uncomfortable about any of these aspects? What is the dominant discourse of Christmas constructed here? (Note in the news item how all the participants are White—this is very much a White Christmas!)

Figure 4.2 Happy Christmas: interviews and photos from *Local News: Claremont*
Source: *Local News: Claremont*, 18 December 1996

Figure 4.3 Christmas cartoon
Source: Bestie, The Ink Group, 1994

EVERY YEAR AS A FAMILY THEY
ENACTED A LITTLE PLAY TO REMEMBER
WHAT CHRISTMAS IS ALL ABOUT.

THE LIMITATIONS OF DOMINANT IDEOLOGY THEORY

We now return to the theory of dominant ideology. Although it is a useful frame-work, there are limitations to this way of thinking. It paints ideology as too much of a one-way system. It suggests that the dominant ideology is always imposed from above and accepted unproblematically by people. It holds that people are compliant in accepting these beliefs. This does not account for people who refuse to accept these values or for the two-way struggle that goes on between dominant and subordinate groups in establishing social values. It also does not fully allow for the fact that many people working in the media challenge the dominant systems. As John Hartley has argued in analysing media representations of ethnicity and Aboriginality: '[I]f we accept that the media … encourage racism in certain of their ways of reporting the world, then we have also to believe that they can influence … for positive change as well as negatively … that the media are forces for progressive social change as well as for negative social stereotyping' (Hartley 1996, p. 73). The theory of dominant ideology is thus too rigid and simplistic. It does not allow for contradictions and variations within the development and establishment of ideology.

HEGEMONY

The theoretical framework of hegemony has more flexibility than that of dominant ideology, and it can be used alongside the concept of ideology. Theories of hege-mony were developed by Antonio Gramsci, a leader of the Italian communist party in the 1920s and 1930s who was imprisoned by the fascist Mussolini regime.[4]

Hegemony is a way of understanding how one social group maintains its power over subordinate groups. It means power and control. So when we speak of the maintenance of hegemony we are referring to a way of maintaining power. The major point about hegemony is that it suggests that maintaining power over others is always a process in struggle: it is never stable; it involves participation and negotiation on both sides; and it is a two-way process (in contrast to ideology, which tends to be conceived of as a one-way process, imposed from the top down).

Hegemony is maintained through consent. While power can be maintained in many ways, including force, hegemonic power is maintained consensually and it entails a degree of complicity in one's own subordination. Hegemony can not be maintained by use of force because coercion does not win consent; it wins obedience and it is imposed from the top down. Coercion is a method of maintaining power that parallels the way in which RSAs are maintained through force by institutions such as the police, the law, and the army, all of which have the capacity to enforce compliance and punish dissidents (see p. 215). Consent as a method of maintaining hegemony parallels the way in which ISAs are maintained. Gramsci saw consent as the basis of the social organisation of the democratic societies that predominate in Western culture. The notion of hegemony as maintained by consent is very useful in media studies. It brings us back to a question posed at the beginning of this book: how do the media win support for their representations?

We can see how hegemony works by imagining an example of it at a micro social level: the interactions of a parent and child. The parent holds the main power (in the same way as the dominant groups in society hold power) over the child, yet the parent cannot always make the child do what he or she wants. Children have wills of their own, and parents constantly have to resort to bribery or blackmail—'You can watch TV if you do your homework'—or to the granting of concessions—'You can have half of the sweets now and half later'—in order to get their way. (They could use force as well, but this would not win consent.) Parent and child are involved in a process of negotiation and struggle.

At a macro social level, similar negotiations and struggles go on between bosses and trade unions, political parties and lobby groups, men and women, Whites and Aboriginals, and so on. The main qualitative differences between the micro level of the parent–child relationship and the macro level of struggles between the groups just mentioned are that the parent–child relationship is usually based on love and that the child is clearly dependent on the parent. In contrast, the struggles between the social groups are based on factors such as monetary exploitation (of course, it is a moot point whether workers depend on the bosses for their jobs or whether the bosses depend on the workers for their profits!).

Analysis of the continual negotiation and struggle between dominant and subordinate social groups must take into account the following:
- There must be some positive reward for the subordinate groups in order for them to accept the social conditions: for example, Western democracies must offer enough freedoms, pleasures, comfortable lifestyles, and media entertainments for members of subordinate groups to accept the status quo.
- While subordinate groups can win many concessions and benefits, the dominant group will never allow power to be completely taken away from them. Struggle

between groups may result in lots of gradual changes, but ultimately the dominant groups will not give up power and control completely.

- This second point is important politically and socially. The logic of this argument is that radical change necessarily involves violent struggle. The opposing view, described as gradualist or reformist, holds that social change can and will be achieved through gradual, minor shifts, and that equality can be achieved peacefully.

You can test out this theoretical model of hegemony in your understanding of the media. Use the example of gender. Ask yourself whether, despite all the changes and concessions won by women and feminism, the hegemony of men, of patriarchy, is still maintained. Men have let many of their powers go but still maintain power overall. In the media this might be reflected in the fact that while many media texts show major changes in gender relations, overall, media output still supports male dominance.

Finally, relate hegemony back to the idea of ideological work (pp. 217–21). Hegemony stresses struggle and negotiation, the way texts present different points of view and the way they include new perspectives, partly by accommodating them. Many media texts are contradictory: they include radical and conservative aspects, and regressive and progressive aspects, all at the same time. The ideological work they do in the course of addressing issues of social struggle can be seen as part of the way hegemony is a process of struggle between dominant and subordinate groups. In this model, ideology is not just imposed from above. Rather, it is a much more complex interaction of social groups and forces. The concept of hegemony fits in with media theory that, instead of seeing texts as having total control over audiences, understands that audiences can 'do things' to texts in the readings they make of them and the pleasures they derive from them.

SUMMARY

In Part 4 an extended analysis of the term 'ideology' has been developed and applied widely to society. The term 'ideology' has been closely associated with discourse, but has also been distinguished from it because not all aspects of discourse form a naturalised part of our world-view. We have suggested that hegemony is a theoretical tool that is similar to the concept of ideology but allows greater understanding of the two-way processes of struggle and negotiation between dominant and subordinate groups. We have suggested that all three concepts are useful for understanding how the media work and we encourage you to use them and test them out in your media analyses. Part 5 explores these concepts further by considering them in the context of gender and ethnicity.

Part 5

BOYS AND GIRLS, BLACKS AND WHITES:
GENDER AND ETHNICITY

I knew nothing about sex before I got married. When my mother told me that the man goes on top and the woman on the bottom, I bought bunk beds.

Joan Rivers, comedian

OVERVIEW OF PART 5

In Part 5, we will use the concepts of ideology and discourse to examine media representations of gender and ethnicity. We will also consider how gender and ethnicity are experienced in the real world.

16 Gender and Contradictory Ideologies of Femininity

SEX AND GENDER

In thinking about the categories of male and female, masculinity and femininity, it is useful to make a distinction between two defining terms: 'sex' and 'gender'. Sexual difference is a biological distinction between male and female. Gender is about social and cultural roles, about behaviour that is deemed socially acceptable for men and women, and about 'masculinity' and 'femininity'. Gender study arises from concerns about the relative social positions of men and women, and about the social inequalities and the social struggles between them. Many of the examples already used in this book have explored representations of gender. Our interest in the question of gender comes from the fact that sex and gender are two of the most important ways that humans classify themselves and other people: your answer to the question 'Who are you?' may well begin 'I am a man ...' or 'I am a woman ...'.

Gender issues intersect with sexual desire and sexual expression. Sexuality is lived out and expressed in many different ways and many different places. In Western culture it is often connected with heterosexuality, love, marriage, and the family. The social institutions of marriage and the family are ideally meant to include, and be the natural outlet for, sexual feelings and sexual expression. The dominant ideology has been that people find love and sexual satisfaction in monogamous relationships and in families, although the reality is that these social institutions coexist with other forms of sexual and emotional relationships. This ideal of the family connects with the way in which sexuality is constructed, with many media representations, and with many of our own interests in such issues as masculinity, femininity, and sexuality. An explanation of gender identity, sexuality, and social experience enhances our understandings of ourselves, our families, and our roles in the communities and social structures in which we live. We hope you will be able to share this interest in the social construction of masculinity and femininity by relating it back to yourself and your experiences.

The analyses in this chapter look both at media representations of gender relations and at how men and women live in the real world. It is necessary to take account of both to have some understanding of media discourses and wider social discourses.

WOMEN AND ADVERTISEMENTS

This first chapter focuses on the contradictory ideologies and discourses of femininity found in advertising imagery of the 1990s. The aim is to see how certain ideologica shifts have occurred in the 'postfeminist' era (see p. 289) and how these have both progressive and regressive potential. As such, this is a good example of ideological work, of the struggle over the maintenance of male hegemony, and of the simultaneous appearance of different ideological positions in the media. These points extend the discussion of ideology, discourse, and hegemony in Part 4.

Each of the four advertisements reproduced in this chapter demonstrates interesting facets and contradictions in relation to constructions of ideologies of femininity. Take a few minutes to look at each and consider what is significant in relation to constructions of femininity. While we cannot cover all aspects of the construction of femininity in our analysis, we will draw out the most significant aspects in each advertisement. One of the most important things these advertisements have in common is the fact that they all appear to offer women some pleasure and some power, and thus appear to have progressive aspects, at the same time as being traditional and patriarchal.

Advertisement number 1

Figure 5.1 Advertisement for Wedgwood dinner service
Source: Wedgwood; published in *Mode Brides*, 1994, reproduced with permission of Wedgwood, Barlaston, Stoke-on-Trent, United Kingdom

This advertisement (Figure 5.1) is interesting in the way it 'wins' a female audience over to very traditional aspects of marriage. It is the most conservative of the four images. It wins women through its mode of address, through the pleasures it offers, and through masking or displacing potentially problematic issues to do with marriage. Initially it is useful to consider what the implied narrative underpinning the image might be (you may wish to refer back to the section on implied narrative, p. 96). Ask yourselves what has just happened in the scene depicted in the advertisement, and what is going to happen next? It looks as though the wedding ceremony (the service) has just finished, and the couple appear to be relaxing after the reception, at the beginning of their honeymoon. Honeymoons traditionally feature three things: ordering room service from the honeymoon suite in a hotel, the ritual of unwrapping wedding gifts and, of course, consummating the relationship.

Mode of address

Mode of address refers to the different ways in which a text speaks to or addresses its audience. In this advertisement, who is speaking to whom? We read it as though it is a woman speaker addressing other women. We read it in this way for four reasons:

1 The woman in the photograph is looking more directly at the camera (and therefore, at us, the audience) than is the man.
2 The caption talks about 'service' being received, and because it is the woman who is being served by the man holding the bottle, it is therefore her speaking.
3 Weddings are traditionally a feminine topic—men would not normally be represented in the media as discussing marriage in this way.
4 The advertisement appears in *Mode Brides*, a magazine aimed at, and bought and read by, women.

The advertisement thus foregrounds a woman's voice and women's discourses, and consequently gives women power, even if it is within the traditional context of marriage, historically a bulwark of patriarchy. She is the person commenting on, describing, and consequently 'owning' this event. She has the power of naming.

Pleasure

Numerous pleasures for women are made available in this advertisement:

- **humour.** There are three puns in the caption to this advertisement. In addition to the simple meaning of 'wedding service', the word 'service' can mean dinner service (crockery and cutlery), room service, and sexual services.
- **sexual pleasure.** Narratively, the picture suggests that the wedding has just happened and the honeymoon is about to commence. In the context, the bottle and the champagne are phallic, as they suggests the sexual activity that lies ahead for the bride and groom. In the context of the pun on sexual services, the advertisement is also suggesting that the woman will be pleasured by the groom (that he will service her).
- **wealth.** The setting is beautiful and the scene is pleasingly photographed, suggesting wealth through the furnishings, the clothing, the garden in the background, and most importantly, through the expensive and tasteful dinner service.
- **the traditionally feminine pleasures of marriage.** The traditionally feminine dreams of, and excitement over, marriage are referenced here, as is the common perception that a woman's wedding day is the most exciting day of her life.

Masking and displacing

This is a wonderful example of ideological work (see p. 217). Some aspects of the situation are foregrounded at the expense of others. In this picture, women's domestic work is subtly acknowledged, but is then masked behind other pleasures. The advertisement wants us to answer the question 'What will happen next?' with 'She will receive ecstatic sexual pleasure'. But there is an alternative answer: over the years of her marriage, she will do lots of cooking, serving out of meals, and washing up! While this labour is alluded to by the dinner service, which is designed for these domestic routines, it is masked by the way the dinner service becomes an aesthetic object of beauty and pleasure, a gift.

Women's domestic labour is also displaced by the fact that the advertisement depicts the woman being served (and suggests that she will later be serviced sexually)—by her husband—thereby drawing attention away from the fact that women in marriages tend to be the servers rather than those who are served. A feminist saying of the 1970s states 'It starts when you sink in his arms and ends with your arms in his sink'. This nicely points out the way that, for women, the discourse of romance and pleasure can often turn into the reality of domestic drudgery in traditional gender relations. In this advertisement the discourse of romance and pleasure is used to outweigh the realities of marriage for most women. While the wedding gifts are potentially a reminder of this housework, their beauty distracts the audience from this unsavoury allusion.

This advertisement shows how the foregrounding of interests and pleasures may win women over to traditional feminine roles.

Advertisement number 2

Figure 5.2 Advertisement for Mills & Boon romances. The caption to this advertisement reads: 'Not even her dentist had gone that far with his instrument. You'd be surprised what happens between the covers of the world's best-selling romances. Available now from newsagents, bookshops, supermarkets, chain stores, and department stores'. Source: Harlequin Enterprises; published in *Cosmopolitan*, 1992

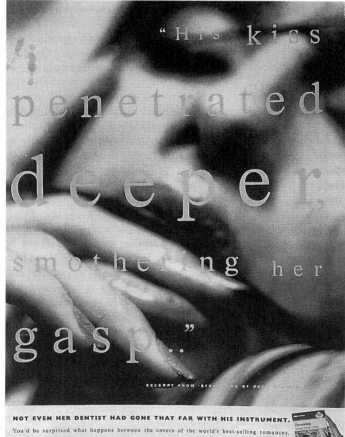

By combining two different discourses, two different voices about femininity, this advertisement (Figure 5.2) shows changes in the ideology of femininity. It wins women by offering them something new, a new aspect of femininity.

Romance discourse

Mills & Boon books are paperback romance novels, read mostly by women. They are denigrated for their formulaic and clichéd literary style, and also because romance writing has traditionally been vague and euphemistic in its representation of women's sexuality and conservative in its portrayal of gender. These romances perpetuate stereotypes in that they portray women being attracted by tall, strong, powerful, domineering men. The discourses of romance novels have been part of women's culture for a long time (although initially, in the eighteenth and nineteenth centuries, romance novels were considered rather risqué) (Radway 1987).

The discourse of soft porn

In its overtly sexual nature, the advertisement aims to make people think Mills & Boon are offering something new. Both the image and the words of the caption relate to photographic and literary codes and conventions, not of romance or melodrama, but of soft pornography (soft porn). They imitate typical soft porn photographs, imagery, and language. Pornography has traditionally been seen as a male discourse, but with the advent of mainstream erotic romances, women readers are being encouraged to take on the traditionally male (and therefore taboo for women) pleasures of pornography.

At one level this is an ideological move forwards. Patriarchy has traditionally felt threatened by and tried to control women's sexuality. One aspect of feminism has been the foregrounding and celebration of women's sexuality. This is reflected in the way that many women's magazines contain explicit features on sexuality. In this advertisement the female reader is being offered sexual pleasure, although note how the humorous element in the caption might undercut the sexual element, in the same way that male strippers for women are often seen as funny rather than a real turn on.

On another level, there are negative aspects to this advertisement. Does it confirm the traditional view of women as primarily sexual beings linked to their biology, rather than as social beings? Since the soft porn discourse is primarily male, does this advertisement ask women to take on a male pleasure, a male way of seeing this world, thereby defining pleasure in male terms and legitimating the pornography industry (which is renowned for objectifying and degrading women)? If so, does this negate the equality instated by the advertisement (the fact that women may enjoy sexual pleasure as much as men)?

Advertisement number 3 (Plate 2)

Ideological contradictions and ideological work are demonstrated well in this third advertisement (Plate 2). Like the previous two advertisements, this one plays with the theme of women's sexuality and their relatively new sexual freedom. But it goes on to place severe limitations on it and finally channels women's desire into more traditional avenues.

Women's desire

Women's desire is foregrounded through the sexually appealing image of the man. The female audience is invited to take sexual pleasure in objectifying the man, thus acknowledging active female sexuality (as do the previous two advertisements).

Restrictions on women's desires

Having invited women to take sexual pleasure in viewing the man, the advertisement then negates this through a focus on health discourses and by playing on the guilt associated with contravening social norms related to body shape and passive sexuality. Safe sex is a major issue confronting us today in relation to sexuality and health. This advertisement advocates safe sex as no sex. Instead of tackling safe sex in terms of safe sexual practices, women are encouraged to displace their desire back on to the safer arena of food. This displacement is reinforced by making viewers feel guilty. Guilt has traditionally been used by Christianity to suppress sexuality, for both men and women. The West represses sexuality in many ways, but at the same time, through advertising and other popular media products, it consistently foregrounds sexual desire. This is one of the fascinating contradictions of Western culture. My belief is that sexual advertising works because people are sexually repressed, since desire works on the basis of absence or lack. If people were sexually happy, these advertisements, which seem to be offering us sexual satisfaction through the purchase of goods, would not work. People would not need to buy the goods because they would already be sexually satisfied. Consequently, advertisers need people to be sexually repressed! This advertisement suggests that if the narrator followed her sexual desire, she would feel guilty.

Food

This advertisement proposes that the substitute for sex is food. The ice-cream is presented as desirable (including the phallic chocolate wafer) but while female desire is acknowledged, it is simultaneously dismissed. Ice-cream, like sex, will not be good for the female reader (even though she might want them both!). Vegetable soup, however, will be! Again this draws on a health discourse (of nutrition). While it is undoubtedly true that vegetables are healthier than sweets, we maintain that the real reason women are being asked to reject ice-cream is because of physical appearance. The suggestion is that consuming ice-cream will make women fat and they will therefore not conform to (male) ideals of femininity. There is indeed an interesting reference to size in the advertising copy ('and because size really does matter') and while this is partly a joke for women about male sexual prowess and how women may enjoy sex with well-endowed men, it is also a subtle reminder to women to be conscious of their own size, weight, and appearance. Consequently, the narrative resolution and structure of this advertisement is to present various forbidden pleasures for women that are then finally denied, in the guise of a health discourse, in favour of traditional values.

Summary

The advertisement is fascinating in the way it offers aspects of a progressive discourse about women's sexuality but then incorporates these back into a traditional view of feminine roles and ideal femininity.

Advertisement number 4 (Plate 3)

This advertisement (Plate 3) was intended to show that fashion is something that is in your blood, or under your skin—a sense of style that is innate and distinctive like the fashionable clothing produced by the Young Designer's Emporium. However, a number of key signifiers in the ad work to convey a more powerful message.

The configuration of the initials Y.D.E. on the page reads 'D.Y.E.' or, phonetically, 'die', thus connoting death and creating an association between death and the fashion industry in which fabric and coloured dyes are so important. The resemblance between the red fabric 'under her skin' and blood reinforce the connotations of death, leading critics to interpret the advertisement as an image of suicide, the ultimate form of self-inflicted harm. To our mind these oppositional readings are extreme, but a semiotic analysis does reveal links between the image and the phrase 'fashion victim', and between that phrase and many other media representations of women as victims (victims of violence and crime and sexual abuse, victims in slasher films, and so on).

The phrase 'fashion victim' and the advertising image itself are particularly powerful because, like *The Big Shave*, a film discussed on pp. 250–1, they depict instances in which young people inflict harm on their own bodies. For many women, being a fashion victim hurts only the bank balance, but it can also lead to plastic surgery and other forms of self-wounding. This is related to the actual site of the cut on the body of the woman in the image. The 'wound' is over her uterus, a part of the body associated with uniquely female forms of power and creativity. While it is true that many young women channel their creativity into designing their own clothing or style, and into many areas other than family and children, the image looks like an attack on the heart of femininity itself, in the form of elective abdominal surgery (tubal ligation, a caesarian, hysterectomy, or abortion).

CONCLUSION

These are complex advertisements in their mixture of discourses and the way they present different aspects of ideologies about femininity. We have read these four advertisements as offering something positive to women but ultimately as reasserting aspects of traditional femininity. In this way we can see a hegemonic struggle taking place: women win something, but the traditional roles and power relations are not ultimately shifted.

In recent years there have been numerous examples of films and television programs centred on young women as the main, heroic characters, for example *Zena: Warrior Princess, Clueless, Tomb Raider, Muriel's Wedding, Buffy, Bridget Jones's Diary*. These can be usefully considered within this same context of hegemonic shifts in, and changing roles and definitions of, femininity. *Legally Blonde* focuses on discourses of femininity. What is interesting is how it seems to celebrate many aspects of 'traditional' femininity—interest in clothes, make-up, 'trivial' talk, and gossip. However, it shows these things as sources of pleasure for women in a female world—the opening scene is all about girls being together and being united in a sisterhood of femininity; they are not dressing up for male pleasure but for each other's pleasure. And it is a film that seems to validate these feminine pleasures—they are not to be seen as trivial, not to be denigrated—and as the plot moves into the 'masculine' world of law and the law courts it is the 'feminine' knowledge that is ultimately more powerful in establishing justice. But this is a 'feminine' discourse that still allows its heroine to wear tight-fitting, pink-leather outfits and marries her off in the narrative resolution. These recent media texts can be considered in the context of postfeminism (see below).

Our aim in this chapter has been to demonstrate how different discourses can be combined in the same media product. Our job is to see these different aspects at work, to draw attention to the way in which they are combined, and to be aware of the possible different ideological readings of the text at hand. In this way, we will be able to see, in media products, progressive and regressive aspects of gender ideologies, as well as contradictions and changes in the construction of gender ideologies. The images allow us to use the critical tools of ideology, hegemony, and discourse as a way of understanding what they are doing.

17 Ideologies of Masculinity

We will now discuss ideologies of masculinity in media representations. We will also discuss masculinity in real life: How do men actually live? What are the current discourses of masculinity? This will involve some reflection on femininity.

To prepare yourself for thinking about masculinity, take some time to reflect on the following questions. Then write down your answers and discuss them with male and female friends.

1 What things do you like best and what things do you like least about men and masculinity (in the real world)?

2 What male film stars, pop stars, and television personalities do you like most, and what are the characteristics they have that you like?

3 Take a moment to consider what options might be available to men who do not see viable male role models or possibilities for identification in the representations of masculinity offered in the media.

You can do the same exercise for femininity as well.

INTRODUCTORY POINTS

Patriarchy: masculinity and femininity are differently valued

We believe we live in a patriarchal society whose ideological values relate directly to men and masculinity, women and femininity. Patriarchy is a system based on the 'law of the father'. This is so in two ways: first, through lineage (children tend to take on their father's family name rather than their mother's); second, through the legal and political institutions that, although no longer given over into the exclusive power of men, have developed as male institutions. In the past women could not hold political office; they were excluded from voting rights (women won the right to vote only after protracted struggle); they had lesser legal rights; and married women were regarded as the property of their husbands. (Churches are one of the last major institutional powers still divided over the issue of whether or not women have the right to hold positions of power—we are thinking here of the struggles of women to be ordained in, for example, the Anglican Church.)

Most cultures have privileged men with greater rights than women, and most continue to give them greater benefits in terms of power and wages. Consequently, our society is based not just on different genders but on unequally positioned genders.

The dominant values of patriarchal society are linked to values encouraged in men and masculinity. Western society encourages competitiveness and individuality. It also encourages aggression and violence as ways of solving problems. All these values are central in the way we work, in the economic sphere, in terms of our education system, in terms of the way we interact socially, and in the way boys are socialised into becoming men. You could say that warfare is the ultimate problem-solving device of patriarchy.[1] Our culture tends to validate such male characteristics at the same time as denigrating female characteristics and femininity. This denigration of femininity, alongside the inequality in power between the sexes, leads to a sexist, misogynist society. Misogyny means hatred of women and femininity (literally, hatred of the womb). Misogyny can also lead to a rejection of men's own feminine and softer side.

Multiple masculinities

Just as with ideologies and femininities, we should remember that there is not only one version of masculinity but many possible variations of male behaviour: there are many masculinities. Referring back to your list of stars (p. 238) may alert you to the different styles of masculinity to be found: for example, Heath Ledger, Noah Taylor, Mark Wahlberg, Chris Rock, Leonardo di Caprio, Robert de Niro, Arnold Schwarzenegger, Mel Gibson, Brad Pitt, Eddie Murphy, Woody Allen, and Ewan McGregor. Be aware also that different ethnic groups may have different masculinities: for example, Afro-American masculinities may be different from White masculinities.

However, as with ideology and femininity, there is a dominant ideal of masculinity. In the 1980s this ideal was epitomised by stars such as Arnold Schwarzenegger and Clint Eastwood, both of whom represent ideals of strength, toughness, coolness, attractiveness, heterosexuality, and Whiteness. While these ideals are still found at the beginning of the twenty-first century—in stars such as Heath Ledger, Nicholas Cage, and Wesley Snipes—there are many other possibilities. However, the ideal version of dominant masculinity presents a problem for real men because the ideal is so difficult to attain. While many comic actors draw attention to the impossibility of achieving perfect masculinity and point to its ridiculousness, heroic film texts still predominate.

Alongside the media ideals there are also dominant versions of actual masculinity and femininity. This is less clear cut, but we argue that as a consequence of our socialisation and upbringing men and women are likely to develop certain patterns of typical behaviour. While the behaviour of some men and women will not conform to these patterns, it is still possible to see general tendencies in masculine and feminine behaviour, in how men and women act and feel. This is illustrated by Stephanie Dowrick's table on pp. 242–3.

Masculinity in crisis?

Since the 1970s masculinity has become an 'issue' in Western culture; people speak of masculinity being in crisis. This suggests that the old masculine ideals are no longer universally accepted and that people have begun to question what it means to be a man. Bookshops have sections on men's health and men's issues and universities have courses in men's studies.[2] Jokes are made about and against men in the way they used to be made against women. This crisis was prompted by two movements: feminism and the gay rights movement.

Feminism

The growth of feminism from the 1960s onwards has had an enormous impact on society. Initially the focus was directly on women: feminism fought for women's social, legal, political, and economic rights, and attempted to understand how the construction of femininity was related to the status of women. This led to important social changes that had far-reaching impacts on both women and men. Then feminists began to explore masculinity, problematising masculinity for the first time, and seeing it too as a social construction. Consequently, some men began to question and look at their own masculine identities.

The gay rights movement

In parallel with the growth of feminism, the gay rights movement challenged the oppression of lesbians and gay men by our heterosexist society. The gay movement offered many insights into both homosexual and heterosexual masculinity and challenged some of the stereotypes of 'normal' masculinity. Most recently, a body of work called queer theory (see p. 288) is continuing this task in different ways.

These two movements—feminism and the gay rights movement—challenged normal masculinity and suggested new possibilities for masculine identity. In the late 1980s and 1990s the so-called 'men's movement' has been exploring masculinity further. This movement, characterised by the work of Robert Bly (in America) and Steve Biddulph (in Australia), looks to find ways of changing and revalidating masculinity.[3] The result is that as we start the twenty-first century, masculinity is in question. It is seen as more fluid than ever before, in the sense that there are more options available for men as to how to be masculine. The damaging nature of patriarchy to women and men has been acknowledged, and attempts have been made to find new versions of masculinity that challenge the oppression and sexism of patriarchal masculinity.

With awareness of the crisis of masculinity, many popular films, television programs, newspaper and magazine articles, and advertisements address the question of what it means to be a man today. Gay culture has become much more acceptable and has influenced ideals of masculinity. Figure 5.3 is the opening text from an article published in *Cleo*. The article imagines a world in which men have become redundant. The text is a mock encyclopaedia

Figure 5.3 Extract from an article in *Cleo* magazine
Source: text from *Cleo*, May 1998; photograph by Jasmine Martin

entry on homo sapiens. This article is typical of the recent spate of media products that comment on or make reference to a crisis in masculinity.

Essentialism versus social constructionism

One of the major arguments about gender is between essentialist definitions of gender and views that hold that gender is a social construction. The essentialist position sees gender as based on genetic, biological, and psychological differences. It holds that men and women are essentially (inevitably) different in their biological and emotional make-up, and that this determines how they feel and act. The social construction position sees gender characteristics as purely a consequence of how people are socialised. We cannot resolve this very complex position here. Our approach is to accept elements of both, but to stress the socialisation position. Your position on this question will emerge as you progress through this Part.

Consider these lyrics to the popular song 'Only a Woman':

> The tears that drip from my bewildered eyes, taste the bitter sweet romance;
> You're still in my hopes, you're still on my mind, and even though I manage on my own,
> My heart is low, my heart is so low, as only a woman's heart can be,
> As only a woman's, as only a woman's, as only a woman's heart can know.

Do you think these words suggest an essentialist/biological or a social constructionist division between men and women?

Exercise commentary

You could argue that the text supports both positions. It supports the essentialist, biological difference stance because it suggests that certain experiences inherent in the nature of women and femininity are available only to women. But it can also be interpreted as supporting the view that these experiences are socially based; they grow out of women's experience of oppression, exploitation by men, and patriarchy and, because only women have experienced these situations, they alone can feel and express them.

MASCULINE AND FEMININE CHARACTERISTICS?

The points above suggest that masculinity is not only in crisis but is also a problem for our society. As a man, how do I feel and write about this? In many ways I am critical of masculinity and patriarchy, and I recognise ways in which men are sexist and oppress women. I would like to see social changes. But I am also sympathetic towards men's position in our society. I think it is important to see that men too have suffered under patriarchy, in trying to live up to its limiting and impossible ideals. Men's failings hurt themselves as well as others, and they are predominantly the result of society, not biology. But criticism alone won't always help matters; we need to understand the processes that have produced patriarchy and we need to make changes in masculinity. At the same time, I want to validate the positive aspects of masculinity alongside the positive aspects of femininity; I see them as complementary.

In her book, *Intimacy and Solitude* (1991), Stephanie Dowrick examines the way men and women grow up in Western society. She concludes one section by suggesting that there are dominant male and female characteristics. Her argument is not that these are genetic (that is, inherent) biological male and female characteristics, rather that they are the result of social causes—for example the fact that men work outside the home more than women, and so are absent from children for more time than women—and upbringing (for example, the different psychological patterns caused by the different ways in which male and female children are treated by their parents).

Read the following characteristics. How appropriate are they are for you, your friends, and your relatives? Remember that these are not judgmental descriptions; they are simply the way Dowrick and others see men and women behaving. Note which descriptions you strongly agree or disagree with, and then consider why men and women might act like this.

A WOMAN IS LIKELY TO:

feel incomplete when she does not have close relationships
find it difficult to compartmentalise her life (forget the children when she is at work, forget the fight when her partner leaves the house)
use her primary relationships rather than her work as her measure for self-acceptance
see her mother rather than her father as largely responsible for problems in her family of origin
blame herself when a relationship or interactions with other people are not going well
value friendships with other women
find it difficult to tolerate differences of opinion in close friends
believe that his role is to initiate and her role is to respond
believe her male partner's opinions and experience carry more weight than her own
protect her male sexual partner from unpleasant 'truths'
protect her male sexual partner from his emotional inadequacies
wait a while before getting into another relationship, should she and her partner split up
feel children and home are primarily her responsibility, even when she and her partner are both doing paid work
need solitude as a time to be self-caring
doubt her entitlement to solitude
have difficulty distinguishing thought from feeling
feel insecure about her personal appearance
feel relatively free to risk being no one important, without feeling that she is no one at all

A MAN IS LIKELY TO:

have difficulty listening to other people
blame others rather than taking self-responsibility
feel uncared for when he is alone
collapse on being left
compartmentalise his life with relative ease
express anger more readily than tears
use anger as a shield against deep feeling
find it difficult to be intimate or even open with other (heterosexual) men

measure people according to their 'differences' from him
mistrust women
put more effort into his work life than his intimate relationships
gain his self-acceptance through his work rather than love
replace his partner quickly should she leave him, die or be dismissed
assume that small children are better off cared for by women
find it difficult to empathise
perceive he has more worldly (physical, economic) power than his female partner
want his partner to recognise and tend his 'little boy' within
believe that his command of rational thinking makes him more often 'right'
believe that at times of crisis he should take command
find it difficult to describe his feelings (Dowrick 1991, pp. 96–7, 103–4).

Exercise commentary

These lists are generalisations, so they will not apply to all men and women. They are also written at a particular historical moment, 1991, as a description of Western gender traits. Feminism, the gay rights movement, and the crisis of masculinity have changed men and women, and these changes continue. Consequently, the characteristics Dowrick proposes may not be so applicable now. The younger you are, the more likely that you will be less susceptible to these stereotypes. If you do not feel that these usefully describe men and women, take note that this may be because you are part of a changing generation—they may well be valid for those born earlier and so are still important. It can be very useful for you to understand what your parents and their generation went through in terms of their positioning as masculine and feminine. If you do recognise these as accurate descriptions of men and women, think about why this should be the case: what social and psychological factors push men and women towards these typical behaviours? Dowrick goes on in her book to give her explanation of why this is the case.

MEDIA REPRESENTATIONS OF MASCULINITY

In this section on media representations of masculinity, our comments refer to both media representations and to masculinity in the actual world, and we suggest some themes and areas for analysis that you can pursue. We refer mainly to traditional aspects of masculinity (or dominant masculinity) although we recognise that there are new kinds of representations available now.

Men and women together

Since masculinity and femininity partly define themselves in relation to each other—masculinity defines itself in relation to femininity, and vice versa—it is useful to look at images of men and women together and to consider the limitations of oppositional thought. Such representations tend to highlight the binary opposition that makes discourses of masculinity and femininity work. Men and women are often represented together in a context of heterosexual coupling.

Figure 5.4
Advertisement for
Creda heaters, circa 1980
Source: General Domestic
Appliances Ltd

Figure 5.5 Billboard advertisement for Channel 9, *circa* 1990, Perth
Source: Channel 9, Perth

Figure 5.6 Biff cartoon, 1989
Source: Mick Kidd

Figure 5.7 Advertisement for Pino aftershave
Source: Vidal, 1995

Collect advertisements that feature images of men and women together. Note what relationships are set up and pay particular attention to: power relationships, who looks or is looked at; and what different, complementary, opposite, and desirable characteristics are depicted for men and women.

Do the same for the images in Figures 5.4–5.7, and for Plate 4 in the colour section.

Defining masculinity

The major attribute, both in the media and real world, that is seen as the key signifier and definer of masculinity is power. Masculinity is achieved by having physical (see, for example, Figure 5.8) and/or social power.

We see the valuation of physical power in sports and in stars such as Stallone and Schwarzenegger. This is confirmed in countless media narratives in which the hero proves himself and wins the day through physical contest. The message 'might equals right' still predominates in texts that conclude with fighting. Male body attractiveness is also often linked to developed muscularity.

The ideal male also has social power, meaning wealth and influence in the world of business. Richard Gere's character in *Pretty Woman* is typical. His desirability is linked to his social power—in this way power functions as an aphrodisiac. Gere's beauty is expressed through his clothes, which are, significantly, professional clothes (he wears business suits and ties). This links male identity to the professional world.

Figure 5.8 Advertisement for
Levi's jeans
Source: Levi's Jeans 1993

Men are often defined by their jobs: a successful man is a man who does well profes-
sionally. This locates masculine identity in the public world of work rather than the
private world of domesticity (the feminine world). Men who are purely domestic are
not considered 'real men'.

Figure 5.9 is an advertisement for men's shirts. The caption of the advertisement,
which is not shown in Figure 5.9, is 'There's a decision-maker inside all our shirts'.

Figure 5.9 Advertisement for Van Heusen
shirts. The caption to this advertisement
reads 'There's a decision-maker inside
all our shirts'.
Source: Van Heusen Company, 1985

This caption draws attention to the rational qualities of the well-dressed man depicted, whose professional skills confirm his successful male identity.

Male power inevitably involves power over something or someone. This includes not only male power over women, but also over other men, over the environment, and over themselves. This is linked to the fact that male relationships are often competitive or controlling. Masculinity is consequently not just a problem for women but also for men and the environment as a whole. The ability to control (controlling others and self-control) is linked to power and rational abilities. Thus control is a defining feature of ideal masculinity.

Women, in contrast, are conventionally given power in representations in just one way: they have sexual power, which they can use over men. This has positive aspects in that it acknowledges female sexuality and in the simple fact that women are shown as having a measure of power. But it also has negative aspects: it reduces women to their sexuality (we cannot see them as separate from this), it encourages us to see women primarily as sex objects, and it denies women other forms of power. The logic is that the only way women have power is through their sexuality, which encourages women who want power to learn to use this attribute in a manipulating way rather than attempting other ways of gaining power. In addition this trend devalues women who are not stereotypically sexy, and it diminishes the worth of attributes such as intelligence, eloquence, practicality, agility, humour, and kindness.

Men together

Many media representations present stories about men relating to other men. Two themes predominate: struggle and friendship between male buddies. Many stories show both: male rivalry turns to male friendship when the protagonists find themselves fighting alongside one another or against each other. Depicting male characters fighting alongside one another allows them to be physically close and provides a situation in which each can earn or win the respect of the other, leading to friendship. Other narratives involving fighting encourage men to distrust each other, to see men as rivals. These narratives have also have been interpreted as the playing out of the psychological father–son relationship and have been discussed by thinkers such as Joseph Campbell (pp. 172–5): for example, in his notions of the quest and the hero's journey. Such work has informed writers such as Robert Bly, author of *Iron John*, one of the most well-known men's-movement books about masculinity.

We suggest that these hero stories can be seen as dramas of masculinity. The stories are about men finding their true masculinity, their masculine identity. The process of testing they go through initiates them into masculinity. Westerns, gangster movies, thrillers, and police dramas, which make up a huge proportion of popular television and cinema entertainment, tell stories about masculinity. Traditionally, these stories have validated typical masculine characteristics (for example, in stars such as John Wayne and Clint Eastwood), but many stories today carry an interesting tension as to whether they are celebrating or critiquing masculinity. Films directed by Martin Scorsese and featuring Robert de Niro (for example, *Taxi Driver*, *Raging Bull*, and *Cape Fear*), and dramas such as *Reservoir Dogs*, *Fight Club*, *Chopper*, *Bad Lieutenant*, and *American Beauty* seem to revel in moments of male aggression and male power, and at the same time, show how futile and destructive, to self and others, such masculinity is. These films can be read as both celebrations and critiques of masculinity. Other stories, such as those in the films *Stand By Me*, *The Fisher King*, *Dead Poets' Society*, and *Strictly Ballroom*, present softer, more supportive versions of ideal masculinity.

Buddy films contain an interesting tension: they validate male friendship but reject any homosexual possibilities. Homophobia is fear of same-sex intimacy. Men's fear of intimacy with other men is often a fear of homosexuality. The medium only depicts intimacy between men in certain situations: war films when a buddy is dying; sports, after goal-scoring exploits; and in other dramas in which men fight, drink, or joke together. Male bonding has also been interpreted as a rejection of femininity and hence as part of male misogyny. Yet some critics argue that these buddy movies unconsciously suggest strong love and erotic attraction between men. They argue that the male stars are filmed in such a way as to make them visually attractive not only to female characters in the film and women in the film audience, but also to male characters in the film and men in the audience. The actual narrative structure may deny or disavow male attraction, but the way it is filmed suggests homoeroticism.

The central relationship in the Australian film *Chopper* is between Mark 'Chopper' Read (Eric Bana) and his best mate Jimmy, played by Simon Lyndon. In one scene the depth of emotion between these two men erupts into physicality and Chopper is stabbed by his friend—the two are gripped in what looks like a dying embrace as Jimmy plunges the knife into Chopper's torso again and again. 'If you keep stabbing me I'm gonna die, mate', Chopper says without any evidence of anger. The two characters lock eyes and it looks for a moment as though they are about to kiss. It is an ambiguous cinematic moment, charged with a twisted kind of homoeroticism. The film *American Beauty* features a more stereotypical view of the restrictions surrounding intimacy between men and the malignancies these restrictions can lead to.

Look at the ways men relate to each other in films and television programs. See how many times men are subjected to tests that prove their masculinity. Pay special attention to father–son relationships. Ask whether these stories are celebrating or critiquing traditional masculinity. Look for any homophobic and homoerotic tendencies. Study the images of male bonding in Plates 5 and 6. Is the way this bonding is depicted powerful, ridiculous, or homoerotic?

Men and feelings

It has been suggested that men learn to hide their feelings (or that they don't have many feelings) and that they learn to value rationality over emotion. In reality, I think men's feelings are repressed in many ways as they grow up. The most obvious example is the way that men are taught not to cry. However, this does not mean they do not feel. It just makes the realisation and expression of feeling more difficult. While women are encouraged to show their tears but not their anger, men are encouraged to hide their tears but show their anger. The socialisation of boys teaches them that anger and aggression are legitimate feelings for men: it is OK to be angry; indeed it can confirm masculinity. This is shown repeatedly in media representations. Men are not encouraged to discuss their feelings and are not represented as doing so. Instead their feelings are expressed through violent action.

Male violence

Male violence has two aspects to it: destruction of others and self-destruction.

Destruction of others

Male violence towards women, children, and other men is prevalent throughout the world. It occurs in private/domestic spheres and in public spheres (including large-scale armed conflict). Anger may sometimes be a useful and appropriate response for men and women, but how that anger can be appropriately expressed is a vexed question. The male solution (fighting) permeates the media, and this may endorse this behaviour for individual men and may promote it as the best way of solving social problems. The ubiquity of violence as a problem-solving strategy endorses warfare as a legitimate problem-solving strategy. We are not arguing a direct-effects response mechanism here: that is, we are not arguing that men see violence on television and imitate it. Nor are we arguing for repressive censorship of media violence. Both these views are too simplistic. Rather, we want to draw your attention to the issue of male violence and to media representations of male fighting and anger towards others. Hopefully this will make you think about what model of masculinity the media offer us and how this might relate to the way men act in the real world. We think the question of how to work with male anger and violence is one of the major social issues the world faces at present.

Self-destruction

Violent actions are not always towards other people. Many male feelings of anger are turned inwards masochistically. (Note the ironic similarity between the words 'machismo' and 'masochism'!) The culture of pain and masochism is found in sport, one of the defining arenas of traditional masculinity. Sport is often presented as an arena of endurance: 'no pain, no gain'; 'when the going gets tough, the tough get going'; and so on. (It doesn't have to be this way, but male sport is typically understood in terms of power, strength and competition—winning and losing—rather than grace, elegance, transcendence of time, beauty of the human form, and so on.) The following comments by professional sportsmen show sport as a regime of endurance and punishment for the body:

> Your thigh muscles swell up as if you were going to burst. You zig-zag along. The whole body is under terrible pressure (P. Trentin, cyclist).
>
> The feeling of lack of air is terrible. You think you're going to pass out—that you're not far from dying. It's true you say to yourself maybe that's what dying feels like (B. Thevenet, cyclist).
>
> Up to the middle of the race the fatigue increases. You're practically dead but you have to carry on. To reduce the pain you think about how much the others are suffering. Your thighs swell up, your arms hardly make it and your back stops responding. When you get to 1,500 metres you tell yourself that if you had any sense you'd stop there, and then.

But you have to keep going. Right up to the end the burning sensation gets worse—you feel as if your whole body is on fire from head to toe … rowing involves 100% effort and that means 100% pain (Y. Fraysse, oarsman) (Brohm 1978, p. 25).

What these quotations demonstrate is that the body is being disciplined and controlled. Pleasure is not involved or, if it is, it is the pleasure of pain, masochism. To illustrate such tendencies in the media, consider films directed by Martin Scorsese and featuring Robert De Niro. The characters De Niro plays invite people to attack him and hurt him. In *Raging Bull* this reaches its climax when De Niro beats his own head and fists against a brick wall. This self-destructive violence is directed specifically against the head, the source of rationality and control. Film theorists such as Yvonne Tasker have also noticed how many male heroes in films undergo testing rituals that involve them undergoing extreme pain and often body-wounding (Tasker 1993). This certainly relates to male initiation ceremonies of many traditional cultures. Such ceremonies test young men by inflicting pain on them. It also resonates with Robert Bly's (Bly 1990) idea that masculinity is about wounding. Clearly, masculinity and pain are strongly linked. Pain is a way in which men can express their feelings.

Fight Club explores similar themes. Here the pleasure, emotional release, and bonding found in fighting with other men is initially shown as beneficial and health restoring (despite the physical injuries involved) for Edward Norton's spirit and for many other men. It is contrasted with the self-help support groups shown earlier in the film and it is noticeable that the character played by Meatloaf, who has lost his testicles to cancer and grown breasts (the threat of castration is a recurrent theme in the film) thus becoming emasculated or feminised, finds more in this ultra-male brotherhood than in the support groups. The film seems to be suggesting that fighting is better than hugging! It seemed to resonate with male audiences, and it may be that this reassertion of the value of traditional male expression and aggression is part of a reaction against the influences of feminism and the emergence of the sensitive new-age man. As Amy Taubin has argued, in dealing with issues of masculinity, the film is another example of homoeroticism:

> Shot in a wet-dream half light that gilds the men's bodies as they pound each other's heads into the cement, the *Fight Club* sequences are a perfect balance of aesthetics and adrenaline; they feel like a solution to the mind/body split (Taubin 1999, pp. 16–18).

In the same week that Scorsese's film *Bringing Out the Dead* was released in Perth in 1999, one of his first films was screened to an audience of about 250 media students. This early film, *The Big Shave*, elicited a strong reaction. During the film the audience squirmed and flinched, muttered uncomfortably, and averted their eyes. Within moments of the final credits, two viewers fainted and one had to be escorted to the medical suite to recover. 'I was glad that the woman three rows down fainted and attracted so much attention', one young man said after viewing *The Big Shave*, 'because nobody noticed when I keeled over too'.

The Big Shave lasts only six minutes (though it is difficult to tell whether the events depicted in the story world unfold over the course of one day or a hundred days). The use of jump cuts, a technique in which each shot lurches into the next with a slight but awkward shift of perspective, is jarring for the audience because it

Figure 5.10 A masculine wounding ritual
Source: Aaron Elliot, 1998

disrupts expectations of spatio-temporal continuity. This dissonant repetition of imagery is central to the film's impact.

The protagonist, a young, 'clean-cut' all-American type in a spotless white bathroom, shaves before a mirror. The pleasant, fresh-faced results of this process emerge from beneath the lather of suds, only to be nicked by the razor as the man looks with satisfaction at his own image, then moves to touch up a few remaining bristles. Appearing not to notice the small cut, he continues to shave his clean-shaven face until the screen is awash with blood. Finally, he slits his own throat.

The film is not disturbing because of the blood—most modern viewers are thoroughly desensitised in that respect. Rather, it is distressing to watch because the violence is self inflicted, ongoing, and motivated by a desire to conform to the popular vision of an ideal man.

Even though it is becoming more acceptable for men to be concerned with looking good, men still do not tend to openly discuss or raise objections to the unattainable images of masculinity projected by the media. This may be because, by admitting an overt concern with 'image' and appearance, they would be entering a territory traditionally branded as the domain of women and thus they would run the risk of being considered effeminate.

Men in frocks

A number of current media texts feature cross-dressing—men in women's clothes. For example, in *What Women Want*, Mel Gibson plays an advertising executive who dresses in women's hosiery and wears make-up in an attempt to find a way of 'getting inside women's minds' to target the female market more effectively. In a magical electrical accident that occurs while he is using a hairdryer and applying cosmetics, he develops the ability to hear women's thoughts and exploits this talent to climb the corporate ladder, seduce women, and win over his teenage daughter. Interestingly, cross-dressing provides the key to the two major transitions in the film. Gibson first tries on feminine apparel and cosmetics in an attempt to understand what women want so that he can help his clients exploit the female market. It is during this act of cross-dressing that he gains, then later relinquishes, the power to read women's minds, thereby re-entering the world of masculinity as a better person. Such texts are interesting in that they present a transgression of dominant masculinity. Note the following points:

1 This transgression is threatening to the establishment because it blurs the normal gender definitions that give people their identity and are used in the support of patriarchy.

2 Men in drag are often represented humorously, thus making the situation less threatening. The male figures are made to appear ridiculous. Some argue that the laughter generated by such representations is directed against femininity, in that femininity is being parodied. This would make these texts misogynist. Others argue that the humour arises from the fact that these texts reveal that gender identity is a construction or a mask, and that these texts therefore challenge patriarchy.

3 When men in women's clothes really look like women, this is more disturbing than when their cross-dressing leaves no doubt as to their biological sex. In such situations there is uncertainty about the stability of gender categories. (Figure 5.11)

4 While in films such as *Tootsie* and *Mrs Doubtfire*, the male characters find that assuming a female persona means they can express their feelings better and be more emotional, the films nevertheless emphasise the skill of male actors at

Figure 5.11 Image from *Men in Frocks*
Source: photograph by Ed Heath, published in
C. Kirk, *Men in Frocks*, GMP Publishers, Norfolk 1984

impersonating women. Thus it is masculine skills that are being applauded rather than feminine attributes. Both films reassert normal gender positions in their narrative structure by having the main characters reassume their masculine identity at the end, thus avoiding any possibility of gender uncertainty.

5 Cross-dressing seems to be more transgressive when men dress as women than when women dress as men. You may wonder why this is the case. One suggestion is that because masculinity is valued more highly than femininity in patriarchy, women dressing in men's clothes is seen as a positive thing, whereas men dressing as women are seen to be losing power and authority. Men dressing as women are seen to be devaluing themselves and, more importantly, masculinity (and consequently patriarchy). This makes cross-dressing a subversive act that can be a powerful attack on patriarchy.

How do you read these cross-dressing images (Figures 5.11–5.12)?

Figure 5.12 Advertisement for 17 Cosmetics
Source: 17 Cosmetics, 1998; photograph by Mosche Brakha

Gay representations

There have always been underground films, stories, and magazines made by and about gay men: for example, the films of Kenneth Anger and the stories of Jean Genet. There have also been many gay film-makers and stars working in apparently heterosexual films. Their work in mainstream film has often been read from a gay perspective by gay audiences, as exemplified in Vito Russo's book *The Celluloid Closet* (Russo 1981) and in the documentary inspired by this book. Mainstream films that are overtly about gay issues have tended to pathologise gay characters as sick or criminal and, as we have already noted, even sympathetic representations tend to provide unhappy narrative resolutions for gay characters. However, since 1980 there have been more films celebrating gay men (and lesbian women) and providing much more optimistic resolutions: *My Beautiful Laundrette*, released in 1985, shows this change.

Men advertising cosmetics

The cosmetics market, traditionally aimed at women, has realised it has a huge potential male market. In order to win this market, it has to overcome the perception that the purchase and use of cosmetics are feminine activities. There is a tension between selling products that will make men look and smell desirable, thereby

Figure 5.13 Advertisement for Paco Rabanne XS perfume
Source: Paco Rabanne; published in *Cleo*, September 1994

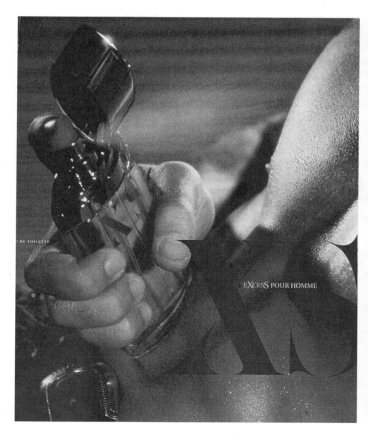

focusing attention on men's appearances and making men objects of desire, and traditional masculinity. Shaving advertisements are a rich source to examine. They manage to maintain the ideal of masculine strength and proximity to physical danger by showing razors as instruments of technological power, capable of providing dangerously 'close shaves'. Many are framed in terms of competition (beating rival products), and many link shavers to sports activities and achievements in sport.

Advertisements for perfumes marketed at men are similarly linked to physical activities (for example, advertisements for Old Spice feature surfing). The 1995 advertising campaign for the Chanel perfume Egoiste featured a man, presumably wearing the perfume, fighting with his own shadow. Such names and images of fighting and strength ensure that men wearing male perfumes are not challenging traditional masculinity and the virility with which it is associated. Rather, these advertisements suggest that in wearing male perfumes, men are strengthening their traditional masculinity. The imagery of the advertisement for XS (Figure 5.13), a perfume produced by the house of Paco Rabanne, emphasises phallic strength.

Male pin-ups

The advertisements, which feature attractive males, are a good lead-up to a discussion of male pin-ups. Since the mid 1970s, representations of the naked male body as an object of desire have become more frequent (this may be partially linked to the increased visibility of gay culture). Richard Dyer was one of the first critics to explore this (Dyer 1982a). Representations of naked men have often been a source of humour (in contrast to representations of naked women). It is as though humour is being used as a way of defusing feelings of unease about the portrayal of naked men. This tendency is still evident in films such as *The Full Monty*, which ultimately refuses to show 'the full monty' (full frontal male nudity including penis). But while humour still persists in many representations of male nudity, many are now explicit about showing the male body as an object of desire, and these representations aim to provoke not laughter but desire. Such images have become very common, demonstrating that there is a trend towards men being seen as objects of the sexual gaze. In this context, it is interesting to note that the advertisement for Wolf shoes (Figure 5.14) combines humour and sexual desirability.

Given that many critics have argued against the portrayal of women as sexual objects in the media, how do we assess the fact that men are now being portrayed in similar ways? Does this show equality? Does it validate the active sexual desire of women and gay men? Does it encourage women to construct their own feelings and sexuality in a different way such that women look at men the way men have traditionally looked at women? Does it denigrate men by making them sexual objects? Does it threaten ordinary men who can't live up to these visual ideals? In what ways are male pin-ups and male exhibitionism different from the portrayal of females as sexual objects? Do male pin-ups work? Or are they funny rather than sexual?

Explore these questions by collecting and examining media images of men as sexual objects. How do you and your friends feel about these images? Is there a difference between male and female attitudes towards them? Note particularly how imagery of strength, work, and

Figure 5.14 Advertisement for
Wolf shoes
Source: *Intransit International*, 1988

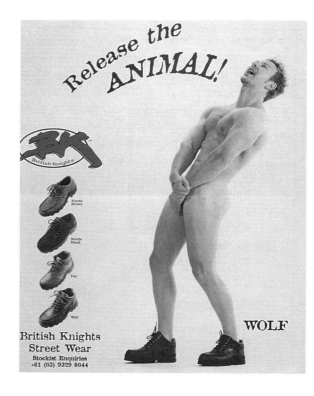

Figure 5.15 Advertisement for
Ella Baché sunscreen
Source: *IDD Agency*, 1998

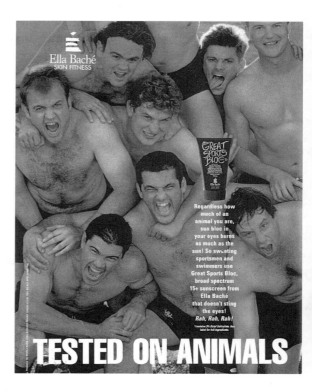

sport, as well as the fact that male models tend not to look at the camera, may help to maintain masculine identity. Note the considerable emphasis on the body and skin, including the taut muscularity and smooth hairlessness of the bodies depicted (suggesting masculinity and femininity simultaneously). Keeping these questions in mind, look at Figures 5.14 and 5.15 in terms of how they represent male power and desirability.

Finally, look at Figures 5.16 and 5.17, which are images from a campaign for Kolotex hosiery that promote Voodoo pantihose. The image in Figure 5.16 was the first image to appear on billboards, and at that stage it was clear that it was part of a larger image. How do you read this image? Note its combination of humour and sexual desirability. After a couple of weeks, the entire image (Figure 5.17) was revealed to show the couple. How do you read Figure 5.16 in terms of issues of the relative power of men and women, and in relation to Figure 5.17?

Figures 5.16–5.17 Billboard advertisements for Voodoo pantihose (Kolotex hosiery)
Source: Oddfellows Billboard Advertising, 1998

Exercise commentary

The following quote is from Janet Hogan, the managing director of Oddfellows Billboard Advertising, the advertising agency behind the campaign for Voodoo Control pantihose. It makes for very interesting reading. It is a good example of how authors' intentions can be important in the construction of meaning, how images are produced in relation to contemporary ideas about sexual representations, the changing roles of men and women, and how audiences can read texts.

> In keeping with past Voodoo advertising, the billboard for Voodoo Control pantihose was designed to reinforce Voodoo's positioning as the pantihose for women in control; women who believe that promoting their sexuality does not in any way compromise their liberated status.
>
> The campaign has been so hugely successful ... because it deliberately challenges political correctness and recognises that the vast majority of women aren't hung up over gender stereotyping. Most think the whole issue of gender politics is boring, academic, counterproductive and out of touch with everyday women. They enjoy risqué advertising and the irony and humour implicit in the role reversal strategy which underpins Voodoo marketing.
>
> To create maximum impact and intrigue, the ad was designed in two stages: a teaser ad followed by a reveal of the product.
>
> The first stage shows on the left hand side a scantily clad male trying to cover himself with a piece of cloth. The message on the right: 'Ladies please control yourselves' leaves the audience to assume that the fellow is struggling against some over zealous females trying in vain to disrobe him.
>
> With the reveal, Stage 2, it becomes clear that it is in fact him pulling on the cloth, engaged in a sort of sexual tug of war with a woman wearing Voodoo Control pantihose. The gold cloth pulled tightly around her waist and thighs emphasises the firming, flattering quality of Control top pantihose.
>
> It is up to the reader to read as much or as little as she/he likes into the ad. Most consumers would undoubtedly read very little. They simply respond to the cultural cues present.
>
> On one level the ad is simply a sexy demonstration of the product being advertised. On another, the struggle between the sexes; a (vulnerable?) male trying to dominate the female, but unable to.
>
> If she epitomises the role model most modern women aspire to: feminine, strong, and ultimately in control, the ads epitomise the complexity of contemporary sexual mores, where really anything goes. Indeed, Voodoo is being rewarded with massive sales by the majority of women who are grateful that someone has dared to take on the thought police and do it with style and humour (correspondence to author from Janet Hogan, Managing Director, Oddfellows Billboard Advertising, July 1998).

Changes in masculinities

Masculinity, as we have said, is in crisis, and has been going through significant changes. Correspondingly, so have media representations of men. Look out for traditional representations of dominant masculinity but also for new and changing representations such as the image of the SNAG (sensitive new-age guy). In the last decade or so films and television programs have tended to deal more sensitively with male issues, with relationships between fathers and sons, and with men's emotions and vulnerabilities; advertisements play with role reversals; and documentaries focus on male issues. The influence of gay culture has affected many areas of mainstream masculinity, through areas such as clothing styles and popular music (groups such as Frankie Goes to Hollywood, the Pet Shop Boys, and Take That produce mainstream popular music). All these factors have affected our ideas about sexuality and gender. Many young people are now much more fluid in their understandings of and feelings around gender and sexual identity.

Note media texts that deal with or represent new and different aspects of masculinity. Are there many media texts that make relatively obvious allusions to masculinity?

The changes in masculinity dovetail with changes in femininity: both areas are going through processes of exploration and development. We think this is an exciting and sometimes confusing period. Women may be more conscious of this through feminism's direct impact on their lives. Men's awareness of how these issues impinge on them is more recent. In discussions among my students, there has been a broad trend towards women saying that while they feel oppressed in many ways and are critical of media representations, they actually enjoy being women. In contrast, men, who tend not to have the same complaints about their place in society and the way they are represented in the media, often feel confused about being men. It is as though contemporary male roles are more uncertain than current female roles. Whereas women feel they have something to gain from these changes, men feel threatened. We think we should strive to create a climate in which both women and men feel they have much to gain from such changes.

CONCLUSION

The discussion in this chapter has explored some issues around masculinity and the way it is represented by the media. You can pursue these questions further in your reading. Keep questioning the different ideologies of masculinity that are being constructed in the media. Ask yourself how these relate to the real world and how they compare with ideologies of femininity.

18   *Ethnicity, Ideology, and the Media*

Let us start with three points about ethnicity:

1   Like gender, ethnicity and nationality are major ways humans classify their own and other people's identity: 'I'm Australian', 'I'm Aboriginal', 'I'm from Italy', and so on.
2   The world is divided into different and unequally positioned ethnic groups and cultures; there are many inequalities of power and wealth between these groups, who are, consequently, often in conflict both internally and with other ethnic groups.
3   The media are important in giving us constructions, images, and representations—discourses—of ethnic difference. As such, they offer us ways to understand ethnicity and ethnic issues.

In this chapter, we refer to images and ideologies of ethnicity in the media, as well as to how ethnicity is lived and experienced in the real world. While we use the terms 'ethnicity' and 'race', it is important to point out that there is a major problem with the term 'race'. Not only is it without scientific basis, but because it suggests biological differences, using it is tantamount to accepting the proposition that these essential differences exist. To speak of ethnic groups and ethnicity, on the other hand, is to refer to cultural differences between social groups. While we do not accept the baggage associated with the term 'race', we do use it occasionally because it is so much a part of common-sense understandings and definitions.

REPRESENTATION OF ETHNIC GROUPS AND ETHNICITY

Consider the significance of the following scene from the film *Do the Right Thing*, directed by Spike Lee. This film is set in a multi-racial New York inner-city ghetto. It explores tensions between a number of ethnic groups, focusing mainly on the struggle between Afro-Americans and Italian-Americans. The local pizza store is owned and run by Italian-Americans but is frequented, and therefore financed, primarily by Afro-Americans.

Early in the film one of the Afro-American customers, called Buggin' Out, complains to Sol, the owner of the pizza store, that all the photographs on the walls are of famous Italian-Americans. As he puts it, 'Why aren't there no brothers on the wall?' Sol argues that it is his right as owner of the store to decorate as he wishes. Buggin' Out argues that since the customers finance the store through purchases, they should be represented by the photos on the wall. He is so upset by this lack of representation that he tries to start a boycott of the store, and this eventually leads to the store being wrecked and burnt down.

The film thus puts issues of representation right at its centre. Representation is an important political issue. It is important for ethnic groups to be represented in the media. Buggin' Out's argument goes right to the heart of race issues in America.

Afro-Americans, like Australian Aborigines, have consistently been denied their own images, stories, representations, histories, social customs, and rituals, and until it is redressed this lack will continue to contribute to ethnic and racial inequality. It is necessary to fight for these representations.

The absence of representations of Afro-Americans in the media affects the way Afro-Americans see and understand themselves (remember Ngugi's argument that indigenous Africans have been deprived of their own language and thus their cultural identity—pp. 45–6). *Do the Right Thing* is itself a representation that gives a voice and a face to Afro-American points of view, and Lee's film is one of a number that have emerged recently from Hollywood, suggesting that Afro-Americans are beginning to gain a foothold in Hollywood from which to represent themselves (Reid 1997; Bogle 1973; Diawara 1993).

The other major concern is the misrepresentation of ethnic groups. It is important to see who is accorded the right and the ability to make representations, who has access to the media. The tendency within Western culture has been for media representations to be produced by Whites and thus most epitomise a White view of the world and of other ethnic groups. We explore this further after considering the Black/White opposition and the historical realities on which relationships between non-Whites and Whites have been built.[4]

BLACK/WHITE OPPOSITIONS

Central to the argument about representations of ethnicity is the idea that Whites and non-Whites have fundamentally opposed natures. This simple opposition is actually complex. 'Race' is a term without scientific basis, and similarly, the descriptions 'Black' and 'White' do not do justice to the multiplicity and range of different ethnic groups. But because they are popular labels they are useful for understanding the discourses surrounding ethnicity.

The opposition Black/White carries within it notions of inequality, of subordinate and dominant groups, of groups who are both different and opposed to each other. This points to the idea that ethnic groups are in conflict over power. Ethnic conflicts have existed throughout history. Many wars that have complex economic and social causes are also cultural conflicts between different ethnic groups. Ethnic conflict is involved in many of the armed conflicts around the world today. The White/Black opposition can be expressed in at least four other ways, all of which point to its historical origins:

White	Black
White	non-White
European descent	non-European descent
West	East

The last two sets of oppositions—European descent/non-European descent, and West/East—draw attention to the history behind these oppositions: the realities of global European expansion since the fifteenth century. Note that once again this oppositional form of thought polarises groups in extreme ways that make it seem as though there is no middle ground, and they have nothing in common. In actuality, each of these pairs of terms is situated on a continuum with subtle gradations of difference linking the extremes at each end.

THE HISTORY OF THE WEST AND 'THE REST'

The historical relationship between Europe and the rest of the world has a number of elements, all of which demonstrate European domination of, and abuse of, other cultures.

Exploration and discovery

These were, and still often are, the terms used to describe the invasion of other lands and cultures by Europeans. The Americas and Australasia were said to be discovered despite the fact that they had indigenous populations at the time of the so-called 'discovery'.

Extermination

In colonised lands, the colonisers employed repressive policies against the indigenous peoples, and in many cases virtually exterminated them.

Colonisation

Europeans started to settle and live in these 'new' lands, setting up a number of European colonies.

Colonialism

Colonialism refers to the acquisition and maintenance of colonies. Colonialism involved control and domination of the indigenous population, who were subjected to laws originating in Europe. Colonialism was established in, among other places, Africa, the Middle East, India, Pakistan, and parts of the Asia–Pacific region.

Exploitation

The prime motives behind colonisation were the exploitation of the natural resources of colonised lands, the exploitation of the labour of indigenous peoples, and the opening up of new markets for European goods. Colonised lands were an enormous source of wealth for Europe. These lands were exploited for their natural resources (for example, through mining and agriculture), for their human resources (for example, slave labour), and as a market for European goods. In more recent history, America's economic domination of some countries (particularly in Latin America) has been called neo-colonialism. (Note how in modern times, cigarettes and tobacco, which are being subjected to increasing regulation in the West, are being aggressively promoted in the majority world (the Third World), which is providing new markets for tobacco and cigarette companies.) The wealth and dominance of Europe and America (also called the First World, the minority world, and the Western world—we will call it the minority world) are largely built on the exploitation of the wealth and resources of these other countries.

The relationship between the majority world and the minority world has been described in ways that make the exploitation involved in this relationship invisible. First, the term that the United Kingdom used in relation to its empire was 'the Commonwealth' (meaning the wealth held in common by all the nations). The idea expressed is one of sharing, equality, and mutual interests, whereas the reality was that its aims were to siphon wealth to the United Kingdom from the other countries of the Commonwealth. Second, the advantages of imperial exploitation have become culturally naturalised in relation to products such as tea and coffee. Tea-drinking is seen as a quintessential British activity, and coffee has become a marker of European sophistication, the essence of cafe culture. Both drinks are available in these countries thanks to the plantations, cheap labour and imperial trading companies established by Europeans in South America and Asia.

Imperialism

Out of colonialism grew a number of European empires—predominantly the Dutch, French, German and British empires—and subsequently America's neo-colonial empire. These empires were initially about control over lands and peoples. Nowadays we think of empires in terms of financial power and control such that even if countries have regained their independence, as in most of Africa, they are in many ways subject to the power and control of the World Bank and multinational corporations owned by the minority world.

Cultural imperialism

Cultural imperialism is, according to Herbert Schiller, the theorist who coined the term, transnational corporate cultural domination (Schiller 1992, p. 39). The theory of cultural imperialism argues that the globalisation of communication, which is driven by economic, political, and military interests of giant transnational corporations and their host countries, results in the domination of traditional cultures and the intrusion of Western culture and Western values such as consumerism.

Cultural imperialism describes how one culture spreads its values and ideas culturally, rather than through direct rule or economic trading. The global reach of Hollywood films and US television is the most obvious example. Economic trading is also important because commodities from toys to tennis shoes, soft drinks to CDs, are carriers of culture. The term 'coca-colonisation' (Klein 2000, p. 131) succinctly expresses the links between colonisation, the global spread of commodities and brands, and cultural imperialism.

Most theorists now acknowledge that the globalisation of communication has not led to straightforward American dominance, but has resulted in a complex process of adaptation, appropriation, hybridisation, and mutual incorporation of different cultural texts and traditions as the media spread knowledge of different cultures around the globe. Power relations of domination and dependency certainly do exist, but the exchange of culture through the media is certainly not one-way or entirely negative.

Integration

Integration and assimilation indicate the absorption or incorporation of ethnic groups or minorities into the dominant or colonising culture in a manner that eradicates difference and renders it invisible once the language and culture of the dominant group are adopted. Multiculturalism champions the idea of unity in diversity, or a kind of cultural pluralism, in a positive way. However, it is still a form of integration that serves the interests of the dominant group by uniting the nation within a common or shared identity in order to reduce dissent.

Postcolonialism

This term describes the situation in existence since majority world countries achieved their political independence. It is an important critical term and is discussed in Chapter 19.

Figure 5.18 Advertisement for Drop the Debt campaign
Source: Photo courtesy of Red Cell, Drop the Debt, and photographer Tif Hunter

The advertisement (Figure 5.18) is a wonderful example of the media's capacity to be an agent of positive social change. Created with the intention of shocking people into awareness and action, it is intended to represent the fact that Westerners and developed nations are literally sucking Africa dry. A Drop the Debt press release states that 'African nations currently spend approximately $13.5 billion per year repaying debts—more than double the amount they spend on healthcare, and roughly equal to the amount needed to combat HIV/AIDS each year' (http://www.dropthedebt.org, June 2001). The image of the healthy white baby sucking much-needed nutrients from an emaciated African woman encourages those of us from developed nations to examine our personal consumption habits. It is part of a global campaign aiming to put pressure on governments to change foreign aid policy, and on the World Bank and International Monetary Fund to waive loan repayments owed to them by poor nations. The scale of the figures in the image reminds us that the first world consumes far more than its fair share of the earth's resources. When we consume more than we need, we are using money and resources that could help save lives and thus we inadvertently deprive others of what they need to live. The caption, 'Haven't we taken enough?' anchors the meaning of the image, and prompts us to remember that we are all consumers; thus we are all implicated in the global economic relations that widen the gap between the rich and the poor.

Homi Bhabha and the shadow history of the West

The nine elements discussed above are useful for understanding the relationship that has existed between Europe and the rest of the world from the fifteenth to the twentieth century. What follows is an excerpt from an interesting interview with the cultural theorist Homi Bhabha. Bhabha notes that the major twentieth-century ideas of Western culture have their basis in the eighteenth and nineteenth centuries, the time of colonialism, which he describes as 'the founding moment of modernity'. Thus, according to Bhabha, the West's ideas about itself are linked to the moment and realities of colonialism.

Interviewer: I'd like to refer to your comment that the founding moment of modernity was the moment of colonialism … You said 'the colonial moment is the history of the West'. Can you elaborate on this remark?

Homi Bhabha: I think we need to draw attention to the fact that the advent of Western modernity, located as it generally is in the eighteenth and nineteenth centuries, was the moment when certain master narratives of the state, the citizen, cultural value, art, science, the novel, when these major cultural discourses and identities came to define the 'Enlightenment' of Western society and the critical rationality of Western personhood. The time at which these things were happening was the same time at which the West was producing another history of itself through its colonial possessions and relations. That ideological tension, visible in the history of the West as a despotic power, at the very moment of the birth of democracy and modernity, has not been adequately written in a contradictory and contrapuntal discourse of tradition. Unable to resolve that contradiction perhaps, the history of the West as a despotic power, a colonial power, has not been adequately written side by side with its claims to democracy and solidarity. The material legacy of this repressed history is inscribed in the return of post-colonial peoples to the metropolis. Their very presence there changes the politics of the metropolis, its cultural ideologies and its intellectual traditions, because they—as a people who have been recipients of a colonial cultural experience—displace some of the great metropolitan narratives of progress and law and order, and question the authority and authenticity of those narratives. The other point I'm trying to make is not only that the history of colonialism is the history of the West but also that the history of colonialism is a counter-history to the normative, traditional history of the West (Rutherford 1990, p. 218).

This is a complex and important statement. Try to answer the following two questions: What is the difference between and the relationship between the two 'histories of the West' that Bhabha discusses? How does he understand the current relationship between Western peoples and postcolonial peoples? It might help to consider what the key characteristics of democracy are and what the term 'enlightenment' means.

Exercise commentary

Bhabha suggests that there are two histories of the West, dating from the eighteenth and nineteenth centuries. The first is full of the sorts of positive ideals expressed in the French Revolution (liberty, fraternity and equality) and 'The Rights of Man', a document central to the American Revolution. These democratic and liberal ideals are the basis of the commonly accepted view of the development of the West until the present. They have had, and continue to have, an enormous impact on the development of democracy, democratic ideals, and human rights across the world. Bhabha does not deny these and indeed values them as positive and progressive. But his view is that at exactly the same time as the struggle for the 'rights of man' was being conducted, the West was also involved in instituting and perpetuating slavery, racial extermination, and exploitation in the colonies. This second, 'shadow' and often hidden, history is the other side of the democratic, enlightened ideals. Bhabha exposes the obvious contradiction between these and argues that globally we have to acknowledge the historical consequences of these two histories and begin to try and reconcile them.

Bhabha also points to the fact that since the 1950s, when many former colonies achieved independence, many people from Asia, Africa, and the West Indies have migrated to what had become, through colonialism, their 'mother' countries. The processes of immigration have forced minority-world countries to face the consequences of colonial exploitation.

Returning to the discussion of the history of the West and the rest (the non-West) it is important to note the following three points about our contemporary situation:

1 The twentieth century saw a gradual fight back by the majority world. Many countries, African, Asian, and Middle Eastern states in particular, have achieved various forms of political independence since 1945. However, economic independence has been more difficult to achieve: multinational conglomerates are still able to dominate in majority world markets, even without Western political rule.

2 Two non-Western powers, Japan and China, have maintained more independence, and Japan has established its own economic empire that penetrates the Western world.

3 Economically, Asian countries may be coming to the fore in the world, raising the possibility of a new world order for the twenty-first century, in which the countries of the Asia-Pacific may have considerable economic power.

In relation to the media, it is important to understand that racial attitudes and beliefs have been built on both the official and the shadow history of the minority and majority worlds, and that these histories therefore provide a framework for understanding the European/non-European opposition.

'THE OTHER'

Another way of characterising the oppositions referred to above (White/non-White, East/West, and so on) is significant in media studies and cultural studies. This characterises everything that is not Western or European, or basically everything that is 'foreign', as 'the other'. It should be noted that this term is used to highlight the political nature of such oppositions. It is not a straightforward description. The term 'other' highlights the fact that that which falls into the category of 'other' has historically been seen as deviant, unnatural, and strange because it exists outside the boundaries of what the West deems normal and considers to be part of itself, or the same as itself. The use of the term 'the other' draws attention to the way this judgmental stance supports the notion that Europeans are superior to their 'others'.

EUROCENTRISM

Yet another way of expressing the oppositions East/West, us/the other, minority world/majority world, and so on is core/periphery. This opposition draws our attention to eurocentrism. A eurocentric approach is one that takes European values, judgments, beliefs, and cultures as normal, natural, and ideal. It makes European values central, relegating others to the outside, the margins, the periphery. Many ethnic groups, their values and beliefs pushed to the edges of society, feel marginalised by this tendency on the part of dominant groups.

The core/periphery opposition has immediate resonance for a White Australian audience. Populated predominantly by people of European descent, Australia can be said to be part of the core. At the same time, it is geographically located almost as far east of Europe as you can go (c. 113–153 degrees latitude East—New Zealand beats it at c. 168–178 degrees East); it is part of the southern hemisphere, which is made up predominantly of the majority world; and as a colony, it has a history of 'cultural cringe' in that has perceived its culture and achievements as inferior to those of Europe. For all these reasons, Australia can also be said to be located on the periphery. Such a dual positioning may mean that the Australian psyche is split. You could also look at this in a more positive light. It may be that Australia is in a unique position to appreciate both the benefits of being part of the core and the disadvantages of the marginalisation that stems from being part of the periphery.

One of the major issues in relation to multiculturalism has been the notion of integration of cultures and what this means. Some argue that integration means the 'outsider' group taking on the values and identities of the 'host' culture or the dominant culture: the danger here is that a monoculture would result. Others suggest that both cultures can change by drawing from each other. The dominant tendency in terms of White/non-White relationships has been for White cultures to expect non-Whites to take on White values. The consequence of this has been that non-White cultures have lost much of their cultural identities. Consequently, some groups have refused this option. They have sought out their own cultural heritage as an important source of their identity and have tried to sustain a separate cultural identity. This process of maintaining cultural distinctiveness has been reinforced when migrant groups attempting to integrate have met with continued racial discrimination by the host population. Films such as *Wog Boy* and *Looking for Alibrandi* celebrate the cultural distinctiveness of ethnic groups who are labeled 'wogs' in Australia, and explore the complex issues of discrimination and identity formation in a warm and humorous way.

Many 'outsider' groups integrate through adopting markers of mainstream identity: for example, clothing styles, hairstyles, particular sports, and other cultural pursuits. Many do this at the same time as searching for and preserving their own cultural roots and histories. In Australia this dual pursuit applies both to Aborigines, who have faced the problems of invasion and colonialism, and to non-British immigrants to Australia who have made Australia multicultural. The issue of what integration means for these groups and for White Australians, as we all struggle over multiculturalism and land rights, is critical. As we enter the twenty-first century, we must continue to investigate issues relating to our cultural and national identity.

All the oppositions discussed above are central to questions about representation of ethnicity in the media. We have located these oppositions within a historical context: the real relations existing between Whites and non-White. It is important to understand that real relations of ethnicity are always represented and understood by us within the discourses of race and ethnicity that use these oppositions. We need to examine these discourses in order to understand current media representations of ethnicity.

DISCOURSES OF RACE AND ETHNICITY

We have discussed the meanings and use of 'discourse' already. Media studies is interested in looking at the various voices or discourses of ethnicity and race, both in the past and in contemporary culture. It aims to see if and how these voices link together, to see what overall discourse of ethnicity and race they produce. Different discourses, or ways of thinking, come from a range of fields—for example medical, philosophical, anthropological, and aesthetic. Put together, these constitute and organise our discourses of ethnicity and race. When we say 'organise' we don't mean that these ideas are deliberately put together. Rather we mean that, through the culture's 'common sense', they shape the way we see particular issues.

One example of Western discourse in the nineteenth century is the European belief in racial superiority. This belief justified Europe's imperial exploits. This belief was supported by religious, scientific, and philosophical discourses, which 'demonstrated' that Whites were more advanced, civilised, and moral than the peoples whom they were colonising. This discourse of superiority was crucial in justifying the colonialist actions of Europeans. Despite the fact that contact with colonised cultures and peoples was beneficial to European culture and detrimental to non-European cultures, many Europeans thought they were actually helping these indigenous peoples. This was only possible because of the European belief in European supremacy, a belief supported by the combined discourses of Christianity, the scientific rationality of the Enlightenment, and (later) Darwinian philosophies of evolution. European philosophers held that Europeans were more fully evolved, more civilised than other races; hence, other races needed 'civilising', and Europeans felt they had been charged with this task. The phrase 'the White man's burden' was used to refer to this 'duty' to civilise the colonies. The notion of White superiority and moral responsibility meant that Whites felt that they carried the burden of maintaining order and control, establishing right and wrong. Ironically, this belief was self-perpetuating because when Western structures, rules, regulations, political systems, literacy standards, and languages were imposed, of course the Westerners themselves were more accomplished in all fields because their background knowledge and experience gave them an advantage. Any mistakes that were made as the colonised group adapted to or resisted the new system were taken as proof of inferiority. Colonial exploits, which included mass murder and wide-scale plunder, were carried out on the basis of this religious, missionary, 'do-gooding' belief.

Thus discourses of White superiority, which are discourses of race, justified exploitation of the colonies and the colonised peoples.

ORIENTALISM

One of the key texts relating to discourses of race is *Orientalism* by Edward Said (1980). Said examines the way in which Western countries have understood cultures of the 'Far East' and 'Middle East', countries beyond the 'Oriental line' (which divides the globe geographically between East and West). He suggests that there were a set of discourses about race that together constituted a discourse of Orientalism.

Said defines Orientalism in various ways. First he sees it as a European method for understanding unfamiliar cultures: 'Orientalism is the generic term ... to describe the Western approach to the Orient; Orientalism is the discipline by which the Orient was (and is) approached systematically as a topic of learning, discovery, and practice' (Said 1980, p. 73).

This definition does not refer to the exploitation inherent in Orientalism, but his second broader definition draws attention to the relations of power involved in Orientalism:

> Orientalism can be discussed and analysed as the corporate institution for dealing with the Orient—dealing with it by making statements about it, authorising views of it, describing it, by teaching it, settling it, ruling over it: in short, Orientalism as a Western style for dominating, restructuring and having authority over the Orient (Said 1980, p. 3)

This definition shows that Orientalism contributes to maintaining European cultural hegemony over the Orient.

Said's work focuses on Europe's relation to Eastern countries, but his approach has also been used to think about Europe's understanding of other non-European cultures, particularly African cultures, but also Aboriginal culture and the culture of Native Americans.

STEREOTYPES AND BINARY OPPOSITIONS

We will examine discourses of ethnicity circulating in the media by looking at:
1 the use of stereotypical representations of non-Europeans and Europeans
2 the use of binary oppositions as a way of depicting the differences between Europe and its others.

We would like to reiterate that we are aware that the category 'race' has no scientific basis and that it is highly politically problematic. We have, however, used it in the discussion that follows for the purpose of pointing out the construction of discourses of race and ethnicity.

Stereotypes

Stereotypes act as a shorthand for delineating character. Though they may involve some truth about the social realities of people's lives (Dyer 1993), they are limiting because:

- they suggest that particular characteristics are shared by many people
- they suggest that these characteristics are part of the nature of these people (that is, they are genetic/biological) rather than connected to any social realities
- in many instances stereotypes are used pejoratively by dominant groups to describe subordinate groups.

We are mainly going to explore White representations of non-White people and a number of problematic stereotypes that can be found in many twentieth-century media representations, both fictional and factual. Some of these may now seem outdated, but they are still apparent in films such as *The Mummy* and *Indiana Jones and the Temple of Doom*, and they were historically important in reflecting and maintaining dominant racist discourses through the twentieth century. But in doing this it is useful to focus not only on the non-White stereotypes but also to consider the White characters involved and ask what kinds of stereotypes of whiteness are being presented. Perhaps two of the most recognisable White stereotypes are the blonde bimbo (or the prostitute with a heart of gold) and the cold, calculating business person whose life is governed by time and money. These characters are rarely played by non-White actors. Richard Dyer was one of the first critics to suggest that Whites can also be seen as a specific ethnic group. As analysts, we can begin to think about how Whites and Whiteness are being represented, what particular characteristics and stereotypes are involved. Many people believe that only media texts depicting non-White characters and racial conflict are 'about race', but it is worth noting that texts that have an all-White cast are also making implicit ideological statements about race by 'naturalising' whiteness and portraying it as the norm.

As a starting point consider this 1930s representation and celebration of white masculinity in Figure 5.19. This cover of a British boys' annual, *The Top-All Annual for Boys*, 1939, shows how children are introduced to stereotypes at an early age. *The Top-All Annual* was awarded as a Methodist Sunday School prize (Figure 5.20), legitimating it within an official religious discourse. The title of the book, *Top All*, and the illustration—one boy elevated over others on a cricket field—demonstrate the stereotypical ideology of masculinity, involving in this instance male sporting competitiveness. Such a cover might appeal equally to young White boys in England or Australia. I was particularly interested in this book because the contents included stories set in India and Africa (then parts of the British Empire) and thus provided images of non-Whites and Whites and a way of understanding the relation between the two races. One of the stories has many similarities with the film *Indiana Jones*: clearly racist discourses from the 1930s were still prevalent in the 1980s. I include some other illustrations from the annual below.

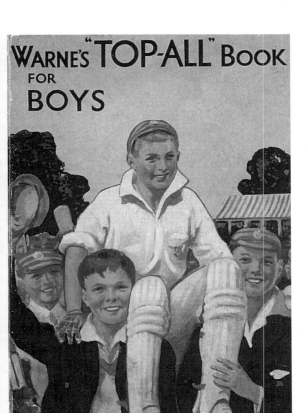

Figure 5.19 Cover of *Top-All Annual for Boys*, 1939
Source: Frederick Warne

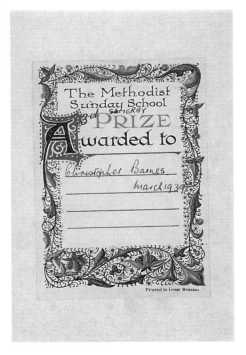

Figure 5.20 Certificate awarding *The Top-All Annual* as a Methodist Sunday School prize
Source: Frederick Warne

The dangerous savage and the civilised White

This stereotype portrays non-Whites as dangerous and animal-like. It suggests that non-Whites are uncivilised and want to attack and harm Whites, that they are 'savages' threatening 'innocent' women and children (Figure 5.22).

The perceived threat to women is understood as a sexual threat. This perception relates to the fear of miscegenation—sexual mixing of races—understood as a potential for the 'contamination' of the 'White race'. Mixed-race sexual relations have been a taboo area for official White culture, although throughout the history of race relations, White men have used non-White women sexually.

In the past, representations of attacks by indigenous peoples on Whites have depicted such attacks as the result of the savage, evil nature of indigenous peoples. They are rarely presented as the last resort of peoples whose lands are being stolen and whose lifestyles are being destroyed by White invaders. The representation of these attacks as savage and animal justifies White violence as a defence against savagery and as an attempt to impose restraint on animal-like savages (see Figure 5.21). The stereotype of the Black savage is thus very useful in justifying White oppression of indigenous populations (Figure 5.23).

Figure 5.21 Illustration from *Top-All Annual for Boys*, 1939
Source: Frederick Warne

The Bravest Thing

'Down dogs!' he stormed.
'Do you dare snarl at me?'

Such stereotypes have been popularised by Westerns that show Native Americans as savage, by Tarzan stories that show Africans as savages, and by numerous other stories, set in Africa, Asia, and Australia, that deal with relations between non-Whites and Whites. When Whites and non-Whites are portrayed together it is invariably to demonstrate a fundamental opposition in their natures that then justifies White violence against non-Whites—coded as a form of honourable retribution against savages—and suggests that Whites need to exercise control over native populations in order to 'tame' them. The Whites are thus shown to be heroic, more intelligent, and more in control of their emotions, more rational.

This stereotype has been used negatively in White representations. However, some texts have reclaimed the stereotype, reworking it to positive ends. Some US films made in the early 1970s began to capitalise on Afro-American cinema audiences: Afro-American heroes were introduced in films such as *Slaughter*, *Shaft* (recently remade with Samuel L. Jackson in the lead role and the actor who played Shaft in the original film playing his uncle), *Foxy Brown*, and Tarantino's *Jackie Brown* (with Pam Grier, star of the 1975 film *Sheba Baby*). These films redefine perceptions of race and gender.

The Afro-American heroes in these movies are strong, powerful, and sexually potent figures who elicit positive identification from young Afro-American audiences and envious admiration from White audiences. But while this genre, known as blaxploitation, was a move forward in some ways, as D. Leab puts it, the shift 'from Sambo to Superspade' (Leab 1975) is still, in some ways, a reconfirmation of the stereotype of the Black savage. Many fictional characters in films, comics, television programs, and pornographic movies still draw on this stereotype (Baker and Boyd 1997; Hernton 1970).

Figure 5.22 Poster for the film *The Battle of Elderbush Gulch*, *circa* 1920
Source: British Film Institute

Figure 5.23 Illustration from a boys' comic of the 1960s. The text accompanying this image reads: *I felt that if only I could kill this one man I should be happy.*
Source: British Film Institute

The noble savage

The noble savage stereotype is a variation on the Black savage stereotype. It too sees non-Whites as uncivilised, but puts this in a positive light. The noble savage draws on European ideas established by Rousseau and developed by American thinkers such as Thoreau, eighteenth- and nineteenth-century thinkers respectively. These writers regarded civilisation as corrupted and unnatural; they thought that people living outside European civilisation were pure and noble because of their relationship with nature, their distance from the decadence of European civilisation. Non-Europeans were thus thought to have a higher morality. This stereotype draws on Christian traditions in that it sees the 'savage' state as similar to the state of Adam and Eve in the Garden of Eden—a before-the-fall state. This is a great example of eurocentrism, whereby non-White cultures are understood in terms of White beliefs, religions, and mythologies. This shows the way White culture projects its own beliefs and values on to other cultures.

While this stereotype portrays non-Whites as morally superior to Whites, it is still limiting in that it locks non-Whites into a predetermined mould, denying them their own histories, glossing over the specificity of different non-White cultures, and portraying them as incapable of change. The stereotype of the noble savage can be found in films such as *Walkabout* (Figure 5.24), *Geronimo*, and *Dances with Wolves*, in which Aboriginal culture and Native American culture are portrayed as morally superior but essentially static and without internal diversity or a history of cultural development. In the first part *Walkabout*, the White girl and boy are shown wearing school uniforms as signs of their civility. In the course of the film they gradually remove them.

Much recent interest in indigenous cultures and ways of life, for example in the context of the New Age movement—also idealises such cultures as nobly savage. This takes little account of the current social realities faced by indigenous people living in the modern world. The noble savage stereotype romanticises lost values in a nostalgic way, rather than exploring actual social realities and relations between Whites and

Figure 5.24 Image from the film *Walkabout*, 1971
Source: Scott Murray, *Cinema Papers*

non-Whites. Despite this, the renewed interest in indigenous cultures shows a dissatisfaction with European values and an opening up to other traditions. This may be a positive development in that it has the potential to widen the cultural perspectives of Whites. It also coincides with the re-emergence of a number of indigenous cultural perspectives. The television series *Northern Exposure* locates Inuit culture in a modern (if somewhat remote) setting, rather than in the past, and mingles Canadian, US, and

Inuit perspectives. *Northern Exposure* often portrays Canadian and US views on the modern world as limited in comparison to Inuit approaches. Current representations of indigenous cultures can also be analysed in terms of the debates over incorporation, discussed in Part 4 in relation to ideology (pp. 218–19).

The childlike primitive and the responsible adult

This stereotype is also linked to the noble savage stereotype. The connection is that both see non-Whites as innocent. While both the noble savage and the childlike primitive, with their respective connotations of beauty and cuteness, seem the complete opposite of the dangerous savage, they share an important characteristic with the dangerous savage. Just as the dangerous savage needs to be controlled (by Whites), so both the noble savage and the childlike primitive need to be looked after (by Whites): the noble savage needs to be protected from corruption by White civilisation so that he or she can continue to serve as an inspiration to Whites, and the childlike primitive needs to be protected in the same way that children need the protection of their parents.

The stereotype of the childlike primitive involves showing adult non-Whites as having a simple, childlike, innocent nature, as well as making children in general representative of non-White cultures. Portrayed as childish, non-White adults are amusing, but are clearly in need of a sensible White authority to look after them because their childishness makes them backward, stupid, and unsophisticated. Childishness is used to suggest that non-Whites and non-White cultures are underdeveloped, thus supporting ideas of White superiority.

The use of children in general to portray non-White cultures is common in reports of wars and famines in African and Asian countries. Such reports often use images of starving, deprived, and helpless children. We are not arguing that these children do not exist, or that they do not need help. Rather we are suggesting that the recurrent image of defenceless, helpless children stands in for the whole culture, which is seen, by implication, as similarly defenceless and helpless. The repeated use of images of children in such reports encourages White culture to see its efforts to help victims of famines and wars in the majority world as fulfilling the White man's burden. Such images avoid the politics and history behind the crises, deflecting attention away from the fact that colonisation has played a significant role in current majority world conflicts and disasters. The focus on innocent victims does not encourage full historical understanding. Nor does it seek to find answers to the current situation beyond the continuation of charity, aid, and loans (loans often perpetuate dependency through interest repayments). This way of portraying majority world famines again confirms White superiority.

The child stereotype is a comforting one for Whites since it seems to defuse racial tensions and threats by focusing on children, who are perennially innocent.

Uncle Tom and the Black mammy

The Uncle Tom and Black mammy stereotypes are also non-threatening. The image is of a faithful retainer or servant, whose main aim in life is to service and look after his or her White master, or White family, and who is understood as benevolent. Non-Whites depicted in this way are shown as old (and therefore not potent physically or sexually) and supportive of White culture. Uncle Toms and Black mammies need White authority to look after them, and in return they serve their masters by doing the manual work (in the case of Uncle Tom) and the domestic work, including caring for children (in the case of Black mammy). They are often not very clever, although they are portrayed as possessing a kind of mystical or spiritual knowledge, and this is why they need the support of White rationality to look after the important, big issues in life. Fictional non-White characters portrayed in this mode are viewed and presented with affection and humour: they are virtuous and loyal, and are often shown caring for White children.

The Black mammy is a physically large woman (again defining race in relation to the body) who, like an earth mother, looks after everyone. (The film actress Hattie McDaniel played many of these roles in Hollywood in the 1930s and 1940s.) Her devotion and loyalty to her White employer family allows her licence in how she speaks to Whites. Both she and Uncle Tom present an image of racial complementarity, showing Blacks and Whites fitting together and benefiting each other through their different characteristics and abilities. Both these types are warm-hearted and can be contrasted with the White stereotype of the cold, calculating business person, whose life is governed by time, money, and responsibilities.

The entertainer

One of the major means by which Afro-Americans have been able to win cultural acceptance has been through the entertainment industry, particularly comedy, music, and dance. The stereotype of non-Whites as having natural rhythm, as being more naturally attuned to their bodies, supports this. Non-Whites are acceptable if they are funny or can sing and dance. They are not expected to play serious roles. Paul Robeson was an important figure for Afro-Americans because, alongside his sporting and entertainment prowess, he demonstrated great intellectual capabilities, and played serious roles (Dyer 1987). The visibility of a number of Afro-American stars and personalities—such as Michael Jackson, the Artist Formerly Known as Prince, Eddie Murphy, and Bill Cosby—is still built on this stereotype. If they are comic, are we being invited to laugh with them or at them?

The sexually exotic and alluring woman

Whereas the Black mammy's sexuality is negated by her role as a mother figure, there is also a stereotype of non-White women as being powerfully sexually attractive. This stereotype portrays non-White women as exotic, as more sexually daring than White women. While some non-White women characters portrayed in this way seem powerless, others seem dangerous. Their sexuality is linked to the White view that non-White cultures are inherently more sexual than White cultures because non-Whites are seen as more connected to nature, and therefore to their bodies (and because non-Whites are perceived to be free from religious injunctions against the expression of sexuality).

Just as the Black mammy figure has its male counterpart in the figure of Uncle Tom, so the figure of the sexually voracious Black woman has its counterpart in the figure of the sexually potent and sexually aggressive Black male. This sexually potent Black male figure is linked to the stereotype, discussed above (pp. 271–3), of the dangerous Black savage. As mentioned, this figure has been reclaimed by the blaxploitation film genre, which has reworked this figure as heroic.

The figure of the dangerously sexual non-White woman draws on mythological and historical figures such as Cleopatra, Delilah, Salome, and the Indian goddess of destruction, Kali. Such stereotypes are perpetuated in novels such as Rider Haggard's *She*. Such non-White female characters are excessively desirable: they need to be tamed or avoided. They have their counterpart in White culture, in the figure of the *femme fatale*, the sexually exciting but ultimately destructive woman. Another very common White female stereotype is the blonde bimbo.

Many images of Asian women offer a representation of unthreatening sexuality in that Asian women are often portrayed as passively inviting and sexually obliging. The sex is, of course, on offer for White men, not White women, and it is based on the realities of the Asian sex trade: parts of Thailand, for example, have been established as places devoted to the tourist sex trade. The perceived sexual freedom of non-Whites makes these stereotypes appealing to Whites.

The rich, evil tyrant

Non-white leaders are often depicted, in both fictional and non-fictional representations, as corrupt, excessive, and despotic. They are seen as over-indulgent in respect of all aspects of the body, and are portrayed as enjoying their riches while their subjects reside in extreme poverty. They are shown as neglecting and oppressing their subjects. These images suggest that non-Whites are incapable of ruling fairly, and that, given power, they will tend towards deviant excess. Once again, this stereotype provides a justification for White rule, conceived of as necessary to restore fairness and equality. Once again it pays little attention to the historical realities whereby White imperialist powers have often, for their own benefit, supported dictators such as Idi Amin and Saddam Hussein.

We might also consider that the stereotype of the rich, evil tyrant is a projection of the shadow side of Western colonialism and economic imperialism: it is a part of our cultural identity that we refuse to acknowledge and that we displace on to others.

The clever, devious trickster

Depictions of non-White men in power who are Western-educated often portray such characters as particularly dangerous to Whites. This perceived danger is understood as deriving from the fact that these characters are thought to possess both the powers of 'black magic' and the powers they have gained by taking on Western education. While combinations of White and non-White cultural knowledges can, in reality, be very productive, in media representations such characters are normally shown as evil and dangerous. The 'veneer' of European civilisation they have taken on is perceived as dangerous since it conceals their 'real' evil nature (which is seen as inherent in the fact that they are non-Whites), which is often revealed as the narrative comes to a climax.

In 'The Flying Death', one of the stories from the *Top-All Annual* (see p. 270), an ancient cult is revealed (Figure 5.25). It is presided over by an Oriental trickster who is the high priest. This story is almost identical in terms of both plot and visuals (the *Top-All Annual* is an illustrated picture book) to the discovery that the character of Indiana Jones makes about the ancient 'Thuggee' cult in the film *Indiana Jones and the Temple of Doom*. In both stories, Whites discover and witness underground rituals of torture that are presided over by a priest-like Oriental figure.

Figure 5.25 Illustration from 'The Flying Death', in *The Top-All Annual for Boys*, 1939. The caption for this image reads: *It was a military catapult, such an engine as had been used centuries ago in siege warfare.*
Source: Frederick Warne

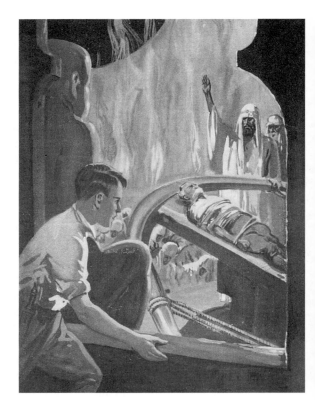

Stereotypes summary

Some of these stereotypes are affectionate, but they nevertheless put non–Whites in subordinate positions, confirming their inferiority. Most of them are negative. Taken together, what is interesting is that they are able to take a number of different and opposed characteristics and make them all negative for non-Whites. So whether non-Whites are portrayed as savage or childlike, poor or rich, stupid or clever, they are always presented as in need of White control and authority, and therefore as inferior to Whites. So although the stereotypes may seem contradictory, they do cohere to present an unfavourable view of non-Whites. It is as though all the possible behaviours of non-Whites have been accounted for as contributing to their inferior status, while all the White stereotypes of rationality, responsibility, and heroism make them appear superior.

Let us stress again that these stereotypes are not a true account of the real world. They are found across a range of popular media representations, factual and fictional, and these representations draw on and contribute to the maintenance of racist discourses.

Look closely at any of the Indiana Jones films, and at other popular representations involving ethnicity, to see which stereotypes are being used.

Binary oppositions

You can develop the stereotypes model by using binary oppositions as a framework for looking at race. White, Orientalist definitions work by defining non-Whites in terms of their differences from Whites. A series of categories/oppositions is used by White culture to define and delineate non-White culture and, by implication, White culture:

Non-White	White
primitive	civilised
savage	sophisticated
body	mind
irrational	rational
natural	cultural
eternal	historical
ancient	modern
mysterious	known
magical	scientific
heathen	Christian
evil	good
innocent	knowing
exotic	ordinary
erotic	repressed
free	controlled

To explore these oppositions, look for them in texts that include White and non-White characters. What aspects of the left-hand column of the above table are signified in the advertisements for Persian carpets (Figure 5.26) and Thailand (Figure 5.27)?

Figure 5.26 Advertisement for Persian carpets
Source: *Claremont/Nedlands Post*, 1993

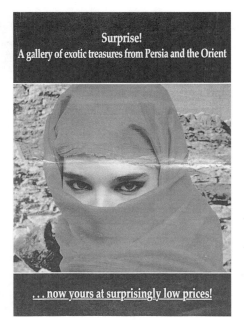

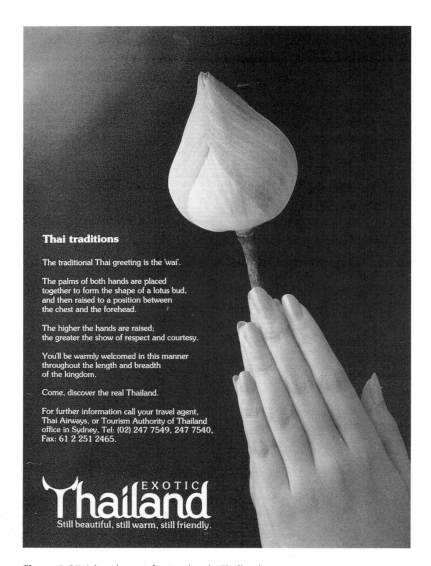

Figure 5.27 Advertisement for tourism in Thailand
Source: Tourism Authority of Thailand, Australia, 1993

Exercise commentary

Both advertisements draw on the **Oriental** characteristics given in the left-hand column of the above table. The first advertisement (Figure 5.26) tells us that it offers exoticism but also 'treasures'. The word 'treasures' connotes a world of piracy and fairy tales, the world of '1001 Nights'. This takes us to fictional worlds or historically past worlds. It contains sexual promise through the signifier of the alluring woman made mysterious through costume, through the veil that hides her from us and connotes the harem. The landscape places her outside time in a natural environment that is outside or beyond the modern, civilised world, stretching back timelessly so that the image and the costume could come from the past. This advertisement thus offers escape from the modern world. It also clearly positions the non-White woman as an exotic treasure, an object that can be bought or possessed.

This is echoed in the Thailand advertisement (Figure 5.27), which stresses tradition through customs and through its use of the term 'kingdom', which connotes a feudal society. The advertisement's copy places Thailand in the past and attributes a static quality to it: '*still* beautiful, *still* warm, *still* friendly' (our emphasis). This also constructs an opposition between the idealised past and the ugly, cold, unfriendly modern world. The image of the lotus again signifies nature, and the advertisement suggests a correspondence between the human hands and the lotus, placing Thais within the world of the natural. The greeting depicted here, with the hands held together in front of the body, is one of respect and courtesy in Thailand. We cannot help but read through the lens of our own culture: to a Christian/Westerner the greeting looks like an act of prayer, implying that the person being greeted has a god-like status. The suggestion here is that Western visitors will be treated with great respect, approaching reverence.

The perceived eroticism of the Orient is suggested by the alluring feminine hands in conjunction with the lotus. Considered in the context of the tourist sex trade in Thailand, the lotus image, with its particularly fleshy, pink shape connotes a penis, and the hands (they could have been male but this would not have suited the sexual message) are servicing the lotus/penis sexually. The exhortation 'Come' may also be a knowing sexual innuendo. Thailand is thus depicted as a place that offers escape to a sexual, timeless, pleasurable world that exists to serve and pleasure the White (male) Westerner. The modern realities of Thailand are hidden behind the tourist stereotypes and the binary categories used in the advertisement. This is a typical example of the way that indigenous cultures and customs are valued purely in terms of the pleasures they offer tourists.

The oppositions in these advertisements also draw our attention again to the construction of whiteness since, in both cases, the implied and interpellated audience is White (male).

This discussion has focused on White representations of race. Within Western culture these are still predominant; however in the last 20 years there have been significant developments in this area: non-Whites are producing their own representations, and there is increased visibility of non-White characters in film and television fictions and in the media generally. Legislation regarding representation of minorities in American media has led to increased roles for non-White actors; there are now Black 'stars' such as Eddie Murphy and Denzel Washington. Within the music industry and the sports world many Black performers have achieved huge success and a space for Black voices and images. Many advertisements aimed at a youth market include positive representations of sexy, street-wise non-White characters. A number of non-White writers and directors have produced hit films in America, notably Spike Lee and Ang Lee. An indigenous African cinema has emerged led by directors such as Ousmane Sembene. There are a number of Aboriginal film-makers such as Tracey Moffat and Rachel Perkins working in Australia. A tradition of Black British film-making has also developed. We should of course remember that the biggest film industry in the world is the Indian cinema, famous for its Bollywood productions.

From all these perspectives there has been an increased visibility of non-White characters and concerns, but also, in a form of reversal, representations of White characters by non-White writers and directors. One of the most humorous and early examples in Australia was the short film *Babakiueria* (1986), which told the story of a group of Aboriginal sailor explorers discovering an 'indigenous' White native population who were engaged in exotic rituals around the 'barbecue area'!

Choose a film made by a non-White director/writer and examine its representations of race and ethnic issues.

The Orient as a 'projection' of the White psyche

We want to put forward one more way of understanding the White/non-White relationship. 'Projection' is an important psychological term that was used by Freud and Jung. As discussed in Part 3 (pp. 179–81), it suggests that what we see in the world and other people are aspects—projections—of repressed features of our own personalities, our own psyches. Projections are aspects of ourselves or our desires that we normally disown or repress. Freud saw these unacceptable parts of our personality as repressed in the unconscious; Jung suggested that we all have a 'shadow' side that incorporates these rejected parts of ourselves. According to Jung, rather than recognising that we have these aspects by acknowledging our shadow side, we project them on to other people. Thus, if White culture officially denies and rejects aspects of bodily nature in favour of rationality, if it represses sexuality, if it denies savage wildness in favour of civilised behaviour, if it limits its thoughts and beliefs to

Figure 5.28 Illustration from *The Top-All Annual for Boys*, 1939
Source: Frederick Warne

As fine a state of frenzy as can well be imagined.

Christianity, then all its negative or denied aspects may well be projected elsewhere, such as on to the Orient or the other. In the caption to the illustration in Figure 5.28, the reference to imagination gives the game away. This illustration is from the White imagination; the non-White figures play out the repressed White side.

The consequence of this understanding is that Orientalist discourse can be seen as an incredibly rich source of information, not about the Orient, but about the West itself. A study of Orientalist discourse as a projection of the repressed side of the White psyche reveals a great deal about the West. The theory of projection also begins to explain some of the fascination that 'other' cultures have always held for the West. They have been used by the West as a kind of shadow or mirror in which the West, without realising it, was exploring itself.

Such a notion is obvious if we consider the concept of exoticism. For something to be exotic it has to be strange, foreign, and exciting. To anyone born in a so-called exotic culture everything there will seem quite normal—far from exotic. Things can only seem exotic to the foreign eye. Thus a description of a culture or a person as exotic tells us about the beholder rather than the beheld.

CONCLUSION

In this chapter we have given an overview of some of the issues relating to representations of ethnicity by focusing on the relationship between Whites and non-Whites, both in historical realities and in media representations. Using the concept of discourses of ethnicity, we have offered a number of ways of thinking about and understanding the White/non-White connection. You should be able to use these methods to think about representations of different ethnic groups.

Part 6

BUT THEY KEEP MOVING THE POSTS:

POSTMODERN PERSPECTIVES

I sometimes think that I'm too many people, too many people at once:

The husband or the hedonist, the businessman or the communist,

The artist or the show-biz creep, the lover or the nervous geek.

The question of identity is one that's always haunted me,

Whoever I decide to be depends on who is with me

The Pet Shop Boys, 'Too Many People'

OVERVIEW OF PART 6

Chapter 19   Postfeminism and Third-wave Feminism, Poststructuralism, and Postcolonialism

Chapter 20   Postmodernism

In an ever-expanding universe nothing is static: societies change, the media change, and theories change. Much of what we have presented so far has been an attempt to pin down the meanings of texts, to give definitions of concepts, and to outline approaches for understanding the media. In many ways these methods are fruitful and illuminating, but they have their limitations. You have probably already realised that our readings of texts such as *Thelma and Louise* tend to become ever more complicated as more and more theoretical approaches are introduced. It's important to recognise that the complexity of theory carries with it a great deal of explanatory power. Without it we would generally have a disorganised array of opinions and responses to media texts. Theory enables us to ask deeper questions about media texts and what they reveal about society, and it gives credibility to our answers to these questions. In essence, a theoretical approach is a structured way of thinking that enables ideas to be organised and substantiated within a certain framework.

Most of the theories we have discussed in this book were developed during the 1970s and 1980s. Since then, there have been significant changes in media, society, and theory. Some of these changes are encapsulated in the 'post' words: postmodernism, poststructuralism, postcolonialism, and postfeminism (alongside third-wave feminism). These words suggest that we have moved into a new era, new ways of being and understanding. It is hard to say exactly when this new era began (for example, considerable argument has taken place over the issue of when postmodernism began, and there has even been debate over whether it should be one word, two separate words, or a hyphenated word). But these terms were being used by cultural theorists in the 1980s and are now part of common currency for talking about and describing the world in which we live.

19 Postfeminism and Third-wave Feminism, Poststructuralism, and Postcolonialism

POST

It is useful to consider the use of the prefix 'post', because this shows differences and connections between the terms 'postmodernism', 'postfeminism', 'poststructuralism', and 'postcolonialism'. Using 'modernism' (see pp. 307–8) as an example, the prefix 'post' is used for these reasons:

- 'Post' means 'after'. Postmodernist ideas, beliefs, and feelings are new discourses about art, culture, and society that have emerged after earlier ideas of modernism.
- The term 'postmodernism' recognises that we live in a world in which modernist ideas and actions are important and have changed the world. A postmodernist world is one that is built on the theories and practices of modernism.
- Connecting 'post' to 'modernism' does two more things. First, it shows that this new discourse about culture and society is still linked to modernism: it carries on with modernist concerns so it is, in fact, another version of modernism. Second, it challenges or goes against earlier modernist discourses, and in so doing it breaks new ground.

The use of 'post' as a prefix for 'modernism' has similar implications for the other 'posts'. They are all movements that have come after, are built on, are linked to, and challenge the previous movements.

A CRITIQUE OF THIS BOOK SO FAR

Taken together, these new perspectives—postfeminism and third-wave feminism, poststructuralism, postcolonialism, and postmodernism—might produce the following general critique of what this book has done so far:

1 We have tried to fix the meanings of texts, but postmodernism sees meanings as indefinite and mobile; it conceptualises audiences as having more power and suggests that meanings only come into play in specific social situations. The context in which texts are read and the nature of the audience are more important than the text, in terms of the readings that can be made of that text. Signs and signifiers are more fluid and open; readers and contexts give them meanings. Semiology is thus considered to be a flawed approach because it legitimates or

privileges preferred or dominant meanings over the infinite possible meanings that might arise for other readers in diverse contexts.

2 We have worked with oppositions as a structuring framework in two ways: first, we have used binary oppositions in relation to analysis of language and text; second, we have discussed them as ways of understanding gender, sexual orientation, and ethnicity. These oppositions perpetuate discrimination against women, homosexuals, and ethnic groups, and are a major factor in the continued subordination of these groups in society. Although we have raised the problem of the oppression of women, homosexuals, and non-Whites, in critiquing the systems set up by binary oppositions we have been forced to use these oppositions as key terms in my arguments. The danger of this is that focusing on critiquing such oppositions keeps our understanding fixed within this adversarial framework, rather than facilitating the search for different conceptual frameworks. The search for such frameworks is central to queer theory. It can be found in the work of Judith Butler, who has suggested that the distinction between male and female may not be a helpful way to understand people (Butler 1990). Many young people today seem less bothered by these differences and can mix easily across gender, sexual, and ethnic divisions.

3 Our focus on issues of language and representation seems to point to a need for ideal, positive, forms of representation—politically correct representations—that will satisfactorily represent reality. Postmodernism questions that there are ideal forms of representation, arguing that all representations are relative and partial. Postmodern theory is happy to play with stereotypes, and its ironic tone also makes readings more complicated.

4 Structuralism, Marxism, and theories of ideology run the risk of being too fixed; at times they paint a picture of a world in which people are easily controlled and positioned by texts, social structures, and organisations. Structuralism, in particular, implies that a linear, sequential, coherent structure underlies all aspects of life from media narratives to myths and kinship groups. This suggests that we can use such theories to discern and follow these underlying pathways to meaning, truth, and understanding. Such theories do not do justice to social complexity or to the range of possibilities available to us in our identities, behaviour, and actions. For example, in relation to identity and subjectivity, it is now clear that we can occupy multiple identities—feminist, Australian, ethnic-Australian, raver, student, worker, and so on—in a multitude of social situations and spaces. These different positions give us different ways of seeing and acting in the world. Our social position is more open than Marxism, structuralism, and theories of ideology would suggest.

5 Our analysis of the media is too focused on cinema and television, and on specific texts—that is, particular films and television programs. More concern needs to be placed on how the media are positioned in society (the political economy approach), on how they are actually used and experienced by people, and on how they are part of a wider media flow that is developing new forms. While cinema may have been the dominant form of the first half of the twentieth century, and television the dominant form since 1950, these media are currently being replaced by a new set of technologies, particularly the Internet, which offer new forms of interactive communication.

There is validity in each of these points. Nevertheless, we think that the approaches offered so far in this book are important for the following reasons:

- They establish initial skills in reading texts, skills that are relevant to media practitioners and critics alike.
- They give a history of developments in media and media studies. This history forms the foundations for contemporary work and analysis, and you need to understand these developments to engage fully in the debates around postmodernism.
- The theoretical concepts discussed so far are still relevant for understanding current media.

POSTFEMINISM AND THIRD-WAVE FEMINISM

The history of feminism (the movement for women's equality and liberation) has many stages. Currently, the most well-known is the strand of feminism that emerged in the late 1960s and was the dominant form of feminism throughout the 1970s. This strand of feminism, known as second-wave feminism, has had enormous influence on Western society. It was built on earlier feminist movements, such as the efforts of first-wave feminists such as Mary Wollstonecraft, author of *A Vindication of the Rights of Woman*, written in 1792; the struggle for emancipation and suffrage (the right to vote) in the early twentieth century; and the raising of questions by people such as the novelist George Eliot and political theorist John Stuart Mill about women's rights, duties, and responsibilities in the nineteenth century. The late 1960s and the 1970s was a time when feminist writers became significant voices in public discourse. First- and second-wave feminism should be understood in the context of a long history of patriarchy and the oppression of women stretching back through the centuries.

Since the 1980s, there have been many new developments and debates in relation to the social roles of men and women, and the construction of gender and sexual identities. Different strands of feminism have developed, and there have been reactions against feminism. These developments are built on earlier feminisms: some identify positively with earlier feminisms; others challenge them. The term 'postfeminism' tends to be used in relation to theories and ideas that reject much of earlier feminist orthodoxy. 'Third-wave feminism' tends to be used as an umbrella term to describe a new era of feminist thinking that has developed since the 1980s and 1990s, and we will use it in this way.

How is third-wave feminism distinctive from the feminism of the 1960s and 1970s? How is it built on and linked to this feminism, and how does it challenge it? While we will outline some significant factors in the answers to these questions, there is a significant body of research and writing related to this field that you may well want to pursue further yourself.[1]

Earlier feminist concerns and struggles produced many social changes that are now part of the landscape of contemporary life for women:

- equal rights in terms of pay and job opportunities
- challenges to sexual discrimination and sexual harassment
- acceptance that women can enter any field of work
- acceptance that having children does not preclude full participation in the paid workforce and in public life generally, because caring for children is not 'women's work' but a shared parental and social responsibility

- increased maternity benefits
- more freedom in terms of marriage and divorce
- a greater understanding and privileging of women's feelings, skills, and sexualities.

This rosy picture should not disguise the fact that women are still discriminated against in numerous ways: women's political power, in terms of parliamentary representation, is low, and struggles around equal pay, child-care facilities, violence against women, and general misogynist tendencies continue.

Earlier feminism was not a simple, unified set of ideas. It was a variety of developing positions that, despite sharing the overall objective of developing women's lives for the better, differed on how this was to be achieved. By the 1990s, feminism had become part of popular consciousness, and it is now a common reference point for the media: everyone knows about feminism. Many current female students are members of a third-wave feminist generation; they were born into a world where they are treated differently from the way their mothers were treated, and they have opportunities that their mothers never had (the male students have also been affected by these new ways of living). It is interesting that many of them take these 'new' rights for women—the ones that first- and second-wave feminism fought for—as given and many do not want to label themselves as feminists. While they are the product of feminism and support many of its ideals, they also challenge it. There are two significant aspects to this challenge.

First, there has been a backlash against feminism. *The Backlash Against Feminism* is the title of a book by Susan Faludi. This book looks at developments, particularly in the USA, that suggest that men and patriarchy have been fighting the advances that women have made over the last few decades (Faludi 1992). Faludi cites the men's movement and commentators such as Robert Bly as part of this backlash, and she points to the misogyny in films such as *Fatal Attraction* and *Basic Instinct* as further examples. This backlash has been successful in so far as feminism has taken on negative connotations, including, ironically, that feminists are unfeminine (hairy, power-hungry, butch lesbian separatists who aim to oppress men). This perception has led some women to reject it.

The limitations of second-wave feminism

Second, some women have seen limitations in earlier feminisms. We are referring here to third-wave feminist theorists such as Naomi Wolf, Judith Butler, and Catharine Lumby, all of whom grew up in a world familiar with feminism. As writers, critics, and thinkers, they endeavour to take theoretical understandings of feminism beyond the confines of second-wave feminism. The limitations such theorists have identified in second-wave feminism can be broadly categorised as follows:

1 Second-wave feminism and sex

Recent feminist theory suggests that earlier second-wave feminist thought around sexuality was restricted and restrictive. The second-wave feminist struggle against sexual oppression and harassment focused on how women were exploited through sex. In feminist analysis of the media, much was made of the way women tend to be visually represented as sexual objects, and a body of theory developed to analyse and understand this tendency. In the struggle to shift definitions and representations of women away from the purely sexual, second-wave feminism objected strongly to media texts in which the female body was sexualised. These feminists argued that such representations interpellated the audience into a masculine subject position, encouraging viewers to take pleasure in the controlling, possessive gaze and participate in the process of sexual objectification. These critiques of objectification still have force and we may still rightly object to women being reduced to images that sell commodities by making men think about sex. However, the danger is that the attempt to control objectification also censored women's efforts to represent and express their own sexuality, or to enjoy media representations of female sexuality. While this aspect of second-wave feminism can be seen as repressive of women's sexuality, it should be noted that women's magazines today do not display any such aversion to sex or sexuality. They are full of articles, information, stories, and pictures that explicitly explore issues of female sexuality. If second-wave feminism was ever leading towards advocacy of censorship and restrictions around sexuality, this seems to have been headed off.

There are currently a host of new possibilities for women in terms of the expression of sexuality (McRobbie 1997; Lumby 1997). The opening up of these possibilities is partly related to the reappropriation or the reclaiming of particular signifiers of femininity. I can still remember my confusion when a feminist friend started wearing lipstick again in the early 1980s. Make-up had been seen as part of the objectification of women and was decried by many feminists, because it signalled the fact that the wearer cared about how she looked to others, but here was a feminist wearing it. This at first seemed to undermine the feminist statement that a woman's worth is not located in her appearance, or in her status as an object that is sexually appealing to men. However, the manner in which she wore the make-up was also very deliberate: instead of make-up that is not obvious (that is, make-up that makes the wearer look 'naturally' beautiful, and that the observer may well not notice) she was wearing make-up that drew attention to itself. The obviousness of such make-up draws attention to the artifice involved in beautification. It invites the viewer to recognise that a mask is being worn. It can thus be worn with irony, humour, and playfulness, and thereby becomes part of a game that involves playing with identity. This play with identity challenges essential notions of the self (see pp. 209–11), and makes it acceptable, in feminist terms, for women to create different identities for themselves through make-up, hair styles, and clothes. While men can also change identities

Figure 6.1 Advertisement for 17 Cosmetics.
Caption: It's not make-up, it's ammunition.
'I'm the last bird you'll peck on the cheek, mate.'
Source: 17 Cosmetics, 1998;
photograph by Mosche Brakha

through changing their appearance, this 'putting on' of a persona has been more part of women's culture, and so it can be said that it has been reclaimed by women for different purposes. Apart from giving women the freedom to be ironic and knowing about their assumption of feminine identities, make-up can also be used as an instrument of power in relation to men, allowing women to assert their sexual attractiveness as power over men. For example, some recent advertising campaigns for make-up (see, for example, Figure 6.1) show it being worn aggressively rather than enticingly.

Figure 6.2 Advertisement from Ella Baché's Every Body is Beautiful campaign
Image courtesy Ella Baché

At the same time there is a new exploration of women's sexuality in popular culture, making earlier theories about visual objectification seem limited. For instance, Ella Baché's campaign Every Body is Beautiful positions skin care and beauty therapy within the discourse of health and well-being. Because the campaign celebrates natural beauty and offers a non-stereotypical image of female sexuality, it draws together the discourses of femininity and feminism. Some critics claimed that the campaign was guilty of the commodification of Polynesian culture (although the model looks Eurasian, her ethnic identity is ambiguous), and others claimed that it was a condescending attempt to reach the lesbian market or mature women, but these readings are oppositional and were clearly not the intended meaning of the advertisement. The significant thing about the Every Body is Beautiful campaign is that, although it still foregrounds beauty as an important attribute of bodies, it also reclaims the female gaze and female sensuality. It aims to transform the way women look at other women, and the way they see themselves, rather than being about the way men look at women, or about how women see themselves through the lens of the sexualised male gaze (Figure 6.2).

Figure 6.3 Australian *Big Brother* (2001) contestant, Sarah Marie
Source: *Cosmopolitan*, October 2001

This image of Sarah Marie (Figure 6.3), one of the most popular members of the Australian version of the reality TV program *Big Brother*, was featured on the cover of the *Body Love* edition of *Cosmopolitan* magazine (October, 2001). The magazine, and others like it, invariably feature very slender, classically beautiful covergirls. In contrast, this issue depicted a 'real woman' looking good and feeling good about herself. However, it was considered such a great risk to break away from the norm that a picture of a thin model was included on the back cover, so that storekeepers could choose which image would face the public on the magazine stands.

Sarah Marie was very popular on *Big Brother* because she was confident and uninhibited. She was unashamed of working as entertainment manager of a club called 'The Doll House', featuring exotic dancers; she was comfortable with her body shape and size; she was warmly affectionate (and received friendship and affection from both her male and female housemates); and she celebrated her femininity by 'bum dancing' with her friends. All these attributes made her a positive role model for young women and a welcome alternative to other media texts that promote unattainable body types and less bold, assertive, outgoing images of femininity. Like many other reality TV participants, Sarah Marie has used *Big Brother* as a springboard to launch a media career.

While Ella Baché is working with sensuality and the female gaze, and Sarah Marie offers a role model of a real woman who is uninhibited about her body, Madonna's work and her media profile provide the most obvious examples of changing images of women's sexuality in popular culture. Whereas critics such as Berger and Mulvey decried the way men look at women (and the way women are looked at generally) as a system of unequal power relations, Madonna has subverted these systems of looking by showing that men can take up passive or subordinate viewing positions in relation to women who are in charge of the way they present their sexuality to the world.

Another form of asserting 'girl power' is evident in a clothing brand called 'Bad Girl', which is marketed using a logo with a halo over it (subverting the good girl/bad girl division by celebrating the deviance of the 'bad girl'). The postfeminist theorist Catharine Lumby has written a book called *Bad Girls: The Media, Sex and Feminism in the 90s* (Lumby 1997) that explores the positions of a new generation of feminists in debates about pornography, censorship, and the media. Signs of oppression (such as the label 'bad girl', or even images of sexism and objectification) can thus be reclaimed and reused by the oppressed group, in this case women, as a sign of power and agency.

Nobody Denim offers a good example of postfeminist advertising strategies (Figure 6.4). The label itself is playfully reworking the idea that most media images of women feature models so thin that they have practically 'no body', and are 'nobodies' lacking in individuality because they all have the same stereotypical kind of beauty. The caption 'Do u measure up?' (using the modern email abbreviation of 'you') is a self-conscious reference to the famous Levi's campaign, 'Do you fit the legend?', implying that Nobody Denim is in the same league as Levi's and that it is the customer that has to be good enough to fit the clothes, rather than the other way around. The advertisements feature models tied up with tape measures, with another tape measure visible in the background linking a series of images. This could all be interpreted as yet another media message that young people have to be thin and wear designer labels in order to 'measure up' to media ideals of beauty. However, the advertisement's playful appropriation of stereotypes and its incorporation of gender ambiguity situates it firmly in postmodern terrain and betrays an awareness of feminist critiques of the beauty myth. One panel of the advertisement shows a young woman in heavy make-up wearing a T-shirt with the word 'Foxy' across the breast, and another shows three figures from the waist down, with their backs to the camera, posing as though they are at a urinal. These three models wear jeans, and nothing else. At least one of the models has a clearly defined waist, signifying femininity. At least one could be either male or female, so the advertisement makes us laugh by manipulating our expectations about gender and making fun of the feminist slogan 'Anything a man can do, a woman can do better'. However, the implicit critique of media images that exploit female sexuality and promote unhealthy ideals is subtle and can readily be overlooked, in which case the advertisement may reinforce the norms of which it is making fun.

The danger with postfeminism's 'devil may care' attitude about gender and sexuality, evident in some postfeminist media texts, is that it assumes that gender relations and the power dynamics they entail are issues that have been resolved, rather than being ongoing concerns linked to race, class, and other forms of identity and opression. Many depict assertive female characters who don't give a damn about issues such as sexism because they already have the benefits of equal opportunity. For example, the models in the Nobody Denim advertisement are all slender, young, fair-skinned, and beautiful, and they look as though they come from privileged, middle-class backgrounds.

There is a tension between two different understandings of postfeminism. On the one hand postfeminism is associated with antifeminist discourse, and with the sense that we have entered an era after feminism, in which resistance to patriarchal oppression is no longer necessary. On the other hand, postfeminist theory is a sophisticated postmodern or

Figure 6.4 Advertisement for the clothing label Nobody Denim
Source: Courtesy Avant Card

poststructural critique of earlier approaches to feminism that were seen as being extreme, essentialist, caught up in dualisms, or flawed, and misguided in other ways. Interestingly, feminism has had such an impact on both the media and society that its fundamental insights and goals have, in many ways, been internalised and affirmed in both these strands of postfeminist discourse. Young postfeminists take the benefits of first- and second-wave feminism for granted: it is from a position of increased equity and changed attitudes that they are able to critique earlier feminist positions.[2]

2 Valuing differences between men and women

The second general limitation of second-wave feminism has been seen as its approach to questions of differences between men and women. While first- and second-wave feminism stressed the construction of femininity and fought for equality with men, some third-wave feminists argue that there might be important differences between men and women, and that traditional feminine qualities and characteristics need to be revalidated and endorsed. Many third-wave feminists have also recognised that while patriarchy privileges men, men also seem to suffer from it in various ways. For example, health research points to the fact that women live longer, and many men have come to feel the privilege of paid employment (being, or having to be, 'the breadwinner') and the exemption from parenting duties as a burden in the first instance and a sacrifice in the second.

Other third-wave feminists develop the point about the construction of femininity further, suggesting that all gender roles for men and women are socially constructed and that gender categories are themselves subject to question.

Thus, third-wave feminism attempts to understand what constitutes women's identities, and it explores the issue of whether or not gender identity is essential or constructed (Butler 1990). This is a continuing area of debate that we consider below.

3 Class and ethnicity in feminism

Finally, third-wave feminism has asked about the implications of the fact that much second-wave feminism was the product of a White, middle-class elite. The African–American feminist theorist bell hooks spells her name with lower-case letters to signify the fact that she is a member of a doubly marginalised group and that being a woman of colour differentiates her experiences from those of White women. Feminism, hooks claims, should be opposed to all systems of domination. This careful attention to difference, diversity, and the historical or contextual specificity of women's experiences is a core characteristic of third-wave feminism, and it arose from feminist critiques of homogeneity that date back to civil rights movements in the 1960s and 1970s.

Third-wave feminism challenges the perceived dominance of White, middle-class voices in second-wave feminism by taking care to include a range of women's voices and positions. For example, the experiences and concerns of a Black or so-called 'coloured' South African woman will have similarities with, but not be identical to, the experiences and concerns of a Maori woman, a well-off Singaporean business woman, or a White female academic from California or London. Each of these women will experience patriarchy in distinct ways, and no woman can speak for all of them.

Conclusion

The exploration of the limitations of second–wave feminism has fuelled the development of feminist concerns in the present era. Alongside the productive nature of these explorations and the freedom they give to women to challenge the legacy of feminism, is the potential for them to be used in the ongoing backlash against feminism.

1 Explore the question of the limitations of second-wave feminism, as discussed above, by looking at any of Madonna's videos. How does her celebration of female eroticism, display, and power relate to second-wave and third-wave concerns? Look for elements of irony, excessiveness, and overt performance.

2 The following images (Figures 6.5, 6.6, and 6.7) show different aspects of 1990s representations of women. How do you 'read' these advertisements? How is the audience invited to look at them?

Figure 6.5 Advertisement for *RALPH* magazine
Source: *RALPH* magazine, 1997

Exercise commentary

This advertisement (Figure 6.5), which is aimed at men, is deliberately politically incorrect and as such can be seen as part of the backlash against feminism. It combines a 'knowingness' about feminist debates around the sexual objectification of women with the suggestion that men have certain instinctive, essential sexual drives that can only be satisfied by treating women as objects of (male) visual, and ultimately sexual, pleasure. Note that the context of reception also influences our interpretation of the image in significant ways. For instance, in South Africa, a country sensitive to racial discrimination, the advertisement would still be read within the discourse of gender politics and postfeminism. However, the punch line 'You should never mix your Whites with your coloureds' (which revels in political incorrectness) takes on added significance.

Figure 6.6 Advertisement for Panasonic computers
Source: Matsushita Electric Corporation
of America, 1998

Exercise commentary

This advertisement (Figure 6.6) is an example of advertising that plays on the audience's knowledge of feminist issues: the woman is portrayed as professional, as conversant with technology, and as capable of playing with stereotypes of femininity (this advertisement plays on the stereotype of women as flighty and incapable of being seriously immersed in paid work) to her advantage. However, while this advertisement suggests that women can take pleasure in being ironically sexy, it may still be suggesting that beauty is a prerequisite for success.

Figure 6.7 Advertisement for
Hestia lingerie
Source: Hestia Lingerie, 1996

Exercise commentary

This advertisement (Figure 6.7), which is aimed at women, again plays on feminist issues and the kinds of things with which feminism is associated in the popular imagination—women's support for each other, bra-burning, and venturing out into traditionally male terrains.

Look at other media examples. Consider whether and how they are built on and linked to earlier feminisms. Ask yourself whether, and how, they challenge these earlier feminisms.

POSTSTRUCTURALISM

The same points about the 'post' prefix apply to poststructuralism: poststructuralism comes after, is built on, is linked to, and challenges structuralism. The main problem with structuralist approaches is that they are too rigid, too limiting in understanding media and culture. In particular, they suggest that people are determined by structures, that they are dominated by them and therefore have little autonomy or freedom. Poststructuralism opens up more possibilities.

Structuralism is linked to semiology and theories of ideology; together they formed a central part of media studies theories about media texts and their relationship to society, as outlined here in Parts 2, 3, and 4. Structuralism, which flourished in the 1970s, was opposed to what was called 'culturalism' or theories that drew on 'lived experience' (Hall 1986). This opposition lead to a poststructuralist critique of structuralism (Hall 1985).

Structuralists argue that people are determined and controlled by the social and aesthetic structures that they live in, and that dominant ideology is transmitted through these structures to a relatively powerless population. In contrast, culturalists argue that people actually have some say in whether they accept or refuse dominant ideology. According to culturalists, people can challenge dominant ideology and can live it in different ways. In relation to media, this difference between structuralism and culturalism corresponds with the difference between, on the one hand, textual analysis that shows how dominant ideological values are inscribed in a text through its processes of signification, representation, and its narrative structure, and on the other, analysis that asks what audiences are actually doing with texts. The stress on audiences and their uses of the texts is crucial to poststructuralist approaches (Weedon 1987).

With multiple readings of texts and our use of hegemony as a conceptual tool, we have already begun to present poststructuralist analyses. The broadly based approach recognises that structures are important for understanding the world, and at the same time it acknowledges that there is more to understanding the media than texts alone.

POSTCOLONIALISM

'Postcolonialism' is a term used in various contexts, and in each context it has a slightly different meaning. It relates to colonialism, which is explored in the discussion, in Part 5, of the historical relations between Europe and the rest of the world and the discourses associated with non-Western cultures. 'Postcolonialism' is a descriptive term that recognises that the colonialist era, in which European countries established overt control over majority world (colonised) countries, has ended; nearly all the former colonies have achieved political independence. But the reference to colonialism reminds us that the nineteenth century and much of the twentieth century have been colonialist periods and that the influence of colonialism is still being felt throughout the world.

Postcolonialism can operate as an attitude: to be a postcolonialist is to hope and presume that we now have equality between people of different ethnic backgrounds, that old colonial power bases have thankfully gone, and that we do not need to dwell on or examine the colonial past (it can be left behind).

Postcolonialism can also be a way of looking at the world, a way that understands the present postcolonial situation in the light of the past colonial situation, and draws our attention to this link—not to remind us or make us feel guilty, but to see how this past is still relevant and still has an influence on power relations and social attitudes.

Some argue that we now live in a neo-colonialist world. While the traditional forms of colonisation have disappeared, the previously colonised nations are still dominated economically through the powers of multinational corporations and thus a new form of power, neo(new)-colonialism, has been established.

Postcolonialism is often used to study literature and media products that come from previously colonised countries or that specifically address postcolonial issues (Rivkin and Ryan, pp. 851–1024). The work of many indigenous writers and film-makers is interpreted from a postcolonial perspective. In Australia, the films made by Tracey Moffat and the paintings by Gordon Bennett explore these issues from, among other positions, Aboriginal perspectives. Their work shows how histories of colonialism and discourses of racism are inscribed in present-day Australia. Such discourses and histories are often referred to in their work. For example, Tracey Moffat's *Nice Coloured Girls* relates contemporary experiences of Aboriginal women, in particular their relationships to White men, back to a colonial history. Gordon Bennett's painting *Altered Body Print* (*Shadow Figure Howling at the Moon*) (Plate 7) plays on and challenges the binary oppositions (and discourses) around race that were used to construct his identity (McLean and Bennett 1996). In this painting, he mixes up the oppositions that structure discourses of ethnicity so that they are not neatly paired opposite one another. This breaks the structure of such discourses and also suggests the confusion of an identity positioned within these discourses. He comments:

> There came a time in my life when I became aware of my Aboriginal heritage. This may seem of little consequence, but when the weight of European representations of Aboriginal people as the quintessential primitive 'Other' is realised and understood, within discourses of self and other … then you may understand why such an awareness was problematic for my sense of identity. The conceptual gap between my sense of self and other collapsed and I was thrown into turmoil.
>
> It is the collapse of the conceptual gap between the binary opposites of self/other, civilised/savage, sophisticated/primitive, or perhaps more appropriately its gradual disintegration and my process of integration, that forms the substratum of my life and work (McLean and Bennett 1996, p. 9).

Bennett's painting is produced out of a knowledge and awareness of cultural theory; it is built on and extends notions of structural binary oppositions, thus linking cultural theory and practice in significant ways.

Essentialism also enters the debate about ethnic identity: this comes up in relation to discussion of people's 'roots'—where they come from in a historical sense. *Roots* is the title of an influential novel by Alex Haley, which was made into a television series about the history of Afro-Americans (Haley 1976). This series celebrated the rediscovery of Afro-American history and saw this history as significant in terms of the identities of modern Afro-Americans. Similarly, many people today seek connection and understanding with their 'roots'; this now extends to White Anglo-Celtic ethnic groups in Australia seeking to understand their historical and spiritual connections. One of the main issues surrounding this search is whether these roots are cultural/social or genetic/biological ('in the blood'). Many ethnic groups seem to call on both these understandings of their roots. Roots can be romanticised, as happens when Australians looking at Aboriginal spiritual connections with the land make these connections seem 'eternal', representative of something beyond culture. Even those who believe only in social construction sometimes lapse into the common-sense view that cultural differences are based on genetics.

20 *Postmodernism*

Postmodernism[3] is the most complex and the most inclusive of the four terms: all the other 'posts' can be seen as part of postmodernism. So what is it? Where did it come from? And where can we find it?

THE ORIGINS OF THE TERM 'POSTMODERNISM'

Where does 'postmodernism' come from?

The term 'postmodernism' was first used (as early as the 1960s) to describe a style or movement in architecture (Jencks 1986). This style worked by taking various elements of past architectural styles and mixing them together in new buildings. Consequently, there was nothing new or original in it other than the way it combined and reworked past styles.

Frederic Jameson

The term was taken up by the political and cultural theorist Frederic Jameson, among others, to describe contemporary Western and global society. Jameson argues that a shift that began in the late 1960s and that was driven by economic changes is changing the world and its culture (Jameson 1991). He maintains that society is moving into a phase he describes as 'late capitalism'. By this, he means that the capitalist system—some people investing wealth in the production and distribution of goods and others selling their labour for wages—that has been developing since the end of feudalism, is developing a new form. He argues that:

- Economic power is increasingly concentrated in multinational companies whose businesses cross national borders, and that through their ability to sell goods globally, these companies are changing the face of production (so that, for example, American-based multinational companies can produce goods much more cheaply in Asian countries than they can in the USA) and distribution.
- In the drive to sell more goods, emphasis is now placed more on consumption than on production. The emphasis on consumption means that people are becoming more aware and more concerned with issues of lifestyle, image, and appearance, leading to a society focused on appearances, on spectacle, a designer-label mentality.

Postmodernism as a style of cultural production

Jameson's focus on spectacle and appearance leads to a definition of postmodernism as a style of cultural production. This is the most common way of using the word, and it is a use that you are probably familiar with. When people describe things as postmodern, they are often drawing on this meaning. Postmodernism as a style of cultural production is relevant to aesthetic products (for example, films, advertisements, and television programs) and to lifestyles (how people live, feel, and act in everyday life). Thus 'postmodernism' is a term that can be used to describe the media and the way we live in real life (see the quotation from Lyotard on p. 303). Jameson's analysis links postmodern styles of living and cultural production to economic changes. Others see postmodern styles, postmodern cultures, as an aesthetic response to, and reflection of, at least three other aspects of the world we now live in. These aspects are described below.

1 New scientific theories

New scientific theories have changed our understanding of the world. Previous theories in both the physical (biology, physics, chemistry, and so on) and social sciences (politics, sociology, and so on) aimed to classify and understand the human and physical world; semiology, Marxism, and psychoanalysis, which have informed so much of media studies theory, were part of this project. Scientists have tended to think they can rationally explain the world we live in and how we behave, but current scientific discoveries and theories have undermined these certainties. Developments in nuclear physics, in chaos theory, and in complexity theory suggest that all knowledge about the physical world is relative, partial, and uncertain. The search for ultimate truths, for objective impartiality, is futile. Among social scientists, it has become commonplace to assert that even individual identities are not 'real', since we are just a collection of constructed social masks. 'Reality' cannot be pinned down. There are no certainties except uncertainty and continual change.

2 We live in a media-world

The spread of the media, particularly television, has produced a new way of seeing the world. First, people are saturated, as never before, with media-provided images, information, and knowledge. We have an amazing archive of media images available to look at, and we also store many in our brains. Second, media representations and the real world have begun to blur: we see the real world in terms of media images. This is apparent in the way we viewed the 1991 Gulf War, which appeared on our television screens, and was reported, like a series of video games. More recently, images of the War on Terror and the collapse of the twin towers of the World Trade Center in America have been compared with footage from an action film (in fact, the release of an Arnold Schwarzenegger film featuring a terrorist attack on an office building was delayed, and *Fight Club* was pulled from some play lists because it suddenly seemed disturbingly realistic in light of the news footage). So much experience, knowledge, and feeling comes by way of media images that the media dominate our ways of seeing the world. Reality TV offers a clear example of this closure of the gap between reality and representation—other examples include interactive television situations in which the viewer has a degree of control over the image, and television programs such as Cartoon Network's *Flash Force Five*, which features animated versions of real children.

3 Postmodernism as a reaction to politics in the 1990s

Lastly, postmodernism is a reaction to post-1960s politics. The 1960s was an important historical moment that crystallised in 1968. This revolutionary period ended the Vietnam war; saw the rise of student and trade-union power; brought new social liberation with the hippies; brought down the corrupt Nixon government through Watergate; increased freedom and liberation movements throughout the Third World; and in Australia, led to the famous Whitlam Labor government. All this seemed to herald a new beginning, a new optimism in society. But it did not produce a new social utopia. Inequality, war, and social struggle persist, and the postmodernist generations, who know so much about social change, seem to be able to do little but look ironically or dismissively at the world we live in.

Postmodernism is an expression and response to all the above factors. The big questions about postmodernism as a style or practice are: Does it celebrate this new global, economic, social system? Does it offer a critique and challenge to it? Does it offer a way of coping and surviving in the system? We think it can do all three. To explore these questions, we need to examine specific instances of postmodernism, since it is not limited to one position.

GLOBALISATION, FRAGMENTATION, AND HOMOGENISATION

Globalisation

The following quotation from Jean-François Lyotard gives an excellent flavour of postmodernism as described so far; it also points to two other significant terms and tendencies: 'globalisation' and 'fragmentation': 'One listens to reggae, watches a Western, eats McDonald's food for lunch and local cuisine for dinner, wears Paris perfume in Tokyo and "retro" clothes in Hong Kong' (Lyotard 1984).

This description could be of an 'ideal' lifestyle for a global, postmodern individual. It stresses consumption and style, it involves mixing 'high' and 'low' culture (see p. 311), and it involves combining different cultures in one's everyday life. Globalisation means that these different styles are now easily available in all parts of the world for a large number of people. Our world is approaching what theorist Marshall McLuhan has called a 'global village', in which we are linked by culture and in which technology makes distances largely irrelevant. Globalisation can lead to homogenisation. Used in this context, the term 'homogenisation' refers to the way that cultures are beginning to look the same everywhere. This is clearly becoming true in big cities: American patterns of architecture, and American-style fast food, and Hollywood films are so common that sometimes it is difficult to tell if you are in the USA, Asia, Europe, or Australia.

Homogenisation can also refer to the global domination of one culture over others; in other words, it is a description of a form of cultural and economic imperialism. In a sense it can be said that since World War II many countries have indulged in economic warfare rather than military warfare, realising that social power can derive from economic power. Globalisation through multinational production and distribution can mean the elimination of other cultures. In terms of language, globalisation could mean that we will end up with just one global language (most likely English).

The cover of the Benetton magazine, *Colors* (Plate 9), presents a powerful image of globalisation. The liquid splattered across the page is bright red, forming an image recognisable as the Disney character Mickey Mouse. If we read this image as an image of bloodshed, then the question we must ask is 'Who, or what, has died, and how is Disney implicated in this death?' Students have come up with several different answers to this question, many of which point to the positive and negative aspects of globalisation. One answer is that globalisation and cultural imperialism tend to produce a monoculture, which leads to the death of cultural difference and diversity, and the loss of non-American cultural traditions and customs. The other answer, based on the signifier of the Internet address turned into a smile on Mickey's mouth, is that the Internet and other media have linked people across the globe together into a 'global village' or a virtual community. These positive aspects of globalisation are specifically linked to communication media and their ability to bring us closer together, inform us of issues and events in distant places, and create a sense of 'oneness': one culture shared by all humanity. In the case of this advertisement the media are helping to counteract the prejudice and exploitation that arises from ignorance of the difficulties faced by other peoples struggling to maintain their cultures.

Being a media giant and powerful transnational corporation that has exported images and aspects of American culture around the world, Disney is an agent of globalisation. As media analysts, we need to consider the meaning and the impact of global media products, as well as the employment practices and ethics of corporations that circulate media texts on a global scale. For an interesting discussion of this point, see *No Logo* (Klein 2000, esp. p. 328 and p. 331).

Fragmentation

Fragmentation is the opposite side of the same coin. Where the discourse of globalisation suggests a unified world, postmodernism's observations of fragmentation point to the way that emergent trends feature the break-up, dispersion, and redistribution of previously unified social groups and cultural practices. Entities such as the family, the community, and traditional costumes, foods, and customs that were once associated with a particular place or locale are now dispersed across the globe and available over the Internet, on television, or in an international franchise. Perhaps fragmentation is illustrated most clearly in relation to media forms: for instance, a community of Internet users can be located in different parts of the world, whereas traditional communities were defined at least in part by a shared geographical location.

Fragmentation is also associated with the process of breaking apart and recombining parts of older structures in new ways. For example, the film *Pulp Fiction* playfully and inventively fragments the traditional narrative structure, prising apart the beginning, middle, and ending in order to rework them to create something fresh. The resulting postmodern text builds on audience members' knowledge of the old system and its components, challenging the claims that the old style of storytelling has to being the best or only way of making sense. Hybridisation, another characteristic feature of postmodernity, often results from the recombination of fragments of conventional texts and structures. For instance, we speak of generic hybrids in cinema and television, hybrid identities and styles emerge from the meeting of different subcultures, and 'culinary fusion' is a new kind of cuisine that blends foods and flavours from different cultures.

So, on the one hand, traditional boundaries—which used to separate people in terms of time, space, and culture—are now easily broken. Satellite and Internet technology connect people instantly, and national governments have little power to stop the transmission of ideas and goods across these previously policed boundaries. We have a global culture.[4] On the other hand, at the same time, groups define their own identities at levels below that of national identity; through increased access to media technology, they celebrate their difference.

In themselves, these changes are not necessarily good or bad. Just as at the beginning of this book we note arguments for and against the media, we could do the same thing in relation to the trends towards globalisation and fragmentation. Value judgments about these trends really only make sense if they are related to particular issues: for example, 'How do multinational companies benefit from global markets?' 'In what ways does global culture increase potential access to knowledge and communication?' 'In what ways does it promote democracy?' As ecological and social problems develop, new global connections may help us to recognise our interconnectedness across the planet and may enable us to work together towards equitable solutions.

World music and global television

World music is an interesting case to examine in relation to trends towards globalisation and fragmentation: majority world (Third World) music, particularly African and Latin American music, is now played and marketed around the world, and it influences European and American styles. Perhaps this demonstrates that eurocentrism is coming to an end: rather than focusing on European and American culture, thereby suggesting it is the best, world music invites openness to other cultural influences. This is not cultural imperialism but a flow of culture back from previously colonised states (my own identity as a European who has been influenced by Native American rituals and traditions, is also an example of this flow). World music is also influenced by Western music styles and by Western recording technology.

However, it is important to note that the production and marketing of world music is still largely in the hands of a few European and American companies; they receive a bigger percentage of profits than do the artists who produce the music. In some cases, songs include recordings of indigenous music but no money goes to the original artists. While such instances may suggest that world music is an example of the continuing exploitation of the majority world, we think that on the whole, world music amounts to more than this: it celebrates majority world music and values and its increasing popularity is slowly changing dominant cultural values. Nevertheless, the economic exploitation of indigenous musicians is a problem; the economic rewards flowing from global music must be shared.[5]

Similar points can be made about global television, television networks that span many countries. Sinclair, Jacka, and Cunningham have recently explored how the global television market is developing (Sinclair et al. 1996). They note that it is not a simple case of domination by Australian media mogul Rupert Murdoch and by

American television. There are new possibilities for many other countries as the television market opens up.

Democratisation of the media?

Developments in media technologies are reshaping how information is transmitted; technological devices such as CD players, computers, and video recorders are becoming cheaper to produce and sell, and are thus becoming available to more people: from our own homes we can record and market music, make and edit our own television, and print and publish our own books. As media communication opens up to many more people, a multitude of voices can speak and be heard via the media.

How much is globalisation part of your everyday life?

1 *Consider what factors influenced your decision to buy the different items of clothing you are wearing. Nike and other big-brand companies use the media extensively to increase brand recognition, and most retail outlets rely on advertising to communicate information about sales and new products. Consumers rarely remember the first time they see an advertisement for a particular brand, but they rarely forget the brand if they see the advertisement enough times. In her thought-provoking book* No Logo, *Naomi Klein cites a 1998 United Nations National Development Report estimating that global advertising spending stands at over US$435 billion, a figure that has risen so fast it outstrips the growth of the world economy by a third (Klein 2000, p. 9). If that figure represents the importance of the media in modern life, it also indicates significantly misplaced priorities—considering how the money could have been used productively to improve the quality of life for those suffering in poverty and hunger world-wide.*

2 *Is the music you listen to influenced by the music of different cultures? How global are your music listening habits? Chances are, your choices in music and your knowledge of music have something to do with music videos and the promotional machine surrounding bands signed to large record labels. Whether you watch MTV (Music Television, an American television program and entertainment network specialising in popular music videos) or not, many radio stations and music stores do monitor MTV and use it to guide what they play, promote, and sell. MTV itself is more than a marketing machine for the products it advertises between songs and the albums it promotes with its music videos; it is also a medium of communication and a truly global brand in its own right. Music is also used to sell non-music products and build brand images (Sprite's association with hip hop and the Gap's 'Jump, Jive'n'Wail' Khakis Swing advertisements are good examples). The implications of this are that there are both positive and negative outcomes of globalisation: the media play a positive role in helping us learn about and share in each other's cultures, but it is also implicated in wasteful and exploitative marketing practices that primarily benefit the top tier of corporate executives.*

3 *You might like to consider further implications that arise from how global your lifestyle is, and how your choices and habits in both media and product consumption have unintended consequences.*

POSTMODERNISM IN CONTEXT

Postmodernism is built on an earlier movement that we have not discussed: modernism. Since postmodernism is both a reaction to and a continuation of modernism, modernism needs to be briefly described here. To place postmodernism in its proper context, it is also necessary to discuss its relationship to realism.

Realism	Modernism	Postmodernism
Nineteenth century onwards: painting, literature, and mainstream film	1900–60s: modern art and modern architecture, some literature	1960s–present

These three umbrella terms—realism, modernism, and postmodernism—give an overview of aesthetic tendencies in Western culture over the last two hundred years. Realism can be described as an attempt to portray things as they 'really are', as they appear to the human spectator. Realist art often involves portraying ordinary humans in their social situations, and realist art and media products tend to reflect and comment on society. Realism dominated painting and literature in the nineteenth century, and it is still common today. In film, realism is characterised by naturalised conventions of represention, acting, and editing that do not draw attention to the process of construction because they resemble 'normal' ways of seeing and experiencing the world. The realist style is thus not unusual or difficult for audiences to 'read'; much mainstream film is made using realist principles.[6]

Modernism describes the art and aesthetic movements of the first half of the twentieth century. These movements were a reaction against realism (Bradbury and McFarlane 1976; Lunn 1985). Modernism marks the beginning of the modern world; it grew out of enormous political and social changes that were linked, in many ways, to revolutions in technology and communication. Modernism is characterised by:

1 an optimistic belief in the power and possibilities of machines, technology, science, rationality, and progress
2 a range of new art movements that saw and represented the world in new and revolutionary ways (these include cubism, dadaism, surrealism, futurism, stream-of-consciousness writing, and all forms of abstract art). Many of these movements were interested in producing art and architecture that draws attention to the processes of construction involved in making the objects and art. Modernist artists were interested in exploring and foregrounding the very means of representation: paint, the canvas, celluloid, narrative structure, and so on. Modernist artists also questioned how they could represent the world, which involved asking how people see and experience reality. They showed that this process of experiencing and representing reality is more complicated and fragmented than earlier realist aesthetic styles suggested.

Despite the terrible history of the modernist period—two world wars, and major turmoil in China, Russia, and throughout the globe—modernism was essentially an optimistic movement. It looked for ways to organise human society that would deliver happiness and fulfilment.

We can see this in the aims of modernist architecture. Its abstractly styled buildings were functional. The angular, box-like constructions with little ornamentation or elaboration that we have come to associate with modernist architecture were designed as utopian housing spaces that would cater for all human needs. People were grouped together in these modernist buildings: housing estates made up of tower blocks are a modernist legacy. But the utopian dream of this sort of housing has rarely been realised, and housing estates made up of tower blocks are probably the most damning indictment of this dream. In Godfrey Reggio's film *Koyaanisqatsi* (see pp. 123–5) there is an extended sequence that shows the blowing up of one of the most famous modernist housing estates in the USA. Before its demolition, the site had become derelict and deserted because it did not cater for people's real needs. Its destruction can be seen as a metaphor for the death of modernism and the death of the modernist dream. As discussed above, the genesis of postmodernism involves many factors (pp. 302–3), and one of these is this perceived failure of modernism. While postmodernism is linked to modernism, it also challenges it.

CHARACTERISTICS OF POSTMODERNISM

In reading about postmodernism, you will probably come to realise that it is associated with various characteristics (Solomon 1988): for example, irony, the blurring of traditional boundaries, fluid identity, intertextuality, pastiche, appropriation, bricolage, hybridity, self-reflexivity, and self-referentiality. Where structuralism and semiotics look for deep structures and underlying meanings, postmodernism celebrates superficiality, spectacle, and surfaces. What follows is a discussion of some of the most significant of these. Look for examples of these characteristics in media products: you should be able to find them easily. Some of the media products previously examined—for example the films *Blue Velvet* and *Koyaanisqatsi*, the Barbara Kruger photographs, and various advertisements—can be classified as postmodern, and you can reconsider them in this light.

Irony

Let us start with irony. To be ironic is to mean the opposite of what you say. Something is ironic when it indirectly contradicts its surface meaning. The opening of *Blue Velvet* is ironic. It appears to say 'Here is a beautiful, ideal community', but it sees through this to the dark side of the American dream. Irony is witty and cool, knowing and cynical. Todd Gitlin notes '[the cultural critic] Paul Fussell has made the point that irony became standard in English writing after World War I as a way to navigate around the unspeakable' (Gitlin 1993). Why did irony emerge as such an important form of cultural expression in the late twentieth century? What is unspeakable now? What is this ironic mode built on?

Knowingness

Postmodernism is very knowing and self-reflexive. It is built on knowledge of the world, knowledge of media products, and knowledge of countless theories and critiques of society, modernity, and the media. We have a glut of knowledges, accumulated over twenty centuries and more, with which to make sense of the world. However, whereas modernism thought that it was possible to make sense of the world and to rationally organise the future, postmodernism, after modernism's failure, recognises the futility of such a dream. Furthermore, postmodernism embraces non-rational modes of knowledge: for example, it is open to Tarot, astrology, intuition, and so on. Perhaps the most important feature of postmodernism is the way that it is comfortable with lack of certainty. The popularity of *The X-Files* reflects this: each program depicts, in essence, a repeated failure to provide rational explanations; each program suggests new possibilities. Postmodernism suggests that we can pick up whatever theoretical framework feels right to us at any particular moment and that we can use that for a while before moving on to the next one. While we are urged to demonstrate our knowledge, we are reminded that there is no ultimate way of making sense of the world.

Cynicism

Our knowledge has given us the power to 'see through' things. We are no longer naive; we know that the media are all constructions, and that we cannot trust media products to represent reality truthfully; we know that the capitalist world is out to exploit us; we know that we are being controlled by family, church, education, and media systems; and we know that Big Brother is watching us.

Powerlessness

Despite our knowledge and our ability to 'see through' things, we remain powerless because nothing is certain, everything is relative, and the corporate powers that, to a large extent, control our lives are too strong. What can we do as individuals? We can see the world's problems and injustices but they seem too overwhelming for us to do anything about them. This intractability of our problems, the fact that the system is too strong, is what is, in Gitlin's terms, unspeakable. As Gitlin says, 'the fear is that what's underneath hurts too much, better repress it'.

Pleasure

What can we do with all our knowledge, uncertainty, and powerlessness? We can at least use it to indulge in humour, wit, and pleasure: we can make ironic jokes about the system; we can live 'in the moment' and celebrate our (limited) power to be what we want to be; we can play; and we can look good. In the words of a song by the Pet Shop Boys, 'Shameless':

> We're shameless: we will do anything to get our fifteen minutes of fame; we have no integrity, we're ready to crawl to attain celebrity we'll do anything at all.

We can celebrate uncertainty as a freedom from limitations. The feeling that there are no boundaries, that we are in a state of continual change, fluidity, and expansion can lead to excitement and hedonistic experimentation. Postmodern pleasures are also less elitist than modernist ones.

Aspects of these constituents of irony are at work in the Biff cartoons in Figures 6.8 and 6.9, and are also evident in much contemporary advertising (see, for example, Plate 8).

Biff cartoons are a series of postmodern cartoons, often reproduced on postcards, made in the United Kingdom during the 1980s by a company called Biff Products.

In a sense, they are a comic and ironic response to media theory and cultural studies theory. In these cartoons we see the inclusion of multiple realities: a 1950s world, in terms of dress and appearance, is juxtaposed with 1980s knowledge. Postmodernism often uses the perceived idealism and naivety of the 1950s (as lived in the West) as an ironic comparison with the cynical, knowing 1980s and 1990s. *Blue Velvet*, for example, sometimes looks as though it is set in the 1950s, sometimes the 1980s. Biff cartoons also include different levels of discourse:

- The statements of the characters contrast with their real thoughts.
- Authorial comments or captions draw our attention to the divide between high and low culture and set philosophical and art theories in low-culture contexts such as the genres of pulp fiction and popular romance.
- They use 'dirty realism' (for example, in Figure 6.9) there is dandruff on the man's jacket).
- They comment on commodification and marketing.
- They are politically aware.
- They demonstrate awareness of narrative theory, feminism, and philosophical movements such as existentialism.

In Biff cartoons, these knowledges and discourses are set in an arena of sexual politics and relationships, in which women's consciousness is usually shown as more developed than that of men. The pleasure that readers derive from these cartoons is partly dependent on recognising the references to such knowledges, time periods, and sexual politics. Biff cartoons are produced by authors and cartoonists steeped in theory and knowledge. But these theories and knowledges are mocked: it is as if the cartoons ask, 'Where do they get you?'

The CAT boots advertisement (Plate 8) displays another element of the post-modern mix. What we find here is the popularisation of theories of the social construction of reality. This time we are not invited to mock knowledge but to take

Figures 6.8–6.9

Biff cartoons

Source: Mick Kidd, 1988

it on board and work productively with it. The caption 'We shape the things we build, thereafter they shape us' parallels our arguments, presented throughout this book (for example, p. 41), about how our society conditions us, how 'we don't speak language; language speaks us'. Cultural studies knowledge surfaces as part of popular discourse in this advertisement, which appeared in the British magazine *The Face* in 1996. The advertisement recognises how we are caught up in urban deserts in which we have become machine-like, and it suggests a way through this: the answer is not another course in cultural theory; the answer is to buy a new pair of CAT boots! The advertisement suggests that these boots can give our lives in cities shape, and that our identities are shaped by what we wear and where we live. This advertisement proposes that we can escape from the urban jungle by purchasing stylish commodities. Moreover, the figure in the advertisement is an older, Black man. In terms of age and ethnicity a person from a subordinate group in society is shown as fashionable (clothes and hairstyle add to this): Blackness and age become powerful in this advertisement. These advertisements play with signifiers and signification in an exhilarating and pleasurable way, but they do so in the realms of commodification and consumerism.

Blurring the boundaries

Before postmodernism, aesthetic products could be classified into discrete areas—fiction, fact, high culture, low culture, Westerns, musicals, documentaries, plays, films, operas, pop music, and so on. But postmodernism knows no such boundaries or rules; it delights in the blurring of cultural boundaries and in hybridisation. Todd Gitlin cites Australia's Circus Oz, who draw on 'Aboriginal influences, vaudeville, Chinese acrobatics, Japanese martial arts, fireman's balances, Indonesian instruments and rhythms, video, Middle Eastern tunes, B-grade detective movies, modern dance, Irish jigs, and the ubiquitous presence of corporate marketing' (Gitlin 1993). Traditional notions of circuses are blown apart in this mixture of influences and in the blurring of categories. The inclusion of various non-European elements is an example of the fact that Eurocentrism is coming to an end as postmodern culture embraces other cultural traditions. There is freedom in this loosening of the traditional boundaries between cultural forms.

Within film and television, similar changes have been taking place. The development of music videos and the MTV channel is one of the most important and influential in this respect. The music video has provided a space for visual experimentation in the context of a popular art form (pop music) (Goodwin 1993; Frith et al. 1993). Young audiences have grown up familiar with the wide range of techniques used in these videos: non-narrative structures, experimental editing, the mixing of film formats (for example, Super 8 and 35 mm), and so on. This is linked to the freeing up of styles in mainstream film and television. The film *Natural Born Killers*, directed by Oliver Stone, combines elements of traditional narrative with documentary conventions, and includes an extraordinary mock television sitcom. Standard rules of continuity in film-making are disappearing. For example, Stone combines colour, black and white, 35 mm, and Super 8 footage in his films. He also uses jump-cuts, shaky camera, flash forwards, and fast-paced editing. Similar rule-breaking techniques are apparent in many films, for example, *Breaking the Waves*, *Moulin Rouge*, and *Wonderland* and in television series such as *NYPD Blue*, *This Life*, *Wildside*, and *Good Guys, Bad Guys*. Television's realist premises, which dictate the requirement for continuity, have been challenged with great energy, and the innovations in this regard are often well received by the public, particularly by young audiences who have grown up watching television programs and films that use these new styles.

Documentaries

The blurring of genres and boundaries is clear in the field of documentary film-making. Many recent documentary films mix fact and fiction. The aims of modernism included making people aware of the construction involved in all media products, making them question the reality effect of media products, and encouraging them to deconstruct these products. In this light, documentary's realist premise—that it can innocently, impartially, and objectively record the world—is challenged. If all representations are constructions, this should discredit documentary film-making. Alternatively, this realisation can free up documentary film-making from its link with realism: in its documentation of 'the real world', it can now use any techniques and can include all manner of representational modes. This is what it has done, and by embracing many postmodern cultural techniques it has dramatically increased its popularity, the pleasure it provides, and its aesthetic repertoire. Since 1980, documentary film-making has enjoyed a resurgence and a renewed popularity.

The Thin Blue Line is an extraordinary documentary. In its search for 'truth' and 'reality', it reveals that all we have are ways of representing, re-enacting, and reconstructing events. It shows how our lives are now so imbued with media realities that it has become difficult to tell if we are living life or watching a movie! Crossing the boundaries of film noir and documentary, *The Thin Blue Line* combines a mixture of elements into a tense and pleasurable narrative. Its great strength is that its postmodern depiction of our postmodern reality offers insights into how we understand the world. One of these insights is that we may not be able to ultimately know the world, that we may not be able to find 'the truth' (Williams 1993).

One of the ways this is achieved here and in other documentaries is by including a plethora of different voices, or discourses, that cannot be placed into a simple hierarchy. There is no overall dominant discourse, no expository voice of God or commentary that makes the subject of the documentary clear. In this way, meanings in postmodern texts such as documentaries are more open, and are dependent on readers. These texts challenge the certainties of realist texts as well as some of the modes of textual analysis discussed earlier in this book, making it difficult to discern preferred readings.

The subject of the film *True Stories* is tabloid newspaper stories. The film dramatises its subject using actors, but sets this dramatisation in a documentary format. Its opening five minutes recounts a million years of history using a combination of footage from popular fictional and non-fictional films and television programs, as well as pictures, photographs, maps, and an ironic voice-of-God commentary. It presents and questions history, showing how history and memory are currently constructed.

No longer bound by the demands of realism, documentary makers can play with a host of other techniques, using, for example, soap opera and documentary in *Sylvania Waters*, non-realist techniques of time lapse and slow motion in *Koyaanisqatsi*, and re-enactments and techniques of narrative suspense in other documentaries. The blurring of boundaries is evident in films such as *Cane Toads*, which makes the audience question whether the film is a documentary at all, and in so-called 'mockumentaries' such as *Zelig*, *This is Spinal Tap*, and *Forgotten Silver*. A mockumentary encourages questioning of what reality is, and as Jane Roscoe argues, blends fact and fiction, 'thus questioning and challenging documentary's authority' (Roscoe 1997, p. 78), which otherwise tends to be accepted at face value. At the same time, new media techniques mean that the 'real world' can be made to erupt into fictional films such as *Forrest Gump*. Aardman Animations, the team of animators that produce the popular films featuring the characters Wallace and Gromit, combine documentary and fiction in their animations. For example, *Creature Comforts* uses recordings of real people talking about their everyday lives. It puts these voices in a different context—the fictional zoo setting of the film—where the voices become the voices of the animal characters in the story.

Fluid identity

The documentary *In Bed with Madonna (Truth or Dare)*, is an excellent case study of the postmodern documentary. It explores issues relating to postmodern identity and the possibilities of signification (Pribram 1993). Madonna is well known for her constant changes of images and identity. For some, this is a sign of her shallowness; for others it is a cause for celebration of the possibilities of postmodernism. Madonna's career raises the question of how we can think about the relationship between identity and gender in the postmodern world. In a realist world, we would look for our real identity; we would try to find out who we are. In a modernist framework, we would recognise that we have many different facets to our identity, and we would hope to find ways of successfully integrating these facets. In a postmodern world, identity becomes a series of masks and possibilities, and we realise that there is no true self behind these masks. Madonna is happy to 'vogue', to adopt and discard different identities; she has at her fingertips the possibility of multiple subjectivities. She is thus experimenting with identity, which is liberating as it allows her to access feelings and behaviours not traditionally sanctioned for women (it also allows her to exploit successive markets, capitalising on the fact that diverse groups of women relate to the different personas she adopts). Postmodernists would argue that she is going further than this in that she is actually denying that there is any final, true identity to be discovered, that her career demonstrates that all identity is a mask. This protects Madonna from some of the negative aspects of publicity. By refusing to deliver up to spectators her 'authentic self' (Dyer 1991), she remains ultimately safe from the inquisitive gaze of the audience, who see only a series of masks. This play on reality is reflected in the question that is the subtitle of the documentary, *Truth or Dare?* In one scene near the end of the film the cast is playing the game 'Truth, Dare or Torture' and Madonna has to answer, truthfully, a question about her private life. As an audience we are 'dared' to question the veracity of the answer she gives in front of the camera, and thus to question whether any of the 'documentary' (or any other media images of Madonna) offers intimate, accurate insight into the reality of Madonna's life or identity.

Are these roles just performances, or is there something in them that comments on the essence of femininity, or the essence of gender relations? The postmodern view is that the film is just a dare; it is about the impossibility of knowing the truth; it exposes the myth of a real self.

Gender and postmodern identity

Judith Butler argues that all gender behaviour is 'performance' (Butler 1998). Men and women learn to play gender roles through 'the structure of impersonation by which any gender is assumed ... Gender is a kind of imitation for which there is no original' (Butler 1998, p. 722). Hence there is no essential reality behind these roles. Women are socialised into a compulsory performance of 'normal' gender roles, which they must perform on pain of ostracism, violence, punishment, and repression. Madonna's transgressive play with gender roles, her performances of gender identities, and her refusal of the normal categories associated with gender offer a way out for women. Two questions are crucial here: first, 'What range of roles and identities are available for women (and by implication men)?'; second, 'Are these roles just performances or is there something that makes them essentially feminine, essentially gendered?' You will have to decide on your own answers to these questions.

In Bed with Madonna also raises postmodern questions about the process of signification, about the making of meanings. While semiotic analysis seeks meanings and attempts to relate signifiers and representations back to reality, postmodern approaches challenge these aims, seeing texts as simulations (a term popularised by the theorist Jean Baudrillard) rather than representations. Deirdre Pribram puts it as follows:

> In our culture of information and the mass media, we are inundated with an overabundance of images and signs that no longer have referential value but, instead *interact solely with other signs*. This marks the advent of simulation. Rather than the previous vertical connection, if you will, between sign and meaning, there is, instead the horizontal relationship of sign to sign [my emphasis] (Pribram 1993, p. 201).

The point about *In Bed with Madonna* is not whether we will find the true Madonna, but that Madonna is just a series of signs. The film, as Pribram says: 'raises the question of the "real"—Which is the public persona and which private individual?—but refuses to answer it. Or it does answer it by saying that the question itself is absurd and irrelevant' (Pribram, p. 202). *In Bed with Madonna* illustrates the postmodern proposition that texts cannot give us reality or knowledge about reality; they just give us signs, appearances, and simulations. This relates to the openness of signs and meanings in the postmodern text. As Madonna has said, 'everything I do is meant to have several meanings'.

This is complicated material. We hope it shows you that postmodernism challenges our ways of understanding identity and of reading texts. According to this view, texts relate not to reality but to other texts; they become 'intertextual'. Indeed reality itself is knowable only as a series of texts and discourses.

Figure 6.10 Advertisement for Ursa computers
Source: Videolab, 1995

Relate these ideas to the images of masculinity in the following advertisement (Figure 6.10). Does it offer realistic new masculine identities for men, or does it merely play with signs and signifiers of masculinity? Is it possible to make any clear preferred reading of this advertisement? Whatever your answers to these questions, it is clear that texts designed for a popular audience are able to present a range of very different masculinities. My reading of the cross-dresser in Figure 6.10 is to see him as more powerful than the other men depicted; we are invited to laugh not at him, but at the surprise and shock of the 'normal' men.

Intertextuality, pastiche, appropriation, and bricolage

A pastiche is an imitation of a style or various styles, and it is often affectionate and humorous about its sources. Bricolage builds on the artistic techniques of collage and montage. While collage involves some form of cutting out and pasting together images from many different sources, montage refers to the process of editing together images from different spaces and times in film and video. 'Bricolage' means the appropriation and combination of different cultural elements into a new form. It involves appropriation: the original sign/signifier takes on a new meaning/signified in its new context, where it is combined with other signs. The work of artist Barbara Kruger (pp. 105–8) is an example of bricolage.[7] Intertextuality involves reference, borrowing (some would say plagiarising), and making links with other texts or sources. Postmodern architecture is a good example of bricolage.

Nowadays, the recycling of cultural genres, codes, and conventions, and intertextuality generally, are rife in media products. Here are some examples:

- *The Simpsons* frequently adapts mainstream film plots (for example, *Goodfellas*) as the basis for its stories, and it often parodies famous film scenes (for example, the shower scene from *Psycho* and the 'Rosebud' sequences from *Citizen Kane*).
- Many music videos recycle old film footage: for example, Madonna uses *Metropolis* and the Pet Shop Boys reference Andy Warhol's famous statement about everyone having fifteen minutes of fame.
- Individual episode titles for the television series *This Life* include 'When the Dope Comes In' (reworking the popular television series *When the Boat Comes In*) and 'The Plumber Always Rings Twice' (reworking the book and film *The Postman Always Rings Twice*).
- In Australia on *The Science Show* on ABC Radio National, a discussion segment involving academics is entitled 'The Good, the Bad and the Cosmic', a title that reworks the title of a famous Spaghetti Western, *The Good, the Bad and the Ugly*.
- Advertising for the Lotteries Commission of Western Australia reworks a famous painting by Edvard Munch, *The Scream* (Figure 6.11).

The last example shows how irreverent postmodernism is. The tortured expression on the face of the figure in *The Scream* signifies fear and anxiety; the painting is a

Figure 6.11 Advertisement for Lotteries Commission of Western Australia
Source: Lotteries Commission of Western Australia, published in *Festival of Perth Programme*, 1998

WATCH'A GOING TO DO WHEN YOU WIN?

Every time you play Lotto, Scratch 'n' Win or Soccer Pools, you're helping to support fine art, theatre, dance and music in Western Australia.

Western Australia

Principal supporter of the Festival of Perth

commentary on early twentieth-century society, and has, over time, become an icon of high art. In the Lotteries Commission of Western Australia advertisement, however, it is used to make us laugh and buy lotto tickets! Nothing is sacred for postmodernism.

All the above examples draw on and rework known cultural artefacts, producing new meanings through recycling them. They demonstrate how the media-world reflects inwards on itself, looking forward by looking back at other media products. What is the connection between the past and the present in this recycling of images? How do these images and representations relate to reality? Dick Hebdige argues that:

> The past is played and replayed as an amusing range of styles, genres, signifying practices to be combined and recombined at will. The then (and the there) are subsumed in the Now. The only history that exists here is the history of the signifier and that is no history at all (Hebdige 1985, p. 47).

The past is used, but simply for visual play and pleasure. This is what is meant by 'the disavowal of history': we are not interested in history as a truthful or factual account of the development of our current socio-cultural position, or as a way of learning about relationships between different parts of the world over time—it is simply a treasure trove of unconnected, fascinating images and stories. For those 'in the know', there is the pleasure of spotting the reference; for others there is the simple pleasure of spectacle. You do not need to know all the cultural references to enjoy a postmodern media product. Knowing them is a sign of your cultural knowledge; it indicates that you are a connoisseur of signs and images, not of truth and reality.

In the following cartoon (Figure 6.12), the cartoonist Judy Horacek draws attention to the mixing of genres, the crossing of boundaries, and the practice of intertextual referencing. This cartoon also signals the way we construct our identities in terms of media images; we picture ourselves as dealing with the world as a hero or heroine in a Western or science-fiction movie. Our psyches are being structured in terms of media realities.

Figure 6.12 Judy Horacek cartoon
Source: Judy Horacek, first published in *The Australian Magazine*

Look for examples of postmodern media products and postmodern lifestyles. Can you find examples of the characteristics of postmodernism we have listed above? What, if any, social messages and meanings are being disseminated by these products and lifestyles?

Self-reflexivity and the excess of surface

Finally, let us consider self-reflexivity and surface. The self-reflective nature of much postmodern culture represents a strong link with modernism.[8] Self-reflexivity is a modernist technique whereby a text draws attention to its own construction: for example, the characters in a fiction film might talk directly to the camera or the boom microphone (a microphone on a long pole that hangs over the action), or the clapperboard might be shown intentionally. Self-reflexivity means that the audience sees the processes of construction involved in making the media product. We are made aware, for example, that we are watching a film being made, that we are watching constructed representations, not reality. In 1978, Sylvia Harvey gave an interesting summation and criticism of modernism's tendency towards self-reflexivity:

> Modernist aesthetics induces a reflection upon, a consideration of, the means of representation, and for lovers of art it generates aesthetic pleasure out of a series of 'frame-shifts' (the procedures whereby the work of art playfully refers to itself and its own processes of production). But too often it fails to lead its audience 'through' this first consideration and towards a second, namely, a consideration of the action represented. It is this second area of consideration which opens up the possibility of introduction of knowledge of the social world and its processes, what Brecht would have called 'instruction'. And if there is a sense in which modernism offers the only way forward, there is also a sense in which it constitutes a dead end, a graveyard. Only those who pass through it can learn from it; the rest remain buried within it (Harvey 1978, p. 82).

Her argument is that reflection on representation—self-reflexivity—is not sufficient; it is a potential dead end; we must aim to understand the real world and gain 'knowledge of the social world and its processes'. Harvey is arguing here that modernism can tend to forget this project.

How does postmodernism look in the light of her critique of modernism? Postmodernism seems to have extended the self-referential nature of modernism: it remains heavily self-reflective, drawing attention to the processes of construction involved in cultural products and knowledges, and it derives great pleasure from this. But it has gone further than modernism in seeing that the world has become full of, as Pribram has put it, 'images and signs that no longer have referential value but, instead, interact solely with other signs' (Pribram 1993). Does it therefore become difficult to find instruction about reality in the postmodern world?

While there seems to be a clear political project in modernist self-reflexivity (this project is described by Harvey as 'knowledge of the social world and its processes'), postmodernism often seems content merely to play with processes of production: for example, the use of deconstruction techniques in the end credits sequence of the television series *Melrose Place*. The following questions address this issue:

- Does postmodernism's focus on surface reality, style, and appearance produce a depthlessness that makes postmodern texts uninterested in understanding the real world?
- Do postmodern texts play with techniques and signifiers merely in order to ensure that their meanings are up for grabs, thereby providing the audience with the pleasures of decoding the text using their cultural knowledge, or can the postmodern style still produce some Brechtian 'instruction' about the real world? In other words, is postmodernism caught up in consumerism and style, to the detriment of effective critique?

Some, myself included, see that the techniques of postmodernism can be used to provide 'instruction' and new perspectives. Because we now realise that the world is more complex than the contemporaries of Brecht and Harvey could have imagined, the 'instruction' provided by postmodernist texts is inclusive of more possibilities and uncertainties than would have been thought possible from the 1940s to the 1970s. In enabling the inclusion of new modes of thinking, in opening up identity, and in challenging eurocentrism, postmodernism can be liberating and powerful (Jagtenberg and McKie 1997). There is also an interesting connection between postmodernism, New Age philosophies, and traditional meditation practices, since all these exhort us to live in the present moment: postmodernism problematises grand historical narratives of progress, while Buddhism and meditation stress that what is important is the present moment, that in order to be fully alive we need to bring ourselves into this moment. These philosophies recognise that much contemporary Western life is built around living in the past or the future: at any one time, we tend to be either ruminating about what has happened or planning for what will happen—in other words, we rarely live in the moment.

The danger, as we see it, of postmodernism as a way of thinking about the world is that its view that everything carries a multiplicity of meanings and signs, and its acceptance of the coexistence of different theories and viewpoints, threatens to leave us with no certainties. This is what Baudrillard is describing when he writes: 'All the great humanist criteria of value, all the values of a civilisation of moral, aesthetic, and practical judgements, vanish in our system of images and signs. Everything becomes undecideable' (Baudrillard 1988, p. 128).

The problem with this perspective is that it may deny us some hold on the real world. For myself and for many others, finding a connection to and knowledge of the real world through various systems of representation (at the same time as recognising their subjective nature and their partiality) is very important. It is worth repeating (see p. 50) Richard Dyer's view of the relationship between reality and representation: 'Because one can see reality only through representation it does not follow that one does not see reality at all. Partial—selective, incomplete, from a point of view—vision of something is not no vision of it whatsoever' (Dyer 1993, p. 3). Dyer argues that material reality is important and that representations can tell us something about it. Linda Williams, discussing *The Thin Blue Line* (p. 312), asserts that 'some form of truth is the always receding goal of documentary film' (Williams 1993, p. 20). She recognises the impossibility of finding *absolute* truths but insists on the importance of attempting to find some possible truths about the world.

Junot Diaz, a writer from the Dominican Republic, puts it even more simply. In his writing he aims to be 'representing as honestly as I can' (Diaz 1998) his experience and his society from his perspective, and he sees writing (representation) as allowing him this possibility.

SUMMARY AND CONCLUSION TO THE BOOK

These comments by Dyer, Williams, and Diaz bring us back to the materiality of the real world. This book has been about the media and their relationship with the world. We have argued that there are a series of complex media–world relationships, or media influences on the world, and we have attempted to unravel them. Our focus has been on language, texts, representations, discourses, and ideology; these are the ways in which we apprehend the world, the ways in which we give it shape and form (this book is itself just another text). We have looked at various media products closely, taking them apart bit by bit, and mixing, we hope, appreciation with criticism.

The analysis of postmodernism in this chapter brings the discussion to the present climate in cultural studies and media studies. Having read this book, you should be able to draw on a body of theory, past and present, with which you can begin to make sense of the media-world in which you live.

This book has combined the two areas of knowledge that we have found most illuminating in understanding the world, the media, ourselves, and other people: first, an understanding of the role of ideology and discourses in organising how we live and think; second, psychological insights into how we act and feel. We hope that these ways of understanding the world, along with Marxism, feminism, and semiotic and structural analytic techniques, prove useful for you.

Important social and psychological questions remain: Will 'late capitalism' continue or will we move into a new phase? Will it collapse or grow? What direction should we take in the twenty-first century? Can we reach new heights of sophisticated, cultural development, especially through the evolution of new technologies? Will progress be accompanied by new difficulties such as economic inequalities, social disruptions, and environmental uncertainties? What will the role of the media be in this new era? How will we find fulfilment and satisfaction in this brave new world?

We suggest that we need to look carefully at five important areas in relation to our future lives, areas that cover the personal, the social, and the global:

1 **Gender, sexuality, and the family.** How do we live out our gendered and sexual lives? Is the family the place for this or should we evolve new forms? How do men and women resolve issues relating to power, oppression, intimacy, sexuality, and love?

2 **Work.** What forms of work will be fulfilling for us and provide balanced growth, material and spiritual, for the planet as a whole?

3 **Issues of ethnicity and race.** Together these issues form one of the major sources of social division in Australia, the United Kingdom, and globally. They are connected directly to issues of economic inequality and global economic inbalance. We have not paid detailed attention in this book to questions of the oppression of Aboriginal Australians and to the way in which the media represent them. However, we hope that the frameworks given, and many of the examples from

other countries, will allow you to explore these issues further. Any ideal of the future has to address and resolve issues of racism and discrimination, and must involve finding ways in which people can live together harmoniously.

4 **Ecological and environmental issues.** Media studies has tended to focus on humans. Today, ecological issues relating to all living species, and to the planet as a whole, are pressing. Questions about how we and the planet can survive in the twenty-first century are paramount. While this book has not examined how the media deal with such issues, this question will become even more important in the near future. We hope that you have found, in this book, useful insights about the relationship between the media and our ecological future.[9]

5 **Technology, interactivity, and globalisation.** Keeping abreast of technological advances, particularly new forms of interactive communication technologies, is an important aspect of media studies and social change. Being well-informed and conscientious consumers of the media and other cultural products can help to make sure that the interconnections linking humans all over the world result in positive influences on other lives, rather than inadvertently widening the gap between the rich and the poor or between those with access to resources, opportunities and information, and those without.

The media will continue to explore and represent these five broad issues, which will continue to be crucial aspects of the world you live in. We hope that your engagement with both the media and society is enriched by the ideas and insights offered here, and that media studies connects in relevant ways with the interests and ideals that you pursue in your everyday life.

Appendix 1

MODEL ESSAY: ANALYSIS OF AN ADVERTISEMENT

This model essay is presented here as an example of how to write a student essay that demonstrates the use of semiological analysis. It includes endnotes and a bibliography. Note that the bracketed references in this essay refer to books listed in the bibliography of this essay, rather than the bibliography of this book.

In all academic essays it is important to give evidence of reading and research. You must always include references to and terminology from the course material in the unit you are studying, and it is also advisable to include quotes from external sources, to support and substantiate your ideas and opinions.

ESSAY QUESTION

Using a semiological approach, give a detailed textual analysis of an advertisement, showing how meaning is constructed. Consider signs, signifiers, connotations, codes, and conventions, as well as the possible ideological meanings of the advertisement.

Introduction

Advertisements exist primarily as a means of selling products. They do this by appealing in various ways to the spectator. Many advertisements (such as the one I will analyse here) try to create an association between the product or brand and a desirable lifestyle or identity. Within these images of desirable lifestyles and identities, a range of ideological messages and meanings are encoded.

The term 'ideology' can be understood as 'the practice of reproducing social relations of inequality within the sphere of signification and discourse' (O'Sullivan et al. 1986, p. 107). In other words, ideology refers to a 'world-view' or a set of beliefs, feelings, and attitudes that are taken for granted as being natural and normal, but that are actually socially constructed. The body of ideas within a certain ideology is not neutral; it is always implicated within power relations that privilege certain people over others. It is the aim of this essay to denaturalise these power relations by looking beneath the surface of one particular advertisement and using the terms and techniques of semiotic analysis to decode and interpret its messages. The advertisement I have chosen is for a fast-food product called Chiko (see Plate 10 in colour section). The advertisement was considered offensive by some members of the public, and it was withdrawn from circulation. I will argue that while the image clearly reinforces patriarchal ideology, it also communicates more subtle ideological messages about class, race, and age. The public response to the advertisement reveals changing attitudes and ideologies. Hodge and Kress, authors of *Social Semiotics*, write:

Semiotics has been defined as 'the science of the life of signs in society' (Saussure 1974) … In its terms everything in a culture can be seen as a form of communication, organised in ways akin to verbal language, to be understood in terms of a common set of fundamental rules or principles (Hodge and Kress 1991, p. 1).

The principles of semiotic analysis were originally developed by Ferdinand de Saussure to analyse how language produces meaning. However, as Hodge and Kress suggest, semiotic analysis can also be used as a means of understanding other signs such as media texts.[1] This essay will use semiology as a tool for exploring the connotations of the advertisement's signs and signifiers. Following the 'principles' of the semiotic method, I will stress the importance of the reader or viewer's cultural knowledge and awareness of context and intertextuality in the process of interpretation as I analyse how each element of the image relates to the overall meaning of the advertisement.

CONTENT AND CONTEXT

The Chiko Roll advertisement (Plate 10) appeared on billboards across Australia in September 2000, and was also available internationally on the Chiko Roll website. On a denotative or descriptive level, the advertisement depicts a young, blonde woman wearing a low-cut black swimsuit or lingerie-like garment, sitting on the ground in front of a motorcycle. She is leaning slightly forward, looking directly into the camera lens, and holding a Chiko Roll between her widespread legs. The photograph is on a dark background, and it carries the caption 'grab a Chiko', accompanied by a picture of a male hand holding a Chiko Roll. The Chiko web address is visible in the top left corner of the frame.

The advertisement is a complex sign, consisting of iconic, indexical, and symbolic elements. For instance, the photograph is an iconic sign because the markings on the billboard resemble a woman and a bike. The Internet address is indexical, because it points us to a location in cyberspace in which more information about Chiko can be found. The letters C-H-I-K-O are symbols. Each of the elements that I have just described is a signifier that carries many possible connotations or associations.[2] 'The structures of message systems are linked to the structures of referents via codes which organise signifieds and signifiers' (Hodge and Kress 1991, p. 262). Here the referent means the concept or idea to which the sign refers. This range of possible meanings (polysemy) can be narrowed down when we take into consideration the target audience of the image, and the context in which the image is located.

Chiko's target market is young men in their early teens through to their early thirties[3] and the advertisement interpellates the viewer into a masculine, heterosexual subject position. The advertisement invites the viewer to gaze with desire at the model and the motorcycle, and to displace that desire on to (or link it to) the Chiko Roll. However, the advertisement was available to a large cross-section of the public (people of all ages and from all demographics were able to see it on billboards in public spaces, and it was even accessible to the global public on the Internet). The mismatch between the people who saw the advertisement and the people at which it was aimed was part of the reason that the image was so controversial. I am going to focus on the target market (young men) in order to construct the implied

narrative underlying the advertisement and work out what the most plausible connotations of the different signifiers in the advertisement might be.

Gender and ethnicity

The model in the advertisement is looking directly out at the viewer, as though she is
meeting our gaze, and she is leaning forward and displaying her legs and breasts in a
way that connotes sexual availability. The implied narrative is that the viewer is the
owner of the bike, and the person at whom the model's inviting gaze is directed.
(The model herself is clearly not the owner of the bike as she has no helmet, and is
not dressed to ride.) The woman is hungry, and the kind of food that will satisfy her
is a Chiko; hence we assume that the kind of man who will satisfy her other appetites
will also like to eat Chiko Rolls. That man is not pictured in the advertisement, but
the male fist holding a Chiko is a metonym for the model's male counterpart.
According to John Fiske in *Introduction to Communication Studies*, 'Metonymy works
by associating meanings within the same plane. Its basic definition is making a part
stand for the whole' (Fiske 1988, p. 97). In this case the hand stands for the whole
man. As the masculine hand is not attached to a particular body or identity, it is easy
for male viewers of the advertisement to put themselves into the picture as the man
who rides the bike, gets the girl and, most importantly, eats Chiko Rolls.

The physical appearance of the woman is also ideologically charged. She is blue
eyed, fair skinned, and blonde and she is presented to the viewer as an object of desire.
The male hand that is pictured is also White. Thus we could argue that the advertisement is racist by omission because it assumes Whiteness to be both the norm and the
ideal. I am not suggesting that the advertisement is deliberately racist, but it does work
to naturalise the ideological belief or assumption that even in multicultural Australia
(indeed, even globally), the leggy blonde White woman is universally desirable. If this
is the 'ideal human type', what place do redheads, Africans, Chinese, and others have?
How are such identities constructed by the media? Are we left to assume that it is less
desirable and less than ideal to be anything other than slender and blonde? I think this
is a good example of the way in which beauty, which is often coded as thin, blonde,
and fair skinned, carries ideological and racial implications.

The position of the Chiko and the way in which the woman is grasping it has
unmistakable phallic connotations, which are mirrored by the male fist enclosing
the Chiko near the bottom of the ad. It is important to note, however, that the male
grip on the Chiko doesn't have the same connotations because it is not at crotch
level. Instead the Chiko is held aloft triumphantly. The meaning of these two images
of fists grabbing a Chiko Roll is anchored by the words 'Grab a Chiko'.[4] On a
denotative level, this is an instruction to the audience to buy a Chiko at the nearest
fast-food shop. The word 'grab' has connotations of snatching something quickly,
which is consistent with the whole fast-food lifestyle, in which people don't have
time to prepare meals but instead just eat 'on the run'. However, when we move to
the level of connotation, the words 'Grab a Chiko' convey a more complex message.

The word 'Chiko' is an abbreviation of 'chicken roll' (although there isn't actually
any chicken in the product). The words 'chick' or 'bird' are also slang terms used
to refer to women, so the written instruction to 'grab a Chiko' neatly reinforces the

association that is constructed in the image between the woman's availability and the man's appetite, and the Chiko Roll and the man's appetite. The notion that women are 'chicks' who can be 'grabbed' when a man desires them is very problematic, not least because 'grabbing' is often a rough gesture and has connotations of taking something from an unwilling giver. 'Grab' also has connotations of criminality, as suggested in the phrases 'snatch and grab' or 'smash and grab'. Interpreted in this light, the advertisement provides a clear example of sexual objectification and commodification in which the woman is 'constructed as an object for the "look" of the male spectator, or the male voyeur' (see Walters 1995, p. 51). Although the woman in the image seems to have physical appetites, this is a very limited form of subjectivity. She is not represented as a thinking, feeling, human being; she is no more than an object that functions to satisfy desire, like a possession (the bike) or food (the Chiko).

This reading is supported by the photographic codes and conventions used in the advertisement, which closely follow those of soft porn. For instance, the model's pornographic gaze, her posture, the revealing dominatrix-style costume made of black lycra or leather, the stilettos, and the slightly open mouth glistening with pink lipstick are all typical of 'raunchy' images. In addition, the nondescript grey background gives a sense of anonymity that is also a conventional feature of pornography. It implies that the man who is involved with the model could be anyone, anywhere. This allows the viewer to situate themselves and the details of their own fantasy inside the picture more readily, without being identifiable. As these sorts of images seem to be becoming increasingly acceptable in mainstream media, especially on the Internet, the incorporation of such codes and conventions situates the advertisement within a heated debate about sexual expressiveness and sexual exploitation.

The association between the Chiko Roll and the other desirable object in the advertisement (the motorcycle) is also significant. The motorcycle is a Harley-Davidson, which is one of the most powerful bikes on the market. Such motorcycles are associated with a wild kind of masculinity that might be considered sexy. Motorcycles also connote freedom and rebellion through intertextual links to films such as *Easy Rider*. While the bike is not in motion in the advertisement, and the word 'roll' is not written anywhere in the advertisement, the food is commonly called a Chiko Roll, and Chiko advertisements have included the combination of a woman (chick) and a motorcycle (that rolls) for more than three decades, so the association of words and images is not accidental. The website, which the advertisement invites us to visit, features a gallery of such images. It has become common to include an Internet address on ads only in recent years, so this signifier functions to suggest that Chiko Rolls are up to date and part of the modern lifestyle.

Age and class

The ideal of 'untamed', rebellious masculinity associated with motorcycle riders links in with two other ideological messages embedded in the advertisement. The humour of the wordplay about grabbing a chick and/or a Chiko is specifically directed at people who use the word 'chick' to describe women. I will argue that certain signifiers in the advertisement suggest that sexism is permissible within the context of a young, male, working-class subculture. (Calendars and posters of scantily clad models posing on cars and bikes are common in mechanics' workshops and the like.) First, the colour combination of the Chiko wrapper—tomato-red and egg-yolk yellow—are widely associated with inexpensive fast-food franchises, and such eating places are frequented by middle- to low-income people such as labourers who need a quick, high-kilojoule meal to give them the energy for hard, physical work. Such a colour scheme is not generally used to advertise the expensive bars, cafés, and restaurants in which wealthier people nibble seafood salads and sip chardonnay. Furthermore, the heavily made-up model (wearing a costume that would not look out of place on a raunchy dancer or a *Playboy* pin-up) and the powerful, flashy motorcycle are status symbols that young, working-class men would be most likely to covet. Although mature, educated, professional men may find these images desirable on some level, they would probably openly classify them as being 'in poor taste' like the Chiko itself. Hence, although the images may be desirable to individuals from a range of social circumstances, the connotations of rebellion, sexiness, and status that the image of the woman and the bike carry operate predominantly within a class-specific context that targets readers of a certain age and gender.

Interestingly, the fact that the advertisement is directed at a young, male, working-class audience is precisely what invites a tolerant, humorous reading or response. In Australia, if not elsewhere, there is a cultural stereotype of young men being 'lovable larrikins'; playful and harmless easygoing pranksters. Youth (and lack of education, if we bring class into the picture) make their actions and attitudes seem somehow more excusable. There is a kind of permissiveness associated with late adolescence (even if such behaviour persists into middle age!) that is best summed up by the phrase 'boys will be boys'. Within this ideology or view of masculinity and class, it seems perfectly acceptable and natural for 'boys' to make fun of political correctness. This ideological perspective turns the serious issue of sexual objectification into 'a good lark' or 'a passing phase'. This ideological reading is supported by intertextual evidence that clearly shows the advertising strategy is meant to be playful, harmless, fun, and funny. Visitors to the Chiko website are invited to play a video game in which the aim is to chase 'chicks' and gain power by eating Chikos.

Conclusion

In conclusion, I have shown how the image works through naturalising certain ideological beliefs. The different signs and signifiers in the advertisement draw on cultural codes and conventions and combine to present an image that is desirable because it has connotations of youth, sexiness, rebellion, freedom, and playfulness. The product is thus desirable by association with this set of attributes. It is important to stress that the image 'works' only for those who have the relevant cultural knowledge and who share in the belief system that positions these attributes and images as desirable. The advertisement is open to oppositional readings by those who fall outside the target audience. Feminists, for instance, may interpret the advertisement as being a problematic instance of commodification and objectification rather than harmless fun. Younger audiences, even those who are familiar with and generally supportive of feminist ideas, might interpret the advertisement as poking fun at gender stereotypes and rebelling against conservative, politically correct attitudes. Sexually conservative audiences may see it as offensive because of its explicit sexuality.

While Chiko advertisements have included a beautiful woman and a motorcycle for more than 35 years, as the images on the website illustrate, interpretations of the imagery and reactions to them have changed significantly. Sex is still being used to sell products, but social responses to such images have become more complex. An advertising strategy that was uncontroversial in the 1960s now gives rise to debates about sexuality, commodification, ethics, humour, and authority structures. Such advertisements are now interpreted as either problematic and exploitative, or harmless and funny, but they are no longer simply accepted as 'the norm'. The fact that the advertisement was replaced with the image of the Chiko chick clad in less revealing red leather, seated astride the Harley-Davidson (Plate 11), indicates that the degree of sexual expressiveness and objectification considered acceptable in advertising is subject to an active process of negotiation between image producers, image receivers, and regulatory bodies. The range of responses to the advertisement, and the controversy and public outcry that made the company decide to withdraw the advertisement from circulation, shows the power of sexual moralists and the denaturalisation of patriarchal ideology over time. This does not mean that patriarchy has been usurped, just that it is no longer invisible and taken for granted. The discourse of sexuality and the ideology of patriarchy are now both much more explicit, and much more vocally contested in both the media and society.

Endnotes

1 For an example of the use of semiotics in media analysis see D. Lusted (ed.), *The Media Studies Book*, 1991, Routledge, London.
2 According to Hodge and Kress, 'The material realisation of a sign in a message is its *signifier*, and the referent it constructs is its *signified*' (Hodge and Kress 1991).
3 In an article entitled 'Flashy Flesh Gets Chiko Rolled', the journalist Vivienne Stanton states that 'The advertisements were aimed at 12 to 29-year-old-males' (*West Australian* September 2000).
4 According to John Fiske, the term 'anchorage' describes the 'function of words used as captions for photographs' (Fiske 1988, p. 112). Fiske points out that visual images are polysemous (they have many possible meanings), and therefore words can be used to anchor the meaning of an image by reducing the range of plausible meanings.

Bibliography

Dyer, G., 1982, *Advertising as Communication*, Methuen, London.

Fiske, J., 1988, *Introduction to Communication Studies*, Routledge. London.

Hodge, R. and Gunther, K., 1991, *Social Semiotics*, Polity Press, New York.

Lusted, D. (ed.), 1991, *The Media Studies Book*, Routledge, London.

O'Sullivan, T., Hartley, J., Saunders, D., and Fiske, J., 1986, *Key Concepts in Communication*, Methuen, New York.

Walters, S. D., 1995, *Material Girls: Making Sense of Feminist Cultural Theory*, University of California Press, Berkeley.

Appendix 2

MODEL ESSAY: ANALYSIS OF THE OPENING SEQUENCE OF *BLUE VELVET*

This is a model essay. It includes endnotes and a bibliography. Note that bracketed references in this essay refer to books listed in the bibliography of this essay, rather than in the bibliography of this book. It also includes a shot list that lists and briefly describes the shots discussed in the essay.

ESSAY QUESTION

Give an analysis of the opening sequence of the film Blue Velvet *showing how the language of film—mise en scène, cinematography, editing, and sound—contribute to its meaning and to its affective power ('affect' refers to feelings and emotions). Consider also how this sequence relates to the whole film.*

ESSAY

Introduction

The opening of *Blue Velvet* (1986, directed by David Lynch) illustrates the main themes of the film and is an affective piece of film-making. Lynch has described the film thematically as 'a journey into small town America' and 'a journey into the unconscious' and, stylistically, as a 'technicolour sandwich' (Ross 1990). It is a film that gives the viewer a fascinating, sometimes humorous, sometimes shocking, viewing experience.

The major theme of the film is the revelation of the dark, shadow side of an idealised, small American town. This exploration is personalised through the film's focus on the psyches of its main characters, Frank, Dorothy, and Jeffrey. Lynch examines American culture and its ideals of community, equality, and fulfilment—the so-called American dream—exposing its 'other' side, and revealing what Robin Wood calls 'the American nightmare' (Wood 1986).[1]

Wood sees horror as the main genre that explores the dark side of the American dream, in contrast with melodramas and television soap operas, which tend ultimately to celebrate community and its values. *Blue Velvet* mixes cinematic conventions from all these three genres. It also includes elements of the genres of film noir and the thriller, and it has ironic and satirical aspects. This combination of conventions produces a piece that hybridises genre, resulting in confusion and unease for the audience, who become uncertain as to what type of film this is and as to how they are being invited to respond to its moments of satire, exaggerated emotion, extreme violence, graphic sexuality, and horror.[2] The opening sequence exemplifies this by including shots from different generic conventions. In fact both the opening and the closing shots are satirical (there is no simple, perfect world, and the film is making fun of the idea that we might believe there is).

Unease is also produced through surrealist elements. Lynch has described the influence of early surrealist film-makers on his own career. (*Arena* 1987). Their thematic interests of the unconscious, the world of dreams, and extreme states of desire (*l'amour fou*—crazy love), coupled with stylistic methods that present ordinary objects in an extraordinary light or that juxtapose objects to reveal disturbing connections, are all evident in this film (Matthews 1979, pp. 23–34).[3]

I aim to show how the opening sequence of *Blue Velvet* exhibits the above characteristics and uses 'film language' to produce both meaning and emotional affect for its audience.[4] Drawing on the conventions of surrealist art and using binary oppositions and the concept of irony, I will argue that the opening sequence sets up the themes of depth and surface and the ambiguous nature of good and evil that the film explores. The audience's affective responses (their embodied, emotional, gut reaction to what they see and hear in the cinema) are rendered more complex by the use of irony throughout *Blue Velvet*. For instance, a certain tension between laughter, confusion, and uneasiness is produced by the ironic juxtaposition of images in the opening sequence, especially when Jeffrey's father collapses in the garden and the dog jumps playfully on his crotch and laps at the water spurting from the hose he is holding. The contradictions between different layers of meaning, and the dissonance between, on the one hand, intended meanings or effects and, on the other, unexpected effects or subtexts, constitute irony and are characteristic of many postmodern texts, including *Blue Velvet*.

Shots 1–4: Light vs dark; idealisation, irony, and dissonance

Shot 1 involves the camera panning down, descending from clear blue sky to reveal brilliant red roses and a white picket fence.[5] The camera position is close to the ground. This single shot has considerable significance. The whole movement of the opening sequence is downwards: the camera pans down, the man will fall down, and the camera concludes by going down into the underground world of the insects. (The camera's position in shot 1 is at a low angle, eventually descending, in shot 3, to ground level to give us a beetle's point of view.) We are involved in a visual descent—into the earth, into darkness, into the animal world—that is also a metaphoric descent into evil. The film creates an opposition between innocence and darkness, and chooses to explore the latter. The opening sequence sets this up cinematographically, through one simple camera movement. At the end of *Blue Velvet*, when order has been restored, the camera ascends to the clear sky, the world of light, neatly mirroring, in reverse, the opening shot.

However, this ending is not straightforward. Both the opening and the closing shots are satirical (there is no simple, perfect world). Lynch, as mentioned above, has described the film as a Technicolor sandwich. The opening and closing sequences are the bright Technicolor borders, inside which is the main body (the filling) of the film that is filmed in darker tones and portrays a sinister world. Technicolor was the first major Hollywood colour process and is conventionally associated with films from the 1930s through to the late 1950s that show spectacle, fantasy, and idealised worlds, particularly musicals and Disney cartoons (Neale 1985, pp. 44–51). While *The Wizard of Oz* used Technicolor to render the fantastic dream-world of Oz, it used black and white film stock to portray the 'real' world of Kansas because audiences of the time were used to seeing reality depicted in black and white. However, technological advances change the codes and conventions of representation, and modern film-makers are inclined to use black and white to depict fantasy sequences, dreams or flashbacks, because audiences are now used to seeing 'the real world' in colour on television. As colour processes are now more realistic, the bright Technicolor appearance of shot 1 connotes the past and unreality. Interestingly, references to *The Wizard of Oz* form part of David Lynch's signature as an 'auteur' (the artistic author of the films he directs).[6]

As colour processes are now more realistic, the bright Technicolor appearance of shot 1 connotes the past and unreality. This prepares us for the satirical view of Lumberton, the fictional town in the film. The film suggests that while the town appears beautiful, the image it presents to the world is unreal; it is purely surface, cosmetic, and idealised. This effect has been created by the use of a particular type of film stock and certain camera exposures—both of these are cinematographic techniques, and as such are part of film language. In addition, shot 1 has a two-dimensional quality (there is no depth of field): the fence, flowers, and sky are presented as flat, furthering the sense of unreality.

Iconographically, the white picket fence is part of the *mise-en-scène*.[7] Images of white picket fences have been used in countless films as a symbol of the ideal family home.[8] Lynch uses it as an obvious cliché, imparting irony to the opening shot (shot 1).[9] According to Dyer, icons are signs that resemble what they refer to, and symbols are signs that are arbitrarily associated with a particular concept that they neither resemble nor indicate (1982, pp. 124–6). Hence the white picket fence in the setting of *Blue Velvet* is both an icon (it looks like a fence), and a symbol that has been used in countless films in association with family life (it is symbolic of the ideal family home, and thus the 'American dream').

Sound is very significant throughout the opening sequence. The main layer of sound is the song *Blue Velvet*. The film uses several popular songs of the early 1960s, which, seen from the perspective of the 1980s, appear innocent, suffused with nostalgic connotations of a golden age. But Lynch presents this innocence ironically by choosing songs that have a dark and ambiguous side to them and by having them as the soundtrack to disturbing images. For example:

- The context in which 'Candy Coloured Clown' is played makes it clear that it refers to drugs and drug dealing. It is also mimed by a grotesquely lit, dangerously violent man.
- 'In Dreams' points to the surrealist world of the unconscious and nightmares, and is played while Jeffrey, the hero, is being beaten up.
- The positioning of, and the visual images that accompany, 'Love Letters' makes it clear that the 'letters' of the song's title refer to bullets (the song plays while people are being killed).
- 'Blue Velvet', as sung by Dorothy (the female lead in the movie) watched by Frank (her sadistic lover), suggests depth, pain, extreme sensuality, and sexuality, in contrast to the associations it conjures up when sung by the 1960s crooner Bobby Vinton

(in the opening shots of the film). In the film's opening shots, the innocent song (the Bobby Vinton version) complements the idealised Technicolor-like images, acting as an ironic counterpoint to the disturbing images that accompany Dorothy's version later on.

Innocence is also signified through the birdsong heard during the first nine shots of the film. This natural sound is significant to the film as a whole, since the character Sandy hears the song of the robins during her dream. She believes that the robins will bring peace and love to the world. At the end of the film we finally see a robin, showing the realisation of Sandy's dream and the triumph of good over evil—the latter is signified by the fact that the robin eats a beetle, which in the opening sequence signifies savagery and evil. However, once again, the portrayal of the robin involves irony, since the robin is obviously a mechanical model: the triumph of the natural (and therefore good) world is undermined by its artificiality, its unreality.[10] Here the distinction between diegetic sound (sound originating in the story world and heard by the characters, as when Dorothy sings) and non-diegetic sound (sound of which only the audience is aware, such as the musical score) is significant. The distinction is blurred because the song could be playing on the radio. The fact that the old fashioned version of the song 'Blue Velvet' sounds innocent, but the diegetic version sung by Dorothy has dark, sadistic undercurrents is yet another way in which the distinction between depth and surface, reality and illusion, are being explored. What looks or sounds like a dream from the outside, turns out to be more like a nightmare once you are fully inside the story.

The first four shots are images of the community. Peace is signified through editing and *mise-en-scène*.[11] Dissolves, providing smooth and gentle transitions between shots, are used for the first four cuts, and the length of the shots (the rhythmic editing) contributes to the sense of calm. As you can tell from the respective lengths of these shots—15 seconds, 10 seconds, 7 seconds and 16 frames, and 7 seconds and 16 frames—there is some acceleration of shots. While the first two shots give the audience time to enter the world of the film and register what is happening, shots 3 and 4, which are of equal length, are shorter. This balance in time between, on the one hand, shots 1 and 2, and on the other, shots 3 and 4, is mirrored in the balance in content: shots 1 and 2 are of flowers (roses) and then the fire truck; shots 3 and 4 are of flowers (daffodils) and then children. In terms of graphic editing (Bordwell and Thompson 1997, pp. 273–8), the fire truck and the children move slowly across the screen: the fire truck moves from left to right; the children from right to left. Although the truck and the children are moving in opposite directions, the way in which the shots are intercut with flowers produces symmetry and balance rather than a graphic clash of movement. The red fire truck and the children crossing are idealised icons, filmed in sunlight and bright colour. The fire truck and the fireman, complete with friendly dog, represent the caring nature of male authority (a concept questioned in the body of the film), while the children represent innocence, as does the caring female authority figure who guides them across the road.

While the setting and staging of these shots suggest that everything is all right in this world, the ordinariness and innocence of these images are also ironically exaggerated. The fireman is waving in slow motion (although the film is normal speed) like an automatic model or puppet. His waving is strange because, since there are no people visible, it is as though he is waving to no one, unless it is us, the audience. For a moment he seems to look directly at the camera, violating one of the conventions of narrative cinema. But his gaze is similar to the credit sequences of many television series in which characters look and smile at some offscreen person: for example, the opening credit sequence of the American melodrama *Beverly Hills 90210*. The children and the woman directing them across the road move at a similar, regimented, robotic pace. All this suggests a dehumanised, artificial, child-like, puppet world. This theme is developed by other two-dimensional characters and acting styles throughout the film—for example, Jeffrey's aunt, the recurring image of the man walking his dog, and some of Sandy's mannerisms (particularly her open-mouthed silent screams, which often provoke audience laughter)—but also by placing humans next to real puppets, thereby suggesting that humans are like puppets. This happens in the scene in the brothel and in shot 7 of the opening sequence (in which Jeffrey's mother sits next to a doll and a lampstand with a carved face on it). In the opening sequence, the puppet-like quality of the town and its characters encourages the audience to take an ironic view of the community. This depiction of humans and communities as artificial and puppet-like is a familiar theme in horror films and science-fiction films, where it is used to undermine the assumption that the community depicted is normal.[12]

This short four-shot sequence establishes the community in a particular way. Its exaggeration of idealised, clichéd images that are traditionally used to validate the American dream invites a cinematically literate and aware 1980s audience to watch ironically.

Shots 5–8: the dark side of the ideal of the family, voyeurism, and film noir

Shots 5 to 7 begin the narrative, establishing a personalised situation in the community. Through the conventions of establishing shot, relational editing, and the depiction of typical family life, the audience is invited to link these three shots together in such a way as to construct a vision of a normal, middle-class family in which the husband is performing outdoor gardening jobs, while the wife relaxes inside watching television. The mood of these shots continues the established theme of peace and order.

The shot of the television screen (shot 8) shatters this normality and provides the first moment of rupture in the film. It is thus very important. The image is dark. It creates foreboding as we see a close-up of a gun moving threateningly across the screen from right to left. The editing makes it seem as if the gun is pointing at Jeffrey's mother—who was looking left to right (towards the gun) in the preceding shot (shot 7)—and Jeffrey's father, who is shown facing the gun in shot 9. The implication is that both parents are under threat—a threat that is quickly realised when the father collapses. There is a further implication: within ordinary, suburban homes is a mysterious and violent side that ordinary people are fascinated by. This suggests that such homes harbour perversity. This suggestion is strengthened by the calmness with which Jeffrey's mother watches the sinister images on the television screen as she drinks her tea (shot 8). Jeffrey's mother and aunt are regular watchers of television thrillers, as is shown in a later scene. The iconography of these thrillers is that of film noir, a genre that explores the 'shadow side' of human impulses. *Blue Velvet* draws on film noir's visual style as well as its sexual focus on the figure of the femme fatale (Kaplan 1978, pp. 1–15).

One of the major themes of the film is the perversity and voyeurism that we are all prone to, shown particularly through the voyeurism implicit in the scene in which Jeffrey spies on Dorothy from a closet, a point of view that we are invited to share as audience. The theme is made explicit when Jeffrey suggests to Sandy later in the film that he is either a detective or a pervert, implying that all detection is perversity. Shot 8 (of the gun on the television screen) points the audience towards this theme through its film noir connotations, and through the fact that the image of the gun is being watched (voyeur-like) by Jeffrey's mother. There is also a self-reflexive quality in this shot: a television fiction is being shown within the film fiction that we are watching. At the same time as the violence of shot 8 disturbs the calm of the previous shots, its self-reflexivity invites the audience to watch with irony, amusement, and distance.

Shots 10–18: surrealism, animated objects, and the use of sound

Shots 10–18, which show a hose and Jeffrey's father collapsing, illustrate Lynch's affinity with surrealism, particularly through the editing. The first viewing of this sequence often confuses viewers. How do we, as viewers, explain the sudden collapse of the father? We are left to come up with our own explanations: he has been shot, he has been stung by an insect, he has had a heart attack, and so on. We are not given a clear answer at this stage, which adds to the mystery of the whole sequence. The confusion is created partly through the crosscutting between Jeffrey's father, the hose-tap, and the blockage in the hose. This crosscutting creates tension by moving between these three elements, by using an extreme close-up of the hose-tap in shot 14 (which is repeated in shot 16), and by increasing the pace of the editing (shot 11 is 3.13 seconds, and then shots 12–16 become progressively quicker until Jeffrey's father collapses in shot 17).[13]

The ordinary, domestic hose is made to appear extraordinary: it is as though it is alive, a character itself. The editing between the hose-tap, the hose blockage, and the collapse of Jeffrey's father encourages the audience to make a connection between the two, inviting them to see the hose as somehow responsible for the collapse of Jeffrey's father. An inanimate object has thus been surrealistically animated and given power through the use of close-ups and relational editing.

Sound is again important. While the image of the gun in shot 8 first fractured the aura of peace and order, now the sound of the hose-tap intrudes harshly on the melody of 'Blue Velvet', providing a second moment of fracture (heard also as an interruption because the sound of the hose-tap jars with the beat of the music). 'Blue Velvet' gradually fades and is replaced by a series of disturbing noises that grow ever louder. These noises include the sound of the hose, the dog, and the sounds of the beetles that we see in shot 24. The contrasting qualities of innocence/light and corruption/darkness are expressed through sound: the sounds associated with the world of darkness and corruption take over from the innocence of 'Blue Velvet'.

The sounds used include some savage animal noises that fit the film's portrayal of the animal nature of men, particularly through the character of Frank. But Lynch also uses industrial sounds. He used these to sinister effect in two earlier films, *Eraserhead* (1976) and *The Elephant Man* (1980). These noises appear to symbolise the powerful, destructive threat that the industrial world poses to humanity (Ross 1990). Lynch once lived in Pittsburgh, a heavily industrialised town, and Lumberton, the fictional town featured in *Blue Velvet*, is a community founded on the destruction of nature through the timber industry. The industrial noises point to the destruction of Lumberton's natural environment as well as giving the beetles a mechanical quality.

Shots 19–24: life vs death, innocence vs savagery

The shots following the father's collapse—shots 19–24—play on the oppositions life vs death and innocence vs savagery. Shots 17–19 continue the downward movement of the sequence, bringing the audience closer to the earth and preparing them for shots 23 and 24. Shots 17 and 18 use a 'match on action' (Bordwell and Thompson 1997, pp. 290–1) of the father falling, but in contrast to his collapse, the water, a symbol of life and fruitfulness, continues to flow. Shot 19, which pans downward, is a close-up of drops of water spraying over the garden. The lighting, the gentle, flowing movement of the water, and the way this is shot out of focus all give the image a softness and lyrical beauty that creates an ironic juxtaposition with the father's shocking collapse. This ironic juxtaposition is heightened by the fact that 'Blue Velvet' continues to play on throughout his collapse.

Once the father has collapsed, the hose continues to gush forth; symbolically, and ironically, it is at his crotch—he appears phallically powerful at the moment of his collapse. Two characters are introduced as witnesses, a dog and a young child. Neither understands nor can help the father. They both signify life and innocence (the dog, man's best friend, is puppy-like), in contrast to the collapsed old man. In shot 21, the dog laps at the water while jumping on the father's crotch. Shots 21 and 22 are perverse in that they violently contrast life and death: on the one hand there is the vitality and savagery of the dog as well as the phallic water, and on the other there is the lifeless father. (The power of sexual and animal instincts crops up again later on in the film when Jeffrey confronts Frank.)

In terms of film language, the violent contrast between life and death is intensified by the fact that shots 21 and 22 are close-ups of the dog—shot 22 is a more extreme close-up than shot 21. The second close-up emphasises the savagery. By very slightly slowing down the action of this shot and by giving the image a grainy texture, Lynch creates a disturbing effect, suggesting that reality is entering another dimension. This prefigures the movement, in shots 23 and 24, towards the world of the beetles.

Shot 23 is an extreme low-angle and close-up position: the camera tracks through the grass. The sound has changed dramatically at this point: 'Blue Velvet' has completely faded, and there is a moment almost of quiet before the animal/industrial noises recommence, crescendoing throughout shot 24, thus increasing the drama and suspense. This camera movement forward and inwards is an investigatory move that mirrors the way in which the narrative of the film is itself an investigation and journey. It is a camera motif that is repeated later in the film when the camera tracks into the ear Jeffrey discovers, illustrating Lynch's idea of a journey into the unconscious (the movement is reversed when the camera tracks out of Jeffrey's ear towards the end of the film). Hand-held camera shots that track through vegetation are common in horror films; they serve to create suspense and they tend to lead to, or suggest, some strange sight or revelation (exactly what happens here with the visual suggestion, in shot 24, of insects frenziedly eating some other creature, or each other, and the accompanying disturbingly vivid sounds of eating). Thus Lynch adds a horror convention to the earlier soap opera conventions and surrealist techniques.

Shot 24 (the edit between shots 23 and 24 is hardly noticeable) continues the camera movement into the beetles' nest. The image gradually gets darker until finally the audience is immersed in blackness. The metaphorical theme of darkness is suggested by the literal darkness of the image, and this connection is repeated several times in the film when there are fades to black (the Technicolor of shots 1–4 has been left behind). Once again, this is reversed towards the end of the film, when there is a fade to white that symbolises the triumph of good over evil.

Shots 23 and 24 are quite long—7 and 24 seconds—creating suspense and paralleling the longer shots (shots 1 and 2) at the beginning of the opening sequence. The length of these two shots signals that this particular opening sequence is coming to a close. We are given no explanation of what the beetles mean, but in terms of affect, the conventions of the horror movie, the suspense, and the intensity of the close-up of the insects are meant to frighten and sicken us. In attempting to make sense of the opening sequence, audiences may link the two events—the collapse of the father and beetles. Just as the inanimate hose was earlier related to his collapse, now his collapse may be seen as linked to the underground beetles. This confusion and ambiguity suggests a disturbed world that is in complete contrast to the order and beauty of the world depicted in shots 1–4. This disturbed world is the one that Jeffrey will discover through his investigations.

Conclusion

The opening sequence sets up the themes of the film. In particular, it introduces the contrast between the world of light (and goodness) and the world of dark (and evil), and it begins to suggest that unknown evil forces lurk beneath the surface. The collapse of the father also suggests the collapse of stability and order (fathers are culturally associated with order) and sets the scene for the hero, Jeffrey, to discover himself by taking on his own adult male power. The opening sequence affects us through its manipulation of filmic codes and conventions, its use of cinematography (particularly the downward pans, close-ups, and investigative camera style) and its use of *mise-en-scène*, editing, and sound. The combination of idealistic, ironic, surreal, and horrific images results in a two-minute sequence that operates as a short film in its own right. While it has little to do with the film's actual narrative, it establishes the themes of the film and provides the top layer to the Technicolor sandwich that is the film. As the character Sandy says, 'It's a strange world, isn't it?'

Endnotes

1   American literature and film have a long tradition of exploring aspects of the American dream. See, for example, the work of the writers Nathaniel Hawthorne, Herman Melville, Mark Twain, and F. Scott Fitzgerald. Horror films such as *Psycho* (1959, directed by Alfred Hitchcock), *Carrie* (1976, directed by Brian De Palma) and *The Stepfather* (1987, directed by Joseph Ruben) show the dark side of this dream. While melodramas and soap operas tend to depict problems within communities, such problems are usually positively resolved (Gledhill 1987, pp. 5–43).

2   The blurring and borrowing of different generic conventions, often referred to as one of the distinguishing features of postmodernism (Collins 1992, pp. 327–54), has become increasingly common in popular film and television since about 1980. Thus, *Blue Velvet* may not be as disturbing to a 1990s or twenty-first-century audience as it would have been to a 1986 audience. A friend has described to me how she felt extremely shocked and disturbed when she first saw the film, finding it distasteful. Such was her reaction that she was most unwilling to see it again. However, she was working as an usher at a cinema where the film was playing and she found herself drawn to watching it repeatedly. As she watched it over and over again, she found herself laughing at particular moments. Her laughter was not at the film but with the film: she was seeing its satirical and humorous aspects. This double-edged reaction of horror/fear and laughter is elicited throughout the film, particularly in the opening sequence.

3   The surrealists' desire to go beneath the surface to reveal a deeper reality is graphically illustrated in *Blue Velvet*. Lynch's juxtaposition of different filmic conventions can be seen as surrealistic, as surrealism uses juxtaposition as a formal method.

4   'Film language' is a term used to describe four features of film-making: *mise en scène*, cinematography, editing, and sound. These are the four features of film language, as listed by Bordwell and Thompson (1997).

5   See the 'Shot list' below, which lists and briefly describes the shots discussed in this essay.

6   See A. Sarris, 'Notes on the Auteur Theory in 1962', in G. Mast, M. Cohen, and L. Braudy (eds), *Film Theory and Criticism: Introductory Readings*, 4th edn, 1992, Oxford University Press, New York, pp. 585–88.

7   *Mise en scène* is described by Bordwell and Thompson (1997, p. 169) as 'staging an action', and is said to include settings/objects, costume, lighting, and figure position.

8   See for example *Shane* (1953, directed by George Stevens) and *Meet Me in St Louis* (1944, directed by Vincente Minnelli). Awareness of the icon's associations is evident in the television series *Picket Fences*, which looks at the life of a supposedly ideal American community, revealing many bizarre aspects that lurk below the surface. *Picket Fences*, a postmodern text that is more humorous and less violent than *Blue Velvet*, uses the icon of the picket fence self-consciously.

9   A final comment on this shot is that its almost exclusive use of the colours red, white, and blue— the familiar colours of the American flag—might be an invitation for us to see the film as exploring the ideals of America through reference to the national flag.

10 An irony compounded by Lynch's refusal to admit publicly that the robin portrayed at the end of the film is a mechanical model rather than a real bird (Ross 1990).

11 Editing is the joining or splicing together of any two shots (Bordwell and Thompson 1997, p. 271).

12 See, for example, the films *Invasion of the Body Snatchers* (1958, directed by Don Siegel) and *The Stepford Wives* (1975, directed by Bryan Forbes).

13 The use of close-ups of people and objects is a conventional way of creating greater intensity and revealing truth (Dyer 1979, pp. 133–4). See Bordwell and Thompson (1997, pp. 278–80) for discussion of rhythmic editing. Note how whereas the camera panned slightly to the right to follow the father's actions in shot 11 (a camera movement we don't notice as we are watching him, not the movement of the shot), in the collapse shot, shot 17, the camera does not follow him; consequently, he appears to fall out of the frame, emphasising his collapse.

Shot list

Key

CU = close-up; ECU = extreme close-up; EECU = very extreme close-up; LS = long-shot; MLS = medium long-shot; MS = medium-shot

Shot number	Time in seconds and frames	Description
1	15	Pan down from sky to CU of roses, followed by a dissolve; sound of birds intermittently (continuing through to shot 10); 'Blue Velvet' begins to play, continues at same level until it starts to gradually fade in shot 18
2	10	MLS of fire truck moving left to right, followed by a dissolve
3	7.16	CU of daffodils (beetle's-eye view), followed by a dissolve
4	7.16	MLS of children crossing the road from right to left, followed by a dissolve
5	5.06	LS establishing shot of house
6	4.18	MLS of man in garden; soft noise of water; the cut to the next shot is not in keeping with the beat of the music
7	4.14	MS of woman indoors drinking tea—she looks from the left to the right of the screen
8	3.05	ECU of television screen showing a gun—the television shot pans from right to left
9	3.18	MS of man in garden—he is facing left to right; the water noise that began in shot 6 becomes louder
10	2.13	CU of hose-tap; loud discordant noise of tap and water
11	3.13	MS of man (same as shot 9); camera pans to follow the action (match on action with shot 12); he jerks the hose; water noise is now not so loud as shot 10, and it continues at this medium level through to shot 13
12	1.17	CU of hose being snagged (matches action in shot 11)
13	1.17	MS of man (same as shot 9)
14	1.14	ECU of hose tap; loud discordant noise of tap, which then continues more quietly through to shot 23
15	1.05	CU of snagged hose (same as shot 12)
16	1.03	ECU of hose-tap (same as shot 14)
17	3.07	MS of man (same as shot 9); sound of a gasp; he collapses and falls down out of the camera frame—the camera does not follow him; match on action with shot 18

Continued

Shot number	Time in seconds and frames	Description
18	4.20	High-angle MS of man falling to ground; match on action with shot 17
19	3.16	Out-of-focus CU of drops of water from hose; camera slowly pans downwards
20	2.17	Re-establishing LS of man, child, dog, and picket fence; sound of dog begins and continues through next two shots
21	3.14	CU of dog lapping water and jumping on the man
22	3.17	ECU of dog filmed in (slightly) slow motion; film stock may be different as the picture is grainy; music fades
23	7.06	Ground-level ECU of grass; camera pans slightly and tracks forward; music has gone and the noise of the tap (introduced in shot 14) increases and then fades; there is then some silence and other unidentifiable industrial-sounding noises begin
24	24.17	EECU at the same angle as shot 23; camera tracks into the darkness and shows what looks like beetles moving; the sound level increases; intense noise of animals eating is introduced alongside the industrial sounds of shot 23

Bibliography

Arena: David Lynch Presents (presenter: H. Gallagher), BBC Television, United Kingdom, 1987.

Bordwell, D. and Thompson, K., *Film Art*, 6th edn, McGraw-Hill, New York, 2001.

Collins, J., 'Postmodernism and Television', in R. Allen (ed.), *Channels of Discourse, Reassembled*, Routledge, London, 1992.

Creed, B., 'A Journey through *Blue Velvet*', *New Formations*, 1989, pp. 97–117.

Denzin, N., 'Blue Velvet: Postmodern Contradictions', *Theory, Culture & Society*, vol. 5, 1988, pp. 461–73.

Dyer, R., *Stars*, British Film Institute, London, 1979.

Gledhill, C. (ed.), *Home is Where the Heart Is*, British Film Institute, London, 1987.

Jonathan Ross Presents David Lynch, Channel 4, United Kingdom, 1990.

Kaplan, A. (ed.), *Women in Film Noir*, British Film Institute, London, 1978.

Matthews, J. H., *Surrealism and American Feature Films*, Twayne, New York, 1979.

Neale, S., *Cinema and Technology*, British Film Institute/Macmillan, London, 1985.

Wood, R., 'The American Nightmare', in R. Wood, *Hollywood from Vietnam to Reagan*, Columbia University Press, New York, 1986.

NOTES

PART 1

1   Steve Neale illustrates this well, exploring Hollywood's history in S. Neale, *Cinema and Technology: Image, Sound, Colour*, Macmillan, London, 1985; so does Douglas Gomery in his two chapters, 'The Coming of Sound', and 'Economic Struggle and Hollywood Imperialism', in E. Weis and J. Belton (eds), *Theory and Practice of Film Sound*, Columbia University Press, New York, 1985. For other histories of media institutions see P. Kerr, (ed.), *The Hollywood Film Industry*, Routledge & Kegan Paul, London, 1986; A. Crisell, *An Introductory History of British Broadcasting*, Routledge, London, 1997; S. Dermody and E. Jacka, *The Screening of Australia*, vols 1 and 2, Currency Press, Sydney, 1987/88; S. Dermody and E. Jacka (eds), *The Imaginary Industry: Australian Film in the late '80s*, Australian Film, Television and Radio School, Sydney, 1988.

2   The best starting point for looking at the media as industries and for political economy approaches are, for Australia: S. Cunningham and G. Turner, *Media and Communications in Australia*, 2nd edn, Allen & Unwin, Sydney, 2001; I. Ward, *Politics of the Media*, Macmillan, Melbourne, 1995. For a fascinating and readable account of the economics of a feature film see S. Bach, *Final Cut: Dreams and Disaster in the Making of Heaven's Gate*, Faber & Faber, London, 1986. For an analysis of the British situation see J. Curran, *Power without Responsibility: The Press and Broadcasting in Britain*, 5th edn, Routledge, London, 1997.

3   Further information about the media and democracy is available in J. Habermas, *The Structural Transformation of the Public Sphere: An Inquiry into a Category of Bourgeois Society*, Polity Press, Cambridge, 1989; and J. Thompson, *The Media and Modernity: A Social Theory of the Media*, Polity Press, Cambridge, 1999.

4   H. Jenkins, *The Children's Culture Reader*, New York University Press, New York, 1998.

5   As an example of this inoculation approach see D. Thompson, *Discrimination and Popular Culture*, Penguin, Harmondsworth, 1964.

6   The most significant works of the Frankfurt School are T. Adorno, (edited by J. Bernstein) *The Culture Industry: Selected Essays on Mass Culture*, Routledge, London, 1991; T. Adorno and M. Horkheimer, *The Dialectics of Enlightenment*, Allen Lane, London, 1973; H. Marcuse, *One Dimensional Man*, Routledge & Kegan Paul, London, 1964; H. Marcuse, *An Essay on Liberation*, Penguin, Harmondsworth, 1972.

7   For coverage of effects research see D. McQuail, 'Processes of Media Effects', in D. McQuail, *Mass Communication Theory: An Introduction*, Sage, London, 1987; Ward, chs 2 and 3; S. Lowery and M. Defleur, *Milestones in Mass Communication Research: Media Effects*, 3rd edn, Longman, USA, 1995; J. McLeod et al., 'On Understanding and Misunderstanding Media Effects' in *Mass Media and Society*' in J. Curran and M. Gurevitch (eds), *Mass Media and Society*, Edward Arnold Press, London, 1991; D. Gauntlett, 'Ten Things Wrong with the Effects Model', http://www.leeds.ac.uk/ics/theory/effects.htm, 1998. For an initial overview of media audiences and effects see Cunningham and Turner, *The Media in Australia*, part 5.

8   For an account of Innis's work see 'Space, Time, and Communications: A Tribute to Harold Innis', in J. Carey, *Communication as Culture: Essays on Media and Society*, Unwin Hyman, London, 1989. For an introduction to McLuhan's work see M. McLuhan, *Understanding Media: The Extensions of Man*, Ark, London, 1987; T. Gordon, *McLuhan for Beginners, Writers and Readers*, London, 1996. For Ong's work see W. Ong, *Orality and Literacy: The Technologising of the Word*, Methuen, New York, 1982.

9   For more on television news coverage see P. Schlesinger, *Putting 'Reality' Together—BBC News*, Constable, London, 1978 (this is one of the best studies of the news gathering processes); Glasgow University Media Group, *More Bad News*, Routledge & Kegan Paul, London, 1980; 'Home Help for Populist Politics: Relational Aspects of TV News', in J. Hartley, *Tele-ology: Studies in Television*, Routledge, London, 1992; S. White, *Reporting in Australia*, 2nd edn, Macmillan, Victoria, 1996;

M. Alleyne, *News Revolution: Political and Economic Decisions about Global Information*, Macmillan, Sydney, 1997.

10 For an assessment of this work see G. Turner, *British Cultural Studies: An Introduction*, Unwin Hyman, London, 1990. An excellent anthology of cultural studies perspectives is L. Grossberg, C. Nelson, and P. Treichler (eds), *Cultural Studies*, Routledge, New York, 1992.

11 For extensive discussion of these debates and other important issues relating to popular culture, see B. Waites, T. Bennett, and G. Martin (eds), *Popular Culture Past and Present*, Routledge, London, 1982; J. Fiske, *Reading the Popular and Understanding Popular Culture*, Unwin Hyman, Sydney, 1989; R. Dyer, *Only Entertainment*, Routledge, London, 1992.

12 For a discussion of the media's coverage of sports, see G. Whannel, *Fields in Vision: Television Sport and Cultural Transformation*, Routledge, London, 1992.

13 For further discussion of the appeal of Australian drama to British audiences see M. Wark, *Virtual Geography: Living with Global Media Events*, Indiana University Press, Bloomington and Indianapolis, 1994. For a discussion of soaps and documentaries that refers to Australian suburban families, see J. Stratton and I. Ang, 'Sylvania Waters and the Spectacular Exploding Family', *Screen*, vol. 35, no. 1, pp. 1–21.

14 For an excellent critique of reality TV see B. Nichols, 'At the Limits of Reality (TV)', in B. Nichols, *Blurred Boundaries*, Indiana University Press, Indianapolis, 1994.

15 For discussion of censorship issues see M. Barker (ed.), *Video Nasties*, Pluto Press, London, 1984; 'Censorship and Pornography', *Continuum: Journal of Media and Cultural Studies*, vol. 12, no. 1, 1998.

16 For an in-depth discussion of the relationship between the circulation of media texts and the construction of popular common sense, see J. Hartley, *The Politics of Pictures*, Routledge, London, 1992.

17 The newspaper story reports that this comment was made by a man named Mark Garner, who watched the arrest from the balcony of his nearby flat in the city centre.

18 The most extensive explanation of this is found in P. Berger and T. Luckmann, *The Social Construction of Reality*, Penguin, London, 1967.

19 Theories of how languages have evolved in societies and how language relates to an individual's learning, growth, and understanding of the world are complex. The best places to look in more detail at this are M. Montgomery, *An Introduction to Language and Society*, 2nd edn, Routledge, London, 1995; J. Britton, *Language and Learning*, Penguin, Harmondsworth, 1970; N. Chomsky, *Language and Mind*, Harcourt Brace Jovanovich, New York, 1972.

20 Sapir and Whorf were two American language researchers. Their famous thesis is the starting point for much work on language. See D. G. Mandelbaum (ed.), *Edward Sapir: Culture, Language and Personality*, University of California Press, Berkeley, 1949.

21 This view is put forward by Chomsky, *Language and Learning*.

22 For an introduction to queer theory see M. Warner (ed.), *Fear of a Queer Planet: Queer Politics and Social Theory*, University of Minnesota Press, Minneapolis/London, 1993; A. Jagose, *Queer Theory*, Melbourne University Press, Melbourne, 1996.

23 L. Gilbert and C. Kile, *Surfergrrrls: Look Ethel! An Internet Guide for Us*, Seal Press, Seattle, 1996. E.K. Garrison, 'US Feminism—Grrrl Style!: Youth (Sub)Cultures and the Technologies of the Third Wave', *Feminist Studies*, vol. 26, Spring 2000.

24 Morley's book gives an excellent overall account of audience research. See also 'Active Audiences', in J. Fiske, *Television Culture*, Methuen, London, 1987, ch. 5.

25 L. Green, *Technoculture: From Alphabet to Cybersex*, Allen & Unwin, Sydney 2001.

26 For an account of this approach see M. O'Shaughnessy, 'Promoting Emotions: Understanding Films, Understanding Ourselves', *Metro*, no. 97, 1994, pp. 44–8.

PART 2

1 The questions and analysis relating to Figures 2.4 and 2.5 derive from work and images presented by Guy Gauthier in a package made up of slides and notes: Guy Gauthier, 'The Semiology of the Image', British Film Institute Education Advisory Service, London, 1976.

2 For further analysis of Australian 'myths', including a section on homes and gardens, see J. Fiske, B. Hodge, and G. Turner, *Myths of Oz: Reading Australian Popular Culture*, Allen & Unwin, Sydney, 1987. For extended analysis of what the past can mean see R. Williams, *The Country and the City*, Paladin, St Albans, 1975.

3 N. Klein, 'Culture Jamming: Ads Under Attack', in N. Klein, *No Logo*, HarperCollins, 2000, London.

4 If you would like to read more about Peretti's experience and his observations about the power of micromedia and networks of interpersonal communication online, he has published an article available at the following web address: http://www.thenation.com/doc.mhtml?i=20010409&s=peretti. The *Adbusters Magazine* website is http://www.adbusters.org.

5 N. Klein, *No Logo*, HarperCollins, 2000, London.

PART 3

1 There are many books on genre. The best places to start are P. Cook, 'Genre', in P. Cook and M. Bernink (eds), *The Cinema Book*, 2nd edn, British Film Institute, London, 1999, pp. 58–113, which gives an overview of genre criticism and looks at several specific genres; and B. Grant (ed.), *Film Genre Reader II*, University of Texas Press, Austin, 1995, which is an excellent anthology. See also C. McArthur, *Underworld USA*, Secker & Warburg/British Film Institute, London, 1972, for early critical approaches; and S. Neale, *Genre*, British Film Institute, London, 1980, for a more complex formulation.

2 There are several books on the Western: J. Kitses, *Horizons West*, Secker & Warburg/British Film Institute, London, 1979; P. French, *Westerns*, Secker & Warburg/British Film Institute, London, 1973; W. Wright, *Sixguns and Society: A Structural Study of the Western*, University of California, Berkeley, 1975. Books on other genres include R. Altman, *Genre: The Musical*, British Film Institute and Routledge & Kegan Paul, London, 1981; C. Clover, *Men, Women and Chainsaws: Gender in the Modern Horror Film*, Princeton University Press, Princeton, 1992; E. Kaplan (ed.), *Women and Film Noir*, British Film Institute, London, 1978; C. Gledhill (ed.), *Home is Where the Heart Is*, British Film Institute, London, 1987.

3 For a detailed account of the American dream of the West and the frontier see H. Smith, *Virgin Land: The American West as Symbol and Myth*, Harvard University Press, Massachusetts, 1970.

4 On road movies see S. Cohen and I. Hark (eds), *The Road Movie Book*, Routledge, London, 1997; M. Williams, *Road Movies*, Proteus, London, 1982.

5 There are numerous essays and articles on *Thelma and Louise* including 'The Many Faces of Thelma and Louise', *Film Quarterly*, vol. 45, no. 2, pp. 20–31; 'Thelma and Louise Review', *Sight and Sound*, July 1991, pp. 16–19. See also the following two articles in J. Collins, H. Radner, and A. Collins (eds), *Film Theory Goes to the Movies*, Routledge, New York, 1992: S. Willis, 'Hardware and Hard Bodies, What Do Women Want: A Reading of Thelma and Louise' and C. Griggers, 'Thelma and Louise and the Cultural Generation of the New Butch-Femme'.

6 Swankmajer's films are available on video.

7 For initial work on structuralism see T. Hawkes, *Structuralism and Semiotics*, Methuen, London, 1977; D. Palmer, *Structuralism for Beginners*, Writers and Readers, London, 1996. In relation to narrative see P. Cook, *The Cinema Book*, British Film Institute, London, 1985. G. Turner, *Film as Social Practice*, 2nd edn, Routledge, London, 1993, offers an excellent and straightforward account of many of the issues relating to narrative, film, and genre.

8 See for example Greenaway's films *Drowning By Numbers* and *The Cook, The Thief, His Wife and Her Lover*, and Watkins's *Edvard Munch* and *The Freethinker*.

9 Star study, like genre study, is another branch in media studies. The best starting points are R. Dyer, *Stars*, British Film Institute, London, 1982; R. Dyer, *Heavenly Bodies: Film Stars and Society*, Macmillan, Basingstoke, 1987; C. Gledhill, (ed.), *Stardom: Industry of Desire*, Routledge, London, 1991.

10 The words 'project', 'projector', and 'projection' are all linked, but have three different uses: 'project' refers to the aim of the film, what it is attempting to convey; 'projector' refers to the cinematic apparatus that projects the film on to a screen; 'projection', while it can refer simply to

the actual images projected on to a screen, is also used in psychoanalytic discourse to refer to how we project our feelings and beliefs on to other people.

11 J. Berger, *Ways of Seeing*, Penguin and BBC, London, 1972, ch. 3; L. Mulvey, 'Visual Pleasure and Narrative Cinema', in L. Mulvey, *Visual and Other Pleasures*, Macmillan, Basingstoke, 1989. Both of these are great starting points. See also R. Betterton (ed.), *Looking On: Images of Femininity in the Visual Arts and Media*, Pandora, London, 1987.

12 Three useful books looking specifically at television are J. Hartley, *The Uses of Television*, Routledge, London, 1999; J. Fiske, *Television Culture*, Methuen, London, 1987; R. Allen (ed.), *Channels of Discourse*, Reassembled, Routledge, London, 1992.

13 See, for example, T. Eagleton, *Criticism and Ideology*, Verso, London, 1978; F. Jameson, *Marxism and Form*, Princeton University Press, Princeton, 1971; R. Williams, *Marxism and Literature*, Oxford University Press, Oxford, 1977.

14 For an excellent account of Brecht's work and its application in film, see S. Harvey, *May '68 and Film Culture*, British Film Institute, London, 1978. See also M. Thoss, *Brecht for Beginners*, Writers and Readers, London, 1995; C. MacCabe, *Godard: Images, Sounds, Politics*, Macmillan, Basingstoke, 1980.

15 For a full account of the tradition of mimetic art, see E. Auerbach, *Mimesis*, Princeton University Press, Princeton, 1968. See also R. Williams, *Realism and the Cinema*, Routledge & Kegan Paul with the British Film Institute, London, 1980.

PART 4

1 Finulla Neville discusses ideologies of domestic space on *The Science Show: Ockham's Razor*, ABC Radio National, 5 October 1997.

2 You can relate this to the way in which our lives today are structured in terms of time. The constraints of an industrial society produce timetables related to the demands of the factory and of work, rather than timetables that relate to the cycles of the human body. For example, no attention is paid to the menstrual cycles of women. These timetables determine nearly all our activities. Think how many times a day you consult the time. Imagine living in a culture where there are no clocks and your activities are directed by your internal bodily feelings and rhythms, and by the cyclical rhythms of the seasons.

3 One of the best accounts of ideology and hegemony, in relation to the media, is S. Hall, 'Culture, the Media and the "Ideological Effect" ', in J. Curran, M. Gurevitch, and J. Woollacott (eds), *Mass Communication and Society*, Edward Arnold, London, 1977. See also S. Hall, *Critical Dialogues in Cultural Studies*, Routledge, London, 1992.

4 Gramsci's original writings are in A. Gramsci, *Selections from the Prison Notebooks*, Lawrence & Wishart, London, 1971. For a discussion of hegemony see Hall 1992; R. Williams, *Marxism and Literature*, Oxford University Press, Oxford, 1977b; T. O'Sullivan, J. Hartley, D. Saunders, M. Montgomery, and J. Fiske, *Key Concepts in Communication and Cultural Studies*, 2nd edn, Routledge, London, 1994.

PART 5

1 For an excellent short discussion of the topic of men and warfare see P. Adams, 'Religiously Programmed to Kill', *Weekend Australian*, 2 November 1997.

2 There are now many books on masculinity. See, for example, A. Metcalf and M. Humphries (eds), *The Sexuality of Men*, Pluto Press, London, 1985; J. Rutherford and R. Chapman (eds), *Male Order*, Lawrence & Wishart, London, 1988; J. Weeks, *Against Nature: Essays on Sexuality, History and Identity*, Rivers Oram Press, London, 1991; S. Nixon, 'Exhibiting Masculinity', in S. Hall (ed.), *Representation: Cultural Representations and Signifying Practices*, Sage, London, 1997; R. Moore and D. Gillette, *King, Warrior, Magician, Lover*, HarperCollins, San Francisco, 1991.

3   R. Bly, *Iron John*, Vintage, London, 1990; S. Biddulph, *Manhood*, Finch Publishing, Sydney, 1994; S. Biddulph, *Raising Boys*, Finch Publishing, Sydney, 1997.

4   The best place to start reading on this subject is M. Langton, *Well I Saw it on the Television*, The Commission, North Sydney, 1993; see also P. Gilroy, *There Ain't No Black in the Union Jack: The Cultural Politics of Race and Nation*, Hutchinson, London, 1987, and K. Mercer (ed.), *Welcome to the Jungle*, Routledge, London, 1984.

PART 6

1   See for example: Mary Evans, *Introducing Contemporary Feminist Thought*, Polity Press, Cambridge, UK, 1997; Sarah Gamble, *The Routledge Critical Dictionary of Feminism and Post Feminism*, Routledge, London and NY, 2001; Sophia Phoca and Rebecca Wright, *Introducing Postfeminism* (edited by Richard Appignanesi), Icon Books, Cambridge, 1999; and Suzanna Danuta Walters, *Material Girls: Making Sense of Feminist Cultural History*, University of California Press, Berkeley, 1995.

2   For a discussion of this issue see V. Trioli, *Generation F: Sex, Power and the Young Feminist*, Reed, Melbourne, 1996.

3   There are many books available on postmodernism. Here are some useful starting points: H. Foster (ed.), *Postmodern Culture*, Pluto Press, London, 1985; S. Connor, *Postmodernist Culture*, Blackwell, Oxford, 1989; D. Harvey, *The Condition of Postmodernity*, Blackwell, Oxford, 1989; L. Nicholson, *Feminism/Postmodernism*, Routledge, London, 1990; R. Appignanesi and C. Garratt, *Postmodernism for Beginners*, Icon, Cambridge, 1995.

4   For an excellent analysis of how media technology is changing global culture, see M. Wark, *Virtual Geography: Living with Global Media Events*, Indiana University Press, Bloomington and Indianapolis, 1994.

5   For a discussion of issues around cultural appropriation and ethnicity, see B. Hooks, *Killing Rage, Ending Racism*, Penguin, London, 1996.

6   For general overviews of realism, see E. Auerbach, *Mimesis*, Princeton University Press, Princeton, 1968; R. Williams, *Realism and the Cinema*, RKP/British Film Institute, London, 1980; L. Nochlin, *Realism*, Penguin, Harmondsworth, 1971.

7   For an account of bricolage see D. Hebdige, *Subculture: The Meaning of Style*, Routledge, New York, 1979.

8   An excellent analysis of the shift from modernism to postmodernism is given by D. Hebdige in 'The Bottom Line on Planet One: Squaring up to The Face', *Ten-8*, no. 19, 1987, pp. 40–9.

9   One of the few books that approaches the relationship between the media and environmental issues from a postmodernist perspective is T. Jagtenberg and D. McKie, *Eco-Impacts and the Greening of Postmodernity*, Sage, California, 1997.

FURTHER READING

There are many books that are useful for further study of the media and society. The following are particularly recommended as a follow-up to the approaches presented in this book.

Barthes, R. 1974, *Mythologies*, Paladin, St Albans.

This is a seminal media studies text. It develops semiology. See especially the chapter 'Myth Today'.

Bly, R. 1990, *Iron John*, Vintage, London.

A key men's movement book that draws partly on Jungian concepts in its analysis of fairy tales.

Bordwell, D. and Thompson, K. 1997, *Film Art: An Introduction*, 5th edn, McGraw-Hill, New York.

An excellent introduction to film studies. Take particular note of Part III.

Branston, G. and Stafford, R. 1996, *The Media Student's Book*, Routledge, London.

An excellent beginner's book on media studies.

Brown-Kenyon, P., Miles, A., and Rose, J. S. 2000, 'Unscrambling Digital TV' at www.mckisney.com/media/undi00.asp

This article contains an excellent diagram of television transmission paths.

Campbell, J. 1991, *The Power of Myth*, Anchor, New York.

This book is, along with Campbell's interviews with Bill Moyers from his television series, the best place to start in relation to Campbell's work. The video series *Joseph Campbell and the Power of Myth* (Campbell 1988b) is also useful.

Cook, P. and Bernink, M.(eds) 1999, *The Cinema Book*, 2nd edn, BFI, London.

An overview of film studies that is particularly useful in relation to understanding genre and narrative.

Cunningham, S. and Turner, G. (eds) 1997, *Media and Communications in Australia*, 2nd edn, Allen & Unwin, Sydney.

The best analysis of the media in Australia (and the best overview of media studies approaches in relation to Australia). A useful and comprehensive book for all media studies students.

Dowrick, S. 1991, *Intimacy and Solitude*, William Heinemann, Australia.

This is a good place to start exploring psychotherapeutic and psychological approaches. Chapters 7 and 8 give a fascinating account of how men and women grow up to be masculine and feminine.

Dyer, R. 1986, *Heavenly Bodies: Film Stars and Society*, British Film Institute, London.

Excellent studies of Paul Robeson and Judy Garland that analyse these stars in terms of ethnicity and sexuality.

―――― 1992, *Only Entertainment*, Routledge, London,

Discusses popular culture and defines key terms used in cultural studies and media studies.

―――― 1993, *The Matter of Images: Essays on Representation*, Routledge, London.

Develops many of the issues dealt with in this book. Dyer writes clearly and illuminatingly. Highly recommended.

Fiske, J. 1989, *Reading the Popular*, Unwin Hyman, Sydney.

―――― 1989, *Understanding Popular Culture*, Unwin Hyman, Sydney.

Both these books by Fiske are collections of fascinating essays that analyse examples of popular culture.

Hall, S. 1996, *Critical Dialogues in Cultural Studies*, Comedia, London.
Hall is one of the most significant cultural studies writers. He is complex but has a brilliant overview of the field.

_____ (ed.) 1997, *Representation: Cultural Representations and Signifying Practices*, Sage, London.
While this is an introductory textbook, its language and the concepts it explores are more complex than those in this book. Representation also delves deeper into media studies and cultural studies.

Hartley, J. 1992, *The Politics of Pictures*, Routledge, London.
An insightful and stimulating cultural studies approach to the media.

_____ 1999, *The Uses of Television*, Routledge, London.

Jung, C. (ed.) 1978, *Man and His Symbols*, Picador, London.
The best starting place for those wishing to explore the work of Jung.

Klein, N. 2000, *No Logo*, HarperCollins, London
Very readable account of culture jamming.

Masculinity and Representation, http://www.newcastle.edu.au/department/so/kibby.htm
This site has a number of articles (available in electronic form) which have been published in various journals and some suggested web pages.

Men and Masculinities
This is a refereed print journal publishing the most recent gender studies on men and masculinities.

Montgomery, M. 1995, *An Introduction to Language and Society*, 2nd edn, Routledge, London.
The best introductory overview of the relationship between language and society.

O'Sullivan, T., Hartley, J., Saunders, D., Montgomery, M., and Fiske, J. 1994, *Key Concepts in Communication Studies*, 2nd edn, Methuen, London.
This is a useful reference book that defines key words.

Rius, 1976, *Marx for Beginners*, Writers and Readers, London.
A simple and accessible introduction to the ideas of Marx. The Beginners series is useful for providing overviews of key theories. See, for example, Beginners guides to Freud, Jung, postmodernism, and semiotics.

Rutherford, J. and Chapman, R. (eds) 1988, *Male Order: Unwrapping Masculinity*, Lawrence & Wishart, London.
A useful collection of essays on masculinity.

Schwichtenberg, C. (ed.) 1993, *The Madonna Connection*, Allen & Unwin, Sydney.
A useful collection of essays on Madonna that includes postmodern, feminist, gay and race perspectives.

Turner, G. 1999, *Film as Social Practice*, 3rd edn, Routledge, London.
Turner writes clearly and gives good overviews here and in his book on cultural studies.

Wells, L. (ed.) 1996, *Photography: A Critical Introduction*, Routledge, London.
A useful view of photography that develops still-image analysis in many ways.

Wolf, N. 1990, *The Beauty Myth*, Chatto & Windus, London.
Wolf is one of the 'new' feminists.

BIBLIOGRAPHY

ABC Radio National 1995 (7, 14, 21, 28 October), 'Talk, Talk, Talk' (originally produced by the Canadian Broadcast Corporation), broadcast as part of *The Science Show*.

Achbar, M. (ed.) 1995, *Manufacturing Consent: Noam Chomsky and the Media*, Black Rose Books, Montreal/New York.

Adams, P. 1997, 'Religiously Programmed to Kill', *Weekend Australian*, 2 November 1997.

Adorno, T. 1991, *The Culture Industry: Selected Essays on Mass Culture*, Routledge, London.

Adorno, T. and Horkheimer, M. 1973, *The Dialectics of Enlightenment*, Allen Lane, London.

Allen, R. (ed.) 1992, *Channels of Discourse, Reassembled*, Routledge, London.

Alleyne, M. 1997, *News Revolution: Political and Economic Decisions about Global Information*, Macmillan, Sydney.

Althusser, L. 1977a, *For Marx*, New Left Books, London.

_____ 1977b, 'Ideology and Ideological State Apparatuses', in L. Althusser, *Lenin and Philosophy*, New Left Books, London.

Altman, R. 1981, *Genre: The Musical*, British Film Institute and Routledge & Kegan Paul, London.

Anderson, B. 1983, *Imagined Communities: Reflections on the Origin and Spread of Nationalism*, Verso, London.

Ang, I. 1985, *Watching Dallas: Soap Opera and the Melodramatic Imagination*, Methuen, London.

_____ 1990, *Desperately Seeking the Audience*, Routledge, London.

Appignanesi, R. and Garratt, C. 1995, *Postmodernism for Beginners*, Icon, Cambridge.

Armes, R. 1971, *Patterns of Realism*, Tantivy, London.

Auerbach, E. 1968, *Mimesis*, Princeton University Press, Princeton.

Bach, S. 1986, *Final Cut: Dreams and Disaster in the Making of Heaven's Gate*, Faber & Faber, London.

Baker, A. and Boyd, T. (eds) 1997, *Out of Bounds: Sports, Media, and the Politics of Identity*, Indiana University Press, Bloomington and Indianapolis.

Bannister, D. and Fransella, F. 1990, *Inquiring Man*, 2nd edn, Penguin, London.

Barker, M. (ed.) 1984, *Video Nasties*, Pluto Press, London.

Barthes, R. 1973, *Mythologies*, Paladin, St Albans.

_____ 1974, *S/Z*, Hill and Wang, New York.

_____ 1977, 'The Death of the Author', in R. Barthes, *Image, Music, Text*, Fontana, London.

Baudrillard, J. 1988, *Jean Baudrillard: Selected Writings*, Stanford University Press, California.

Benjamin, W. 1977, *Understanding Brecht*, New Left Books, London.

Berger, J. 1972, *Ways of Seeing*, Penguin and BBC Television, London.

Berger, P. and Luckmann, T. 1967, *The Social Construction of Reality*, Penguin, London.

Bettelheim, B. 1978, *The Uses of Enchantment: The Meaning and Importance of Fairy Tales*, Peregrine, London.

Betterton, R. (ed.) 1987, *Looking On: Images of Femininity in the Visual Arts and Media*, Pandora, London.

Biddulph, S. 1994, *Manhood*, Finch Publishing, Sydney.

_____ 1997, *Raising Boys*, Finch Publishing, Sydney.

Blumler, J. and Katz, E. (eds) 1974, *The Uses of Mass Communications: Current Perspectives on Gratifications Research*, Sage, Beverly Hills and London.

Bly, R. 1990, *Iron John*, Vintage, London.

Bogle, T. 1973, *Toms, Coons, Mulattoes and Bucks: An Interpretative History of Blacks in American Films*, Viking Press, New York.

Bolen, J. 1989, *Goddesses in Everywoman*, Harper Perennial, New York.

Bordwell, D. and Thomson, K. 2001, *Film Art*, 6th edn, McGraw-Hill, New York.

Bowles, K., Hartley, J., and McKee, A. (eds) 1998, 'Censorship and Pornography', *Continuum: Journal of Media and Cultural Studies*, vol. 12, no. 1.

Bradbury, M. and McFarlane, J. (eds) 1976, *Modernism, 1890–1930*, Penguin, Harmondsworth.

Brecht, B. 1964, 'Theatre for Pleasure or Theatre for Instruction', in J. Willett (trans.) *Brecht on Theatre*, Methuen, London.

Britton, J. 1970, *Language and Learning*, Penguin, Harmondsworth.

Brohm, J. 1978, *Sport: A Prison of Measured Time*, Ink Links, London.

Brooks, A. 1997, *Postfeminisms: Feminism, Cultural Theory and Cultural Forms*, Routledge, London and New York.

Brunsdon, C. 1986, 'Women Watching Television', *MedieKulture*, vol. 4.

Buchbinder, D., 1994, *Masculinities and Identities*, Melbourne University Press, Melbourne.

—— 1998, *Performance Anxieties: Reproducing Masculinity*, Allen & Unwin, Sydney.

Butler, J. 1990, *Gender Trouble: Feminism and the Subversion of Identity*, Routledge, London.

____ 1998, 'Imitation and Gender Insubordination', in J. Rivkin and M. Ryan (eds), *Literary Theory: An Anthology*, Blackwell, Massachusetts.

Campbell, D. 1997, *The Mozart Effect*, Hodder Headline, Sydney.

Campbell, J. 1972, *The Hero with a Thousand Faces*, Princeton University Press, Princeton.

____ 1988a, *The Power of Myth*, Anchor, New York.

____ 1988b, *Joseph Campbell and the Power of Myth* (video), Mystic Fire Video in association with *Parabola Magazine*, New York (distributed in Australia by the ABC).

____ 1991, *Occidental Mythology: The Masks of God*, Arkana, New York.

Carey, J. 1989, 'Space, Time, and Communications: A Tribute to Harold Innis', in *Communication as Culture: Essays on Media and Society*, Unwin Hyman, London.

Caughie, J. (ed.) 1981, *Theories of Authorship*, Routledge & Kegan Paul, London.

Chomsky, N. 1972, *Language and Mind*, Harcourt Brace Jovanovich, New York.

Clover, C. 1992, *Men, Women and Chainsaws: Gender in the Modern Horror Film*, Princeton University Press, Princeton.

Cohen, S. and Hark, I. (eds) 1997, *The Road Movie Book*, Routledge, London.

Collins, J. 1992, 'Postmodernism and Television', in R. Allen (ed.), *Channels of Discourse, Reassembled*, Routledge, London.

Collins, J., Radner, H., and Collins, A. 1992, *Film Study Goes to the Movies*, Routledge, New York.

Colors, Feb/March 2000, Milan, Italy.

Connell, R. 1995, *Masculinities*, Allen & Unwin, Sydney.

Connor, S. 1991, *Postmodernist Culture*, Blackwell, Oxford.

Cook, P. 1985, *The Cinema Book*, British Film Institute, London.

Cook, P. and Bernink, M. (eds) 1999, *The Cinema Book*, 2nd ed, British Film Institute, London.

Coward, R. 1984, *Female Desire: Women's Sexuality Today*, Paladin, London.

Craig, S. 1992, *Men, Masculinity, and the Media*, Sage, Newbury Park.

Creed, B. 1989, 'A Journey Through *Blue Velvet*', *New Formations*, no. 6, Winter, 1988, pp. 97–117.

Crisell, A. 1997, *An Introductory History of British Broadcasting*, Routledge, London.

Culler, J. 1976, *Saussure*, Fontana, London.

Cunningham, S. and Turner, G. (eds) 2001, *Media and Communications in Australia*, 2nd edn, Allen & Unwin, Sydney.

Curran, J. 1997, *Power without Responsibility: The Press and Broadcasting in Britain*, 5th edn, Routledge, London.

Czitrom, D. 1982, *Media and the American Mind: From Morse to McLuhan*, University of North Carolina Press, Chapel Hill.

Datamonitor 2001, 'Is the Channel Dead? The Impact of Interactivity on the TV Industry', www.datamonitor.com.

Davies, B. 1989, *Frogs and Snails and Feminist Tales*, Allen & Unwin, Sydney.

Denzin, N. 1988, '*Blue Velvet*: Postmodern Contradictions', *Theory, Culture and Society*, vol. 5, pp. 461–73.

Dermody, S. and Jacka, E. 1987–88, *The Screening of Australia*, vols 1 and 2, Currency Press, Sydney.

_____ (eds) 1988, *The Imaginary Industry: Australian Film in the late '80s*, Australian Film and Television Radio School, Sydney.

Diawara, M. (ed.) 1993, *Black American Cinema*, Routledge, New York.

Diaz, J. 1998, interview on *Arts Today*, ABC Radio National, 14 May 1998.

Dovey, J. 1995, 'Camcorder Cults', *Metro*, no. 104, pp. 26–9.

Dow, B. 1996, *Prime-time Feminism: Television, Media Culture, and the Women's Movement Since 1970*, Pennsylvania Press, Philadelphia.

Dowrick, S. 1991, *Intimacy and Solitude*, William Heinemann, Sydney.

Dyer, R. 1981, 'Entertainment and Utopia', in R. Altman (ed.), *Genre: The Musical*, British Film Institute and Routledge & Kegan Paul, London.

_____ 1982a, 'Don't Look Now: The Male Pin-Up', *Screen*, vol. 23, no. 3/4, pp. 61–73.

_____ 1982, *Stars*, British Film Institute, London.

_____ 1987, *Heavenly Bodies: Film Stars and Society*, Macmillan, Basingstoke.

_____ 1991, 'A Star is Born and the Construction of Authenticity', in C. Gledhill (ed.), *Stardom*, Routledge, London.

_____ 1992, *Only Entertainment*, Routledge, London.

_____ 1993, *The Matter of Images: Essays on Representations*, Routledge, London and New York.

Dyer, R., Geraghty, C., Jordon, M., Lovell, T., Paterson, R., and Stewart, J. (eds) 1981, *Coronation Street*, British Film Institute, London.

Eagleton, T. 1978, *Criticism and Ideology*, Verso, London.

Eliade, M. 1963, *Myth and Reality*, Harper & Row, New York.

Erlich, Susan 1995, see ABC Radio National 1995.

Evans, J. 1995, *Feminist Theory Today: An Introduction to Second-Wave Feminism*, Sage, London and Thousand Oaks, California.

Evans, M. 1997, *Introducing Contemporary Feminist Thought*, Polity Press, Cambridge.

Faludi, S. 1992, *Backlash: The Undeclared War Against Women*, Chatto & Windus, London.

Fillingham, L. 1995, *Foucault for Beginners*, Writers and Readers, London.

Film Quarterly 1992, 'The Many Faces of *Thelma and Louise*', vol. 45, no. 2, pp. 20–31.

Fischer, E. 1963, *The Necessity of Art: A Marxist Approach*, Penguin, Harmondsworth.

Fiske, J. 1987, *Television Culture*, Methuen, London.

_____ 1989a, *Reading the Popular*, Unwin Hyman, Sydney.

_____ 1989b, *Understanding Popular Culture*, Unwin Hyman, Sydney.

_____ 1991, *Introduction to Communication Studies*, 2nd edn, Routledge, London.

Fiske, J., Hodge, B., and Turner, G. 1987, *Myths of Oz: Reading Australian Popular Culture*, Allen & Unwin, Sydney.

Foster, H. (ed.) 1985, *Postmodern Culture*, Pluto Press, London.

Foucault, M. 1979, *Discipline and Punish: The Birth of the Prison*, Penguin, Harmondsworth.

_____ 1981, *The History of Sexuality*, Penguin, Harmondsworth.

Frank, L. and Smith, P. (eds) 1993, *Madonnerama: Essays on Sex and Popular Culture*, Cleis Press, Pittsburgh.

Freire, P. 1972, *Cultural Action for Freedom*, Penguin, Harmondsworth.

French, P. 1973, *Westerns*, Secker & Warburg/British Film Institute, London.

Freud, S. 1976a, *The Interpretation of Dreams*, Penguin, Harmondsworth.

_____ 1976b, *Jokes and Their Relation to the Unconscious*, Penguin, Harmondsworth.

Frith, S., Goodwin, A., and Grossberg, L. (eds) 1993, *The Music Video Reader*, Routledge, New York.

Gamble, S. 2001, *The Routledge Critical Dictionary of Feminism and PostFeminism*, Routledge, London and New York.

Garrison, E. K. 2000, 'U.S. Feminism—Grrrl Style! Youth (Sub)Cultures and the Technologies of the Third Wave', *Feminist Studies*, Spring, vol. 26.

Gauntlett, D. 1998, 'Ten Things Wrong with the Effects Model', www.theory.org.uk http://www.leeds.ac.uk/ics/theory/effects.htm.

Gauthier, G. 1976, 'The Semiology of the Image', *Educational Advisory Service*, British Film Institute, London.

Gilbert, L. and Kile, C. 1996, *Surfergrrrls: Look Ethel! An Internet Guide for Us*, Seal Press, Seattle.

Gilroy, P. 1987, *There Ain't No Black in the Union Jack: The Cultural Politics of Race and Nation*, Hutchinson, London.

Gitlin, T. 1993, 'Style for Style's Sake', *The Australian*.

Glasgow University Media Group, 1980, *More Bad News*, Routledge & Kegan Paul, London.

Gledhill, C. (ed.) 1987, *Home is Where the Heart Is*, British Film Institute, London.

_____ (ed.) 1991, *Stardom: Industry of Desire*, Routledge, London.

_____ 1997, 'Genre and Gender: The Case of Soap Opera', in S. Hall (ed.), *Representation: Cultural Representations and Signifying Practices*, Sage, London.

Golden, K. (ed.) 1992, *Uses of Comparative Mythology: Essays on the Work of Joseph Campbell*, Garland, New York.

Gomery, D. 1985, 'The Coming of Sound' and 'Economic Struggle and Hollywood Imperialism', in E. Weis and J. Belton (eds), *Theory and Practice of Film Sound*, Columbia University Press, New York.

Goodwin, A. 1993, *Dancing in the Distraction Factory: Music Television and Popular Culture*, Routledge, London.

Gordon, T. 1996a, *McLuhan for Beginners*, Writers and Readers, London.

_____ 1996b, *Saussure for Beginners*, Writers and Readers, London.

Gramsci, A. 1971, *Selections from the Prison Notebooks*, Lawrence & Wishart, London.

Grant, B. (ed.) 1995, *Film Genre Reader II*, University of Texas Press, Austin.

Gray, J. 1992, *Men are from Mars, Women are from Venus*, Harper Collins, New York.

Grossberg, L., Nelson, C., and Treichler, P. (eds) 1992, *Cultural Studies*, Routledge, New York.

Habermas, J. 1989, *Structural Transformation and the Public Sphere: An Inquiry into the Category of Bourgeois Society*, Polity Press, Cambridge.

Haley, A. 1976, *Roots*, Doubleday, New York.

Hall, S. 1977, 'Culture, the Media and the "Ideological Effect"', in J. Curran, *Mass Communication and Society*, Edward Arnold, London.

_____ 1980, 'Encoding/Decoding in Television Discourse', in S. Hall, D. Hobson, D. Lowe, and P. Willis (eds), *Culture, Media, Language*, Hutchinson, London.

_____ 1985, 'Signification, Representation, Ideology: Althusser and the Post-Structuralist Debates', in *Critical Studies in Mass Communication*, vol. 2, no. 2.

_____ 1986, 'Cultural Studies: Two Paradigms', in R. Collins, J. Curran, N. Sarnham, P. Scannell, P. Schlesinger, and C. Sparks (eds), *Media, Culture and Society: A Critical Reader*, Sage, London.

_____ 1992, *Critical Dialogues in Cultural Studies*, Routledge, London.

_____ 1994, 'The Question of Cultural Identity', in (no editor) *The Polity Reader in Cultural Theory*, Polity Press, Cambridge.

_____ (ed.) 1997, *Representation: Cultural Representations and Signifying Practices*, Sage, London.

Hartley, J. 1992a, *Tele-ology: Studies in Television*, Routledge, London.

_____ 1992b, *The Politics of Pictures*, Routledge, London.

—— 1999, *The Uses of Television*, Routledge, London.

Hartley, J. and McKee, A. (eds) 1996, *Telling Both Stories: Indigenous Australia and the Media*, Arts Enterprise, Edith Cowan University, Mount Lawley, Perth.

Harvey, D. 1989, *The Condition of Postmodernity*, Blackwell, Oxford.

Harvey, S. 1978, *May '68 and Film Culture*, British Film Institute, London.

Haskell, M. 1974, *From Reverence to Rape*, Holt Rinehart & Winston, New York, 1974.

Hawkes, T. 1977, *Structuralism and Semiotics*, Methuen, London.

_____ 1996, *Semiotics for Beginners*, Icon, Cambridge.

Hebdige, D. 1985, 'The Bottom Line on Planet One: Squaring up to The Face', *Ten-8*, vol. 19, pp. 40–9.

_____ 1979, *Subculture: The Meaning of Style*, Routledge, New York.

Herdt, G. 1989, 'Introduction: Gay and Lesbian Youth, Emergent Identities and Cultural Scenes at Home and Abroad', in G. Herdt (ed.), *Gay and Lesbian Youth*, The Haworth Press, New York and London.

Hernton, C. 1970, *Sex and Racism*, Paladin, London.

Hobson, D. 1982, *Crossroads: Drama of a Soap Opera*, Methuen, London.

Hoggart, R. 1958, *The Uses of Literacy*, Penguin, Harmondsworth.

Hooks, B. 1996, *Killing Rage, Ending Racism*, Penguin, London.

Hovaness, H. 2000, 'The Revolution Will Not be Televised: Personal Digital Media Technology and the Rise of Customer Power', white paper by KPMG Digital Media Institute, www.kpmgconsulting.com/DMI

Innis, H. 1951, *The Bias of Communication*, University of Toronto Press, Toronto.

Institute of Contemporary Arts 1987, *The Real Me: Postmodernism and the Question of Identity*, ICA, London.

Jackson, R. 1981, *Fantasy: The Literature of Subversion*, Methuen, London.

Jagose, A. 1996, *Queer Theory*, Melbourne University Press, Melbourne.

Jagtenberg, T. and McKie, D. 1997, *Eco-Impacts and the Greening of Postmodernity*, Sage, California.

Jameson, F. 1971, *Marxism and Form*, Princeton University Press, Princeton.

_____ 1977, 'Dog Day Afternoon', *Screen*, vol. 18.

_____ 1991, *Postmodernism or The Logic of Late Capitalism*, Verso, London.

Jencks, C. 1986, *What is Postmodernism*, Academy Edition, London.

Jenkins, H. 1992, *Textual Poachers: Television Fans and Participatory Culture*, Routledge, New York.

_____ 1998, *The Children's Culture Reader*, New York University Press, New York.

Johnson, R. 1987, *The Psychology of Romantic Love*, Arkana, Penguin, London.

Jung, C. 1967, *Memories, Dreams, Reflections*, Fontana, London.

_____ 1978, *Man and His Symbols*, Picador, London.

Kaplan, A. (ed.) 1978, *Women and Film Noir*, British Film Institute, London.

_____ (ed.) 1990, *Psychoanalysis and Cinema*, Routledge, New York.

Kerouac, J. 1958, *On the Road*, Andre Deutsch, London.

Kerr, P. (ed.) 1986, *The Hollywood Film Industry*, Routledge & Kegan Paul, London.

Kitses, J. 1969, *Horizons West*, Thames & Hudson, London.

Klein, N. 2000, *No Logo*, HarperCollins, London.

Koestler, A. 1975, *The Act of Creation*, Pan, London.

Kuhn, A. 1982, *Women's Pictures*, Routledge & Kegan Paul, London.

Langton, M. 1993, *Well I Saw it on the Television*, The Commission, North Sydney.

Lapsley, R. and Westlake, M. 1989, *Film Theory: An Introduction*, Manchester University Press, Manchester.

Lasswell, H. 1960, 'The Structure and Function of Communication in Society', in L. Bryson (ed.), *The Communication of Ideas, Institute for Religious and Social Studies*, New York.

Lazarsfeld, P. and Stanton, F. 1949, *Communication Research*, Harper & Row, New York.

Leab, D. 1975, *From Sambo to Superspade*, Secker & Warburg, London.

Leader, D. and Groves, J. 1995, *Lacan for Beginners*, Icon, Cambridge.

Lévi-Strauss, C. 1978, *Myth and Meaning*, Routledge & Kegan Paul.

Lowe, P. 1989, *The Experiment is Over*, Roximillion, New York.

Lowery, S. and Defleur, M. 1995, *Milestones in Mass Communication Research: Media Effects*, 3rd edn, Longman, USA.

Lumby, C. 1997, *Bad Girls: The Media, Sex and Feminism in the 90s*, Allen & Unwin, Sydney.

Lunn, E. 1985, *Marxism and Modernism*, Verso, London.

Lyotard, J-F. 1984, *The Postmodern Condition: A Report on Knowledge*, Manchester University Press, Manchester.

MacCabe, C. 1974, 'Realism and the Cinema: Notes on Some Brechtian Theses', *Screen*, vol. 15, no. 2.

_____ 1980, *Godard: Images, Sounds, Politics*, Macmillan, Basingstoke.

Mandela, N. 1995, *Long Walk to Freedom*, Abacus, London.

Mandelbaum, D. G. (ed.) 1949, *Edward Sapir: Culture, Language and Personality*, University of California Press, Berkeley.

Marcuse, H. 1964, *One Dimensional Man*, Routledge & Kegan Paul, London.

_____ 1972, *An Essay on Liberation*, Penguin, Harmondsworth.

Martin, A. 1979, 'Chantal Akerman's Films: A Dossier', *Feminist Review*, no. 3.

Marx, K. 1974, *The German Ideology*, 2nd edn, Lawrence & Wishart, London.

Matthews, J. 1979, *Surrealism and American Feature Films*, Twayne, New York.

McArthur, C. 1972, *Underworld USA*, Secker & Warburg/British Film Institute, London.

McKee, A. 1997, Images of Gay Men in the Media and the Development of Self Esteem, unpublished paper, Media Studies Department, Edith Cowan University.

McLean, I. and Bennett, G. 1996, *The Art of Gordon Bennett*, Craftsman House, Sydney.

McLeod J. 1991, 'On Understanding and Misunderstanding Media Effects', in J. Curran and M. Gurevitch (eds), *Mass Media and Society*, Edward Arnold, London.

McLuhan, M. 1987, *Understanding Media: The Extensions of Man*, Ark, London.

McNair, B., 1995, 'Party political communication II: Political public relations', in *An Introduction to Political Communication*, Routledge, London, pp. 110–36.

McQuail, D. 1987, *Mass Communication Theory: An Introduction*, Sage, London.

McQuail, D. and Windahl, S. 1981, *Communication Models for the Study of Mass Communications*, Longman, New York.

McRobbie, A. 1997, 'More! New Sexualities in Girls' and Women's Magazines', in A. McRobbie (ed.), *Back to Reality: Social Experience and Cultural Studies*, Manchester University Press, Manchester.

McRobbie, A. and Nava, M. (eds) 1984, *Gender and Generation*, Macmillan, London.

Mercer, K. (ed.) 1984, *Welcome to the Jungle*, Routledge, London.

Metcalf, A. and Humphries, M. (eds) 1985, *The Sexuality of Men*, Pluto Press, London.

Miller, A. 1990, *The Untouched Key: Tracing Childhood Trauma in Creativity and Destructiveness*, Doubleday, New York.

Montgomery, M. 1995, *An Introduction to Language and Society*, 2nd edn, Routledge, London.

Moore, R. and Gillette, D. 1991, *King, Warrior, Magician, Lover*, Harper Collins, San Francisco.

Morley, D. 1992, *Television, Audiences and Cultural Studies*, Routledge, London.

Morris, E. 1977, Interview with Errol Morris, *Interview*, November 1977.

Morris, M. 1988, *The Pirate's Fiancee: Feminism, Reading, Postmodernism*, Verso, London.

Mowlana, H. 1997, *Global Information and World Communication*, 2nd edn, Sage, London and California.

Mulvey, L. 1985, 'Visual Pleasure and Narrative Cinema', in B. Nichols (ed.), *Movies and Methods*, vol. 2, University of California Press, California.

_____ 1989, 'Visual Pleasure and Narrative Cinema', in L. Mulvey, *Visual and Other Pleasures*, Macmillan, Basingstoke.

Murray, W. 1964, *Boys and Girls: Key Words Reading Scheme*, Ladybird, Loughborough.

_____ 1990, *Read With Me 1: Key Words to Reading*, Ladybird, Loughborough, United Kingdom.

Neale, S. 1980, *Genre*, British Film Institute, London.

Neale, S. 1985, *Cinema and Technology: Image, Sound, Colour*, Macmillan, London.

New Internationalist 1998 (April), 'Map of the World: Peters Projection', p. 6.

New Internationalist, 'An Unequal World', www.newint.org/index4.html

Ngugi, W. 1986, *Decolonising the Mind: The Politics of Language in African Literature*, Heinemann, London.

Nichols, B. 1991, *Representing Reality*, Indiana University Press, Bloomington.

_____ 1994, 'At the Limits of Reality (TV)', in B. Nichols, *Blurred Boundaries*, Indiana University Press, Indianapolis.

Nicholson, L. 1990, *Feminism/Postmodernism*, Routledge, London.

Nixon, S. 1997, 'Exhibiting Masculinity', in S. Hall (ed.), *Representation: Cultural Representations and Signifying Practices*, Sage, London.

Nochlin, L. 1971, *Realism*, Penguin, Harmondsworth.

O'Shaughnessy, M. 1994, 'Promoting Emotions: Understanding Films, Understanding Ourselves', *Metro*, no. 97, pp. 44–8.

_____ 1997, 'Private Made Public: Ordinary People, Extraordinary Stories', *Continuum*, vol. 11, no. 1, pp. 84–99.

O'Sullivan, T., Hartley, J., Saunders, D., Montgomery, M., and Fiske, J. 1994, *Key Concepts in Communication and Cultural Studies*, 2nd edn, Routledge, London.

Ong, W. 1982, *Orality and Literacy: The Technologising of the Word*, Methuen, New York.

Open University 1981, 'Block 2: Social Aspects of Language' in *E263, Language in Use*, The Open University Press, Milton Keynes.

Packard, V. 1957, *The Hidden Persuaders*, Penguin, Harmondsworth.

Palmer, D. 1996, *Structuralism for Beginners*, Writers and Readers, London.

Peirce, C. S. 1958, *Collected Papers, 1931–58*, vols 7–8 (ed. Arthur Burke), Harvard University Press, Cambridge, Massachusetts.

Perkins, V. 1990, *Film as Film*, Penguin, Harmondsworth.

Phoca, S. and Wright, R. 1999, *Introducing Postfeminism*, Icon Books, Cambridge.

Pinkola Estes, C. 1992, *Women Who Run with the Wolves: Contacting the Power of the Wild Woman*, Rider, London.

—— 1997, *Warming the Stone Child: Myths and Stories about Abandonment and the Unmothered Child*, Sounds True (audio tape).

Platania, J. 1997, *Jung for Beginners*, Writers and Readers, London.

Powell, C. and Paton, G. 1988, *Humour in Society: Resistance and Control*, Macmillan, London.

Pribram, D. 1993, 'Seduction, Control, and the Search for Authenticity: Madonna's Truth or Dare', in C. Schwichtenberg (ed.), *The Madonna Connection*, Allen & Unwin, Sydney.

Propp, V. 1975, *Morphology of the Folktale*, University of Texas, Austin.

Rabinow, P. (ed.) 1984, *The Foucault Reader*, Pantheon Books, New York.

Radway, J. 1987, *Reading the Romance*, Verso, London.

Reggio, G., unpublished interview on *Koyaanisqatsi*.

Reich, W. 1990, *Character Analysis*, The Noonday Press, New York.

Reid, M. (ed.) 1997, *Spike Lee's* Do the Right Thing, Cambridge University Press, Cambridge.

Rivkin, J. and Ryan, M. (eds) 1998, *Literary Theory: An Anthology*, Blackwell, Massachusetts.

Robertson, R. 1992, *Beginner's Guide to Jungian Psychology*, Nicolas–Hays, York Beach.

Robinson, C. 1984, 'Indiana Jones, the Third World and American Foreign Policy', *Race and Class*, vol. 16, no. 2, pp. 83–91.

Rodan, D. 1995, *Feminist Theory Today: An Introduction to Second-Wave Feminism*, Sage Publications, London and Thousand Oaks, California.

Roscoe, J. 1997, 'Mocking Silver: Reinventing the Documentary Project', *Continuum*, vol. 11, no. 1, pp. 67–82.

Rousseau, J-J. 1974, *Emile*, Dent, London.

Russo, V. 1981, *The Celluloid Closet*, Harper and Row, New York.

Rutherford, J. (ed.) 1990, *Identity: Community, Culture, Difference*, Lawrence & Wishart, London.

Rutherford, J. and Chapman, R. (eds) 1988, *Male Order*, Lawrence & Wishart, London.

Said, E. 1980, *Orientalism*, Routledge & Kegan Paul, London.

Saussure, F. 1974, *Course in General Linguistics*, Fontana, London.

Schiller, H. 1992, 'A Quarter Century Retrospective' in Schiller (ed.), *Mass Communications and American Empire*, 2nd edn, Westview Press, Boulder, Colorado.

Schlesinger, P. 1978, *Putting 'Reality' Together—BBC News*, Constable, London.

Schwichtenberg, C. (ed.) 1993, *The Madonna Connection*, Allen & Unwin, Sydney.

Scott, R. 1991, interview, *Sight and Sound*, July 1991, pp. 18–19.

Sharp, D. 1996, *Living Jung: The Good and the Better*, Inner City Books, Toronto, p. 32.

Sinclair, J., Jacka, E., and Cunningham, S. (eds) 1996, *New Patterns in Global Television*, Oxford University Press, Oxford.

Smith, H. 1970, *Virgin Land: The American West as Symbol and Myth*, Harvard University Press, Cambridge, Massachusetts.

Solomon, J. 1988, 'Our Decentred Culture: The Postmodern View', in *The Signs of Our Times*, St Martins Press, Los Angeles.

Spender, D. 1980, *Man Made Language*, Routledge & Kegan Paul, London.

Stratton, J. and Ang, I. 1994, 'Sylvania Waters and the Spectacular Exploding Family', *Screen*, vol. 35, no. 1, pp. 1–21.

Sunday Times 1996 (3 March), 'Well Hello Sailors'.

Tasker, Y. 1993, *Spectacular Bodies*, Routledge, London.

Taubin, A. 1999, 'So Good it Hurts', *Sight and Sound*, November.

Thomas, H. (ed.) 1997, *Dance in the City*, Macmillan, London.

Thompson, D. 1964, *Discrimination and Popular Culture*, Penguin, Harmondsworth.

Thompson, J. 1999, *The Media and Modernity: A Social Theory of the Media*, Polity Press, Cambridge.

Thoreau, H. 1973, *Walden or Life in the Woods*, Anchor Press/Doubleday, New York.

Thoss, M. 1996, *Brecht for Beginners*, Writers and Readers, London.

Todorov, T. 1975, *The Fantastic*, Cornell University Press, New York.

Tong, R., 1989, *Feminist Thought: A Comprehensive Introduction*, London, Unwin Hyman.

Totten, N. and Edmondson, E. 1988, *Reichian Growth Work*, Prism, Bridport.

True Romance 1980, 'I Followed My Dream', February 1980.

Tulloch, J. and Jenkins, H. 1995, *Science Fiction Audiences: Watching Doctor Who and Star Trek*, Routledge, London.

Turner, G. 1990, *British Cultural Studies: An Introduction*, Unwin Hyman, London.

_____ 1999, *Film as Social Practice*, 3rd edn, Routledge, London.

Turner, K. 1988, *I Dream of Madonna*, 1st edn, Thames & Hudson, Slovenia.

Ullman, M. and Zimmerman, N. 1979, *Working with Dreams*, Hutchinson, London.

Vogler, C. 1992, *The Writer's Journey: Mythic Structure for Storytellers and Screenwriters*, Michael Weise Productions, California.

Waites, B., Bennett, T., and Martin, G. (eds) 1982, *Popular Culture Past and Present*, Routledge, London.

Walkerdine, V. 1990, *Schoolgirl Fictions*, Verso, London.

_____ 1997, *Daddy's Girl: Young Girls and Popular Culture*, Macmillan, London.

Walters, S. D., 1995, *Material Girls: Making Sense of Feminist Cultural History*, California University Press, California.

Ward, I. 1995, *Politics of the Media*, Macmillan, Melbourne.

Wark, M. 1994, *Virtual Geography: Living with Global Media Events*, Indiana University Press, Bloomington and Indianapolis.

Warner, M. (ed.) 1993, *Fear of a Queer Planet: Queer Politics and Social Theory*, University of Minnesota Press, Minneapolis and London.